SYMPTOMS *of* WITHDRAWAL

SYMPTOMS *of* WITHDRAWAL

A Memoir of Snapshots and Redemption

CHRISTOPHER KENNEDY LAWFORD

WILLIAM MORROW

An Imprint of HarperCollins*Publishers*

Unless otherwise credited, all photographs courtesy of the author.

HarperCollins books may be purchased for educational, business, or sales promotional use. For information please write: Special Markets Department, HarperCollins Publishers, 10 East 53rd Street, New York, NY 10022.

FIRST EDITION

Designed by Renato Stanisic

Printed on acid-free paper

Library of Congress Cataloging-in-Publication Data has been applied for.

ISBN-13: 978-0-06-073248-6
ISBN-10: 0-06-073248-2

05   06   07   08   09   WBC/RRD   10   9   8   7   6   5   4   3   2   1

For David, Savannah, and Matthew
So that you know who I am

*We do not receive wisdom, we must discover
it for ourselves, after a journey through the wilderness
which no one else can make for us, which no one
can spare us, for our wisdom is the point of view from
which we come at last to regard the world.*

— MARCEL PROUST

*. . . there really wasn't any punishment appropriate
for keeping Chris on the straight and narrow.
Presumably, he does what he wants to do when
he wants to do it, and has very little sense
of conscience about it.*

— DAVID SHELDON, HEADMASTER OF
MIDDLESEX SCHOOL IN A LETTER
TO MY MOTHER

PREFACE

The privilege of a lifetime is being who you are.
— JOSEPH CAMPBELL

On a cold fall day in 1997 I found myself sitting across a large mahogany desk from the most current genius in the independent film world. I had walked into his oversized office in Greenwich Village to pitch him a very cool movie idea about Fidel Castro. Having been an actor for ten years, I was getting tired of begging for work. I was forty-two years old and had decided in a moment of clarity or insanity to become a producer so I could make my own movies and hire myself. I developed a number of good scripts and pitches but the one I was going to sell to this wunderkind on a cold day in New York was special. I had met him at the premier for the movie he had managed to get a credit on. It was a huge success, giving him credibility overnight. Our culture thrives on the flavor of the moment, the messiah of the day. The One who will deliver the goods and sell what needs to be sold — and save us. Nowhere is this obsession more prevalent than in the worlds of entertainment and politics. It has always fostered a feeling of mistrust in me. This has never stopped me from paying homage, however.

The current savior of independent film knew who I was and had indicated a willingness to help. That was the only opening I needed. I had been blessed in my life with people who had shown a desire to be helpful — most of them attracted by the Kennedy flame, some trying to take advantage, others genuine. However, I hadn't yet met anyone in the movie business not thoroughly dominated by self-interest, myself included. In Hollywood you need to be thoroughly focused and committed to *your* dream so as not to be overwhelmed and discouraged by the mountains of bullshit. When I walked into this guy's office at the hot new indie studio to pitch the only movie on my plate that meant anything to me, I hoped he would prove not to be just another movie business sleezeball who had his taste up his ass.

The movie was a fictitious account of Fidel Castro, with the help of an ex–CIA agent named Jack, making his way up I-95 to New York to see his illegitimate son pitch the opening game of the World Series. Along the way Jack teaches Fidel about America and Fidel teaches Jack about commitment, all the while being chased by crazy Miami Cubans. *Midnight Run* meets *Melvin and Howard*. It was subversive and romantic, exploring themes political and of fatherhood. It was funny and a great what-if? There was a lot of me in this movie. After I pitched it, the genius turned to me and with great sincerity said, "Chris, you know what I want." I said, "No, I don't," secretly hoping that he was going to give me a mountain of money to make my movie and a first-look deal. That wasn't it.

"I want your story" is what he said.

My story. Wait a minute. I haven't really done anything. I thought in order to tell the story of your life you had to have done something extraordinary. I'm an actor, for Christ's sake. Many of my relatives had told stories: stories about courage, the Cuban Missile Crisis, or the national health care crisis. My grandmother told the story of her life in a book, but she was an amazing woman who was revered and had a rich, profound, long life. Against these examples, I found it difficult to imagine I had much of a story to tell.

This is what went through my mind as I sat across that large mahogany desk. I have a tendency to move to the negative right off the bat. I'm always waiting for the other shoe to drop. It's what I grew up with, the other shoe always dropping.

I did a movie a while back with J. T. Walsh, the wonderful character actor who died in a Jacuzzi while at rehab. Talk about bad luck. We were on Vancouver Island on the set of *The Russia House* with Sean

Connery and I was in the middle of an actor's rant about not having enough work and too little money. "Man, this business sucks! Forget about artistic gratification, I gave up on that years ago. I'm trying to put three kids through school on the Westside of L.A. on three or four scale jobs a year. It's impossible." J.T. nodded sympathetically and, when I was done, said, "Well, it looks like it's time to write the memoirs." Great! If all else fails, I could write a book about my life. Spend a year opening my veins and pissing a lot of people off in the process.

I'll get back to that later.

There was another problem I faced in telling my story. It seemed like a lot of folks already knew it—or a version of it.

What to do when most everyone you come across in your life knows almost as much about your life as you? It makes for some confusion.

Let's take sailing. I grew up knowing that all Kennedys loved sailing and that they were good at it. I got this information from family, friends, and strangers who somehow knew stuff like this about my family. This information was reinforced in books and on television.

My truth was that I hated sailing and wasn't good at it.

It took me a while to accept this. If you read fifty different books on my family you will get fifty different variations of the same story, and the only real consistency comes from years of repetition of the same bullshit. With the exception of my grandmother, Rose Kennedy, none of the principal relatives in my family have ever publicly disclosed the events of their lives. Most of the commonly held beliefs about them come from the recollections of people only tangentially involved in the lives of those they claim to know. My experience has taught me that whenever anything is publicly revealed about someone, it is usually 50 percent wrong.

I don't know whether Oswald acted alone. I don't even know what other members of my family who had a more proximate and profound relationship with my uncle Jack think about it. I have no idea who, if anyone, had sex with Marilyn Monroe. I was thirteen when my uncle Bobby died and sixteen when my uncle Teddy drove off a bridge at Chappaquiddick. By the time I came of age, all that is of historic interest to the general public concerning my family had happened. I was not privy to any of it. None of the events that preoccupied the media and captivated the imagination of the world were discussed with us kids by those who were intimately involved. The only thing I am capable of relating is my experience of the aftermath.

I got a call a while back from a purveyor of Kennedy gossip who was going to write a book about the men in my family. I asked him why the world needed another book about the Kennedys. He responded with a long letter about how the world needed to know the story of one of my cousins overcoming this or that. The truth is: The world doesn't need to know that story. The only reason for that story to be told is if my cousin needs to tell it.

WHEN I think about my own life and how my experience causes me to view the world, it compels me to share it with others. I need to tell this story. I need to tell you what I have learned at great cost. My purpose in revealing my awkward humanness is to free myself to find myself. I grew up in public; it seems that my emancipation must also be public. My hope, too, is that the relating of my experience may help others facing similar challenges.

My experience as an addict in recovery has taught me that one human being sharing their experience, strength, and hope with another is among the most powerful engines for change on the planet.

MY LIFE has been a pilgrimage to freedom. Freedom from a legacy I didn't ask for, a preordained identity, and a manufactured self. There were some very exacting expectations to contend with, and an addiction I didn't want, to overcome. Joseph Campbell said that doing what someone else wants us to do is slave morality and a path to disease and disintegration of the spirit and body. In my case it was not that anyone in my life forced me to do anything, it is that the circumstances I was born into were so extraordinary that it was impossible not to be imprisoned by them. The results for me were the same: disease and disintegration of the spirit and body.

The story of my life is my journey out of this bondage. My intention is to illuminate and codify this journey, messy as it was, toward self-realization. This book is about my search for my authentic self. I do not claim to be realized, only to be on a path toward authenticity. The circumstances of my life have afforded me the opportunity to see through the illusions of what motivates me. My addiction—did I mention I was an addict?—provided the motivation, and my affluence, the opportunity for me to spend much of my life looking at the underlying causes and conditions of my own humanity. I am enormously grateful for these gifts.

The Israeli novelist Amos Oz said that "every true writer becomes a writer because of a profound trauma experienced in youth or childhood. . . . we might venture to say that the flight of the narrator's imagination is as high as the depth of his wound. . . ." This book will testify to the trauma. I will leave it to you, the readers, to determine the depth of the wound.

My story is one of survival and claiming myself in the face of overwhelming ego and circumstance. I was given what everybody wants at birth and the goodwill of most everyone on the planet. I was also given a good dose of alcoholism and the massive dysfunction that exists in a family dynamic where alcoholism doesn't just run, it gallops. I'm Irish, for Christ's sake. I've heard it said that God invented alcohol to keep the Irish from ruling the world. My family almost proved Him wrong.

I have done three important things in my life. I have stayed sober for twenty years. I have been a committed and more or less present father for much of that time. And I have struggled openly and honestly with my human condition by living an examined, conscious, imperfect life.

My purpose in writing this book is to tell you how I did these things.

Kurt Vonnegut said that he writes so that his readers know that they are not alone—that there is someone out there who thinks the way they do. It is my hope that what I write in these pages will be of use, showing that though the circumstances of our individual lives may differ, our underlying humanity is universal. No matter how crazy life gets or you become, there is a way back.

AUTHOR'S NOTE

*Our Destiny exercises its influence over us even
when, as yet, we have not learned its nature: it is our future
that lays down the law of our today.*
— NIETZSCHE

When I was young my mother told me I was a good writer. I ignored her, figuring she was just being the encouraging parent. I was wrong. I was a good writer but because of laziness and a healthy party instinct I rarely put pen to paper unless I had to. Thanks, Mom, for taking the time to notice. I wished I had listened to you.

Growing up there was no worse condemnation of someone than "he's writing a book!" Plenty of books were written about my family — not all of them were nice. My family members have had a lifetime of unpleasantness dealing with the monotonous public recapitulation of their lives.

The narrative I have written is a recollection of my life as I remember it. I have tried to bring the family into it only when needed to shed light on my character or behavior. I wrote this book because I am intensely interested in the human journey — my journey. The greatest legacy we can give our kids is not property, money, fame, or prestige; it is the truth as each one of us sees it. For a year I sat in front of my computer and allowed the events of my life to be disclosed to me. This pilgrimage was not planned. I prayed that whatever was revealed would be poignant, universal, and helpful to at least one other human being. I hoped for humor and pathos. What follows is what was given to me.

My family has been the source and inspiration for much of who I am and what I've done. My life does not belong only to me for I am part of a greater whole. I am grateful to all the members of my family for who they are and for their contribution in making me the person I am today.

I am indebted to my friend and mentor David Black for his tireless support and guidance throughout my whole revelatory process. His unwavering conviction to my vision sustained me. His commitment to my voice gave me the faith I needed to do this. To my friends Dotson Rader, Jack Weeks, Peter Emerson, Kale Browne, Tom Cunneff, Neal Nordlinger, Liza Wachter, and Tom Caruso for their time, guidance, and support. To Milt Ebbins and Erma Lee Reilly for the loyalty and love they gave my parents, and for the memories, which brought the past to life. To my agent, Loretta Barrett, and her colleague Nick Mullendore, who did way more than just get me a good deal. To my editor, Maureen O'Brien, for her tireless efforts in getting the best possible book out of me. To the hardworking staff at HarperCollins for laboring over it.

To all those friends of Bill's, for the wisdom, which they have freely shared and which is the heart and soul of this manuscript.

I want to especially thank Jeannie for sharing so much of her life with me. The love, pain, and lessons we shared are such a large part of my life and this book. I am sorry and grateful for it all. To my children, David, Savannah, and Matthew, who have been my great teachers and my great joy. You are a continuing source of love and inspiration to me.

Lastly I want to thank Lana for listening to all my angst and fear during the writing of this book. Your love and patience sustained me. I could not have done this without you sitting beside me.

SYMPTOMS *of* WITHDRAWAL

Chapter 1

You can always do it wrong.
That's the beauty of life.
— ANONYMOUS

What happens when you are born with the American dream fulfilled? The dreams that drew my ancestors here had been realized for me at my birth. I was born just off the beach in Malibu, California. My father, Peter Lawford, was a movie star and a member of the Rat Pack. My mother's brother Jack would be president of the United States. I was given wealth, power, and fame when I drew my first breath. Now what?

My mother gave birth to me in Saint John's hospital in Santa Monica, California, on March 29, 1955, on the same day that Judy Garland gave birth to her son, Joe, in the same hospital. I was named Christopher because my mom liked the name and had a thing for Saint Christopher—the giant Catholic saint who carried the baby Jesus and the sins of the world on his shoulders. I received a Saint Christopher medal on every birthday until he was decanonized when I was fourteen because the church determined that the evidence of his existence was entirely legendary. My name lost a bit of its luster on that day, and I remember wondering if the Church might be able to negate my existence also.

The circumstances of my birth were further extolled because Judy was up for an Academy Award that year for *A Star Is Born* and the press was keeping a vigil. Western Union delivered a boatload of telegrams to my parents from those known and unknown.

WE'RE SO HAPPY FOR YOU BOTH. HE'LL BE QUITE A BOY.
LOVE—JEANNE AND DEAN MARTIN

DEAR FRIENDS—I'M SO HAPPY FOR YOU BOTH AND MAY I SAY YOU
PICKED MY FAVORITE HOSPITAL FOR THIS EPIC EVENT—AND I'M A
MAN WHO KNOWS ABOUT HOSPITALS. HELLO TO SISTER MARY
DAVID—BING CROSBY

"Quite a boy."

"Epic event."

I was just out of the womb and there were already lofty expectations from some pretty accomplished folk. Uh-oh! I better get my shit together.

SO THRILLED FOR YOU BOTH. LOVE GARY & ROCKY COOPER

My aunt Ethel sent a telegram that read: What a difference a day makes. Whew. Little Ethel

She should know. She was pregnant at the time with her fourth child, David Kennedy, who would be born two and half months later and become my "best friend to the bitter end."

So Judy's son, Joe, and I were born on the same day to movie star parents in Hollywood, California, and the media were paying attention. From the moment I came into this world, I have had a bizarre and constant relationship with the media. They were rarely there to take a picture of me or get a quote from me, but I was always in the mix—in the glow. I have known many people who have been touched by fame. For most of them—whether movie stars, politicians, artists, or criminals—it only lasts a short time. They go from ordinary to extraordinary and back again in the blink of an eye, but the damage done can last a lifetime. Once you have had a taste of the glare, it's hard to step back into shadows.

My family has maintained its currency with the press for most of my life. Very little we did went unnoticed. A flashbulb or television camera highlighted the ordinary events of life. Years later when I got sober, I realized for the first time that I thought everybody on the planet woke up every day and wondered what Chris Lawford and the rest of the Kennedy family were up to that day. In fact, it was something of a rude awakening when a friend of mine pointed out to me that "there are a billion people in China who don't know who your family is or more importantly, Chris, who you are!"

At the moment of my birth, my father was having lunch down the street at one of his hangouts, an ornate and hip Chinese bistro on Wilshire Boulevard named for its proprietor, the mysterious and ever-present Madame Wu. He was throwing down some of Madame's famous Chinese chicken salad with his sidekick and manager, Milt Ebbins, and talking to Cary Grant about the current state of affairs in Hollywood, as he awaited the call announcing the birth of his first child. Cary was reassuring him. Not about becoming a father but about his career.

"Don't worry, old man. As soon as you get a little gray in your hair, you'll work all the time. I didn't work for two years, my temples got gray, and it was a whole new ball game."

My dad began feeling a bit more optimistic, and then the call came. He thanked Cary for the encouragement by paying the tab and beat it to Saint John's, with the ever-present Milt in tow, just in time to see my mom being wheeled, semiconscious, out of the OR. A half hour later, he opened the door to her room to find her sitting up in bed with a bottle of J&B Scotch, ready to celebrate. "Come on in, boys, we've got a big beautiful boy. Let's have a drink." A few minutes later, the big beautiful boy was delivered to his celebrating mom and dad. My father looked down at me, saw my rather pronounced oriental features, and declared, "That's not my kid. He looks Chinese. Hey, wait a minute, Pat, wasn't the gardener Asian?" They laughed. And had another scotch.

My dad was right. I did look Asian. I was born with a Mongolian fold, which means that my eyelids droop slightly over my eyes. This condition is also referred to as "bedroom eyes" and I have milked it happily all my life. Thanks, Dad.

I was the first boy born to a mother who was the product of a family with a long and lusty tradition of glorifying and supporting the male. You can't get more fawned over than a Kennedy male. My

3

mother had struggled against the yoke of being a talented and willful female in a family and society that didn't really care what the women were up to as long as they were having lots of babies. Her marriage to my father and her subsequent life in California were early attempts to find her own identity and be noticed outside of The Family. It's a miracle that I was born at all, given the fact that neither of my parents was the marrying kind. They were both thirty. Although my mom was feeling the pressure of being unmarried, her personality was like my father's. My parents were two willful human beings, from different worlds, used to getting what they wanted and having their own space. They must have really loved one another to give up that freedom.

When I was a kid my mom often recalled how she tried to escape that love. "I fell in love with your father the moment I laid eyes on him. He was so handsome. Grandpa sent me on a trip around the world to get him out of my system. It didn't work. I got to Japan and turned right around."

Like most women of her generation, all roads led to children and the creation of family. Procreation was the necessary evil in the grand purpose of bringing forth God's little angels. I've been told that my mom made the sign of the cross before engaging my father in the necessary evil. I don't know what she was praying for, but she was pregnant with me four months after saying "I do."

My grandmother Rose wrote a letter to my mom not long after I was born, advising her to write to the Lahey Clinic for high-potency vitamins so she could "get built up" and "not to wear falsies that are too prominent as they are not only cheap but tempt you know whom"! I assume Gramma was talking about my father. Well, it didn't work: after me, they had three more children.

Three girls: Sydney, Victoria, and Robin. A blond, a brunette, and a redhead. All the bases were covered. I was the only boy, the oldest, the king. The way it should be. Pure Kennedy.

WHEN MY mother married my father she made a monumental statement of independence from her own father, whom she adored. Joseph P. Kennedy, my grandfather, was the man from whom everything flowed.

He was the power, the money, and the brains. My mother was the sixth child in a brood of nine. Her lightheartedness and vibrancy made her my grandfather's favorite. My mom called him Daddy, and his actions and words were glorified and sanctified. His story was legend: bank president at thirty, friend and confidant to FDR, ambassador to the Court of Saint James, Securities and Exchange Commission chairman, Hollywood mogul, and go-to guy in all things political. More than any male in my life, my grandfather represented everything a male should be. As I saw it, he was the architect of our world. There was a sense that everything the Kennedy family was came about as a direct result of my grandfather's will. On September 7, 1957, my grandfather predicted in an interview in the *Saturday Evening Post* that someday one of his sons would be president, one would be attorney general, and another would be a United States senator—all this simultaneously.

It was not just about money and power with my grandfather. He was first and foremost about family. His will to power and wealth was about protecting his family. His kids loved him more than they feared or respected him. My mom told me when I was young, "Grandpa gave each of us a million dollars when we turned twenty-five. All of his friends told him not to do it, saying his kids wouldn't give him the time of day if they got all that money. It wasn't true. We all still can't wait to come home." You couldn't keep my mom and her siblings away from "Daddy and Mother." Later I figured out that although Grandpa gave his children the money to realize their independence, he never taught them what to do with it. I always assumed this was because he felt they were meant for higher pursuits. But it might have been about control.

There was no more dominant force in our world than "Daddy," and my mom was his little girl. My dad said to me that "your mother's love for her father took precedence over her love for me."

There is a thin line between love and hate. On the other side of this adoration for her father was a deep anger and resentment at not being allowed fully to live up to her potential. My mom also inherited my grandfather's interest in dramatics. And she was good at it.

"You know," she would say to me and my sisters, "before all of you were born and ruined my life I was a television producer for Father Peyton's *Family Rosary Crusade*, the program that made 'the family

5

that prays together stays together' a household phrase and was seen all over the country." She was only half kidding. My mom had the talent to get her share of accolades in the professional world, and though she wore "putting her children first" as a badge of honor, I think she resented the limitation. Her proprietary outlook toward all things Kennedy was her way of participating in the bigger picture of the family's accomplishments.

My mother was more like my grandfather than were any of her siblings. She had a mind for money, a strong independent streak, and she could cut you off at the knees with "the look" just like the Old Man. There was no mistaking it when Joe Kennedy was unhappy with you. His displeasure burned in his eyes and straight into whoever was unlucky enough to cross him. I don't recall ever getting "the look" from my grandfather, but my mom more than made up for it so I have some idea just how unpleasant it might have been. My mother also had her father's instinct and luck when it came to making money. My grandfather often said that, "The one with the best business head is Pat. If she put her mind to it, she could easily take over the business."

I was seven when my grandfather became incapacitated with a stroke. My mom found out about it in December 1961 while she was driving my sisters and me to lunch. A stranger stopped her and said he had just heard on the radio that her "father just had a stroke." The only vivid recollection I have of him before his stroke was in a park in Washington on a cold day in January before going to President Kennedy's inauguration. He was wearing a topcoat and a hat. It was exciting to be with this man, who made my mother beam as he pushed me on a swing, saying, "You are going higher and higher, Christopher. You are going to fly like an eagle." Then he was gone. The next time I saw him he was in a wheelchair, but for the rest of my life, the voice in my head that only allows perfection and questions my choices would belong to my grandpa, Joseph P. Kennedy.

Shortly after the inauguration my mom shipped me back to California while she stayed on in Washington to make sure all was going well at the White House. A month later she sent me a note on White House stationery:

February 22, 1961

Dear Christopher,
I arrived here yesterday to stay with Uncle Jack until tomorrow.
Remember when you were here the day after the inauguration
to see Uncle Bob sworn in as Attorney General? You really
loved all the beautiful chandeliers so you must come back and
see them soon.

Love,
Mommy

Chandeliers . . .

My mother spent a fair amount of time at the White House while my uncle was in residence. I know this because she would always bring me back the place cards and menus signed by some of the folks she was having dinner with: John Glenn, Douglas Dillon, Dwight Eisenhower, Robert McNamara, Lyndon Johnson, and so on. She might have been gone a lot but she was always thinking about her kids. And the White House chandeliers . . .

MY FATHER, Peter Sidney Lawford, was English, Protestant, and an actor, three characteristics that made my grandfather's skin crawl. When my father flew to New York to formally ask if he could marry my mother, my grandfather supposedly said, "If there's anything I'd hate more for a son-in-law than an actor, it's a British actor!" My mom told me that he advised her not to marry my father, "shaking his head as he left the room" after she told him.

My grandfather had my father checked out by everyone from Louis B. Mayer to J. Edgar Hoover and found that he probably wasn't a homosexual or a Communist, and he must have figured that he could live with my dad's philandering.

He ultimately approved the marriage, if only because he probably couldn't prevent it and he didn't want to lose his daughter. My mom was always willful and determined. Still, it took a lot of courage for her to marry my father in the face of my grandfather's misgivings.

I was born a bit prematurely and weighed six pounds thirteen ounces, possibly because my mother didn't like being pregnant and women then did not modify their lifestyles to accommodate fetal needs. She didn't show until the sixth month, ate like a bird, exercised compulsively, even skiing in the Canadian Rockies well into her seventh month. My father moved out of the Malibu house my mom and he had moved into soon after their marriage. It was a small two-bedroom on the beach that once belonged to Gloria Swanson, who, it was said, had once had an affair with my grandfather. My grandfather had offered to buy them something substantial as a wedding present, but my dad didn't want to live in a house bought by his wife's father. My dad was working on a television series called *Dear Phoebe* and had commandeered the guest room at his manager's house in Beverly Hills. My dad had no idea how to deal with a pregnant wife and my eventual arrival. So he left, citing his need to be closer to work. My mom showed up a few days later. She told my dad that he wasn't getting rid of her that easily—she was moving into the guest room too. My dad decided Malibu wasn't that far away after all. I was already causing panic in my parents, and I wasn't even here yet.

Another fact of my birth that was contributive to my budding uniqueness was that my grandmother Rose, for the first and last time, served as a nurse and helpmate at the birth of one of her grandchildren. She reminded me of this often, "You came a few days early, dear, and I was visiting your mother and father at the time, so I took charge and took care of you."

My grandmother might have taken charge, but she didn't hang around very long after my birth. She was a Kennedy, after all, and liked to keep moving, traveling being her remedy of choice. She jumped on a plane to Hawaii as soon as I was handed off to the appropriate caregiver. Still, three thousand miles of Pacific Ocean didn't diminish her ambivalence about leaving: "Heartbroken that I left so soon and I do not know why I did, except I thought I should be leisurely and I could have easily waited till Wed or even Thurs—I did try to leave Tuesday but it was a day flight—It is nice here but we would much rather be with you and Peter and Christopher. . . ."

My grandmother liked to move and rarely stopped moving. Sometimes when you move, it doesn't feel so good. I would come to know both these states.

Later in life, when locked in the battle with my cousins to secure the coveted title of Grandma's Favorite Grandchild, the fact that I was the only grandchild whose birth she actually attended, no matter how briefly, was my ace in the hole.

MY MOTHER and father used to hang out with their friends at the Beachcomber Bar on Channel Road in Santa Monica. Legend has it that we stopped there on the drive home from the hospital, with my parents proudly placing their newborn son with the Mongolian fold on the bar and ordering their favorite cocktails. I suppose they thought of it as sort of a hip Malibu neonatal unit. I wonder if this was when the imprint of alcoholism found me. Or did it always run in my blood? There are certain activities and professions in life that, once you are exposed to them, get into your veins and you're finished. You can't help but give yourself over to them. Show business and politics are like that. Once you get a taste, you're screwed. The fast, boozy beach bar life of my parents in 1955 was like that, too. Once my bassinet found its way onto the Beachcomber Bar I was toast. Yes sirree, we had privilege, power, and wealth. What we didn't know was that alcoholism ignores all that.

I WAS christened a month later by Cardinal Francis McIntyre at Saint Monica's Church in Santa Monica. My mom showed up with her father and a check for a hundred thousand dollars, which she delivered to the Catholic hospital of my birth before the holy water had evaporated from my tiny Catholic forehead. I'm sure all those zeros had something to do with the good cardinal showing up to do the honors. My father was there with his friend Peter Sabiston, who became my godfather and whom I never remember meeting or having anything to do with. My father's mother, Lady May Lawford, also attended, and managed not to make a spectacle of herself by dissing either me, my father, or the Kennedys—which in and of itself was a minor miracle. If my father was my grandfather's worst nightmare, my mother was Lady May's. To her the Kennedys were "barefoot Irish peasants," and my mother was "a bitch" who had trapped her beloved son into marriage.

IF YOU believed the hype, my parents' marriage was storybook and pretty damn exciting. There were the presidential visits, the Rat Pack, Marilyn, weekly poker games with Hollywood's biggest and brightest, Vegas, Palm Springs, helicopters to work and an extra limo just for the bags whenever they traveled, which I guess was a lot because I don't remember them being around much.

In October 1961, *Cosmopolitan* magazine ran a cover story on my parents titled "Mr. and Mrs. Lawford, the Hollywood Branch of the Kennedy Family." The opening of the article read:

> *The tall, slender, athletic-looking young man was moving briskly back and forth between his living-room-sized bathroom and his billiard-room-sized bedroom, packing his monogrammed suitcases. Suddenly, he looked up. A small tousled (first-grade-sized) boy was standing in the doorway, arms akimbo. "Going away again, Dad?" The boy asked. His father nodded. The boy studied his father for a moment or two, then shrugged, lifted his hands, palms upward in a gesture of mock despair, turned on his heel, and walked out of the room. Six-year-old Christopher Lawford, like the rest of his famous parents' friends and family, has become resigned to their everlasting moving about from one of their glamorous worlds to another.*

I don't remember the guy who wrote the article, but he must have been there because he sure got it right.

The article went on to describe a week in the life of my mom and dad where they "whoop[ed] it up at a Hollywood party with a group of the town's most notable, and nosiest, luminaries"; were "demure and decorous" at a high society dinner party in New York; and relaxed "over an informal supper at The White House with the President of the United States and his wife."

"To the average man or woman" the author noted, "an evening in any one of these worlds once in a lifetime might seem so tantalizingly remote as not to be worth wishing for. To Peter and Patricia Lawford, this is their life."

It was also the life I was promised. It was a promise never realized.

Soon after I got home from securing my spot in a Catholic cemetery with my celebrated baptism, two events took place that had a lot to do with how I would view the primary relationships in my life. The first pretty much sums up my relationship with my parents; the other was the birth of my best friend for life.

My father, who had been an only child and was desperately clinging to the remnants of his sacred beach life, decided that having a newborn in the house wasn't going to work for him. I imagine a conversation that went something like this:

"Pat, he cries all the time. I can't show up on the set with bags under my eyes. Plus the house smells like shit, it's getting into my clothes. Why don't we rent the apartment across the street for him."

"I don't know, Peter, have you noticed how pricey rentals in Malibu are these days?"

My mother might have felt that getting her newborn an apartment of his own was a waste of money, but she wanted her marriage to work, so at the tender age of two months I got a place of my own, a couple doors down from my family house, nice and cozy for me and the nanny.

The second event took place three thousand miles away in Washington, D.C., on June 15, 1955. It was the birth of my cousin and future best friend David Anthony Kennedy to my uncle Bobby and aunt Ethel. I would not realize its impact on me for many years.

SNAPSHOT:

I awoke from my afternoon nap irritable and discontented. My diaper was wet, and I wanted off my back and out of this goddamn crib. I spent way too much time in my crib. I was always waiting for someone to do something to me or for me. I spent my life either unconscious or waiting to be serviced. Not a bad life if you can get it. I made this work for me long after I was out of diapers. I wasn't as cute, but I was just as helpless. Too bad it doesn't last. Anyway, on this particular day I was once again waiting for them to come and take me out of the four-sided prison with the stupid puppy dog mobile that dangled overhead in their failed attempt to keep me occupied. Today, three heads appeared over the railing: my mother, Mrs. So-and-So, who had been changing, feeding, and servicing me since the last Mrs. So-and-So, and somebody I had never seen before.

You know, now that I think about it, I don't think I was ever breast-fed. I can't be sure, but I'd lay odds. It was 1955 in America, and not many women in the upper echelon were cramming their mammaries into the mouths of babes. This isn't something I might be able to verify one way or the other. There are definitely no photos, and this would not have been a conversation my mother would be comfortable having, being old-school Irish and all.

My theory goes like this: Because I never bonded with my mother through suckling, I view the world as a dangerous place where everyone's out to fuck me over and no one can be trusted, especially women. The way to survive is to move fast, not commit, and grab as much shit as you can to fill the hole. I see the world this way because my mother never put her breast in my mouth.

So, back to my crib and me, waiting for the tit that would never come, and the new person with the kind face and funny accent. I was captivated. Her name was Mademoiselle, and by the time she showed up, my parents had moved down the beach from Malibu to Santa Monica and into a house that was big enough to accommodate both my father and me. The rented apartment and succession of rent-a-nannies—my life up to that point—must have been unmemorable, because meeting Mademoiselle that day is the very first thing I remember in this lifetime.

Our new house was a beautiful Spanish monstrosity, which according to Hollywood lore had been built by the construction crews from Paramount Studios as a weekend retreat for Louis B. Mayer. It was big, with a large slab of marble surrounding a spectacular pool, nuzzled right on the beach. According to my mother the house was always in danger of being devoured by termites, and we were constantly being evacuated by the Army Corps of Engineers in anticipation of the giant tidal wave that would level everything on Sorrento Beach. None of it happened, but the drama kept us on our toes—and it was fun running up to the top of the Pacific Palisades to wait in anticipation of the monster wave that would swallow our house.

Shit, man, I had a nanny. I've always been in denial about this aspect of my upbringing. There was something too genteel and aristocratic about being raised by a nanny. My father may have been patrician in his outlook and habits, but the Irish rebel of Kennedy dominated our view of ourselves. Having a nanny would never do, so we called her by her name, Mademoiselle, which isn't a name, really, it's a way to greet a young single Frenchwoman. Hey, that's sexy. A young single Frenchwoman raised me. But my Mademoiselle wasn't sexy. She was cute and cuddly. She was warm and safe. And she had nothing but love for me and my sisters. She was the kind of person you couldn't help inventing cute names for. I called her Mammy, Mammy Frudy, and Frud. Mammy was my first relationship with unconditional love. I think this is why I remember the day I met her. This was a woman who knew how to love without an agenda and did what she said she was going to do. And, she gave us sugar tits.

Mademoiselle:
Chrisstofere, I have special surprise for you.
Me:
What is it?
Mademoiselle:
Calmez-tu, mon petit.
Me:
What is it?
Mademoiselle:
I used to have this when I was a little girl in Paris.
Me:
Can I have it now?

13

> *Mademoiselle:*
> *Soyez-sage . . .* Don't tell Mommy.
> *Me:*
> I won't.

A sugar tit is butter and sugar wrapped in a rag. They're meant for sucking, not suckling, and though they may not be quite as meaningful as the real thing, they sure are good. It's hard not to remember someone who gave you a sugar tit.

When I was three years old I moved out of the nursery I shared with Mammy and into my own bedroom. My mom had decorated it with matching curtains, rug, and bedspreads in a motif of little soldiers with drums and bugles. I guess she figured the soldier motif would offset any pansy in me once my sisters started arriving. She was pretty aware that I was growing up in a house full of women. I didn't mind the soldiers, but the room was way too big. It scared the shit out of me to sleep there. One night I awoke in the middle of the night and looked over at the twin bed next to the one I slept in. It was the place in my bedroom where the monsters would hide. I had never seen them, but I knew they were there. I just hoped I wasn't alone when they decided to show themselves. It must have been one or two o'clock in the morning. Everyone was asleep. The house was quiet and dark. The only light was coming from the small night-light that I was mercifully allowed to have in my bathroom. I awoke with the awareness and terror that it was still nighttime and I was alone. I sat up in my bed and looked to where the dreaded monsters might be. Up until this night they were never there, but I always knew my luck would run out. And it did. On the other side of the twin bed, leaning over and leering at me, was the devil himself, horns and all, in the flesh or whatever the devil is made out of. He was as real as anything I had ever seen in my short life, and after a double take I was out of my bed and into Mademoiselle's room before you could say sugar tit. I was only five but the Catholics had done their job.

> *Me:*
> Mademoiselle, there's this really ugly guy with horns in my
> room.

Mademoiselle:
C'est une reve Christofere, you are only dreaming.
Me:
No Mammy, I swear he's there. I think it's the devil.
Mademoiselle:
Mon Dieu.
Me:
Really!
Mademoiselle:
Why would the devil be in your room? You're such a good
boy.
Me:
He was laughing and drooling and smacking his lips like he
wanted to eat me.
Mammy:
Non. the devil wouldn't eat a good boy.
Me:
I don't want to take any chances. Can I sleep in here with
you?
Mammy:
Allons. I'll get a gun and we can go take care of Mr. Devil.

Mademoiselle grabbed a toy gun, which seemed real enough to me, and we crept into my bedroom to see what we would find. Mademoiselle didn't believe Satan was sleeping with me but you'd never convince me of that. When we got there, the devil was gone but I wasn't at all sure he wouldn't be back. Mademoiselle agreed to stay in my room until the sun came up. She was there when I woke up. This impressed me.

My mother never gave me any slack when it came to being a "scaredy cat." After I was given the honor of having my own room, which I never really wanted, I would find ways to sneak into someone else's room when I got scared. My mom would sniff it out and magically appear to herd me back to face my demons. I never thought of going into my mother's or father's room. That would have been worse than what was under my bed.

15

My parents had separate bedrooms. I would go to visit with them when my mom was watching the news with Walter Cronkite and my dad was getting dressed for the evening festivities, but once the door leading to their wing of the house was closed, it was not a door any kid would want to open. It was dark, and both my parents slept hard. My mom slept in a king-sized bed with blinders over her eyes and all the windows open, so the breeze from the ocean was blowing the curtains all over the place—like a wall of dancing ghosts. I would stand there at the side of her bed whispering, "Mummy, are you awake?" She rarely stirred. There is something terrifying in being unable to wake up a parent.

I wouldn't even think about going into my dad's room.

On the nights the monsters threatened, I would beg my mom to stay with me until I calmed down. She would for a while. Sitting on the side of my bed, brushing my hair back and telling me, "There's nothing to be afraid of, Christopher. It's only your imagination. Daddy and I are right downstairs." My eyes closed and she was gone.

When my mother came into my bedroom before going out, it was as if light itself walked into the room. She had lots of jewels, energy, and glamour. My room would be filled with her smell. She was this il- luminated angel who represented a magical world that existed out there—beyond the walls of my scary room.

During the day, one of my parents lay around on the chaise longue reading a script in the sun. One taught me how to play touch football. Guess which was which.

My mom taught me how to play football by taking me out to the beach a couple times a week and sending me out on pass patterns. She was a Kennedy, and the fact that she had moved three thousand miles from the family didn't mean that her only son wasn't going to be profi- cient at the family game. When my mom was in town she drove us to school, helped with homework, and put us to bed every night, making sure we checked in with God before we crawled between the sheets. Once a week she would dismiss the staff and be a full-time mom from sunrise to sunset. I wondered why on these days we went to sleep when the sun was still up. I suspected that on these days my mom pushed the clocks ahead so that we'd go to bed an hour earlier.

This was my least favorite day of the week.

My mother had a breakfast of fresh-squeezed orange juice and toast in bed every morning. It was the one luxury she required. She would leave a note at the bottom of the stairs as to what time the staff should wake her. My father had his breakfast—two three-and-a-half-minute soft-boiled eggs and burned toast with cold butter—in the den. My parents were not morning people and knew better than to be in close proximity to each other during this time of day.

Chapter 2

My childhood on the beach in California was a utopia. I have never been as happy in my life as I was for the eight years I lived on Sorrento Beach in Santa Monica. My time was spent swimming and surfing in Santa Monica Bay. The entire beach was my backyard, from the Hiltons' house in the south all the way to Steele Hunter's house in the north. In between were Jack Lemon and Marjorie Dye. She was a granddaughter and heir to the Merriweather Post fortune. Marjorie was one of those women who was more like a man. Big and strong with a shock of beach blond hair that she kept in a ponytail, she spent her day lying in front of her house. She always seemed to have a glass in her hand and a phone to her ear. Her voice boomed, so you could hear her laugh all the way to the water. She was the only parent on our beach that I remember seeing around. I liked her because she was indifferent to what the kids were up to, but enjoyed seeing us run through her house. Her daughter, Wendy, was my sister Sydney's best friend.

Sydney was sixteen months younger than me, and was named after my father's father, Sir Sidney, who was a general in the British army. He was knighted for heroism in the field during the First World War. My dad kept an article from the *London Times* chronicling how during a charge against German trenches, my grandfather's horse had its head blown off by a piece of shrapnel. The animal continued to run for nearly a minute with my granddad glued to its back, leading the charge. In my six-year-old way of viewing the world, I didn't understand how a horse could continue on without its head or why the horse wouldn't be knighted instead of the man who was just along for the ride. Sir Sidney was in his sixties when my father was born, and dead by the time I was born.

Aside from showing the *Times* article and his medals, my father never spoke about him. The only thing we knew growing up was that he was old, in the army, and his name was Sidney. My dad held on to his father's medals, clippings, and awards long after he had sold or lost his other mementos. There were his swords, which I begged to play with but could only touch. There was the solid silver chalice that read *West London Volunteer Brigade, Pirbright/August 1900/Tent Pegging Competition won by Capt. Lawford.* I thought it was stupid to give such a nice trophy for pounding tent pegs into the ground, but I still wanted the chalice. I learned later that tent pegging is a difficult and demanding competition that takes place while in full gallop on the back of a horse. No wonder my dad wouldn't give it to me.

One of my dad's strengths was his tremendous pride in his father. It provided a strong side to his personal character. To me, there was something incongruous about a hero named Sidney, and I felt bad that my sister had to carry such an odd name through life.

My father's mother, Lady May Lawford, was the kind of crazy relative you wanted to keep locked in the cellar. Embarrassing moments were her specialty. She didn't believe in small gestures. There was the time she hired an elephant, put a big VOTE FOR NIXON sign on it, and rode it down Hollywood Boulevard. There was her autobiography, entitled *Bitch.* Or the time she telephoned Louis B. Mayer himself and just for laughs told him that my dad was a homosexual. She had flair, drank too much, and drove my dad nuts. The biggest knock against Lady May, though, was that—and this was only whispered incredulously—"she doesn't like your grandmother Rose." Proof positive she was crazy.

Lady Lawford might have been nuts and she drank a lot—but she was a Lady. She wore fur collars and hats. To me she was some sort of British royalty. She had that air about her of thinking she was better than anybody, and she knew she was better than the Kennedys. From day one she had groomed my dad for stardom and marriage to European royalty, not the ersatz American variety.

My sister Sydney was my girlfriend and twin-like sibling rolled into one. She was all pudgy cheeks and blond hair. The way she looked adoringly at me became in later life the litmus test for whether any woman appreciated me enough. Sydney also had the annoying habit of grabbing anything that belonged to me and destroying it. I guess it was her way of making sure I was paying attention to her. This would be another trait I would search out in females later.

My parents dressed Sydney and me in these ridiculous identical outfits, tweeds and plaids. I was in the boy version and she in the girl version but it didn't matter. I didn't like the accompanying feeling of preciousness that comes from being dressed like your sister. I had always assumed that this horror was my mother's doing. Later I learned that my father, who was an only child, had been dressed by his mother as a girl until he was eleven. Maybe this was one of my dad's chief contributions to my formative years.

The other parents on our beach seemed to be away as much as mine, and just as infamous.

The Hiltons had nine kids — most of them boys. Ricky Hilton was my age and my best friend. His hair was so blond it was white. The girls loved him but he was too shy to talk to them. Ricky and I went everywhere on the beach together. His parents had an enormous house, like one of their hotels. One day we snuck into his parents' bedroom so Ricky and his brother Davie could show me the gun their father kept under his pillow. It was a small .2-caliber revolver. The gun looked like a toy but had the weight of something real. The three of us were a little awed by the gravity of what we were seeing. This little thing could kill you!

"Why do your parents keep a gun under their pillow?" I asked Ricky.

"In case a robber comes in the middle of the night," he answered as if it was obvious.

This was the first I had heard of robbers hanging around our beach.

"But what if it goes off by accident while he's sleeping?"

I wouldn't want a gun under my pillow when I was asleep with all the squirming I did.

"Doesn't it hurt the side of your dad's head when he puts his head on the pillow," I wondered.

"It's a thick pillow," Ricky surmised.

Davy was getting nervous. "We better get out of here before we get caught." I left wondering why my parents didn't think we needed a gun to protect us from robbers in the middle of the night. Or maybe they had one. I went home to ask.

"Mom, do you have a gun in case robbers come in the middle of the night?"

"Christopher, we don't like guns in our family."

"But what about the robbers?"

"Christopher, there are no robbers on the beach."

I knew it!

My mom lost two siblings in the Second World War. She had an aversion to guns and violence. I had no idea how much that aversion would grow.

Our neighbor Steele Hunter was the actor who played Christ in all those bad movies about Jesus of Nazareth that ran on Christmas and Easter. His kids had a trampoline, which doubled as the neighborhood hangout. After school we would hightail it over to Jesus's house and see how many kids we could cram on his trampoline. We'd play a game called rocket ship, the purpose of which was to catch a bounce that would send you higher than anybody else. It was fantastically danger-ous, and we were allowed to do it because most of our parents were partying and not paying attention. The people they had watching us were not invested enough to intervene. Mademoiselle was the excep-tion, but I learned early and often how to disregard her admonitions with charm and guile. It was also a different time, when everyone wasn't so fucking precious about health and safety.

One day I caught a bounce and soared higher than anyone had ever soared before. It was exhilarating and painful. I came down off center, landing between the bars that formed the base of our launching pad. My leg broke in two places. I was put in a cast from my foot to my chest and relegated to a wheelchair for a month. It was hard to pee, almost impossible to take a shit, and I itched in places I couldn't get to. However, I learned a great lesson: For every bit of adversity God gives you He also sends blessings. Mine came in the perfectly identical eight-year-old bodies of the Roach twins.

I had been in love with the Roach sisters since kindergarten. They were adorable. I didn't have a preference, I would have taken either one, but until my rather dramatic incapacity, they hadn't given me the time of day. As it turned out, I didn't have to choose, I got them both. The Roach twins loved to play nurse and they didn't mind taking turns wheeling me around in my wheelchair. I loved to play patient—and also didn't mind taking turns. God is great.

THERE WERE a lot of beautiful people hanging around our backyard pool on the beach in Santa Monica. Marilyn Monroe was there in her scarf, trying to stay out of the sun. She had a quiet voice, would smile at me and head out to walk on the sand with my mom. My mother told me Marilyn was like "her little sister." It surprised her that Marilyn was so open with her. My mom didn't come from an environment where emotions and feelings were openly shared. Marilyn Monroe trusted my mother's love for her. There was nothing Marilyn had that my mom needed.

Judy Garland, Jack Lemon, Milton Berle, Angie Dickinson, Henry Fonda, Frank Sinatra, all would stop by on a regular basis. Of all the people who came by, my favorite was Lenny Gershe. He was a friend of my dad's and one of the few grown-ups who ever paid attention to me. He always had some wacky story about some odd cast of characters, which he told in a variety of different voices. Milton Berle always had a big cigar, which he would put on a toothpick when it got really small. When I asked him why he did that he told me, "Kid, the end of a cigar is the best part. It's got all the juice."

I didn't really care who was there, because my parents had built me my very own playground in a corner of the property. That was my kingdom. It had a slide, some swings, and enough buckets, shovels, and things to excavate a small city. In the middle of my little kingdom was a flagpole, which I was the master of. Every morning I would unfold the American flag, which I had neatly folded the night before, being careful not to let it touch the ground. I had been warned that it was a sign of great disrespect to let our flag touch the ground. Nobody ever told me why, but it was something I lived in constant fear of. Apparently this rule doesn't apply to the presidential flag, which I was also in charge of whenever uncle Jack stopped by, but I wasn't taking any chances—it never touched the ground either.

Once I recovered from my incapacitation as a result of the mishap on Jesus's trampoline, the Roach twins lost interest, so I set my sights on our beautiful African American housekeeper—Erma Lee Reilly. Erma Lee was in her late twenties and drop-dead gorgeous. At some point I had an epiphany, realizing she was black. I came home from school one day and announced, "Erma, you are black." She was alarmed that one of my friends had said something derogatory about race, so she marched me over to the dark ebony staircase in our house and said, "What color is that?" It was black and way darker than she was—her point was lost on me. I was still in love with her, whatever shade of black she was. Another afternoon, while holding court with my imaginary friends around the flagpole in my little kingdom and dressed in my slicker in anticipation of the tsunami that would never come, I leaned over the fence, looked into Erma Lee's eyes, and said, "You see, I'm in love." Then I asked her to marry me. I was six years old and already a romantic.

SNAPSHOT:

Joe Luft and I didn't have a lot to do with each other after our coincidental births on the same day in Saint John's hospital. We didn't go to the same school, and I don't remember any playdates. Nevertheless, we did have our own yellow brick road and it led straight to the Beverly Hills Hotel, where our parents would get together every year on March 29 with an intoxicated cadre of their friends and throw Joe and me a lavish birthday party. I don't remember how many of these we actually had, but it was enough to leave a lasting impression and to endow both of us with a pile of great birthday gifts.

I spent a lot of time figuring out what gift to get Joe. It was a competitive thing, who would give the cooler toy. The problem was my mom was cheap. She'd only give me five dollars, and no amount of pleading would increase it. On my sixth birthday I found something for Joe that I knew would be the most fantastic toy he was likely to get: a model of Count Dracula. Paint and all. I had to have it but didn't have enough money. This would be a recurring problem for me in my life. On this day I found my solution. I asked Erma for a pen and a piece of paper. I wrote out my first IOU for $1.47 to Erma lee Reilly and thereby was introduced to the great American habit of debt.

The Beverly Hills Hotel was not the ideal place for a kid to have his sixth birthday party. The maître d' wouldn't let us run around, and the chairs weren't high enough, making it difficult to reach the cake, which was way too good to be appreciated by six-year-olds. Joe and I would be seated at either end of a big table and have a whole bunch of expensive gifts lavished on us. We were allowed to invite our friends, but they paled in comparison—the grownups were so much bigger and more dramatic. Whatever room you happen to be in with a movie star, they're always the center of attention—even if it's your birthday. They also buy better presents—no matter how much debt a six-year-old goes into.

Chapter 3

Don't touch what you can't grab.
— EMINEM

Las Vegas was like Oz to me. A magical place on the other side of the mountains. Our parents were always going. It was the land where kids weren't allowed.

My father worked there, doing shows, first with the Rat Pack and then with Jimmy Durante. Jimmy Durante was Sydney's godfather — which wasn't as cool as having your godfather be Frank Sinatra, like my sister Victoria, but it was a hell of a lot cooler than my guy, Peter Sabiston. My mom loved going to Vegas with my dad. She loved gambling, glitz, and the party. And she could keep up with the boys. Not long after my stint on the Beachcomber Bar, my mom walked into the Sands Casino, bassinet in hand: "I loved roulette and I always bet on red. I put you on the roulette table on red. It came up black. I lost but they didn't take you. So I guess I won."

Thanks, Mom.

I always wondered what she would have won if it came up red.

I remained tethered, but the stimuli and excitement were not lost on me. Sometime in early 1961 my sisters and I were delivered to our parents in the gambling mecca by a big limousine. It was the first limo I had been in. It was huge, with all these gadgets that a kid had control over. It had roll-up seats in the back and electric windows. I spent the five hours on Highway 5 seeing how many times I could rearrange the seating configuration and getting my fingers caught in the windows.

Kids aren't allowed in the casinos, but that didn't apply to us. We ran through the casino at the Sands, playing tag and looking for the set where our father and his buddies were making Rat Pack history in *Ocean's 11*, the sounds of chips falling and slots paying all around us. Sydney and I were treated like royal offspring. My parents were too busy to accompany us, but there was always someone to keep tabs. This was the second movie set I had visited, the first being *Sergeants 3*.

I only visited my dad once while he was filming *Sergeants 3*, but it was enough to let that movie-making thing into my blood. My dad and uncles Frank, Dean, and Sammy playing cowboys and Indians, dressed up in cavalry suits that a kid would die for. And now they were these cool burglars about to steal all the money in Las Vegas. I could do without the suits, but having all that money would be all right. By the time I found my way onto the set of *Ocean's 11* I already knew that this was where I wanted to be. I never let on to my father. It was his world and he never showed any inclination to share it with me. He named his production company Chrislaw Productions, which was his way of bringing me into the mix but he would never bring me into his business. One day I was sneaking around the set trying not to bump into anything and I found this long table spread with every kind of junk food. Free. Craft service sealed the deal.

At night we went to the Copa Room at the Sands Hotel to catch the Rat Pack's show. We sat in the front row. Sydney would lean onto the stage sucking her thumb with her eyes glued to the wings waiting for her dad's entrance. She hardly noticed the crooning of Mr. Dean Martin. My dad walked on stage with Sammy and Joey Bishop, all wearing tuxedo jackets and boxer shorts—with their pants folded over their arms. The audience went wild, and Sydney screamed, "Daddy, you forgot to put your pants on"—loud enough to stop the show.

My dad was happy when he was working. He was especially happy working with the Rat Pack: "I couldn't wait to get to work. Everybody was running on the same wavelength. It was a blast. We did two shows a night at the Sands, went to bed at five, got up at eleven to work on the movie. After filming we'd sit in the steam, get a massage, have some pasta, and start all over again. They were betting we'd all end up in a box."

My father was really conscientious about two things—his work and his clothes. He knew his lines, was never late, didn't cause problems on the set, and was impeccably attired. One of my dad's favorite expressions was "I'm not Charlie Movie Star." What he meant was that he didn't want to be treated special because he was a movie star. It spoke to his egalitarian nature and the years spent in Hollywood as a working stiff. But like anybody who has ever become a star, he liked being special, and despite his protestations to the contrary, he liked being treated like a star.

The Rat Pack was a very exclusive club with its own language and rules. They were always joking, making each other and the crew laugh, but underneath ran emotional torrents more common to a dysfunctional family. Watching them was like being on the outside looking in on guys with a special relationship to each other creating something that only they could do. It was very attractive—even to a kid.

SNAPSHOT:

I was hiding in the entrance hall in my pajamas and my red bathrobe, waiting for the explosion of anger and retribution that was certain to come when my father learned of the horrible thing I had done. Up until a few days before, the absolute worst dirty word I had heard in my short life was *asshole*. I knew it was a bad word because my best friend, Gerry, told me that if a grown-up ever heard me say it, all hell would break loose. Gerry was my best friend in second grade at Saint Martin's. We called him Gerry Escalator. That wasn't his real name but I didn't know that until many years later. When I was seven I thought it would be hip to have Escalator as a last name. Now I'm not so sure. Gerry was one of those kids who found out about stuff that kids weren't supposed to know about way before kids were supposed to know about it. I might

CHRISTOPHER KENNEDY LAWFORD

have been young but I knew what an asshole was. I had one, and I knew it was dirty and nasty. I had made the connection that equating a human being with such a place was a pretty horrible offense. Well, if asshole would result in all hell breaking loose, *fuck* would bring eternal damnation and worse. It was such a bad word I didn't know what it meant, and neither did Gerry.

One of the great things about our house on Sorrento Beach was that it sat next to an empty lot. There had been a house there but it had been demolished, and they left behind all the rooms belowground so there were all these really cool places to hide and play for all of us kids on the beach. We went there to make forts, throw bricks at each other, and hunt for lizards and snakes. We played spud with a brick. Spud is a game you usually play with a ball. A kid throws the ball in the air and calls out a number that corresponds to one of the other kids playing, and that kid has to catch the ball while all the other kids run as far away as they can. Not a great game to play with a brick. I learned this one day when the brick found its way into my skull as I was running, I thought, away from its falling trajectory. My mother heard my scream and came running. By the time she got to me, I was barely conscious. Mademoiselle told me there was so much blood covering my mom and me that she didn't know who was bleeding. There was no apparent brain damage, but I was left with a monstrous headache and a warning that if I ever ventured onto the empty lot again I would be grounded for life.

This didn't stop me.

I had already developed a strong appetite for dangerous behavior and questioning authority. I was also pretty good at not getting caught. One day I got caught and Mademoiselle threatened to tell my parents. That's when I thought it a good time to let her know the new word I had learned. Because I didn't know what *fuck* meant, I said it to her without any specific intent. I just put it out there. I was feeling my oats and eager to see what kind of reaction it might provoke. You would have thought I had called Charles DeGaulle a sissy. She was horrified and backed away from me, muttering in French about Jesus and making the sign of the cross. The only coherent English I got was that she was going to tell my father.

Up until this moment I hadn't done anything bad enough in my life to warrant a disciplinary audience with my old man. My dad had a pretty laissez-faire approach toward fatherhood. I don't ever remember him disciplining me. The fact that she chose him as the ultimate threat is curious. He was the man of the house, but not the authority. It did achieve the desired result of striking fear into my tiny heart, however. I hid behind the giant urn and watched as she made her way into the den where my father spent most of his time when he wasn't tanning himself on the chaise longue.

The den was the most important room in our house along with the bar. It was the place where all the parties started and where we kids were always ushered out of. My parents spent most of their time there when they were together, before things went south and my mom started spending more time in her bedroom. Sydney and I would be brought into the den before we went to bed to spend some quality time with the parents. My dad would munch on chicken curry and brussels sprouts. His favorites, not ours. My sister and I would watch my dad watch TV. My mom would read to us, and sometimes there would be a show. One night Marilyn Monroe showed up and taught Sydney and me how to do the twist. Well, actually, she did the twist, and we watched. I don't know if she was any good but the grown-ups sure liked it. After she was done, it was our turn. When you are six years old and you have to perform for your parents and their friends it sucks. If you have to follow Marilyn Monroe it *really* sucks! Sydney and I did our pathetic little twists. It was humiliating. I remember thinking at the time, "Well, I guess that's the end of a career in show business."

Hiding behind the urn, I strained to hear what was being said for some clue as to what my fate would be. I wonder why I was so afraid of what my dad might do. He never got mad—except once when I was sitting in his room watching him get changed for a dinner party. I used to do that whenever he was home. It was the only time we spent together alone and it was one of those intimate male bonding opportunities.

My dad walking around naked, choosing his wardrobe for the evening, and me, sitting on his floor in my PJs, asking questions about life and the world. Well, on this particular night, my dad was doing his thing, walking around naked, and I got it in my head that this was something my mom needed to see. It doesn't make sense. I was five years old.

I ran into my mom's room and dragged her from the mirror, where she was putting on her face, and into my dad's room, so she could have a look at his privates. As we came through his door, I pointed at my father's naked body and said, "Look, Mom, Daddy's nude." My father looked up from the sock he was about to put on his foot—my dad put his socks on before he put on anything else—and instead of placing the sock over his foot, he covered his manhood with it. As he did this, he looked at me with some disdain and said, "Christopher, why did you bring your mother in here while I was dressing? You're a traitor!" My mom came to my defense, saying, "It's just normal childhood curiosity, Peter."

What a sight—my dad standing there with a sock covering his penis, looking daggers at my mom, who was enjoying his moment of discomfort. As for me, I was simply confused.

My dad liked to surf, sit in the sun, read scripts, and go places in helicopters. He loved the beach and all that went with it. The girls, the volleyball, and the surfing. My mom would walk the beach for hours in back of our house; my dad would play volleyball with Wilt Chamberlain and his crew. Dad pretty much single-handedly brought surfing to Malibu. He didn't know how to surf at first, but he learned. He loved surfing at the Malibu Pier. Soon people started showing up to surf the break at the Malibu Pier with Peter Lawford, and a new chapter in California beach life was born.

My father didn't do the things one normally associates with father-son bonding. He didn't teach me how to surf, for instance, but he did take me to my first baseball game, where I saw Sandy Koufax pitch a shutout against the Milwaukee Braves at Dodger Stadium. We sat in a fancy box, and I thought every ball hit to the outfield was going to be a home run. Sandy Koufax became one of my heroes. I never remember actually playing catch with my father. After all, he was English. Years later, during one of his visits to New York, he took me to see Willie

Mays play at Shea Stadium. The "Say Hey Kid" was a god to me. I spent hours trying to re-create The Catch, his over-the-shoulder basket grab in the 1954 World Series. Going to see him play was a really big deal. My father brought us to our seats and then disappeared for pretty much the entire game. When the game was over, he showed up at our seats, said he had a surprise for me, and brought me into the Mets' locker room and to the locker of the man himself. I got to say hi to my hero, watch him get dressed, and have a piece of his bubble gum. He had a whole box of Bazooka—which I thought was so cool it became one of my goals in life. This was my dad in a nutshell: he was great at the occasional flamboyant gesture, but the nitty-gritty, everyday-relationship stuff was difficult for him. He was not comfortable being a father. So what to do with his six-year-old son, who had just told his nanny to essentially "fuck off."

Nothing.

From behind the urn I heard my father say, "It's just a part of growing up"—and that was the end of it. I had dodged a bullet, and another brick was cemented in my budding wall of imperviousness.

Chapter 4

Some alcoholics have bad childhoods,
but most of us have long ones.
— ANONYMOUS

W hen I was five years old, the Democrats came to Los Angeles to nominate their candidate for president of the United States. My uncle Jack was the favorite, and my parents were the alchemists, mixing the power and the glitter. For five days there was a nonstop whirl of activity. An air of excitement and importance pervaded the laid-back movie-star ambience—the normal fare around our house. The phones rang off the hook, and one of my mother's brothers or sisters seemed to be in every room, talking to someone about something important. Whenever my uncles or aunts showed up it was exciting. They seemed to bring so much life and energy to the lazy order that we lived in. In our house we had to be quiet because "So-and-So is asleep." There were strict nap and bedtimes for kids and dress codes to enhance cuteness. In short, there were a lot of rules and regulations and segregation of the adults and children except for specific times.

All of this went out the window when my mom's family came to visit. They overran us, always in a group, moving fast, a continuous flow, stopping for a quick swim, cocktail, or to work the phones. I don't remember seeing my grandfather, but my mom was always yelling out to one of her brothers, "Daddy's on line two." My parents gave a party one night and our house swelled with the best and the brightest from politics and Hollywood. Frank Sinatra, Judy Garland, Marlon Brando, and Nat King Cole. My mother even brought in a donkey to make all the Democrats feel at home. Sydney and I played with it until it took a crap in the entranceway, probably a result of all those little hot dogs we fed it.

The party protocol at our house was that my sisters and I would be bathed, dressed in our pajamas and our matching red bathrobes, and delivered to our parents, after which we were allowed to mingle with the early-arriving guests and shove as many hors d'oeuvres into our mouths as we could from seven to seven-thirty. At seven-thirty we were brought upstairs by my mom to say our prayers and get ready for bed. After we were tucked in and my mom went back to her guests, we would sneak out onto my mother's balcony to watch the festivities from above. On this particular party night we were allowed more time with the guests because most of them were aunts and uncles who had more tolerance for the suntanned little kids running around snatching up all the guacamole and chips. My uncle Teddy taught me how to put a cherry tomato in my mouth and slap my cheeks, projecting the inner contents onto whoever was unlucky enough to be standing in front of me. This proved an amusing party trick with family, but when I sprayed tomato goop all over the director Otto Preminger, it was time for the children to go to bed.

The 1960 Democratic Convention was held at the Los Angeles Sports Arena. My mother brought me there on the night when the presidential nomination took place. It was the hugest room I'd ever seen. There were thousands of people, waving colorful signs and making lots of noise. I stayed up later than I had ever stayed up in my short life, but fell asleep before any of the good stuff happened. My mother brought me back to a hotel room and put me to bed. Sometime later that night, Uncle Jack and my mother came into the bedroom. He sat on the side of the bed, my mom standing over him.

JFK:
Christopher, wake up. I have something to tell you.
CL:
What? Are we going back to that place where the weird people in the crazy hats and carrying the big signs are?

33

JFK:
No. They've all gone back to their precincts. Christopher,
I won. I am going to be running for president of the
United States.
CL:
Wow! That sounds like a hard job.
JFK:
It will be. We are all going to have to work very hard. Will
you help me?
CL:
Sure, Uncle Jack. But can we do it tomorrow?
I'm really tired now.

I had no idea what he was talking about, but I agreed to help, knowing that whatever was happening in my world was going to take a backseat to what was happening in the grown-ups' world. Then my mom lifted me up, threw me over her shoulder, and off we went to the safety of our beach house.

My mother was never happier than when her family was around her. They invigorated her, made her more alive. She was more a part of her family of origin than she was of the family she created. When my uncle Jack went onto the stage at the convention to celebrate winning the nomination, he invited his family to come with him. But my mom stopped my dad from joining, saying to him, "Peter, you can't come. You're not a Kennedy." My uncle came to my dad's rescue. "Pat, he's your husband, I'd say that qualifies him. Besides it doesn't hurt having a good-looking movie star around." My uncle was generous, but wasn't the damage already done? If my mom thought my father was a second-string Kennedy when it came to ceremonial events, one could only imagine how the rest of the family would treat him.

My mom even pulled this shit with me, and I was a Kennedy. She had a proprietary thing with anything Kennedy. I think it had something to do with intimacy and participating in the family's glory. Her family was the one place in her life where she found intimacy. It was also, along with her children, where she got her self-esteem. It was con-

fusing because, for much of my life, she seemed to be continually trying to separate herself from her family.

My mom was never happier than that night in 1960 when her
brother won the Democratic nomination and she cast her vote for him
as a delegate from California. On that night she blended her life with
that of her family and she shone. She stood at the apex between the
worlds of politics and Hollywood. She looked fantastic there.

My father and my uncle Jack really liked one another. Jack
Kennedy was more generous and accepting of my dad than were his
siblings—including my mother. My uncle appreciated my old
man's cool and grace. He valued my dad's proximity to the ladies
and that my dad got good gossip. My uncle Jack liked gossip. I suppose it took his mind off the business of saving the world. My father
also knew how to dress and make the camera work for him. This
proved useful to my uncle. Jack Kennedy didn't spend a lot of time
thinking about his wardrobe and even less time worrying about
where the camera was. That changed before the first Kennedy-
Nixon debate.

PL:
Jack, I called my tailor at Chipp in New York.
He'll see you tomorrow.
JFK:
Peter, are you saying I need help with my wardrobe?
PL:
I know something about looking good on television.
Nixon will look like a used-car salesman. There's a real
opportunity here.
JFK:
Okay. What are your thoughts?
PL:
Wear a dark blue suit, a blue shirt, and the darkest makeup
that still looks natural.
JFK:
That's it?

PL:

No. Don't be afraid of the camera. Look right into it as
though you are talking to a friend across the dinner table.
Every person watching will feel as though you're talking only
to him.

My uncle wore a dark blue suit and maintained steady eye contact
with the viewers throughout the first debate. He kicked Richard
Nixon's ass. Jack Kennedy's performance in that debate was arguably
the most important single factor in the election. My dad was proud of
his contribution.

There is a famous photograph of my uncle and my father on the
bow of a sailboat. My dad loved the picture and the reaction my uncle
had when he first saw it. My dad told me that my uncle picked up the
framed photo, looked at it for a minute, and then said to my dad, "Peter, there's something wrong with this picture."

"What's that?" my father said.

"Nobody's going to believe it, because it looks like I'm listening to
your advice."

On April 23, 1960, Peter Sidney Lawford became a citizen of the
United States. He did this so he could cast a vote for Jack Kennedy to
be the next president of the United States. I remember him telling me,
"I never studied for anything in my life as hard as I did for that damn
citizenship test. I was sure I was going to fail. All I wanted was to cast a
vote for your uncle Jack."

He kept the telegram from my aunts Joan and Ethel congratulating him on his new citizenship:

CONGRATULATIONS AND WELCOME TO AMERICA. HOWEVER, HOLD
YOUR PASSPORT TILL AFTER WEST VIRGINIA, AND IF HUBERT WINS,
WE'LL GO BACK TO ENGLAND WITH YOU.

WHEN ONE of your relatives runs for president of the United States a
couple of things happen. The first is that everybody pretty much drops
what they were doing before and focuses on that. The other thing that

happens is that the person who is running suddenly becomes way more important, to everybody in the family, than they ever were before. If the relative wins, everybody goes back to their lives, which now pale in comparison with what they've just experienced. The elected relative becomes Mr. President, and more important than God, and everybody else in the family — especially the kids — gets to revise their accomplishments and goals.

The bar gets set pretty high; you get some pretty lofty standards to live up to. *Let's see, after elementary school, I become a world leader. I should really get my grades up.*

After the election my parents went to Palm Springs, California, to spend the weekend with the new president of the United States. My uncle stayed at Bing Crosby's house instead of at Frank Sinatra's house. This really pissed Frank off. He was counting on his pad in the desert being the Western White House during the Kennedy years. What he didn't count on was, after the FBI got pictures of Frank's mobster house guests, my uncle had a change of heart about weekending with the Chairman of the Board. My parents stayed at Jimmy Van Husen's house down the street from Bing's. They brought Sydney and me along, with Erma to keep an eye on us.

Our first day in the desert, Erma, Sydney, and I ran into a giant rattlesnake sunning itself in Jimmy's driveway. Erma hated snakes, especially the kind that could kill you. I wanted to hear the rattle. No dice. Erma hustled us into the house, warning my mother, "Mrs. Lawford, don't go outside. There's a giant rattlesnake sitting right in the middle of the driveway."

My mom didn't even blink. "Erma, make sure the kids eat. I will be having lunch with the president."

And with that she headed out the door, past the rattler, and up the driveway to lunch with her brother.

Erma ran to tell my dad of my mother's imminent peril, but he also dismissed it, saying, "That snake won't bite her. It wouldn't dare."

The next morning my dad had some Secret Service guys deliver breakfast to Erma and his kids courtesy of the president of the United States. Now that's room service.

SNAPSHOT:

I didn't know the difference between a horse and a donkey. They both scared the shit out of me, but my mom seemed pleased we had stumbled on a barn full of donkeys. She liked donkeys; it went with the territory of being a Democrat. "Look, Christopher, they're small and they seem so calm." The animal she kept referring to as "mine" was mangy and disagreeable. She called it "my horse." It sounds better to say, "Christopher, get up on your horse," than "Christopher, get up on your donkey."

I was instructed, "Just put your foot in the stirrup and swing your leg over."

"But Mummy," I whined, "it won't stand still."

"Christopher, donkeys are very calm and slow. See his short little legs. He's not going anywhere. Just put your foot in the stirrup and hop up on his back."

What she didn't tell me was that once I was "up on his back," it would be impossible to get the animal to go anywhere. Donkeys are stubborn. Mine had a strong desire for the barn. It was a war, and the donkey had much stronger motivation. I was clinging to the little bit of control I had left. This was not a good time.

Palm Springs, California, is hot and really bright. The sun seems bigger, and there is only desert, nothing to conceal the pulsating light from the tiny sensitive retinas of a six-year-old. I didn't see a lot through my tiny squinting slits. This, coupled with the fear of being on a disagreeable beast who had even less of an instinct to take a walk in the hot desert sun than I did, was making me very nervous.

Why do parents think that riding is fun for small children? It's not. Horses look like wooly mammoths to a six-year-old. My solace was the donkey's mane. I became one with the mound of ratty hair bursting forth like a dirty wave from my donkey's neck. I would release my grip only when my hands were severed or we were safely back at the barn.

The great thing about a landscape of tumbleweeds and cacti from a boy's point of view is the lizards and the unrealized possibility of running into a rattlesnake—but we had already done that. There is danger in the desert and a sense that you are following in the hoofprints of the real cowboys. As we headed out into the glare of this reptilian Eden, following a path that was discernable to no one but our guide, I vacillated between the fantasy that I was a prospector making my way to a river of gold and the reality of being a small kid glued to the back of a bad-tempered beast who was a hairbreadth away from open revolt. Our destination was a giant man-made crater in the middle of the desert. I assume our guide chose it because it was the only discernable point on the horizon, since all cactuses looked pretty much the same. We arrived at the giant hole in the desert without incident. I was cautiously allowing myself to feel that sense of relief one feels when the time comes to head for home.

This relief was tempered by my donkey's infatuation with the edge of the giant crater. He loved clomping his big clumsy hooves up to the edge of its vertical walls of sand tumbling down to a floor far, far below and peering over as if looking for a safe place to land. Well, I may have been only six, but I knew this donkey was no Dumbo and had no feather, so I used all my will and muscle to turn him away from his obsession and back toward the barn. The guide had told me that if I wanted to get my "horse" to go in a particular direction, I should pull the rein in that direction and kick the animal on his flank to motivate him. I was tentative; I didn't want to piss him off by pulling or kicking too hard. I was little. I had six-year-old arms and legs, and though fueled by the adrenaline of fear, I was no match for the three hundred pounds of nasty stubbornness I was sitting on.

Life is wonderful because in every experience there is an opportunity to learn something new. In this moment I learned why cowboys wear cowboy boots. It's not just because they look cool. They actually have a function beyond shit kicking. When you kick a donkey in its flank wearing cowboy boots, there is cause and effect. When you kick a donkey in its flank wearing sneakers, it's like being a rubber fly. There is no effect; you are just an irritant.

So here I was, at the precipice, going nowhere and becoming more and more frantic. The other wonderful thing about life is that change is inevitable. Just when I thought my donkey and I were destined to become a permanent fixture in the desert landscape, he turned—slowly at first, then with more urgency as if answering a call that only he could hear, a call from the barn, maybe, that dinner was ready. Whatever he heard, it motivated him in a powerful way. What had been slow and stubborn became in an instant fast and directional. Like a rocket, he was off. I had no idea a donkey could move that fast. Desire is a powerful thing even in a donkey. As the donkey ignited in his race home I made a desperate attempt to move my grip from the reins to the mane. I did this in midlurch and came up empty. As I tumbled off I had two thoughts. The first was "I hope I don't land on a cactus." The second was "How did my foot get caught in the stirrup?"

There aren't many events in childhood that leave as profound an impression as being dragged feetfirst over a mile of virgin desert by a raging donkey. It will definitely put a damper on riding for a lifetime or two. The cactus will never be a plant I will cultivate.

The only other time I visited Palm Springs was to accompany my father to a sit-down of sorts with Frank Sinatra. My father hadn't seen Frank since Frank got pissed when JFK stayed at Bing Crosby's house instead of his. It was almost as unpleasant as being mutilated on Mr. Donkey's wild desert ride.

FRANK SINATRA was a pretty big deal in my life. The story goes like this: Frank and my dad were buddies of a sort. Frank had threatened to break my father's legs into a hundred different pieces after he read that my father was dating Ava Gardner. Frank threatened all of his friends like this, so it wasn't that big a deal. My mom loved Frank Sinatra, and early on was always after my dad to introduce her. My dad was incredulous: "Pat, are you nuts? The guy wanted to cripple me for dating his ex-wife." My mother was practical. "Oh, Peter, don't be so dramatic. He didn't do it. Anyway, I love his voice, and he might be able to help your career."

My dad held his ground, but my mother was resourceful. She orchestrated a dinner at her good friends Gary and Rocky Cooper's house where she finally got her wish and had dinner with the great man himself. Frank was charmed, and Mom and Dad were back in Mr. Sinatra's orbit, but just as importantly, Frank was in the Kennedy orbit.

There is a strange synergy of mutual career advancement and ego massaging in politics and show business. They are both mercenary worlds where relationships are only relative to the next rung on the ladder of success. Frank figured he got JFK elected. He got pissed at the Kennedys for not being thankful enough, not overlooking his mob connections, and he eventually took it out on my old man because he could.

MY SECOND sister, Victoria, was born on November 2, 1958. Victoria was named for Jack Kennedy's 1958 Senate victory, which occurred on the same day as her birth. Her middle name—Francis—came from Sinatra. How cool is that? Uncle Frank was at our house a lot back then, especially when my uncles were around. I remember him because whenever he showed, he gave Victoria gifts that were so much better than anything I ever got from my godfather. After Frank was informed that his Palm Springs house wasn't going to be the Western White House, he blew up the helicopter landing pad he had built to accommodate the president, along with his friendship with my old man. We didn't see him again around our house. No more gifts for Victoria. We did still see him on occasion after my parents separated. He visited my mother in New York, and one summer spent time on a huge yacht that he anchored off my family's place in Hyannis Port. My cousins and I used to buzz around his giant boat in our little Boston whalers, trying to get a glimpse of the great man and his hot young bride, Mia Farrow, but they were never on deck. One day Sinatra invited the whole family on board for lunch and a cruise. Frank seemed awkward at sea. I guess you can't take Vegas out of the crooner. He was also pissed that he had to share his yacht with thirty pint-sized Kennedys who had no political clout. Mia looked like a deer caught in the headlights.

I twice got a glimpse beyond Sinatra's facade. I was in my early twenties and my mom brought my sisters and me to see Frank at Radio City Music Hall in New York. After the show we visited him backstage. In an awkward moment he asked me, "Chris, how's your old man doing?" This was surprising enough, but he asked in such a way that it seemed as if he actually cared—and that he understood what I might have to endure being my father's son. It was creepy having "a moment" with the Chairman of the Board backstage at Radio City, but in some weird way my heart opened. I was by then a full-blown addict and must have radiated pain and insecurity—something Frank, despite being a mob-influenced hard-ass, knew a thing or two about.

My second peek was a few years later in Palm Springs with my dad. We went to spend the weekend at Sinatra's house. He had summoned my father to make peace, claiming through an intermediary that there were no hard feelings and that he didn't know what all the fuss was about.

I have no idea why my dad brought me along—maybe he figured that if it was a setup, Frank wouldn't have his kneecaps broken in front of his kid, or maybe my dad didn't want to show up in front of his long-time nemesis all alone. Either way, I had never felt this kind of need from him.

Frank looked old and unhappy. If he was glad to see my old man he sure had a funny way of showing it. My father was gracious and open; I could tell he would have liked to rekindle whatever relationship existed before the breakup. But Frank was too far down the road. He was the king, never really looking at my dad and grunting one-syllable responses. I think Sinatra resented my father—his looks, his style, his command of the language, and his fluency in French. Frank had the power and the voice but my dad had the grace and the style. Those who have been given everything always want more.

Frank was a tough guy from the streets of Hoboken, and he would never be anything else, no matter how badly he wanted it. This left him with a bellyful of anger and resentment. And he had been living with that for so long he wasn't about to let it go at this stage of his life. He didn't have to: he was the Chairman of the Board, for Christ's sake.

SNAPSHOT:

Friday night was poker night at the Lawfords'. The poker room was located right next to the bar—one of the two most important rooms in the house. Somebody was always going to the bar for something. On this particular night those sitting around the table with my mom and dad were Dean Martin, Judy Garland, Sammy Davis, Martha Raye, and the producer Joe Naar, one of my dad's best friends. At seven years of age I was allowed into the small room off the bar with the green felt table and the brightly colored chips to serve guacamole and salsa until my bedtime at seven-thirty.

Peter:
What's the game, Bunny?
Pat:
Whatever you say, baby.
Dean:
Let's play two-card monte.
Sammy:
I'm in. Can someone cash a check?
Dean:
Sure, Sammy. But I want Frank to endorse it!
(laughs all around)
Joe:
I saw Edie Gorme the other night. She was fantastic.
Judy:
(drunk)
What the fuck do you know about music, Joe?
Pat:
(pretending she didn't hear)
Okay, let's play. Who's dealing?
Peter:
Come on, Judy. Don't be mean.
Judy:
Fuck you too, Peter. If it wasn't for the war, you wouldn't have a career.

Nice friendly games.

My mom and dad weren't doing very well in their marriage, despite their cute repartee at the card table, but in public they often

43

displayed affection. They had this routine at the dining room table, popping gingersnaps into each other's mouths while making up little love ditties. I don't remember them doing this when it was just us. Only when there were guests.

It was a performance, but they sure loved those gingersnaps. They were like Nick and Nora Charles from the *Thin Man* series. When things were good, they were perfectly happy just to be together, and part of that happiness depended on the exclusion of the rest of the world and on alcohol. When things got bad, you could never really tell what was happening in their relationship. They played things pretty close to the vest. One of our cooks observed that "if they argued, they must be doing it on the beach when it was raining," because nobody ever heard them fight.

IN OCTOBER 1962, I didn't believe that the missiles they kept talking about would ever find their way to the beach where I lived in California. After all, Sister Maria Claire had drilled us for a year and a half in the art of ducking under our desks and nothing had fallen from the sky. I was beginning to think the whole air raid thing was just a way for the good sisters at Saint Martin of Tours to keep us on our knees. But everybody was really nervous. And it seemed the people in my house got nervous before anybody else.

It's conceivable we got some inside information.

I was right. No missiles fell on the beach in Santa Monica, but it was close. The United States and the Soviet Union went nose-to-nose over offensive nuclear missiles on the island of Cuba and brought the three nations to the verge of war. The Cuban Missile Crisis would prove the defining moment of the Kennedy presidency. My uncles Jack and Bobby proved heroic in their strength and restraint. They forced the Soviet bully to back down, kept the bearded guerrilla impotent, and showed the Washington diplomatic and military establishment who was boss. I grew up on the lore; my uncle Bobby's book *Thirteen Days* took its place next to *Profiles in Courage* as sacred text in our house.

I didn't know it at the time but my indoctrination had begun. Not only in the greatness of my uncles' public service but also in the demonizing of the enemies of the Republic and of the family. When it came to Cuba it was difficult for the average American to get a balanced view. For me it was impossible. I bought the story without question. It would take forty years for me to define my own beliefs when it came to Cuba. It would take almost that long for me to find my own political compass.

SNAPSHOT:

I got my first car when I was seven years old. It was Christmas, and we had this enormous tree in an enormous room that we called the living room, but we only went in there for parties and at Christmastime, because it was better for events than actual living. My seventh Christmas was a bonanza. Along with the expected mountain of toys came a really neat battery-powered car from FAO Schwartz that a kid could actually drive. It was a Thunderbird convertible, almost an exact replica of the real thing, shiny with a white laminated steering wheel and leather seats that four tiny asses could squeeze into.

A car for a kid. How cool! It was big and heavy, not something easily hidden, so I discovered it a week before Christmas halfheartedly concealed in a corner of our garage. My excitement was quickly tempered by the fear that it might not be for me. I did have a couple of sisters younger than me. As the oldest male I had become used to the pecking order of getting all the great stuff first, yet it wasn't an absolute given that the car would be mine. My parents could pull one of those "It belongs to all of you" deals that leaves everybody feeling gypped. Another thing that happens when you are a kid facing the possibility of reaping treasure beyond your wildest dreams is denial. You start thinking shit like, "It's probably not for me. One of my parents' friends left it here for one of their kids and he's gonna pick it up any day now."

Kids do this to minimize the disappointment if they're proved right. Well, the car turned out to be mine, and I was surprised, although my parents cooled my enthusiasm by telling me not to be selfish and to "share it with your sisters." I was often encouraged to feel lucky for getting what I got or to show more gratitude or to share. Maybe this instinct comes from the guilt associated with being given so much. My grandmother Rose used to say, "From those to whom much is given, much is expected." It was a family ethic. Noble. But it kind of wrecks the joy of getting stuff.

There was something else under the tree that Christmas morn: a Saint Bernard puppy. He was one in a long line of canines that wouldn't last long at 625 Pacific Coast Highway. Puppies grow fast, and Saint Bernard puppies grow really big really fast.

I named him Bernie for obvious reasons. We invented this game; well, actually Bernie invented it. It went like this: Every day, when I got home from school, I would sneak in the back gate and look around for signs of him. He was there lurking, his big sad eyes riveted on my entrance, his tongue hanging, goop dripping, with that dumb dog smile. I would run like hell for the safety of the house. I rarely made it. More often than not a hundred pounds of slobbering mass would pin me to the ground and have his way with me. It was fun at first, but got to be annoying. After a long day at school battling the good sisters of Saint Martin of Tours, the last thing a kid wants when he gets home is to be mauled by his yet-to-be best friend. One day I got home and he wasn't there.

Me:
Mom, where's Bernie?
Mom:
Christopher, I have some great news.
Me:
What? Is the tidal wave coming?
Mom:
No, that's not it. Bernie got a movie.
Me:
What do you mean, Bernie got a movie? Bernie's a dog, not
an actor.
Mom:
Well, now he's a dog and an actor.

46

Me:

Gee, that's great. When's he coming back?

Mom:

Well, the thing is, the movie shoots in Alaska. It's nice and
cold in Alaska. Bernie's going to have a great life, staying cool
and making movies in Alaska.

Me:

Oh.

I believed them. At the time I didn't know that they weren't making
movies in Alaska.

We had a bunch of dogs when I was growing up on the beach in
California. I don't know whose idea it was. My mother was allergic,
and my dad seemed to like having a dog around but was oddly disasso-
ciated. I suppose, being an actor, he liked the adulation but not the responsibility. Most of our dogs died on the Pacific Coast Highway after
escaping the confines of our property. A spaniel with lopsided ears disappeared after a lifetime of relieving himself daily on our neighbor's
lawn. The neighbor was Dominick Dunn. Coincidence—I wonder.
Dominick Dunn enjoyed the proximity to his glamorous next-door
neighbors. At that time, he was not very well known but courted
celebrities and loved a good party—but he did have a lawn. Dominick
may not have liked our dogs or the Kennedys, but one thing I can say
about him is that he always stuck up for my old man.

Another one of our dogs was allegedly poisoned by one of our
cooks. She was a sweet Mexican woman with no apparent ill will toward animals, but she was a terrible cook, so who knows. The only ca-
nine that survived long enough for me to have a relationship with was
a small pug named Caesar. When my parents got him his name was
Cape Cod Corky. My dad put a fast end to that. He was my dad's dog.
Caesar was the only dog or human I have known who had narcolepsy.
This dog would fall asleep standing up. He'd be in midplay, his eyes
would glaze over, and he would topple over, fast asleep. My dad hardly
noticed, but I thought it was hysterical.

"Look, Daddy, Caesar just fell asleep standing up again!"

"Wait a minute, Christopher, I'm reading a script."

"Look, Daddy, look. Caesar's asleep and he's standing up!"

By the time my dad got his face out of the script, Caesar had top-pled over and was just another dog asleep on the ground.

My mom loved Caesar but she couldn't get near him. Her allergies prevented close proximity, but she wanted her kids to grow up with dogs, so we had them even though they made her sick.

SNAPSHOT:

My parents had this big boat of a station wagon. It had nine seats, which meant I could play musical chairs on my way to school. No seat belt for this hombre. The best thing about it, though, was the seat in the very back. It was so far away from the front seat that it felt like it was all mine. I would sit back there and imagine I was in my very own rocket ship.

It was tricky getting out of our driveway. The Pacific Coast Highway is a six-lane racetrack. Every other month we heard the screeching of brakes and the crunching of metal. When it happened, my dad would yell to Erma, "Get a blanket," and they would run out to the highway to see if there was a fresh car-crash victim who needed help. One morning my mom was taking me to school, and some guy in a white pickup truck was blocking my mom's view out of the driveway. My mother screamed at him to move but the guy was too invested in his coffee and doughnuts. When she pulled out we were broadsided by a blue Thunderbird. It looked a lot like the one I had gotten for Christmas—but bigger. I was sitting in my rocket ship, which probably saved my life. The middle of the station wagon was creamed. The driver of the Thunderbird seemed a little drunk, but my parents had to do the dance anyway. The dance was the celebrity schmooze coupled with a payoff, because even if the big-haired, slightly inebriated woman in the Thunderbird was in the wrong, it's bad PR for the president's sister and her movie star husband to be involved in a car crash with an average citizen—drunk or not. I couldn't figure out why someone who had almost killed us was now having drinks and laughing with my parents in the den. What really pissed me off, though, was that she wrecked my rocket ship.

My mom promised to fix it. She did.

In early 1963 my mom had had enough of my father and was looking to get out. She was heartbroken that the marriage she had willed into existence and sustained in spite of enormous obstacles was ending, but she had her children and her family to go back to. My dad didn't have anybody.

One day around this time, I walked into the den and found my dad with his arm draped around the little pug, Caesar, and he said, "You're all that I have left." I had no idea if he was talking about me or the dog. In either case it didn't sound good.

My father and his manager, Milt Ebbins, went to the White House to talk to my uncle about the split. Legend has it that my dad and uncle sat in the cabinet room and talked about the end of the storybook marriage.

Peter:
Pat wants a divorce.
Jack:
Peter, listen, don't worry about it. If it's going to happen it's going to happen.
Peter:
Jack, I'm so sorry.
Jack:
It's not all your fault. I know Pat better than you do. When is this going to happen?
Peter:
If it were up to Pat, tomorrow.
Milt:
That's not good. The day *after* tomorrow there will be an article on the front page of the *New York Times* with three photographs, Peter's and Pat's and yours, Mr. President.

Jack:
Maybe we should wait until after the election.
Peter:
Okay by me.
Jack:
I'll call Pat.
Peter:
I hope this doesn't mean that you and I aren't going to be
friends.
Jack:
Don't worry, Peter, I will always be your friend.

This statement, my dad later said, brought tears to his eyes.

As it turned out, my parents would not have to wait until 1964 to end their marriage.

MY LIFE on that beach in Santa Monica was the only time I was content. It was also the only time that I felt ordinary.

That changed on November 22, 1963.

Chapter 5

Experience is not what happens to you,
it's what you do with what happens to you.
—ALDOUS HUXLEY

Sister Agnes was one of the strictest women ever to wear a habit. She had a face so hard and mean, it was hard to believe she was a girl. We could tell she was, though, by the massive breasts she had bundled up under her nun's outfit. When we weren't being grilled on our multiplication tables, having our knuckles slaughtered for not paying attention, or hopping under our desks in anticipation of the likely Russian nuclear attack, I would daydream about what the nuns might look like under all that cloth.

Catholicism is pretty sexy as far as religions go. The images of a half-naked Christ being followed around by a flock of adoring women willing to do anything for him. All these brides of Christ full of love and passion but unable to do anything about it—and they're wearing uniforms! All of this couched in the whole forbidden fruit ethic. No wonder many of the Catholics I know are some of the most prolific fornicators on the planet.

Yes, I confess that I've had my share of hard-ons in church and in class watching one of the good sisters erase yesterday's homework. That day, however, was not one of those days.

Sister Agnes was pissed, not at me but at the collective. My classmates and I were sitting at our desks with our hands folded on top, waiting to see whom she'd land on. I knew it wouldn't be me. It never

CHRISTOPHER KENNEDY LAWFORD

was—unless I was caught red-handed—and even then she'd usually let it slide. Sister Agnes had a soft spot for me: there were benefits to being the nephew of the first Catholic president of the United States.

It was in this heavy silence and expectation of impending ass-whopping that the knock was heard on our homeroom door. Sister Agnes rose to answer it, giving us a look that said this would be only a momentary reprieve. There were two people at the door. They were from the office. When the ladies from the office showed up at the class-room door it usually meant something bad had happened and some-body was going home. They were serious, confused, as if they were trying to make sense of something. They huddled with Sister Agnes, whispering and looking at us—well, at me. I hoped it wasn't me. I didn't like it when the focus shifted to me.

Sister Agnes looked me right in the eye and motioned for me to come to the door. They brought me out into the hallway and told me someone in my family had died—or been so badly hurt they might die. It was unclear. They were having a difficult time communicating, and I was having a hard time understanding. What I got was that someone in my family was dead or close to it. I assumed the terrible thing had happened to my grandfather, who'd recently had a stroke.

They said no, it was the president.

I didn't believe them; it seemed impossible. I thought death was for only the feeblest. My uncle Jack was much too alive to be dead. They asked if I wanted to go home, and I said no. I don't know why. Maybe I didn't want to give in to their sympathy, or accept what had ac-tually happened.

WHAT DO you do when a stranger's experience of a death in your fam-ily is more profound than your own?

Within moments of my finding out that my uncle had been shot, everybody in my school knew. Shit, everybody on the planet knew. It's weird to have a relative die and have everyone share in it. In my eight-year-old psyche I felt some kind of obligation to hold up, to carry myself in a way that was more about us than about me. There was for the first time this feeling that there was something profoundly special about my family and—by association—about me. The day my uncle Jack was shot our family had an experience that was unique in its magnitude and commonality of effect. The world would never let us forget it.

I played baseball that afternoon and hit three home runs. Sometimes tragedy on such a scale can be invigorating. I think it has something to do with the attention and the enormous energy focused on you by the people around you, which in my case resulted in a shitload of eight-year-old nervous energy. And a ton of natural denial.

My mother found out her brother had been shot in Dallas from our maid, who received a telephone call from her husband. My mom let out a scream and went to the television to find out what was happening. After her initial emotional outburst, she shut down and took care of business, making calls back East, gathering her kids, and planning the dinner that was already scheduled with some close friends for that evening. My mom was good in a crisis. Afterward she would fall apart. My father was working with Jimmy Durante at Lake Tahoe. He flew home that night. The next morning I found my dad sitting at the flagpole where I used to raise the presidential flag when uncle Jack came to visit. He was crying like a baby. Strangers held a vigil on the beach outside my parents' house for days after the assassination. I walked through them, noticing their attention and kindness.

Judy Garland was the first of my parents' friends to show up. She stayed until my mom and dad left for Washington. I wasn't sure she would ever leave. My mother asked me if I wanted to go with her to the funeral in Washington. I told her no, I didn't. My best friend, Gerry Escalator, was coming to stay overnight that weekend. My first sleepover. This would also be the first time in my life that my desires came into direct conflict with my family. So I didn't go despite the continuous urgings of those around me:

Mademoiselle:
Christofere, why don't you want to go with Mommy?
Me:
Because Gerry's coming over.

Mademoiselle:
I'm sure Gerry can come over another time. You should be
with your mommy at this sad time.
Me:
I want to stay here and have a sleepover with my friend.
Mademoiselle:
Sidnay is going with Mommy. Wouldn't you like to go with
Sidnay, Christofere?
Me:
No.
Mademoiselle:
Allons, what if John Glenn came to take you to Mommy in a
rocket ship?
Me:
That's Okay, Mammy. I have my own rocket ship.

I would've liked to go on a real rocket ship, but Gerry would have been
sad if we didn't have our sleepover so I said no to the rocket ship ride.

I was a softy just like my dad.

This decision haunted me for many years.

If having a relative elected president forced me to reevaluate my
ambitions, having him martyred while in office assured that I would
forever come up short.

ONE OF the interesting aspects of growing up in an environment
where the world participates in your everyday life almost as much as
you do is trying to distinguish between reality and legend.

The only person in my life who ever attempted to pass down any
oral history of my family to me was Lem Billings. Lem was Jack
Kennedy's best friend, dating back to the days when they went to
school together at Choate. He was a tall man with bad eyes, chronic
asthma, and a roar of a laugh that announced his presence in any
room, no matter how vast or crowded. He was as much a part of our
family as anybody could be, traversing generations with his humor,
fearlessness, and willingness to engage in all things Kennedy. When

my parents divorced, my mother whitewashed the Hollywood years and elevated the Kennedy profile in her life and ours. The most tangible results of this for me were that Kennedy became my new middle name and that Lem Billings, family friend and oral archivist, became my new godfather.

Much of what's been written about my family doesn't jibe with what I've experienced, surmised, or been told. My family's history is like the game of telephone, where one person whispers a phrase to another person and it continues around the table until the last person says it out loud and everyone laughs because what comes out at the end has no similarity to what was said at the beginning.

My uncle Jack's assassination was taboo. It was just too big and painful an event to be dealt with on a human—not historical—level. Lem was the only one to try. He told me my uncle Bobby had spent two years investigating and come to the conclusion that the findings of the Warren Commission were correct. Lem had his doubts, but he was certain that there was nobody more invested in finding the truth than Bobby. And if Bobby bought the commission's findings, so would Lem. And so would I. The day he told me this I felt as if I had been let in on a big secret. My uncle's assassination was first and foremost a murder of a family member, and knowing that my uncle Bobby had dealt with it made me feel better. There is a world of difference between an assassination—a historical event—and a murder—a personal event. The murder of a family member is even more personal—it is a private event. Because I never got to deal with any of this on a level where I could feel any real connection to it, it existed way beyond me. Neither of my parents nor any of my other relatives ever found the opportunity or inspiration to discuss it with me. Maybe they thought it was being covered by so many other people they didn't have to. Maybe they were too busy dealing with the aftermath. Maybe it was too painful.

My mother's proprietary relationship with her family made it difficult to share the pain and the glory with us. It was all hers. We just accepted the fact that we were a small part of something far bigger than we were—and the more ordinary family traditions, like passing down an oral history of the family from one generation to the next, didn't apply.

SNAPSHOT:

I went to bed the night my mom, dad, and sister Sydney left for President Kennedy's funeral feeling like I might have made the wrong decision. I crawled into my bed looking forward to Gerry's arrival the following morning and the activity that would take my mind off what was happening in Washington without me. I reached over to turn the light off by the side of my bed and I said good night to Uncle Jack for the first time. It was the beginning of my long relationship with the dead.

Chapter 6

I want to resign from adulthood and go back to a time when M&M's were better than money because you could eat them.
—Anonymous

Nobody sat me down and told me my mother was leaving my father forever and moving three thousand miles from the beach I loved to a big, cold, scary city and taking us along with her. There were whisperings, of course, but my parents never said a word. Well, that's not quite true. I do remember my mom storming upstairs, not long after returning from my uncle Jack's funeral, and saying to no one in particular, "We're out of here." And we were.

It took a while though. I guess my mom spent a lot of time back East making arrangements for our move because after November 22 she didn't spend much time in L.A. I wrote her a note in March of 1964:

Dear Mommy,
I hope I see you soon. I have seen Son Of Flubber at Mis Die House.
(Turn Over)
And one picture of beaver without cooking. I am doing good in school. I hope you are having fun. Love and xxxx
Christopher

I doubt she was having fun and I have absolutely no idea what a "picture of beaver without cooking" might have been.

SNAPSHOT:

In June of 1964 I sat in my rocket ship as my dad drove my mom, my sisters, and me to the Los Angeles airport for the last time. I had no reason to believe that I wouldn't be returning to the beach that I loved. I thought I was going to Cape Cod for the summer. But there *was* something different about this car ride. Something I could feel all the way in the back of that long station wagon with the nine seats—all the way back in my rocket ship. My mom and dad were sad and beaten. Nobody said a word. Whatever ease we'd had as a family was gone.

According to my father, my mom took pretty much everything from the house on the beach that wasn't nailed down. What really pissed my father off, though, was that she took most of the mementos of Jack Kennedy and his presidency. My dad had the last word when he sent a truck packed with five-gallon plastic containers of water to her new place in Manhattan, with a note: "Dear Pat: You forgot to drain the swimming pool."

I wondered in the ensuing years if the loss of Jack Kennedy was more profound to my dad than the loss of his wife and children.

When I was eighteen and went back to live with my father in California, I noticed that there were a good deal more newfound memorabilia around his house involving his relationship with President Kennedy than there were involving us. It made perfect sense to me at the time. Jack Kennedy was a figure of mythic proportions and a hell of a guy. When you are part of someone's life who is this profoundly special, it often diminishes the lives of those around him. One of the by-products of living with such a profound legacy is that those who survive often protect that legacy by subjugating their own lives.

Whatever the truth, my dad was shattered by the split and by President Kennedy's murder.

Erma, too, never knew we were leaving until she showed up for work to find us gone and heard someone crying in the poker room. It was my father.

"He was raining tears all over the green felt," Erma told me. "I never saw anyone cry like that; he was bawling like a baby."

My dad looked up, pulled himself together, and said, "Erma, I'm so sorry you caught me crying."

Erma told him to "cry until there are no more tears" and left my dad to his sorrow.

My grandmother Rose used to say, "God never gives us more than we can bear," but my dad's friend Lenny Gershe observed that "God gave Peter Lawford more than he could bear."

THE STANHOPE Hotel was one of those boutique New York hotels that nobody knew about. Its only magnificence came from its location, Fifth Avenue directly across from the Metropolitan Museum of Art. Its personality came from a halfhearted attempt at a European, moneyed ambience, which did little more than give it a constipated air. My mother fled to the Stanhope in the late summer of 1964.

I had been to New York: it was cold, and there were a lot of cousins there who intimidated me. California was warm and safe. I didn't want to leave, but I was out-voted.

After Dallas, the landscape changed. My mother's family had been shaken to its core. They had—all of them—been brutally attacked and safety was gone. I think my mother fleeing California had as much to do with trying to feel safe as it did with getting away from my father. The monumental nature of that day made it impossible for me to have a problem with anything in my life without feeling ridiculous. Anton Chekhov said it was important to know the difference between tragedy and burned potatoes. After Dallas, everything in my life was burned potatoes.

My mother eventually found us an apartment at 990 Fifth Avenue on the corner of Eightieth Street, four blocks from my aunt Jackie and four blocks from my mother's sister Jean Smith and her family. Ideal, I guess, if you didn't want to be on a beach in sunny California.

It wasn't easy for my mother to find an apartment. A *New York Daily News* headline trumpeted my parents' entry into the wacky and expensive world of New York real estate: "LAWFORDS BARRED,

CO-OPS FOR SALE." The article described an apartment as a "nifty sixteen-room apartment up for sale today at a mere $150,000—but only non-Democrats and non-actors need apply." A family friend, the humorist Art Buchwald, came to my parents' defense in a piece that ran in the *Washington Post*, "Three Cheers for Discrimination," where he asked, "Would you want your children to play with children who have an actor for a father and a mother who is a Democrat?" Republicans worried about all those Hollywood types descending on their Eastern decency and Sammy Davis bringing his friends by for a drink. What they didn't know was that my parents were divorcing and my dad and his friends would not have a whole lot of access to the new Lawford digs.

I was enrolled at Saint David's School on East Eighty-ninth Street. I was nine years old and would begin my education in the East in the fourth grade. There were no nuns at Saint David's, but there were men with jackets and ties, which was almost as bad. Worse, I had to wear them. After the relaxed dress code in L.A.—traumatic.

Saint David's was an elite elementary school full of rich white kids—so I fit right in. The kids had more of an edge than what I was used to, but they were way too comfortable for any real urban angst, and the only rebellion seeping down to the elementary level would come in pill and herb form.

There were several profound effects of my relocation to the East. That first winter in New York, I morphed from a lean, tan surf rat into a roly-poly, pasty-faced fat kid. The most profound effect was that the big important family that would only periodically drop noisily in on our peaceful sanctuary on the beach was suddenly a very real, present, and important part of my life. My mother had made her declaration of independence when she married my father, and it proved a disaster. When she came back East and buried us deep in the bosom of her family, I had no way of knowing that my life would become a struggle, first, to become more a part of that family, and later, to escape it.

After purging the beach from my soul and accepting my immersion in my mother's large, noisy, and less than anonymous family, I began to let myself enjoy the perks of being considered special.

They say fame is a narcotic. Being a Kennedy is like an addiction to a great narcotic. The high of notoriety and feeling unique. The sense that at least for the moment everything is right in the world because of the enormous amount of goodwill that is directed at you. There is a feeling of power ignited by the real and imagined perception that the rules did not apply to us. All of this can be very intoxicating, and like any good addict I wanted more. But as with any good drug, there's the downside. The hangover of knowing that your place in the world has little to do with who you are. The fear of the other shoe dropping—something bad was always just around the next corner. The certainty of not measuring up. And never knowing the ease of having one's own life. My mom was a victim of the good and bad associated with being a member of her family, but unlike her siblings, she yearned to escape, and she passed on that yearning to me.

Chapter 7

A question in your nerves is lit . . .
That it is not he or she or them or it
That you belong to.
— BOB DYLAN

In my mind the entire world seemed to admire and sympathize with my family. Everywhere I went people reinforced the idea that my relatives and the family dynamics and ethics they fostered were beacons and benchmarks. Myth obscured reality. It became impossible to see people or relationships for what they really were. The individual's ordinary human questions and desires were dwarfed by the enormity of the Kennedy drama. It is difficult enough for an individual to forge his or her unique path when it is in conflict with a family's. It is impossible to do it when pretty much the entire world is reinforcing the greatness of your family's path.

One of the stories I grew up with was that my uncle Teddy wanted to start a waterskiing school in California after college. He and his buddy from Harvard, Claude Hooten, were going to teach the beautiful girls of the West Coast the fine art of East Coast waterskiing. But my grandfather put the kibosh on it, forcing him instead into the family business: politics. I have no idea how much truth there was to this tale, but my cousins and I believed it. For me the story illuminated the possibility of escape—and the spirit of rebellion—forever vanquished for the greater good. If my grandfather corralled my uncle, our generation would be corralled by The Legacy. We were put on notice that there were more important concerns than the beat of one's different drummer.

As I grew up, I became gradually aware of my family's commitment to the enslaved. My uncle's commitment to civil rights, the mentally challenged, and the poor filled me with pride. My family fought for freedom for those in need but often could not see that their own children were in bondage, prevented from following their own dreams by the implied responsibility of their shared heritage. Our personal dreams and desires were always connected to the "big picture" of what it meant to be a Kennedy.

IN MY family the bigger picture was everything. Thinking about yourself was probably the worst thing a person could do. It was selfish, and in a family to which much had been given and from whom much was expected, there was no tolerance for it. Most importantly it was a waste of time because it didn't get you anything. Thinking about others on a grand scale can win accolades and amass power. Don't get me wrong, I don't think all the saving-the-world business was motivated by a desire for power and praise. Most of those in the saving-the-world business in my family hate injustice and want to make a better world. But we are a political family and very pragmatic about seeing the world without illusions and we understand how the world works.

SOMETIME IN the spring of 1964, after we had been in New York for a few months, my mother and my uncle Bobby shared a weekend house in Glen Cove, Long Island. Since Uncle Bobby had been my mom's only support through the breakup of her marriage and my uncle's assassination, she was really looking forward to spending time with him, and my uncle needed a New York–based residence for his Senate run in 1964. What it meant to me was the introduction to a branch of our family tree that I didn't yet know but would soon come to find galvanizing.

My sisters and I with our various friends would pile into the back of a station wagon after school every Friday and make the slow exodus out of Manhattan along one of the worst highways in America, Robert Moses's greatest debacle, the Long Island Expressway. We played a game to make the trip go faster of holding our breath whenever we passed a cemetery. Whoever took a breath before the car had cleared the last tombstone was condemned to be next in the ground. Just outside Manhattan, on the other side of the Midtown Tunnel, there is a massive cemetery—dead people as far as the eye can see—impossible for any of us to hold our breath long enough. By the time we hit the LIE we were all doomed. On our first trip to the Glen Cove house, we arrived late on a Friday afternoon and were engulfed by the enormity of the place. The house had too many bedrooms and a great lawn for playing football and capture the flag. It was much too big a place for the Lawfords, yet I would soon learn it was not nearly big enough for the Robert Kennedys.

I stood in front of the house waiting for my cousins to arrive with the queasiness a kid feels when he is about to be introduced to a new gang. The only thing I knew about my uncle Bobby's family was that there were a lot of them. Some of them had visited us in California, but the only memory I had of their visit was that one of them took a crap in the pool.

SNAPSHOT:

> They arrived like an invasion, piling out of two station wagons with absolutely no hesitancy. They completely took over the space, occupying it as if they had been there many times before. They swarmed through the house and out to the lawn, losing bits and pieces of their clothing along the way, which in the boys' case was always a dark suit, a white button-down shirt, tie, and loafers. They looked like mini Rat Packers.

The girls were in some kind of dress, but I hardly noticed. I was only interested in the boys. I'd had enough of girls and wanted in on the RFK males' brand of anarchic irreverence. A window had been opened in a forgotten attic, closed up with stagnant stale air. I could breathe. And my life suddenly had more urgency and excitement. It brought me back to Santa Monica when my mother's sisters and brothers would visit, releasing me from the stuffy confinement of my family.

There was a rush of freedom. In a moment there were too many children for our parents to control, and so they let go, and we were free. From the moment my RFK cousins Bobby and David flew into my life, I gravitated to their orbit. In life with my mother and sisters, I was drowning in a sea of estrogen. The apartment at 990 Fifth was full of closed bedroom doors, an ambience of walking on eggshells, and the occasional emotional meltdown.

But suddenly now the promise of weekends with naughty male cousins was on my horizon. Sadly for me, this was not meant to be. After my uncle won his Senate seat, there was really no need for a family presence in New York, and so, just as suddenly as they appeared, they disappeared. And I was left to swim alone in my own sea of nuclear family dysfunction. But the seed had been sown . . .

I GREW up in a house full of women.

There was my mom, Mademoiselle, and the three sisters. A blonde, a brunette, and a redhead. I was convinced my mom planned it that way through sheer force of will. She was *that* powerful. Sydney was the blond, who only got nicer. I never understood where Robin's red hair came from. I suspected she might be adopted. My mother said it came from Grandpa, but as far as I was concerned my grandfather didn't have any hair and the little that he had was white. My mom was remembering better hair days. Robin was the baby. She was tiny and frail and adored by all. Especially my mom, who even changed her hair color to match Robin's strawberry orange locks. If I bore the burden of being the only male in the family, Robin bore the burden of being my mother's favorite. Robin lived with my mom longer than the rest of us. She has a generous nature and may have put my mom's needs ahead of her own.

Victoria had dark brown hair and looked more like me than my other sisters. She had more of our father in her. This was good and bad. Good looks—but a reminder. Victoria and I had other similarities. She had a restless creativity and a heavy depth. She seemed more invested than the others in having a relationship with my dad.

My sisters were incredibly nice. They were loved by everyone. The

Lawford children had the reputation of being the *nicest* cousins in the family. And this was a rep we had *in* the family—so you know it was true. My sisters weren't as troubled in the way I was. Or as rebellious. I don't know why. Maybe it had something to do with being female. Females are stronger, and they probably weren't as tied into the whole legacy thing. But as daughters they dealt with my mom in a way I couldn't. While she was loving and kind, she *was* a Kennedy and she could be a handful.

As far as I was concerned there were only two kinds of people in the world: boys and girls. I got really good at being one of the girls, but I would always be a boy, and so whatever was going on in their club was not something I thought I would ever be privy to. This left me feeling isolated and misunderstood. This was mitigated by the fact that I could pretty much do whatever I wanted. I was the male, after all. I might be a pain in the ass but I was their *only* pain in the ass.

My mother often radiated pain. Like my father, she was cursed with a big heart in life circumstances more suited to a Machiavelli. My mom was deeply wounded by the major events of her life, assassinations and divorce. She responded to that hurt by trying to escape and by internalizing the resulting anger at not being able to. It made life with her difficult at times. She struggled mightily to pass on to her children what had been given to her, but the wounds may have hindered that. I also think that in some strange way her heart was sometimes somewhere else, dealing with her many sorrows. As for myself and my relationship with my mother I have learned that what we inherit is not always who we are. Sometime even the best of where we come from becomes a burden if our attachment to it is not organic.

We had a map of the world in our dining room just like she had growing up. She would test us during dinner, just as she had been tested growing up, but the red wine usually cut these geography lessons short. My sisters and I would be left sitting at the oval mahogany dinner table with pockets full of liver, which we were served every Wednesday, confused by my mom's sudden speech incapacity. I once asked one of her friends what was happening in these moments and he told me, "She has trouble speaking because she has had such a hard life." Another one of the downsides to the Kennedy elixir is the enabling behavior of those around us. It wasn't that my mom wasn't paying attention to her children, it's that the attention I was getting has often filtered through a glass.

Life at 990 Fifth Avenue was full of pins and needles with a good dose of frustration thrown in. I learned how to tread lightly. I was often confused and learned early the art of avoidance. I grew up thinking my mom was pissed off at me. It wasn't me. It was life.

My mother was most happy when she was walking. She was most at peace when rambling through the city or marching on a beach. Her walks were legendary for their length and gait. No one could keep up with her—few tried. Walking seemed to free her. She seemed during these journeys to be most with herself.

SNAPSHOT:

> My mother could shrink a man's balls with one glance. It was more glare than glance. It was the look she inherited from my grandfather, and after nine years with my old man she shared it liberally with the male sex. After ten years with a movie star my mom wasn't going to take any nonsense from another man. I was the exception—she took a whole lot of nonsense from me over the years.

My mother saw my father as a womanizing spendthrift. She wasn't wrong. This was pretty much the image of him she passed down to me. In spite of that, it became clear that a powerful, charismatic, heterosexual male was what I wanted to be. I figured this out because although my mother didn't think very much of my old man, I think she loved him in the way a woman loves a man when she cannot fully possess or control him. This is a powerful love, one not easily forgotten, overcome, or concealed from your ten-year-old son. I think this is why my mom never remarried. She figured out that there was no way she was ever going to cave to a man again, and she didn't want the aggravation of being married to a guy like her father, brothers, or ex-husband, so she settled for gay male friends and dysfunctional drinking buddies.

Chapter 8

If you go fast enough, you can't tell where you came from.
— ANONYMOUS

I had never been skiing before my mom fled back East and began our indoctrination into all things Kennedy. My uncle Bobby had been going to Sun Valley at Christmastime for years. The RFKs would fly to Boise on the Great Lakes Carbon plane with the bedroom in the back. My uncle Bobby had married into the Skakel family when he married my aunt Ethel. The Skakels owned the Great Lakes Carbon Company, which at one time was one of the largest privately held companies in the world. It made them very rich. It also made them crazy. That's the funny thing about having lots of money. It sometimes can make you either angry or crazy. Add alcohol to the mix and it's virtually guaranteed. Bobby and David regaled me with stories about their uncles on their mother's side while we played hearts in the bedroom in the back of the Great Lakes plane. The Skakel boys provided a balance to the lofty accomplishments of those on the Kennedy side. Like crazy Uncle George, who would race his kid-laden car down icy mountain roads ahead of the cars following so he could stage an elaborate car wreck with children's and adults' bodies strewn all over the snowbanks on the side of the road, ketchup blood and all. Funny. Right?

After arriving in Boise for my first ski trip, we jumped on a bus to Sun Valley, where we spent ten days tearing up the sleepy little resort town. Averill Harriman had a couple of houses on the side of Mount

Baldy and would loan them to the family for the Christmas holiday. For our first Christmas back East, my mom made us a part of this yearly pilgrimage.

It was terrifying.

The first day in Sun Valley, my sisters and I found ourselves standing outside of Averill Harriman's cottage watching my uncle Bobby and all his kids head off to the big mountain. We were dressed in the new ski clothes we had bought in New York, but we didn't have skis or boots and had no idea where to get them. We were waiting for my mother to wake up and tell us. The problem was we could never be sure when that might happen.

So we would wait.

We were used to it, but that morning in the bright cold sun of Sun Valley with the mountains of snow beckoning and the other kids heading out to all that fun, it was hard to wait. These are the times a kid wants a dad—or at least one parent who can get their ass out of bed.

Just when I thought my head couldn't hang any lower, Uncle Bobby arrived to save the day. In a flurry of purposeful and exuberant activity, he scooped my sisters and me up and hustled us off to Dollar Mountain where he negotiated for our equipment and ski school class and accompanied us on our first ski run ever. Then he was off to bigger challenges and his own brood. I thought it would have been nice to have a father like my uncle Bobby.

SNAPSHOT:

> My cousins John and Caroline lived four blocks from us in New York City. My sister Sydney was the same age as Caroline and both went to the convent of the Sacred Heart on Ninety-first Street. I was five years older than John. We didn't go to the same school and, because of the age difference, had very little in common. But our mothers decided it would be a good idea for me to be his surrogate big brother.

I was being asked to be a male role model to my young cousin in a family that had recently lost two very significant males: my grandfather to a stroke and my uncle Jack to an assassin's bullet. Having no present father of my own, I didn't have a clue what was being asked of me. The only thing I knew was that my maleness would be exposed on two levels with two very important people in the world.

John was a cute little kid who wasn't a brat—except maybe to his sister. He was very much the little prince. It made me nervous that they had picked me to be his big brother. He was little, but he was a *big* deal. Manhattan is an anonymous city. It is possible to go anywhere and not be noticed by anyone, unless you happened to be Caroline or John. They were noticed everywhere they went, and in a society that rewards this kind of notoriety with importance, it became impossible for the rest of us not to think of them as important. I would be packed off to 1040 Fifth Avenue one night every week or two to hang out with my very important younger cousin and do the things that five-year-olds like to do. This was not something I would have looked forward to if it weren't for my aunt Jackie and a Secret Service agent named Jack Walsh.

Sometime between the age of ten and thirteen, young boys become very interested in the female anatomy. I was no exception; I just didn't have very many opportunities to appreciate the fairer sex. Saint David's was an all boys school with all male teachers. The only females in the entire building were in the administrative offices, and most of them had blue hair, not fantasy material.

My sister's school was another matter. The Sacred Heart school was full of young Catholic girls in gray uniforms with kneesocks. There were abundant opportunities to explore the female anatomy, in fact and fancy. The only problem was that the boys of Saint David's were never let near the place. What I was left with were my mother's friends and relatives. My mother didn't really have many girlfriends and the ones she did have never inspired me in that way. My aunts were far too scary and they kind of reminded me of my mother. I never had an Oedipal thing going.

But Jackie. Jackie was inspiring.

By the age of eleven, I considered her the ultimate woman. She was beautiful and nice. She wore these great clothes with these amazing sunglasses, which every now and then she would put on top of her head, pushing her hair back. To this day a woman with sunglasses holding up her hair always turns my head. She had this voice that made you feel like it was all going to be just fine. There was her way of not finishing her sentences, making conversation with her effortless. I never saw her angry or hysterical. Her apartment at 1040 Fifth was a safe harbor. Even sitting around the dinner table, her relaxed grace dominated, a far cry from the emotional unpredictability and geography testing at my mom's dinner table.

One night when I was sleeping over and John was asleep, I went looking for Aunt Jackie to ask if I could phone home. I called out her name, but there was no answer. I went into her bedroom and heard running water in the bathroom. I went to the bathroom door to see if she was there. It was slightly ajar, and I could see that she was preparing to take a bath and doing her daily exercises. I stood at that door mesmerized. This was the first woman I had ever seen this way, and I was transfixed. I was ten years old, having an experience probably every male has had, but the woman I walked in on was possibly the most famous woman on the planet. Seeing her like this changed me from the boy I was into something more. I became the keeper of a secret about the most private of women, my aunt Jackie. It was one of the first—and the loveliest—of the many secrets I would come to own. Being a big brother to my cousin John was not something I really looked forward to until the night I stumbled half awake into my aunt Jackie's bathroom.

JACK WALSH was a tall Irishman from Boston with gray hair. He looked like he could be one of my uncles. Mr. Walsh, as he was known to us kids, was the head of John and Caroline's Secret Service detail. He was the first man in my life, after my father, to see me as an individual—separate and distinct from the rest of the family. He would play baseball with me for hours and treated me to pizza once a week at my favorite New York pizza parlor, claiming that my pizza habit was going to land him in the poor house. His job was to protect Caroline and John, but, with the exception of the time he emptied his revolver into a milk snake we had uncovered under a log on the Lake Trail in Palm Beach, I never had a hint of what his real job was. I thought he was just one of those grown-ups that knew how to have a good time with kids. It amazed me when one day I learned he had his own family up in Boston. How the hell did he do it? I wondered if he was as present with his own kids.

The only problem I had with Jack Walsh was that I wasn't his favorite young Kennedy cousin. If John was his point of focus, David was his favorite. He appreciated David's humor and guts way before anybody else. He also saw his frailty, and after my uncle Bobby was killed, he tried like hell to save David's emotional stability, but no human being would prove to be capable of that.

SNAPSHOT:

The boxing ring was of the makeshift variety deep in the corner of the RFKs' backyard by the giant hedge. A simple square of earth, mapped out with imaginary ropes to keep the boxers from running. No one found themselves outside of these imaginary ropes for any length of time no matter how bad a beating they might be enduring lest the C word be uttered. Nobody wanted to be called a coward. There wasn't anything worse than a coward so once you stepped into the invisible ring you were there until Jack Walsh blew his whistle. First up were the two Bobbys—Shriver and Kennedy— who would beat the shit out of each other gracelessly while David and I watched on the sidelines, waiting our turn. I sat next to my best friend feeling the nervous dread of waiting my turn to do something I didn't want to do but was powerless not to do. The only thing worse than a coward was a coward who didn't even try.

It was a little unfair. David was tiny and I was big and fat, probably twice his size. This was my only solace—through the luck of my place in the family hierarchy I got to go up against someone half my size. But appearances can be deceiving. David might have looked like the ninety-eight-pound weakling in need of a meal but he had the heart of a pissed-off lion. He was tough and tenacious, taking enormous punishment with never a thought of surrendering. He looked like one of those cartoon characters, his fists whirling at a hundred miles per hour. Moving ever forward with no capability of reverse.

I felt worse about hitting him than he felt getting hit. He was driven to win, to make his mark on me. He was ruthless and relentless. Jack Walsh couldn't believe it and told anyone who would listen that David was the toughest kid he had ever seen and certainly the toughest in our family. This didn't matter to me. I had realized that being tough wasn't my strong suit. Having grown up in Hollywood with a movie-star father and been raised in a house full of women, I figured lover would be a more suitable and fruitful path than fighter. What *did* matter was that a potential surrogate father had indicated to me that there was a more interesting surrogate son available in my family. This would be a recurring situation for me. All the males circling around our lives liked me enough, but there was always one of my male cousins who seemed more interesting to the adults. I didn't know whether this was because I wasn't that interesting or because my cousins had a better pedigree. Whether my suspicions were real or imagined, they left me feeling sort of like a second-string Kennedy.

After we had been in New York for a while, my father came to see me to have a talk about what the hell was going on. I can only imagine the conversation between my parents.

Pat:
Peter, he's your only son. Tell him that the reason I'm taking him away from you is that you fucked up. That's why you won't be living with us!

Peter:
Why are you always busting my balls, Pat?

Pat:
Because you couldn't keep your dick in your pants, you selfish son of a bitch! What are you going to tell him?

Peter:
I don't know. This isn't my strong suit. If we were talking about clothes or acting I'd feel more confident.

Pat:
Get over yourself. This isn't about you!
Peter:
Maybe I could get your brother Bobby to do this?
Pat:
Not a chance!

Both my parents were practiced in the art of avoidance. Looking back, it's astonishing to me that "the talk" took place at all.

Parents often make the mistake of thinking that what's happening to them is also happening to their kids. This isn't necessarily so. Kids have a shorter attention span. The damage is done and buried deep in the psyche and they move on to the next event. Kids have their own lives. I had moved on and was attempting to deal with mine when my parents in a moment of misguided compassion decided I needed some clarity on their marriage.

I WAS waiting for my dad in the den, watching TV, waiting for the noise of the elevator door opening to announce that someone had arrived at the eighth-floor entranceway. It's the wait that's the real killer. I had a feeling in my stomach that something bad was going to happen. It was preventing me from losing myself in the interplay between Ed Sullivan and his Italian mouse Topo Gigio that night. I knew my dad wasn't coming back even before he said it. The geography told me. My father could never live in New York. He could visit, but he would die without the sun, the beach, and the ease of L.A. I knew it was a done deal, but it still hurt when he said it. It was just he and I when he told me. He had a tough time coming up with the words. I only remember, "I'm not coming back to live with you and your sisters." At least he was direct. I must have felt the pain of my dad leaving but was afraid to acknowledge it, because it paled in comparison with the pain of the assassination of a young and brilliant president.

Then he was gone, and I went to my room to deal with my homework and the certain knowledge that Dad was gone for good.

My mother thought my unhappiness and resulting drug and alcohol addiction were the result of my resentment at her for, as she said, "being taken away from your father." She told me this at different times in my life, and each time she said it, I didn't know what she was talking about. Now that I think about it, I think it was her way of blaming my father for my subsequent difficulties, even though it was she who made the decision to leave. By the way, I don't think she really had a choice. Even today I can't look back on the events of her leaving my father and say I felt any anger or resentment toward her for the decision she made. I think she was right. There are, however, things that happen to us in our lives that are so profoundly upsetting we can never acknowledge them.

After our "talk," which wasn't really a talk at all but more like a brief statement of fact, my dad would show up a couple of times a year to take us out to dinner at Danny's Hideaway. It never occurred to me that this behavior was not the behavior one would normally associate with fatherhood. Danny's was one of those great New York restaurants with red leather and a Rat Pack feel. It was my dad's hangout and when we walked in with him it became ours too. I would order a giant sirloin steak with French fries and a Coke, and everyone in the place, from Danny to the busboy, would ask me what had been happening in my life since my last steak. For the hour and a half I was at Danny's, it felt like I mattered in my dad's world. My father did his usual casual interaction thing, running to the phone every fifteen minutes, but it didn't seem to matter— there were always presents, big steaks, and my father's off-the-charts charm with the ladies that kept my sisters smitten. By then, I had begun developing my natural-born talent of the emotional deep freeze, which allowed me to have interaction with my old man with no expectation or attachment. The apple doesn't fall far from the tree.

After dinner he would drop us off at 990. My mother made sure she wasn't around. I secretly hoped that one of them would mess up and they would cross paths. I didn't have the fantasy that they would get back together—that didn't seem possible—but I still wanted to put my parents together in the same room to see what would happen. An experiment. To see how they would deal with each other and with what they had done to us. I suppose it was my way of wanting to punish them.

One night when my dad had brought us home from dinner at Danny's and my sisters were tearing up saying good-bye, I heard the elevator door open—the way I had always hoped it would—and my mother stepped into the obvious wreckage of her divorce. It was surreal. Everybody was quiet. Nobody said a word. My parents were like strangers, rigidly shaking hands, incapable of familiarity, painfully conscious of their children's yearning and discomfort for their discomfort. It's impossible for a kid to have any sense of what might be happening inside his parents in such moments. The drama that is unfolding between the two adults who hold your life precariously in the palms of their sweating, trembling hands is far too pervasive and consuming. After what seemed like forever, my dad muttered, "Hi, Pat. How are you?" And my mom mumbled, "Good, Peter. You?" Then they both lurched toward us in their attention, my dad said his good-byes, and then he was out the door like a shot. And I was restored to the role I never wanted: the man of the family.

I have no idea what my sisters thought about all the upheaval in our lives. Like everything else, we never talked about it. We always seemed too busy adjusting to and preparing for the next crisis.

SNAPSHOT:

When I was twelve years old and we had been in New York for four years I learned that my parents had been officially divorced. No one told me. I read it in the newspapers—the way I usually found out what was happening in my family. I had wandered into my mom's bedroom at 990 Fifth Avenue to spend some quality time while she got ready to go out. The phone rang. It was for my mom.

"Hi Jackie . . . Oh . . . That's terrific. I'm so happy for you. When? Yes, I would love to come, thank you. Wonderful. Okay. Lots of love."

And she hung up the phone.

"I can't believe she is going to marry that man."

And with that my mom went into her bathroom to angrily powder her nose.

I didn't understand why none of the adults seemed happy that Jackie was going to marry Aristotle Onassis. He was old—yes. But he seemed like a nice enough guy and he was rich, which was a big plus in the family—usually. I had dinner with him once at Jackie's with John and Caroline. He didn't say very much, but he smiled and he brought presents. I figured it was another one of those complicated adult situations that would never be fully explained or understandable to us kids.

As I was pondering all of this, sitting at the desk my mom had in her bedroom, where she engaged in her version of the saving-the-world business, I made the mistake of opening one of the drawers. Inside the drawer that I shouldn't have opened was a clipping from the *New York Daily News* that read "Peter Lawford and Patricia Kennedy Divorce Finalized."

Chapter 9

How dull it is to pause, to make an end, to rust unburnished,
not to shine in use! As tho' to breathe were life!
—ALFRED LORD TENNYSON

After the beach I grew up on in California, Hyannis Port, Massachusetts, was my favorite place in the world. I loved going there in the summers of my youth, always feeling a rush of excitement as soon as I crossed the Sagamore Bridge, which connects Cape Cod with the great state of Massachusetts. Hyannis Port is a tiny hamlet nestled on the coast of Cape Cod looking out at the Atlantic and the islands of Martha's Vineyard and Nantucket. It has a beautiful harbor protected by a huge breakwater that juts out into the ocean for a quarter of a mile. It was the place that made me feel most a part of my family and its history. My boyhood summers on the Cape were when I first tasted the nectar of unbridled activity and ferocious competition and was indoctrinated into the ethic of sucking the marrow out of life.

IT WAS also the place where I cemented my commonality with the other twenty-four cousins who made up my extended family. My experience growing up in Hyannis Port, along with our notoriety as a family, fostered a feeling that we were all one genetically connected unit and that I had twenty-seven brothers and sisters. Having tour buses full of tourists arriving daily to gawk at the summering Kennedys added to the sense of being a part of one super uncommon tribe, separate from the rest of the world.

The family had three houses on a cul-de-sac: my grandparents' house, or the Big House, my uncle Jack's and aunt Jackie's, and the RFK house. The Smiths bought a place right across the street, and the Shrivers were a two-minute bike ride up Sunset Hill. My uncle Teddy and aunt Joan were the pioneers, electing to live way out on Squaw Island, ten minutes by bike — if you dared. It was rumored that Squaw Island had been a Native American burial ground, and all us kids knew there were ghosts running amuck all over the tiny island. That, coupled with the fact that there were no streetlights and only a few houses, made Squaw Island *the* scary place. One of the tests of a kid's courage was whether they would ride their bike to the tip of Squaw Island on a dark and stormy night.

The world called it the Kennedy Compound. We only called it the compound when we were talking to each other. Mostly it was the Cape—as in "When are you going to the Cape?" We spent much of July and August there in the summers of my youth. My mother never bought a house like her brothers and sisters; renting was her way of maintaining independence. Sometimes we stayed with my grandparents, depending on how much family time my mom could tolerate. I liked it when we rented. Like my mom, I learned early to value my own space.

One summer, we rented the house of Jimmy Piersall, who played for the Red Sox. He'd had some kind of mental breakdown, making his summerhouse on the Cape available. One night, I swear my sisters and I saw a ghost in the third-floor bedroom of the baseballer's musty old house on Hyannis Avenue. It was all I needed to beg my mom to spend my nights at the RFKs' or the Shrivers'.

Snapshot:

When I was really young, before all the tragedy came our way, I could sit on the great lawn in front of my grandparents' house, looking out at the ocean beyond the dunes of sand and grass, feeling the wind coming from Nantucket, and truly know peace. On Friday evenings my cousins and I would gather on this lawn and wait for my uncle Jack to arrive from the White House in the big green Marine Corp helicopter. There would be twenty or thirty of us with friends and always lots of dogs. The Secret Service set up a phone on the porch of the Big House to keep tabs on the flight plan and alert the pilots to any changes in the weather. The fire trucks were always at the end of the driveway . . . just as a precaution.

We would listen to see who would be the first to hear the unmistakable chopping roar of the giant blades. My grandfather would be wheeled out onto the porch with a robe over his knees, my grandmother at his side. A wave of excitement would sweep over us as we watched the helicopter swoop in low over the Big House and bank out over the sea before finally touching down gracefully on the small patch of grass in front of the porch where my grandfather waited in his wheelchair. The giant blades would slow and the door would open, officers would step out, then Uncle Jack. My cousins and I would run out to greet him as he stepped into our summer world. My uncle would make his way through the throng of kids and dogs to the porch, where he would kiss my grandparents hello and then make his way to the golf cart for the short ride back to his house.

A space on the back of Uncle Jack's golf cart was one of the most prized pieces of turf in all of Hyannis Port. My cousins and I competed ferociously to cling to a small part of the white laminated cart as my uncle drove back and forth from the dock to his house. Way before the rest of the country was seeing how many people you could cram into a Volkswagen Bug, we were seeing how many Kennedy grandchildren we could get on the back of Uncle Jack's golf cart.

AFTER NOVEMBER 22, there were no more helicopters or rides on the golf cart, but like all the other aspects of my mother's side of my family, the prominence of Hyannis Port in my life increased exponentially.

. . .

My grandparents' house seemed like a museum with great food. When we were young we had to be careful not to make too much noise or break anything. My grandfather was brought down in the elevator from his second-story bedroom every day and would be stationed in his wheelchair in the corner of the large living room with the picture window looking out onto the sea, the photographs testifying to the fullness and purpose of his life surrounding him. My grandfather with FDR, Disraeli, British royalty, and, of course, his family. The "souvenir pillows" on the couches and chairs with the famous phrases, spoken by my grandfather when he could speak. The characteristic expletive *Applesauce!* Or admonitions such as *You're dipping into your capital!* Or a familiar saying such as *You have just made a political contribution.* This last saying was an inside joke, referring to the letters he would send his children whenever there was a family campaign in need of funds. A tithe was levied on the various trust funds of my aunts and uncles in support of the candidate. My grandfather would send out a letter beginning, "You have just made a political contribution ..."

SNAPSHOT:

My mom called to me from the porch of the Big House just as I was about to diagram the play that would send David into the end zone for the winning touchdown. "Christopher, come and say hello to Grandpa."

There was no escaping it. It was my turn to go in. We were all required to do our time with Grandpa. It scared me. I entered the living room with the awkwardness and trepidation of a kid walking into a hospital room for the first time. I was tongue-tied and terrified that whatever had stricken the great man would find its way on to me—always fearing the unexplained, involuntary physical convulsion, which would send my grandfather into painful spasms requiring a retreat back to the elevator and his upstairs bedroom and the lonely isolation of his illness.

My grandfather was sitting in his wheelchair. His satin pajamas and bathrobe crisp and clean. His head tilting to the side with the mouth and eyes of a stroke victim. His mind alive, trapped in a body that no longer responded to his undiminished desire to live. It must have been torture for a man of my grandfather's will and power. I approached him, encouraged by my mom, on the plastic runner my grandmother had laid over the white carpet, kissing him on the top of his head, saying "Hi, Grampa." It seemed the only safe place to do so.

My grandfather would look at me like he wanted to say something. I could see his joy in seeing me below the rigid mask of his illness. He tried to move his mouth, straining to get the words out. Nothing. He would try harder, his whole body shuddering with the effort to communicate, but nothing would come. Then this cloud came into his eyes and he slouched down—defeated. Tears flowed down his cheeks, making little dark circles on his satin pajamas. I looked out the giant picture window behind him, at the great lawn where my cousins were playing, and prayed for my audience to be over.

I walked out of the Big House and life resumed. My grandfather's vision of life flowed through his children and grandchildren at a hundred miles an hour—just the way we liked it. He was in a wheelchair but his spirit ran through our family. I grew up knowing that my grandfather disliked self-pity for any reason and that overt displays of grief made him uncomfortable. We were always encouraged to think about better times tomorrow, and how to bring those about. Tears accomplished nothing. He reminded us of this while he clapped his hands in steady rhythm to accentuate the admonition, said in mock sternness, "No-crying-in-this-house!" It was a cold hard fact—Kennedys don't cry. His children had learned this lesson well, and now it was our turn.

AFTER NOVEMBER 22, Uncle Bobby became the center of our family and the focal point of all the activity at the Cape.

The grown-ups gathered on the chaise longues in front of Uncle Bobby's house, laughing, working the phones, and planning the day. He was brown from the sun, always in shorts, running his hands through his hairy chest.

"Chris, you're coming sailing with us on the *Resolute* today, aren't you? I think today is the day we'll tip over."

And he was back to the gaggle of weekend guests. There was always an army of guests in Hyannis Port, and they were just as interesting as anyone you'd find around the pool in California. Rafer Johnson, the Olympic decathlon champion; John Glenn, America's first astronaut; Jim Whittaker, the first American to climb Everest; the humorist Art Buchwald; and an assortment of atheletes, writers, and politicos. There may have been a lot of important grown-ups walking around the compound, but it felt as if Uncle Bobby's focus was always on the kids. If he was around, you'd better be certain that you were fully engaged in the day. There was no sitting around watching TV when RFK was there.

RFK:
Chris Lawford, why are you sitting inside wearing long pants?
Chris Lawford:
Uh. I don't know, Uncle Bobby.
RFK:
It's a beautiful sunny day. You should be outdoors doing something.
Chris Lawford:
Uh. Okay, Uncle Bobby.
RFK:
And Chris . . .
Chris Lawford:
Yes, Uncle Bobby.
RFK:
Put on some short pants.
Chris Lawford:
Yes, Uncle Bobby.

It was impossible to stay off Uncle Bobby's radar if you were a kid. Whatever he was doing and whoever he was doing it with, his attention was always on the kids. A typical football game involved a dozen kids and some of the best athletes in the world, from Rafer Johnson to Sam

Huff and Rosie Grier, both NFL players. Uncle Bobby was always the quarterback. "Now here's what we're going to do." Then he would outline the play, dragging his finger through the short grass.

"Rosie, ten steps and cut right; Sam, fifteen and cut right; Rafer, go deep right; David, go out to the left and I'll throw it to you! Chris, you hike the ball, go out, and buttonhook. The next play is to you."

That's the way it was. The pros were decoys and blockers for the kids.

Chapter 10

Blood is the fuel for the enormous energy we burn up battling our own. We wouldn't think of expending such effort on strangers.
— ANONYMOUS

My cousins Bobby Kennedy, Bobby Shriver, David Kennedy, and I were tied to each other by age and position in the large extended Kennedy family. The two Bobbys were the same age and a year older than David and I. We were the second tier in the family hierarchy behind Joe and Kathleen. We were grouped together in all things competitive. We skied, swam, boxed, ran, and toasted against each other from the time we could walk and talk. In our parents' generation there was an ethic of interfamily competition, coupled with a credo of Us Against Them. If you messed with one Kennedy, you messed with them all.

This was not true in our generation.

Maybe it was because there were six different families. All I know is that when it came to competition, there was none more ferocious than that which took place between my cousins and me. Whether playing football, trying to steal each other's girlfriends, outdoing each other in acts of daring, and drug-taking, or one-upsmanship in the family art of toasting, you won or lost depending on who got the better of whom.

So it was with the four of us.

We were inextricably tied to each other by this profound, all-pervasive blood circumstance yet locked in a continual battle with each other for attention and notoriety in a vain attempt to stake out our individuality. Bobby Jr. was the king. He was cool, dangerous, daring, and had charisma, which drew people to him. He had also cultivated an interest in wildlife, which had given him his own identity. I admired him and resented him at the same time. I wanted that thing he had that made him "the guy."

Bobby Shriver was relatively normal compared with the rest of us. He had two parents and a father who never lost his humility and kindness despite his successes. He had a lot less angst and often suffered the fate of nice guys by being the brunt of jokes and pranks. "Charge it to Bobby Shriver" was our cry when buying candy at the news shop in Hyannis Port.

David Anthony Kennedy was my best friend.

He was small for his age, with freckles covering a face that was all innocent trouble. David was like Tom Sawyer. He looked like an angel, but if you weren't careful he'd get you to whitewash the fence for him.

We found each other in the maelstrom and clung to one another until the day I turned my back on him.

David had a twinkle in his eye and even a little streetwise swagger. His irreverence was a hint that he knew before any of us that our lives were some kind of cruel joke, perpetrated by a God ironic at best, sadistic at worst. There was a vulnerability not present in the other RFK male cousins. David found himself in the middle of a big cannibalistic family. His closest brother was Bobby, but he was too self-contained and preoccupied with the animal kingdom for attachment. Courtney was closest in age, but although they were close, she was a female. David and I were the same age, and after the death of his father, we had a common loneliness, which cemented our friendship.

Growing up, our role models were uncles Jack, Bobby, and Teddy, the triumvirate, bound together by blood and purpose to save the world and be adored in the process. From an early age our purpose was to become more Kennedy. More brave, more reckless, more teeth, more charisma, better sailors, better football players, better with the ladies. This is what we were looking for—what we would have liked to recreate—but we never had a snowball's chance in hell of doing it. The premature deaths of Jack and Bobby Kennedy elevated them to mythic proportions. Their greatness was undiminished, their human failings forgotten. They were our benchmarks, which on a deep unspoken level we knew we would never reach. I think David knew this before any of us. It's what fueled his sardonic side.

Nobody had the wisdom to let us know we weren't obliged to follow the path, but the glorification of "the path" seemed to compel us to at least make an attempt to follow it. Certainly nobody had the time or inclination to give us the attention we needed to move down a road of our own choosing. This was David's torture. He wanted to walk the path, but his incredible spirit and originality pulled him in other directions—directions he would not allow himself to go in. He was bound to what had been walked before by our parents and grandparents. It really wreaks havoc on your inner self when you realize you have been born to a life so compelling and attractive that finding your own path and own self feels like losing. This is a torturous dilemma—one that for me, at least, would eventually require massive amounts of painkillers.

So we created our own secret life. A life we had some control over, we thought. It was as if we knew it was all a horrible joke, and we acted out in our outrageousness to let *them* know we knew.

UNCLE JACK's house at the Cape was full of scrimshaw and gravitas. It was the President's House, hallowed ground softened by Aunt Jackie's grace and calm. It was quieter than the other houses, the place we went to whisper about things.

SNAPSHOT:

David and I were in one of the upstairs bedrooms with some of our girl cousins and their friends. We were whispering I'll-show-you-mine-if-you-show-me-yours when Bobby Jr. burst in, out of breath. His big brother Joe was looking for me and was going to punch me in the stomach for something I did or didn't do. I remember thinking at the time that whatever I had or hadn't done didn't warrant getting punched in the stomach, but it seemed that by the time Joe hit the testosterone-producing years of puberty he had developed a fairly regular addiction to punching someone over something.

In hindsight I can't say I blame him. I sure as hell would have been angry if I had been the oldest male of our generation. His inner child must have been scared to death by the level of responsibility. Until this moment in time, I had managed to stay off Joe's radar. Now my luck had run out, and as we all knew, there was no avoiding it. You could hide but you'd have to come out at some point, and Joe had a long memory. So it was best to take your medicine and get it over with. This was what we were discussing in the upstairs bedroom of the President's House—having been diverted from the scary and titillating exploration of our first cousins' anatomy, something all of us were sure was a mortal and not a venial sin. Bobby and David, having had a lifetime of beatings from their older brother, were looking at me with pity and the relief of knowing that it wasn't one of them who was going to be Joe's punching bag.

It was decided that I would hide in the attic, and my cousins would venture out and try to distract Joe from his purpose. Off they went, with the laughter and lightness of those who know someone else is bearing the bigger burden. I was left alone to wait in the anticipation of facing one of those male rites of passage that I had managed to avoid in my ten short years: getting the shit kicked out of me. One of the benefits of growing up with three younger sisters and no older brothers.

It's scary waiting in a dark attic alone, not knowing when you might hear the sounds of heavy angry steps clomping up the creaky old New England stairs. I cowered in the dark musty space among the giant clothing storage bags, wishing my dead uncle Jack or some other male were around so I could run to him for protection. I paced back and forth until my nerves got the better of me and I could no longer stifle my overwhelming need to go to the bathroom. Whenever I was afraid as a kid I always had to take a crap. So I lasted ten minutes and then ran out of the attic, into the bathroom, and from there, like a skittish bird, into the great outdoors, where I was vulnerable.

Nobody was around—which was good and bad. The cousins who

were supposed to be distracting Joe and watching my back had long since become distracted. Joe wasn't around, yet, but that could change, and then I'd be fucked, because I really was all alone. As soon as I had that thought, Joe appeared from around the hedge that separates the JFKs' from the RFKs'. He wasn't happy. His arms were rigid at his sides, fists clenched, his face flushed with anger, eyes darting this way and that, looking for a release for all that pent-up rage. And there I stood—the proverbial deer in the headlights. There was no point in running. I was a chubby ten-year-old and Joe was used to running down his brothers who were way faster than me. I stood my ground, closed my eyes, and waited for what was to come. Joe marched up to me and punched me in the stomach. Joe was also in the habit of doing what he said he was going to do. It hurt, but thanks to all those slices of pizza Jack Walsh had been buying me at Have-A-Pizza, the blow was cushioned and didn't cause nearly the discomfort the anticipation had.

WE PLAYED football every day on the Cape. We played in the afternoon when the grown-ups were playing golf or tennis. Tennis and golf were the two sports where real proficiency was required and kids were relegated to spectator status. When I was in my early teens and my tennis had improved after numerous tennis camps, I was invited to play with my aunts and uncles on the court that sat in back of the Big House. Playing in a foursome with Ethel, Teddy, and Jean was absolutely terrifying. Nobody in my family likes to lose. They like it even less when you are the cause. Ethel often played matches for "favors," which meant that if you lost you might end up being her boatboy for the summer. Even the most benign competition had consequences.

When Uncle Bobby wasn't around, football became the purview of the next generation. It was on the football field that we worked out a lot of our issues. Power struggles were dealt with, alliances formed, and resentments confronted. It was highly competitive and often dysfunctional. We played on the front lawn of the RFK house or, if it was a big game, at my grandparents'. Mostly it was just the boys; girls were invited if we needed bodies. As a rule the RFKs were fast but

couldn't throw—except for Joe, whose arm was as powerful and erratic as his demeanor. Joe retired from football after his knee went
and he realized it was impossible for him to play with us without going into a rage. I can't say I blame him—we were really irritating.
Bobby Shriver and I were slow but could throw, which meant that
one of us was more often than not the quarterback. This was a mixed
blessing. It meant that you got to touch the ball but would have to endure every cousin on your team having a better play than the one you
called.

Our version of touch football was "razzle-dazzle," meaning you
could throw the ball from anywhere on the field. It was more like
rugby and favored the RFKs because it rewarded quickness and short
passes. I didn't like it because I was fat and slow. To me it wasn't really
football. As we got older and more of the younger cousins came of age
and came into their own on the gridiron, the games got bigger and
more intense—usually breaking down into the rivalry between the
RFKs and the Shrivers, with John Kennedy playing with the Shrivers,
and me playing with the RFKs. There had been an untold number of
football games over the years, but nothing was ever settled. Who was
the fastest, who had the best arm, who would win against whom remained forever unsettled because there was always tomorrow and another game. There would be a time in the future when old scores and
our feeling of immortality would be settled for good. But that comes
later. . . .

JOE WAS David's favorite target. I don't remember many football
games that didn't end with Joe getting into a fight with somebody. Joe
was a bull on the football field. He was a big, bruising, snorting presence; and if nobody waved a red cape in front of him he was more or
less controlled. But it was only a matter of time before somebody
waved the cape—and it was usually David.

We all knew how to make Joe crazy. It wasn't hard. All you had to
do was question a call or disagree with a play he called, and all hell
would break loose. It was a very dangerous thing to do, and most of us
didn't have the guts for it. But David couldn't wait. It was like a game to

him. He'd show little pieces of red, and Joe's frustration and anger would build until that moment when David let the red cape fly.

David:
Joe, why don't you let someone else call a play?
Joe:
Because I'm quarterback.
David:
Maybe it's time you let someone else be quarterback, Joe.
Joe:
I'm the quarterback!
David:
It just doesn't seem fair, Joe.
Joe:
It's fair because I say it's fair!
David:
You don't have to get mad, Joe.
Joe:
All right, David, that does it!

Joe would explode and chase David all over the field. Joe would almost catch him, and David would slide or duck, and Joe would come up empty. David would laugh and admonish Joe to calm down. Joe would just get angrier and angrier until he would give up and storm off threatening to never play football again. It was like watching Roadrunner torture Wyley Coyote.

SNAPSHOT:

I didn't think Aunt Ethel, or "the Big E," as she was referred to behind her back, was around, but you could never be too sure. We called her the Big E because she was a very big presence. Way bigger than her five feet and four inches. There was nobody who came into a room with more force than Aunt Ethel. The RFK house was always a cacophony of assorted mayhem, most of which went unnoticed, but you could never tell when the Big E would zero in on what you were doing, and then watch out.

I had finally caught David. It had taken the better part of a half hour and all my wind, but I had him. He was on his back, stuck, deep in the squishy chair in Aunt Ethel's living room. We had been fighting our way across the RFKs' house in Hyannis Port room by room, doing little damage but making a hell of a lot of noise.

I outweighed David by thirty pounds, so if I could catch him I could beat the stuffing out of him. The problem was catching him. He was fast and elusive, with an uncanny instinct for escape. He was like a mosquito buzzing around your head and then disappearing until you felt the bite on your arm or leg. His tactics were to provoke until you couldn't help but go after him; then he would go into his mosquito routine, driving whoever was unlucky enough to be chasing him into a frenzy until they gave up, hoping for a future opportunity when he might let his guard down. David rarely let his guard down.

David loved to infuriate. He could do it with his speed on the football field or with his intellect and wit. Nobody was spared, except me. I was his best friend and ally. I was also no match for his speed or wit. This didn't mean we didn't fight—but it was usually at long distance.

Now I was whaling on him, making up for all those times I had come up empty. I had the advantage, but David didn't have the instinct to surrender. He had me by the hair and was yelling, "Chris Lawford's beating me up. Help! Get him off me. Help." I couldn't figure out who he thought might help him. There wasn't anyone who didn't think this whupping was long overdue.

Well, maybe there was one person.

They say a mother's love is blind. And so I found myself in the crosshairs of the Big E. Aunt Ethel, the volatile one, was on her way to his rescue. I could hear her coming. "Chris Lawford, you get off David this minute."

That was good enough for me. My hands flew up into the air in the universally recognized sign of surrender. I knew better than to cross the Big E. We had all tried, and it never worked out too well.

ONE OF the givens of life in Hyannis Port was getting kicked out of the RFKs' house by Aunt Ethel. I had been kicked out of the house pretty much every other week for things like not standing up when Ethel came into the room or slurping my soup at the dinner table. As I remember it, this didn't happen very much when Uncle Bobby was around and became endemic after he died. The punishment for more egregious crimes could be worse.

SNAPSHOT:

> It had been raining for days and our parents were tired of our inactivity, so we were shipped off to Otis Air Force Base where we could swim, climb ropes, shoot baskets, and continue our quest for the Holy Grail—never-ceasing activity. Over a lunch of tomato soup and ham sandwiches I told a joke I had heard from my degenerate friends at Saint David's. It went like this: A lady has a daughter named Fanny. Fanny gets lost. The distraught mother runs up to a policeman and says, "Officer, Officer, have you seen my Fanny?" The officer replies, "No, ma'am, but I sure would like to."

When we got home, somebody snitched. I think it was one of the girls. Bobby and David ended up sucking on bars of soap for a half hour and it wasn't even their joke. I was standing in the living room wondering why everything had gotten so quiet when the Big E appeared on the stairway and launched herself toward me, tackling me and pummeling me out of the house.

I had learned my lesson; it was not healthy to piss off the Big E. From that day on I was on my feet if Aunt Ethel even thought about coming into the room, so I sure as hell was going to stop beating on her son if she told me to.

. . .

SO, BACK to the squishy chair and me with my hands in the air and my head buried deep in David's chest because he still had large clumps of my hair clutched in his hands. If there was one thing that my best friend knew how to do, it was take advantage of an opportunity. When we were older David would hide and leave twenty-dollar bills on the floor of a room to see if someone walking in would pocket them. If you did, he had you. The advantage was his. So you could be damn sure that if he found himself with his adversary's hands in the air, rendered impotent by his rescuing mother, he'd start hitting me in the face with his right while he pulled my hair out of my head with his left, which he did.

It must have looked to the Big E like I was still whaling on her son, because when she got to us, she grabbed my hand with such force that she broke my thumb with a snap. This got my attention fast and got me off David, who sat back and laughed.

SANDY EILER was our physical education guru, hired by our parents to keep us continually engaged in physical activity during our days at the Cape.

He taught us how to swim, play baseball, and do flips on the trampoline. He kept us busy so our parents wouldn't have to. Sandy was the tannest person I had ever seen, and I had seen a few, being from California and all. He marched around the compound in a pair of shorts and sunglasses, looking for my cousins and me as we hid, trying to avoid calisthenics or swim class. I don't remember ever seeing him wear a shirt, which surprised me because he had the biggest stomach I had ever seen. It was as hard as a rock but I couldn't figure why he didn't want to cover it with clothing. Being the fat kid, I was forever trying to conceal my rolls with oversized clothing and lived in terror of any shirtless activity. Sandy was proud of his girth, showed it off even.

"Go ahead, Chris, hit it as hard as you want," Sandy would challenge me as he stuck out his gut. I didn't want to. I had an aversion to hitting people even when invited. David and Bobby were different. Each took his best shot at Sandy's big brown rock-hard belly, always to no effect. Sandy would look down at us and laugh. David just got frustrated and wondered how long it would take for him to get big enough to make a dent in Sandy's belly. Bobby lost interest after the first attempt and turned his attention to things he had dominion over. I wondered what it was like for Sandy to get up every morning and not be able to see his toes.

The daily protocol in Hyannis Port went something like this:

In the morning we would head down to the pier for dreaded sailing class with the sailing tyrant, Johnny Lenihan, one of those weathered New Englanders as salty as the sea. Johnny Lenihan loved sailing and he didn't have a lot of love for those who didn't share his enthusiasm for cutting through whitecaps with your keel halfway out of the water and the salty sea smacking you across the face as you hurtled across the Hyannis Port harbor toward the rocks of the breakwater in your tiny, unstable Beetle Cat. Johnny Lenihan was a crusty old sea dog who viewed sailing as a riotous obligation. If Johnny Lenihan melted, the puddles of seawater would find their way back to the ocean.

For David and me, this was the worst part of the day. We had to endure Johnny Lenihan's disdain. He had little use for kids who didn't like sailing and even less use for Kennedy kids who didn't like sailing. The other drag about sailing class was the other kids and the order of it all. Most of the kids were eager and attentive. David and I didn't understand why we had to wear life preservers. We were required to learn things like how to tie knots and furl sails, which didn't interest us and interrupted our exclusive, messy, anarchistic summers.

We'd rather be bombing around the harbor in the family speedboat, aptly named *The Rest of Us*. Sleek and powerful, made of wood, it was the fastest boat in the harbor. Our parents used it to water-ski, David and I used it for speed. One of the highlights of any day was when Uncle Bobby took us out into the open ocean, placed David and me in front of the giant silver wheel, pushed the throttle all the way down, and we flew over those whitecaps, leaving Johnny Lenihan's Beetle Cats in the dust.

When I was a kid I didn't understand why anyone would want to crawl along at ten knots in a sailboat when they could fly at fifty miles an hour in a speedboat. Plus you had a whole lot more control with a motorboat. You could go where you wanted to go and didn't have to tack to get there.

There were only two times I really liked being on a sailboat. The first was when one of my uncles threw a long rope off the stern so my cousins and I could "drag" through the rough seas trying not to get knocked off by the waves, which meant a long swim to the breakwater. The second was when the Hyannis Port Yacht Club held its annual Pirate Race—an event designed for my cousins and me. The purpose of the race was to sail around the harbor and attack each other's boats with tennis balls. If you landed a ball on another boat, they were out. The boat that managed not to have a tennis ball breach its defenses was the winner. You could construct whatever defenses you wanted to keep the tennis balls out and rig your boat in whatever outrageous ways you could devise. The rules allowed for as many kids as you could fit on a sailboat. Our family would always enter two or three boats crammed with kids and homemade barricades of sheets and garbage can lids. I don't remember winning, but we loved being pirates.

From the pier we would walk the two hundred yards along the beach to the compound where Sandy would be waiting to give our daily swimming lessons. He'd be standing waist deep—which required us wading out through the beds of sea grass with god only knows what living in it. The trick was to endure the half-hour lesson without putting my feet on the ocean floor, or, if I did, to make certain my feet found sand and not the spooky green grass. Sometime in August the Hyannis Port Beach Club had swim races for every kid in town. My family didn't belong to the beach club, but we were allowed to race. We were a big family so we had entrants in pretty much all the age groups. We also had Sandy Eiler, which meant we took all the medals. This bred a certain amount of resentment on the part of the members of the beach club, and after a few years we weren't invited back.

Lunchtime in Hyannis Port meant a cruise and picnic on my grandfather's yacht, *The Marlin*. It was a fifty-foot cabin cruiser piloted by Captain Frank, a favorite of all the kids. He was a real boat captain who let us turn the giant silver steering wheel and who had a far less volatile demeanor as skipper than the skippers we were related to. After my grandfather died we got rid of *The Marlin*, and lunchtime meant sailing to a picnic on Egg Island or, if the tide was high, Great Island. Both islands were a twenty-minute sail or three minutes in *The Rest of Us* if we could convince a grown-up to forsake their beloved sailboat.

We weren't allowed on Great Island. It was private property and the owners could care less that the Kennedys wanted to picnic there. We weren't welcome. We figured they were rich Republicans so we'd go anyway. The rich Republicans hired a guard. We turned it into a game of hide-and-seek.

Ethel always had the best picnic basket, but sailing with her had its perils. There were always too many kids on the boat and chaos reigned. Sailing with the Shrivers was safer but the lunch was never as good. If you went with Uncle Bobby or Uncle Teddy on their boats, you'd end up having to work the mainsail for your lunch and there was never any telling what time you would finally get home.

Art Buchwald reported in a famous column he wrote after spending a summer weekend in Hyannis Port that he had taken an opinion poll among the Kennedy children and grandchildren. The question was "With whom would you rather sail?" The answers: RFK, 8 percent; ESK—"the Big E"—9 percent; Captain Bligh, 83 percent. Teddy would have scored about the same as his brother.

In the afternoon we played football or baseball. Sandy would organize the game on Uncle Jack's lawn, which had a big fence encircling the outfield, one we always swung for but never reached. After 1963 Jackie found other places to summer, but she always made sure Caroline and John stayed connected to Hyannis Port.

At night after dinner we would all go down the stairs to the basement of the Big House, past my grandmother's collection of dolls from all over the world and into my grandparents' movie theater for a movie. On rare occasions there might be a play or talent show. Trust me, though, there were no Shirley Temples or American Idols in our family.

SNAPSHOT:

In the summer of 1967, David, the two Bobbys, and I, along with a few of the locals, introduced the good people of Hyannis Port to the Hyannis Port Terrors. It was our pathetic homage to

CHRISTOPHER KENNEDY LAWFORD

gang activity. Our purpose was to do some mischief and make a public statement demonstrating our incorrigibility brought on by raging hormones and a surge in testosterone. We had two favorite pranks. The first was to fill a paper bag full of dog shit, set it on fire, leave it on someone's porch, and ring the doorbell. The second was to flag down a motorist, and while one of us asked directions, a compatriot would crawl around the back of the car and shove a potato up the muffler. Neither prank worked very well. The fire usually went out before anyone answered the door, and the potato always fell out of the muffler.

One night we had our greatest success and failure when I managed to cram a potato into the muffler of a police car. I had no way of knowing it was a police car. When I scampered out from behind the hedge, all I could see were tires and a muffler. Bobby had flagged down a cop car, and this time the spud fit like a glove. The officer drove off and there was some kind of backfire. We were rounded up and delivered to my uncle Bobby's house where our parents were in the middle of dinner. The cop made his way into the RFK dining room to tell some very prominent and powerful citizens that their children were little criminals. The criminals were left shaking and scared on the porch.

My cousins and I grew up knowing the story of the policeman's cap. Uncle Bobby and Uncle Teddy were caught stealing a policeman's cap to complete their assignment in a scavanger hunt. My grandfather was furious and when Uncle Bobby tried to explain, my grandfather silenced him with the look and apparently said, "No, you keep quiet and listen to me. This is childish behavior, and I don't want anything more like it." And there wasn't.

My cousins and I had managed to best our uncles in our mischief. We sat on Uncle Bobby's porch unsure if we would endure a similar reproach.

We could hear the policeman introduce himself and begin his story. Then there was quiet, then a roar of laughter led by Uncle Bobby. We had been spared. Big Bobby came out with a stern reprimand but we knew how he really felt. The following summer Robert Kennedy was dead and the HPTs would turn to darker pursuits.

Chapter 11

The price of a memory is the memory of the sorrow it brings.
— Counting Crows

I heard the voices of concern for his safety when Uncle Bobby was deciding whether or not to challenge Lyndon Johnson for the Democratic nomination in 1968. I was only thirteen but I knew that his decision to run invoked a level of fear in the family, especially in my mother, who was closest to him in age and experience. Although she never said anything, I could feel it and see it in her face. Whenever the campaign came up, she would get this tightness around her, like she was trying to ward something off.

The Democratic primary season in 1968 for me was all about psychedelic "Bobby" political posters, fending off attacks from my political neophyte friends, and hoping the other shoe wouldn't drop. I awoke on the morning of June 5, 1968, and found that it had.

I remember three things about that day: The first was coming down for breakfast and finding Mademoiselle slumped at the kitchen table, the cover of the *New York Daily News* announcing the shooting held in her trembling hand. She was crying. I looked at the photograph of my uncle lying on the floor of the Ambassador Hotel kitchen for a long time before going to school, not believing what I had seen. The second thing I remember was feeling that the eyes of the world were on me once again, and—again—the strange surge of energy that comes with that level of profound attention. The last thing I remember is walking into school and having one of my friends who had been a McCarthy supporter run up to me and announce somewhat triumphantly that my uncle had been shot, as if I hadn't known. Henry Adams said, "Politics, as a practice, whatever its profession, has always been the systematic organization of hatreds."

I guess this is true even in the young and unaware.

My mother had gone to California to work on the campaign in the final days leading up to the California primary. She had heard her brother make his victory speech in the ballroom of the Ambassador Hotel and was on her way to meet him at the victory party when she was told, by a campaign worker, that there had been a shooting. My mom raced to Good Samaritan Hospital to find her brother clinging to life. She stayed with him until his heart stopped beating, and brought his body back to New York with the rest of the family. My sisters and I stayed up late and waited for her to get home. Mademoiselle had us all huddled in the entranceway waiting for the elevator to bring what was left of my mother to the eighth floor of 990 Fifth Avenue and the terrified children who didn't know how her life and by association our lives were going to go on. The elevator door opened revealing a broken woman. She grabbed me and hugged me, crying, "Oh my God, oh my God. I love you so much." There was desperation and a need I had never felt before. My mom would never again be this open and raw. I was now the male in her life.

THE ENTIRE family descended on New York City for Robert Kennedy's funeral. This time I was fully present and engaged in the drama, but the days went by in a blur, a sea of dark suits and black dresses covering hunched, broken parents. Bobby, David, and I spent most of our time together at the apartment of Lem Billings. This became our refuge from the volatile intensity of our parents' pain and the place where we could be ourselves. With Lem we were connected to it all but had found a place where we could begin to exercise our independence while remaining tethered to the bright Kennedy light.

The death of RFK meant the removal of another male role model. For Bobby and David it was their father. For me it was a surrogate father. For even though my father was alive, he was absent. Uncle Bobby was a much bigger presence in my life. If Bobby, David, and I were close before, this brought us closer. We had a similarity and distinction of wound. Theirs was more dramatic, but mine was also deep. We all had interrupted and fractious relationships with our fathers. We found ourselves entering our teenage years without a significant male influence. Lem saw our need and rushed to fill the void. His love for our parents' generation was transferred to ours. We were grateful that somebody connected to our parents was paying attention to us. There were thousands of people who claimed to love my family but only a few who gave love. Lem was one of them.

When Uncle Bobby died, Lem was the only adult with any proximity to the generation and events that were having such profound impact on our lives who seemed to have an instinct to find out how we might or might not be handling it all. Lem adopted our generation. He cared about us and treated us like the sons he never had.

I always thought my cousin David envied Bobby Jr.'s relationship with Lem. It seemed to me that in David's mind Bobby was lucky to have an adult who was fully devoted to him and ready to help him deal with the tragedy of losing their father.

I was pissed as well, although I was far too shut down to realize it. Lem had become my godfather, after all, when we moved to New York from California. I was a Kennedy, but once again I felt like I was being sent to the back of the bus in favor of a cousin with a better pedigree and more charisma. I spent years competing for Lem's attention and affection. When Lem was angry with Bobby, I became his favorite and the extra bedroom in Lem's Eighty-eighth Street apartment became "Chris and Bobby's room," but when they made up it was back to being just "Bobby's room."

I never really had a chance.

The loss of Robert Kennedy was the loss of one of the most consequential figures of that time. Bobby Jr. existentially got an enormous amount of star power carrying those initials. He also got a lot of magnetism from Lem's fixation. Lem had decided that Bobby was the next bearer of Kennedy greatness—and none of us were about to argue. Lem had been the president's best friend and he was loved by all the aunts and uncles. These facts gave him gravitas. Lem's attachment and anointing of Bobby defined him as the second coming, which gave focus to our drama of recreating what had come before us.

IT WAS hot as hell in New York during those dog days in June. There was a lot to do to get ready for the funeral Mass at Saint Patrick's. The whole world would be watching. There wasn't a lot of time to think about what had happened. My cousins and I played the part of altar boys, and though we were obliged to wear the costumes that transformed us into little angel servants, a trip to Saks was arranged by Lem to make sure we were all properly attired.

On June 7, the day before my uncle's funeral, a telegram was delivered to me at my mother's apartment. It read:

Christopher Lawford
990 5th Avenue NYC

You are invited to attend a requiem mass in memory of Robert Francis Kennedy at St. Patrick's Cathedral in New York City on Saturday, June 8, 1968 at 10:00 A.M. Please enter through the Fifth Avenue entrance by 9:30 A.M.

Interment will be at Arlington Cemetery, Arlington, Virginia, at 5:30 P.M.

You are welcome to travel on the funeral train from New York to Washington. Buses to Pennsylvania Station will leave the Fifth Avenue side of the Cathedral immediately following the Mass.

This telegram will admit only the person or persons to whom it is addressed and must be retained and presented for identification whenever it is requested.

The Kennedy Family

It seems odd to me now, to have received a formal telegram to my own uncle's funeral. But I suppose that it is just more evidence of how the lines of distinction were often blurred between major public events and our own private ones.

The Mass was like being in a sad movie. There were cameras and lights, wardrobe, lines to read, and crosses not to be missed in front of a cathedral full of devastated people. An hour and a half of crucifixes and crosses. It's not easy to cross the width of Saint Patty's with the body and blood of Christ in front of family, the entire U.S. government, and the rest of the world. I wasn't thinking about anything but my cues and all those eyes on me. Of course I screwed up, bringing my chalice full of our Lord's blood to the wrong priest. It bothered him more than it bothered me. What to do with too much blessed wine in front of a star-studded international congregation? I took it back from the pissed-off priest and wandered around until I found the one who was lacking. Nobody in the pews seemed to notice. When my uncle Teddy stood to eulogize his older brother, calling him "a good and decent man, who saw wrong and tried to right it, saw suffering and tried to heal it, saw war and tried to stop it," his voice cracked and I felt the first pangs of that deep reservoir of emotional pain. Tears began to well up. I struggled to push them back down and pull the solid steel manhole cover over the channel that connected me to my feelings, effectively cutting myself off from all emotional response.

SNAPSHOT:

The train from New York to Washington, carrying Robert Kennedy's body to Arlington Cemetery, took all day. My cousins and I occupied the time by running between the cars and trying to make it onto the roof to wave to the tens of thousands of people who lined the way to say good-bye to another member of our family. There was a lot of drinking and laughter, a pretty ordinary Irish wake—except the whole world was watching.

I made my way to the back of the train, the last car, where my uncle's casket lay in state, elevated so the people lining the route could see it. I was looking for my cousins, but the only people in the car were grown-ups, all in black, the enormity of the loss and the shock of this most brutal public murder hanging off them. I stood there for a moment transfixed by the reality of my uncle's casket and the sea of grief surrounding it, the low rumble of voices punctuated by the occasional burst of laughter, the Irish wail.

In the middle of this, I saw my aunt Ethel kneeling by my uncle's casket. Her head was bowed down and her hands were clutched in prayer. She was crying with the grief and pain of a loss unimaginable. It was the first time in these three days that I saw a member of my family cry. I knew in that moment that the necessary theater that surrounded my uncle's death would serve as a distraction from the profound emotional pain that would come after the television cameras had been turned off.

When the train arrived in Washington, night had already fallen. Candles were distributed and a sea of twinkling lights followed my uncle's casket into Arlington Cemetery. The cemetery was dark and the pallbearers became disoriented, uncertain where to place the coffin. I heard Averill Harriman finally whisper to my uncle Steve, "Steve, do you know where you are going?"

Uncle Steve turned back to those behind him and said, "Well, I'm not sure. But I distinctly heard a voice coming out of the coffin saying, 'Damn it. If you fellows put me down, I'll show you the way.'"

After the burial at Arlington we went back to Uncle Bobby and Aunt Ethel's house, Hickory Hill, where the kids played kick the can and the grown-ups drank. After a couple of hours I found myself alone on the great lawn that encircled the antebellum mansion in Mclean, Virginia. I went looking for Bobby and David, finding Ena, the RFKs' version of Mademoiselle, only she was from Costa Rica. I asked her where my cousins were. She said simply, "Chris, they have gone to bed. They buried their father today." It was at this moment I fully understood what Bobby and David had lost.

THE DEATH of Robert Kennedy was devastating. If President Kennedy represented what the family had been, Uncle Bobby represented what we would become. He embodied all that I had come to believe was Kennedy. His presence made me feel we would be safe. The assassination of President Kennedy was an attack on our family. Uncle Bobby became the head of our whole family and saw to it that there was a coming together. He was strong and sure. He made us feel more like Kennedys than ever—proud of what Jack had been, determined that our time would come again. His will and enthusiasm for life refused to consider failure of any kind. He demanded that we be better than we thought we could be.

After Uncle Jack was killed, Uncle Bobby began a tradition of taking the family on white-water rafting trips out West over the summer. The trips were a perfect blend of Uncle Bobby's capacity for fun and danger. He always navigated the biggest rivers with the best white water. There was a sense that we were overcoming something bigger than we were and having a hell of a time doing it. The kids would have their own boat, but as always, we were his focus. Water fights would rage between the kids' and adults' rafts the entire trip. He brought us into the family activities and the family destiny. He always led by example, often jumping out of the larger rafts and onto a rubber mattress to ride through the bigger rapids. The guides were nervous.

"Senator Kennedy, don't take the next rapids, they're too dangerous."

Uncle Bobby wouldn't get back in the boat.

Everybody would begin to yell from the rafts.

"Don't do it, Bobby!"

"Get back in the boat, Daddy."

"Uncle Bobby, the waves are too big."

But he wouldn't listen. He would turn toward the churning maelstrom and with purpose and a glint in his eye take the rapid. All of us on the rafts would hold our breath until we saw him pop out on the other side and a massive cheer would erupt. How could we not be okay with him leading the way?

I remember my mother jumping into a kayak and heading down a stretch of white water that I wasn't sure she would ever come back from. She did this because she was with her brother Bobby—and because she'd had a bottle of Pouilly-Fuissé at lunch.

He was the only head of the family my generation had ever known. Now that he was dead, there was this sense of splitting apart, and for many in my generation the only safety from here on out would be in escape and not giving a shit.

. . .

DAVID HAD nightmares before his father was killed. The nightmares were always the same. He would awaken from them with the certainty that someone was going to do to his father what they had done to his uncle Jack. His father reassured him but David never lost his fear. The night of the California primary he was in front of the television as the results came in and his nightmare became real. He was the only one awake in the California hotel room and he never got over it. He never spoke about it, but he carried it with him throughout his life.

I always felt that David, more than his brothers, was his father's son. He was in the middle of the family: small, fast, and smart. He had a big heart, but was ruthless in its protection and he had a biting sense of humor. He was the one whom Uncle Bobby said was "the one I have to work with." He was the one who was always first in the car when his father leaned over the banister at Hickory Hill and yelled, "Who wants to come with me to . . ."

I remember seeing a picture of David walking with his dad in the New York City St. Patrick's Day Parade. He was dressed in his little suit and overcoat, his mop top hair cut almost hiding his eyes. He was holding his father's hand. There was no mistaking that they were father and son. David was the ten-year-old version of his father and in his eyes you could see that wherever his dad led him, it would be just fine.

The day before big Bobby died he pulled David from a riptide in Malibu. David figured he owed his father his life. He would look for a way to repay him down the road. He never got the opportunity. David used to wear his dad's shoes when he got older; it was one of the connections he kept with him. When Sirhan Sirhan shot and killed Robert Kennedy, he also killed my best friend's heart and soul. Fucker!

MY MOTHER showed me a letter written by my uncle Teddy and signed by my family asking the California court not to give Sirhan Sirhan the death penalty. At the time, I was thirteen years old and was made to understand that this was a gesture of the highest human compassion and reflected a belief the family held that it was wrong to take a life for a life.

I didn't get it. As far as I was concerned they should do to him exactly what he had done to my uncle or worse. I was thirteen years old and angry. I was not allowed to make up my own mind about it.

HAVING A family member killed definitely messes with your sense of safety. What I realize now about my uncles' assassinations is that the massive outpouring of collective grief and goodwill toward the family obscured the underlying realization that there were people in the world who wanted to blow our fucking heads off.

After my uncle Bobby was killed I think I got a little angry with God. It didn't come out that way. It's hard to be angry when everyone in the world is being so nice to you. In addition, Bobby Kennedy wasn't my father and I didn't feel as though I had a right to be angry. That would be overstepping my place in the family. There was a hierarchy of affect, and I was definitely toward the lower end of it.

THE SUMMER after Uncle Bobby's assassination, Uncle Teddy packed up the family and headed for Utah and the Green River to conquer more white water and prove that despite Dallas and Los Angeles the family would go on. We were looking forward to the trip as a healing ritual. With Uncle Bobby there was no distinction between child and adult; we conquered the river together. On this trip, there was a definite chasm between the adults and the children. The adults floated along with their daiquiris and Pouilly-Fuissé and didn't want to be bothered. They were angry and not in the mood to indulge the highjinks of the younger generation. On the second day we brought the kids' raft alongside the grown-ups and initiated a water fight, one of the staples of our trips with Uncle Bobby. The grown-ups told us to stop, and when we didn't, sent the mountaineer Jim Whittaker onto our raft to let us know they weren't fucking around by forcefully tossing Bobby and David into the river.

The glory and happiness of the early days were gone. The days of JFK and RFK were enshrined as the golden years. They would never do wrong again. Uncle Teddy was left to pick up the pieces and be harshly judged for his humanity. The older generation was wounded badly and their wounds were showing.

That night we took our sleeping bags, found the most inaccessible place to sleep, and camped there. We wanted nothing to do with the grown-ups. The mistrust and estrangement from our parents' generation was solidified—hard and fast.

THE MURDERS of my uncles were never really humanized for me. John and Robert Kennedy were public figures and their murders were public events. Bigger than the ending of an individual's life. I never heard any of the grown-ups vent any anger or hatred toward the murderers. I never heard anybody question why they did it or how. I was never able to own what those two assholes who pulled the triggers in Dallas and Los Angeles did to us in our tiny unformed lives. We just ate it and tried to be good little Kennedys and demonstrate that stoic grace that everybody seemed to admire so much. The killings of my uncles were these giant catastrophic events that we were tied to by relationship. But the mythic proportions somehow dehumanized the actual events and prevented any real human association. We had no tools for dealing with any of it, and those who might have provided some were far too devastated themselves to be much help. The only way to survive was to escape.

The journey begins. Me at my baptism surrounded by Cardinal Frances McIntyre; my father, Peter Lawford; mother, Patricia Kennedy Lawford; grandfather, Joseph P. Kennedy; godfather, Peter Sabiston; and flamboyant grandmother Lady Mae Lawford.

My mother and her number one son.

My dad "on location" on the beach in Malibu. Where are my sunglasses?

Did someone say "photo op"?

Frank Sinatra and my father in 1958.

At home in Santa Monica, my mother presides over lunch with RFK, Angie Dickinson, and Frank Sinatra.

Catching some rays with Angie, Uncle Bobby, and Frank.

My favorite photo of my father—with Marilyn.

"Hey, Uncle Jack, where are you going? We're not finished playing Marco Polo!"

Me, with a minor wardrobe malfunction, and my best friend, Ricky Hilton (holding a mouse). I'm sure he never imagined the day when he would be known as "Paris Hilton's father."

Happy days on the beach with my family in Santa Monica, despite my cast, which made me itch in places I didn't even know existed.

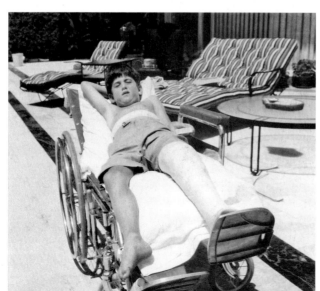

My trampoline mishap left me in a body cast and in dire need of nursing care, eagerly administered by the ever-willing Roach twins.

My mom schooling us in the art of the Kennedy game.

I got the hippest car for Christmas that year. Unfortunately, I had to share it with my kid sisters.

My dad and me on the presidential yacht The Honey Fitz, *off Hyannis Port.*

Asking my cousin John if he wants me to amuse him with some yo-yo tricks.

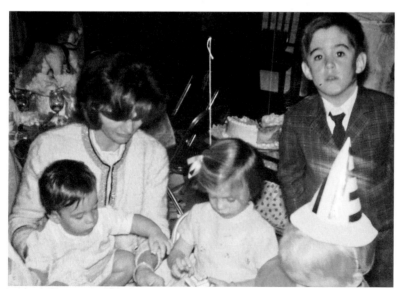

At Caroline's fourth birthday party at the White House with Aunt Jackie and John.

Sun worshippers all: My grandfather with his growing brood of tanned grandchildren. That's me on the far right side of the couch in the back row.

Uncle Jack with me and my sisters, Sydney and Victoria, outside the president's house in Hyannis Port.

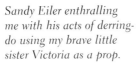

Sandy Eiler enthralling me with his acts of derring-do using my brave little sister Victoria as a prop.

Me and my grandfather
after his stroke.

My mom reading to me while I sit very, very, very still.

Uncle Jack's golf cart: My sister Victoria got to drive that day, leaving the rest of us cousins not very happy.

The original Three Amigos: me and my cousins Bobby Shriver and Bobby Kennedy at one of our regular talent shows held at our grandparents' house in Hyannis Port.

Me and my best friend till the bitter end, David Kennedy.

David and John Kennedy present me with my birthday cake.

Uncle Teddy, David, and me at Uncle Bobby's memorial service. PHOTOGRAPH BY FRANK TETI

A son of the sixties: Here I am at my Grandmother Rose's dinner table, with my mom, Aunt Jackie, and my sister Sydney.

Home for the holidays. I wasn't a rock star, but I could pose like one.

At Disneyland with Elizabeth Taylor. It's a Small World sure is interesting when you're stoned.

My cousin Bobby Kennedy and me with our great family friend and mentor, Lem Billings. PHOTOGRAPH BY FRANK TETI

The Champ and me.

David Kennedy all dressed up, which was a rarity.

Bobby, David, me, and Lem on our first river trip in South America, just before our lunch of chicken salad.

Guarding the "Worm" after a mud bath in the Colorado River. Bobby Kennedy and me.

Letting sleeping pigs lie. Me, Bobby Kennedy, Doug Spooner, and David Kennedy on our first South American river-rafting trip.

Modeling our new plant discovery in the jungles of Venezuela: Bobby and Michael Kennedy with me and our friend Tim Haydock.

Alone on the ascent of Mount Rainier.

Fear and loathing in Boston. Right to left: Bobby Kennedy, me, my friend A.K., Steve Smith, and our Iranian friend Merdad.

I graduated law school despite ingesting enough chemicals to sedate a small city. Celebrating with my mother and sisters at Boston College Law School.

Trying to look tough in Hyannis Port.

All grown up: my sisters and me with our beloved childhood nanny, "Mademoiselle"—the woman who helped give us our hearts.

My Uncle Teddy trying to get Robert Redford away from his very inebriated nephew. Later that night, I would require the services of a hospital emergency room to survive.

Chapter 12

You can't escape until you realize that you are a prisoner.
— ANONYMOUS

When you choose the beginning of a road you also choose the destination. The White House was behind me. I was now ready to follow the white rabbit down the hole.

I was in a dilemma. I was thirteen years old, getting fat on sugar, and facing puberty in a family that was literally dying trying to save the world . . . really kind of a setup for some serious self-loathing.

EVERY MORNING, I used to meet my friends at the Lamstons on Eighty-eighth and Madison Avenue, across from school, for orange juice and a French cruller. They were my apostles. We'd sit at the counter, waiting for the clerk to whip up some eggs and turn his back on us so we could sneak into the back of the store to see what we could steal. We were in eighth grade and well on our way to incorrigibility.

It was the fall of 1968. I was dealing with normal teenage hormone craziness, the certain reality of my parents' divorce—and the repercussions of another assassination. To say I was unstable and on the edge would not be inaccurate. My teachers at Saint David's noted my progressing attitude problem in their reports. My English teacher, Mr. Fagan, wrote, "Your written work in English this marking period has been very good, and I even detect some improvement in penmanship. However your conduct in class and around school is often rude. Sometimes you give the impression that you are totally unaware of your surroundings and the people near you. Good manners are part of a young man's education. I'm afraid I cannot give you high marks in that subject."

What Mr. Fagan didn't get was that I was perfectly aware of my surroundings. I just figured that deference to the good people of Saint David's was not something I need worry about, given the circumstances of my life.

My French teacher, Mr. Bunker, concurred with Mr. Fagan, noting, "While your work in class has been very commendable, I certainly can't say the same for your behavior, which is continually poor. I can't understand why you don't recognize how foolish your attitude is, and how it is interfering with the impression I receive of you in class."

Mr. Bunker didn't understand that I was caring less and less what he or any other adult thought about me.

SOMETIME IN the fall of my eighth-grade year at Saint David's the apostles discovered LSD. One of them brought his discovery to the others, courtesy of a relative who was fully enmeshed in the chemical revolution after a year away at prep school. The apostles became major devotees of seeking alternate consciousness, getting together on the weekends to watch walls melt and the colors explode. My apostles tried to enlist me in their weekend acid-dropping get-togethers, but I had thus far resisted.

It was the last remnants of responsible goodness, preventing me from making the leap to the dark side. There was something deep inside of me that knew it would be the wrong thing for me to do. But my friends were persistent. One day in Bedford, New York, at the house my mother rented as our weekend getaway, we were walking down a beautiful country road. One guy had brought enough Windowpane acid for all of us, and my friends wanted to know, yet again, if I was in or out.

Peer pressure is a bitch.

There was no epiphany, just a calm acquiescence to the thirteen-year-old desire for experimentation and the need to fit in.

I just said yes—and my long strange trip began.

Once I had made the decision to take drugs, there was no hesitation or doubt. It was as if I knew I had chosen the path my life would take, and I was eager to get on with it. We hustled back to the house, my anticipation building along with the fear. One friend pulled out the baggie with four square pieces of paper in it and handed one to each of us one. I put mine on my tongue and waited for its effect. My sister Sydney was there with a friend. I had a crush on her—she had enormous tits for a seventh grader. They were the first breasts I would ever touch.

SNAPSHOT:

> The Coke bottle was pointing straight at me. The opportunity I had been praying for was mine. Our weekend sessions of spin the bottle had provided many trips to first base and I was finally going to try and stretch for a double. Sydney's friend was scared but willing. I knelt in front of her, my knees just inside her rigid thighs. She tensed as I put my lips to hers and moved my hand inside and up her red sweatshirt placing it on her right breast. It was enormous, much bigger than my hand, firm and moist from sweat. Now what? Is this it? Should I squeeze or just let my hand lie there like a dead fish? I had no idea. Then something started to happen. The girl started to change—to soften. Her thighs released as her breath quickened, her head tilting back, and she let out the tiniest gasp. Her tongue hesitatingly made its way around my lips and into my mouth as her chest heaved under my touch. The narcotic of sex was released on me for the very first time. The narcotic being the effect I was having on her. The breast itself was just a round mound, but what my touch was doing to her was what turned me on.

Up until the moment I put windowpane on my tongue, the weekends in the country were full of innocent fun.

LSD was a step up, and meant leaving Sydney behind in her relative innocence.

There was a pool table in the playroom of the house we were

renting; we were sitting around it waiting for something to happen. Sydney was chasing her girlfriend around the table, when she stepped on my foot and it felt as if her foot went right through mine. It was the funniest thing that had ever happened to me, and I didn't stop laughing for six hours. A lot of other things happened in those six hours: colors, hallucinations, weird distortions, and a sense of floating through it all, but the best thing was this sense of being apart from reality coupled with a sense of well-being.

I would take acid pretty much every weekend with my pals. Soon, though, some of the parents must have realized that their sons' strange weekend behavior had something to do with all the time we were spending together, and they were yanked from our psychedelic merry-go-round.

Then it was just two of us—a guy I will call Larry and me.

SNAPSHOT:

Larry's younger brother, Billy had the white pocketbook in his hands but the lady wouldn't let go. Billy was dressed in black, head to toe. He was a year younger than Larry and I, but he had been getting high longer than we had and had progressed on the road of addiction to the point where he no longer had a choice which direction his life would take. He was strong and determined. What he had not anticipated when he chose the slightly inebriated, seriously overweight woman attempting to hail a cab on the corner of Eighty-eighth Street and Park Avenue was just how attached she would be to her pocketbook. No amount of planning or anticipation prepares you for the actual experience of violence, even if it's happening half a block away. Larry and I stood there frozen, watching Billy fling this woman to and fro as he tried to wrest away her belongings. She was screaming. He was frantic. We were in shock.

The three of us had planned this for a while. It took some time to believe that we would actually go through with it. After all, we were young teens from prominent New York families. We lived on the Upper East Side with lives of infinite promise stretching in front of us. Snatching purses from Upper East Side matrons was not what anyone might have predicted we would be doing on a cold night in November. But here we were, fueled by a need for drug money, an insatiable appetite for excitement, and the ever-present aura of invincibility that characterized our youth.

The plan was simple: We would dress in inconspicuous dark clothes; one of us would be on point, while the other two followed a block or so behind. When the guy up front made his move and grabbed the purse, he would run toward the two followers. They would make a show of trying to stop him. Then, one of the two would pretend to chase the attacker and the other would see to the victim, making sure she was all right. It seemed a good plan at the time. I especially liked the attention to the victim after we had robbed her; it made me feel better about what we were about to do.

We agreed to take turns on point, and it was up to whoever that was to choose his mark and make the move. Larry and I had our turn at point but didn't have the balls to go through with it. The first time doing anything is never easy. Robbing and assaulting older women the first time is really hard to do unless you fall into the sociopath category and none of us in our Trio on the street that night did.

The woman hit the ground hard. The bag came loose. And Billy hauled ass, sprinting as fast as his skinny white legs could carry him. Right at us. When Larry and I saw that Billy had done what we had been planning and threatening to do for the past two weeks, the shit got real and our little prank became a nightmare. Everything started to happen in slow motion. We were engaged, committed to a violent assault, and no amount of playacting could conceal that reality. Billy got to us, and this was the part of the plan where we were supposed to make a show of trying to stop him. All we could manage was a tepid little dance and a few halfhearted "Stop thief"'s.

Billy blew by us. Larry and I looked at each other with eyes that wished we could undo all we had agreed to do. Larry took off after his brother, as I stood looking in horror at our victim—sprawled in the middle of Madison Avenue, wailing about being attacked—knowing I had to go to her. Giving aid and comfort to someone you messed up, with them thinking you are some kind of Good Samaritan, does not leave you with a very good feeling about yourself.

She wasn't hurt, but she had a flair for the dramatic. As I knelt down to help her, I noticed a pair of headlights and the sound of a car engine coming to life. It was parked diagonally across the street from us, and whoever was inside had clearly seen the entire purse-snatching fiasco. Eighty-eighth Street is a one-way street running west, so when the car with the headlights started heading down Eighty-eighth street going east I got a little queasy. When the siren went off halfway down the block, I almost hurled lunch. Billy was apprehended a block and a half from where he grabbed the purse by two of New York's Finest who just happened to be staked out on that corner. Coincidence? I don't think so. As I watched the officer approach me, I quietly told God that if he got me out of this, I would never do what I had just done or anything like it again. The cop thanked me for performing my civic duty and said something about wishing that there were more people in the city like me who gave a shit. He gave me a number to call so I could come down to city hall and get some kind of citation. Then he told me to go home.

That was the end of my life of crime—violent crime, at least.

The summer of '69 I brought my new toys to the Cape and introduced Bobby and David to the pleasures of New York City LSD. Meanwhile, they were on their own path to oblivion. That was the summer our paths merged and Hyannis Port became wearing dirty bell-bottoms all day long, sneaking out our bedroom windows for all-nighters full of hallucinations, and showing a burgeoning lack of interest in the more wholesome aspects of that idyllic summer life.

MY PARENTS seemed too busy with their own lives and dramas to intervene in my downward spiral. My mother sent me away to boarding school to be somebody else's problem. And my father only showed up once or twice a year to take me out to dinner. A couple of times during school vacations my mom sent me out to California so that I could bond with my father and he could give me some of that much-needed male influence. What I remember about those trips was that I always got either a sty or an ear infection. I thought it might have something to do with the plane ride, but now I think it was a result of the anxiety I felt about all that "male influence" I was going to get.

My dad was either working or partying the entire week I was there. The only time I ever saw him was at 6 A.M. when I woke up because I was on New York time and he was just coming home from wherever.

My dad had kept Erma Lee on as a housekeeper to take care of the big empty house on the beach. She would stay with me until my dad made it home. It was her least favorite aspect of her job. She was convinced that ghosts roamed the halls of the house L. B. Mayer had built. By then I didn't believe in ghosts, and anyway if they did exist I figured I could outrun them. One night after Erma had put me to bed and fallen asleep in the corner chair I had asked her to sit in just in case I was wrong and the ghosts did exist, we were awakened by the sounds of a party in full swing at the bottom of the stairs. It might have been my dad, but we weren't taking any chances. We locked the bedroom door and waited for daybreak. When the sun came up, we ventured out to find no sign of the party we had heard. Nothing was out of place. And that night my dad had not made it home. Go figure. It put a dent in my denial of the supernatural.

My mother often told me as I was growing up that I was "just like my father." What she really meant to say was that I was irresponsible and bad with money. When I was eighteen and finally spent some major time with my father, I would come to see just how similar we were. Mercifully, my mother never really knew how right she was.

My mom decided before shipping me off to boarding school that she would make the national drug scourge her cause. It probably had something to do with the inexplicable behavior I was beginning to manifest, spending all that time with Larry, but I can't be sure because she never talked to me about it. I just remember a flurry of activity, meetings, phone calls, and campaigns about drug education. It had more to do with my mom finding a public issue than it did with any personal connection she had with the problem. It was a fairly typical family response: solve the problem nationally, and avoid what was going on in your own house.

. . .

WHY IS it that those closest to us have the most difficult time allowing us to live the life we choose? My mother always told me that I could be whatever I wanted when I grew up as long as I was happy doing it. She probably believed this when she said it, but deep down I knew she didn't mean it. Kurt Vonnegut said, "It's true that you can be whatever you want but it's far easier when your ambition is complemented by the ambition of others." But what if ambition is the ambition? Success for the sake of success? Acomplishment for the sake of accomplishment? It becomes impossible to feel any happiness for another's success because everyone is competing in the same arena—the arena of accomplishment. And another's accomplishment necessitates a corresponding reaction of feeling like you're not doing enough. We become animals snarling at each other.

Chapter 13

You shall have joy, or you shall have power, said God;
you shall not have both.
— Ralph Waldo Emerson

My grandfather believed that experience shaped character. My grandmother believed that religion shaped character. I became a perfect hybrid of these two philosophies later in life. In my early years my grandfather's philosophy drove me to a frantic quest for more and more experience. Later the quest—no less frantic—drove me to seek a more intense relationship with God.

My grandmother Rose was a tiny woman, but she could walk a kid into the ground—and did pretty much every day of her life. My cousins and I took turns walking with her in Palm Beach and Hyannis Port. It was an obligation, but one I enjoyed. My grandmother was formidable despite her size. She had the weight of character and faith. She wasn't scary like my other relatives. With Uncle Bobby, there were the constant challenges. With Teddy, there was chaos and laughter. With Eunice, there was purpose. But with Grandma there was the time you spent with her.

She was present in the moment. This didn't mean she wasn't in perpetual activity, but she didn't seem to be planning ahead while doing whatever she was doing in that moment.

She was not warm and fuzzy. If you didn't know her, you might even think she was cold. To those of us who did know her, though, her warmth was revealed by her laugh and her inner spiritual life. She was fortified. Fortified by faith against a life of abundance and onslaughts.

She was quite literally a walking contradiction.

She was a small woman with a faint voice and a delicate sort of presence, yet she held immense importance in our family. Her grand-children engaged her with reverence, humor, and a little fear. All of us had heard the stories of her taking a coat hanger to our mothers and fa-thers when needed. Because she was so sweet, whenever she told those stories she would laugh with a delicacy and humility that made it im-possible to believe she could ever paddle anyone's backside.

SNAPSHOT:

> Palm Beach, Florida, is a beautiful haven for the rich. Very few people of color or limited financial resources live there. The only people you see on that little spit of ridiculously ex-pensive real estate are rich and white unless they're cutting somebody's lawn or working in somebody's kitchen. And if they are—they better have an identity card to prove it. Kind of an odd place for one of the country's preeminent liberal fami-lies to hang out.

My grandfather enjoyed sticking it to the rich WASPs who had little in-clination to allow the Irish or any other minority into their clubs. It was one of the motivating forces of his ambition. Joe Kennedy decided that if they weren't going to invite the Kennedys to their houses, he was going to make damn sure they wanted to come to his.

We grew up with a subversive streak, and it was never closer to the surface than when we were in Palm Beach. My mother loved it when-ever a club turned us down or we were blackballed by a co-op board because of who we were and where we came from. It was a matter of some pride that my grandparents were the only non-Jews allowed into the Palm Beach Country Club.

Well, that's not entirely true, the Duke and Duchess of Windsor were also members. My grandmother mentioned this often. She had a soft spot for royalty. I'm not sure if the Windsors ever took advantage of their membership. The Kennedys more than made up for it. One thing you could be sure of is that if you let a Kennedy into your club, you would get more than you bargained for in terms of usage. An invitation to a member of my family meant a swarm of Kennedys would respond.

The Jews started the Palm Beach Country Club because the WASPs weren't letting them into their clubs either. It was comforting that the Jews suffered the same discrimination as we Irish Catholics—or so we believed—and we were glad to have them on our side. After all, they had all the money, and that's important when you're in the business of saving the world. So membership in the Palm Beach Country Club was thought of as a victory. The club also happened to be conveniently close to my grandparents' house and both of them loved playing golf.

If Hyannis Port felt like a place where my family belonged, in Palm Beach we were a loud reminder to the long-term residents of the ebb and flow of financial and political power in America. The house my grandfather bought in Palm Beach as a winter residence was a noisy, bubbling island of fun and subversion, completely self-contained, surrounded by a sea of social affluence. It was a house anyone would want to visit. Built by the architect Addison Meisner, it was a magnificent Spanish mansion sitting on the beach of North Palm high above the sand. A great lawn stretched out toward the ocean, with six giant, bending palm trees ideal for climbing races to see who would be first to grab the hanging coconuts. The house was protected by a massive sea wall that stood twenty feet high, jutting out over the beach. My cousins and I had competitions to see who could jump the farthest from its top to the soft sand below. A pool and tennis court adorned the grounds. There were ten bedrooms and a special sun box where my grandfather worked the phone in the sun he loved with complete privacy.

After my grandfather's stroke, a cover was put over half the pool to keep the water hot, and a ramp constructed to provide easy access for his wheelchair to the 100-degree water. My grandmother occupied the place with her grace and elegance, complementing the love and ease with which she approached her growing brood of grandchildren.

I loved going there. It reminded me of California with its sun, beach, and wind. It was also the place where I really got to know my grandmother. I usually had no competition from other cousins when we visited Palm Beach. In the early years, I visited with my other cousins, but as the individual families grew larger, my grandmother restricted visits to one or two families at a time. I was there in 1962 with my uncle Jack and a lot of my other cousins. I remember playing kick-the-can with some Shrivers and Robert Kennedys. We played at night and drove the Secret Service guys crazy by jumping from the bushes without warning and running like screaming banshees as we tried to reach the can before whoever was unlucky enough to be guarding it.

SNAPSHOT:

> The living room in the Palm Beach house was on the first floor, just to the right as you passed through the cavernous oval entranceway guarded by the massive oak door with wrought-iron hinges. The door looked like something from medieval times. I could see knights in armor crashing through it and sacking the place. The living room itself was enormous, taking up fully half the entire first floor. There were couches everywhere and giant picture windows that fronted two tiny, cushioned alcoves where an eight-year-old could read a book in the late afternoon or hide from marauding cousins. Kids had to be careful entering the room, making sure there were no adults; otherwise you might be invited in to say hello to Ambassador So-and-So or His Excellency and Mrs. Whoever.

On this particular day I wasn't thinking about who I might get trapped by in my grandparents' living room; I was thinking about hiding someplace where Bobby Shriver couldn't find me. I ran into the giant room and into my uncle Jack. He was sitting in one of my grandmother's overstuffed chairs. My mom was sitting next to him on a couch with her weekend friends Tony Curtis and Janet Leigh, the woman whom I heard about getting whacked in the shower in the movie I wasn't allowed to see—*Psycho*. They were all focused on a man I had never seen before, who was carefully placing giant teeth on a cloth-covered table in front of him. The president of the United States was holding one of the giant teeth in his right hand, a lit cigar in his left.

Me:
What's that, Uncle Jack?
JFK:
Scrimshaw.
Me:
What's scrimshaw?
JFK:
Whale teeth that the sailors of the eighteenth and nineteenth century carved designs on.
Me:
That's a whale's tooth?
JFK:
Yes, it is. This is a sperm whale's tooth. See the carving of the clipper ship on it?
Me:
I didn't know whales had teeth that big. Can I hold it?
JFK:
Sure.

He handed me the tooth. It was half the size of my arm and heavy. I couldn't believe there was a fish big enough to have a mouth full of these teeth and I prayed I would never run into one.

Me:
This is neat.
JFK:
It's yours, Christopher.
Me:
Mine! Really?
JFK:
Yes. A present. Take good care of it.

Me:
I will. Thanks a lot, Uncle Jack.

I couldn't believe it. My uncle had given me one of the giant teeth. This was big. I had never been singled out like this before. I had an inkling that my mom had something to do with it but she had concealed her hand, and the only thing I knew, as I ran from the room to show my treasure to my cousins, was that *the man* himself had given me one of his prized possessions.

I bounded down the stairs, out through the heavy oak door with the wrought-iron hinges, and into the courtyard with the large, uneven Spanish tiles, and just as my scream left my lips, "Bobby, look what Uncle Jack gave me," I stumbled and my tiny hands lost their grip on the smooth piece of ivory and it flew from my hand. It was one of those slow-motion moments. I watched the giant tooth sail into the air and crash down on one of the Spanish tiles. I held my breath. It didn't break—or did it? I ran over and picked it up, noticing for the first time that a small piece of tooth was missing from the curved, pointed end. I never found the missing piece. I never told any of the grown-ups what had happened. It put a bit of a crimp in showing off my new treasure.

My grandmother's cook was a wonderful Irish lass from the old country named Nelly. She was all orange hair, big teeth, and pounds of butter in everything she cooked. Her specialties included bacon sandwiches, creamed chicken, lobster bisque, sugar cookies, and a special cake she made for my grandmother that was drenched in sugar, butter, and vanilla. I would crawl on my belly over broken glass from New York to Palm Beach for Nelly's bacon sandwiches and a piece of grandma's cake. My sisters and I would eat with my grandmother in her massive dining room around the dark oak table that could seat twelve comfortably, feeling small and of insufficient number. She had a foot buzzer to the right of her chair that was used to call the servants. Buzzing for the help was not my grandmother's style, but she liked showing it off to her grandchildren. She would step on it and laugh like a guilty little girl. Every day at about five-thirty she would take her walk along the Lake Trail, which went along the canal on the opposite side of Palm Beach. The walk lasted an hour or so depending on which way we went. North, the trail ended. South, we could go on forever—which would have been fine with my grandmother. The only limitation she ever felt while walking was the one imposed on her by the long face of the grandchild trying to keep up with her.

During our walks, she would talk about anything and everything.

She was completely comfortable with who she was and what she had done in her life, so her words and thoughts came forth without a filter or subtext. She was more interested in my life and thoughts than she was in reexamining her own. I always came away from the walks feeling heard.

My grandmother appreciated her grandchildren as individuals. I never had the feeling she was dealing with me out of obligation or merely as one of twenty-eight. In the mid-1970s she was writing her autobiography. She wrote in Palm Beach and Hyannis Port, spending long hours in her room with the door closed. During this time I received a note from her in response to some flowers I'd sent her for her birthday.

> *Dearest Christopher:*
> *Thank you so much for the lovely little basket of white roses, which is in my bedroom and which gives me great pleasure all day, as I do most of my work here.*
> *You and Sydney were very thoughtful to remember me and I deeply appreciate it. I always say I have the nicest grandchildren, who give me few worries and bring me great joy. Thanks a million.*
> *Jean is here this week with the four children. I miss you older children a great deal because all of you are away and so it seems to me there is something missing.*
> *Come back soon, dearest Christopher. Much love until then.*
>
> > *Affectionately,*
> > *Grandma*

My grandmother had more investment in her way of life than anyone I have ever met but she never pushed or sold it to me. There is great power in that. I once heard a person describe a guru I followed later in life as the most loving person he had known—not because he broadcast a loving attitude but because when you were in his presence you couldn't help feeling love. When I was around my grandmother I felt at peace—I couldn't help it.

> Dear Chris,
> Thank you very much for the picture [she forgot the comma, very uncharacteristic] which is very clear and very characteristic of the Cape.
> It was wonderful down here for a week but now there is a big chill so all the electric blankets and heaters and hot drinks have been brought out.
> Eunice is here with two of her children and later they are going to Antigua on a boat with their father.
> That is all the news, dear Chris. Come down when you can and bring a pal.
>
> > Much, much Love
> > Grandma

Like my grandmother, the house she occupied on Ocean Avenue in North Palm Beach was a contradiction. A contradiction that flowed directly from the two individuals whose personalities had brought the place to life—Joe and Rose Kennedy. Like my grandmother, the house was a peaceful sanctuary, a place where I could rest and feel the sense of being at home as soon as I dropped my bags. As I grew older and invited more turmoil and excitement into my life, I plugged into the energy and exuberance of the place, which I imagine radiated from my grandfather and which made the Palm Beach house one of the great party houses on the planet.

I partied from the moment I arrived until the moment I left. My grandparents had created a house that everyone wanted to visit. My mother let me stay in "The President's Room," which was on the first floor and had its own wing on the side of the house right off the pool. My uncle Jack had written much of his book *Profiles in Courage* in this room and spent many days there in agony recovering from his back injury and the resulting dependency on painkillers. Lem told me that my uncle Bobby had stood guard in front of the door to his brother's room for days, not letting anyone in or out, until my uncle had vanquished the demons of withdrawal. After hearing this I remember thinking how lucky Jack Kennedy was to have someone care about him as much as his brother Bobby did.

My uncle Jack gained a profound existential component because of the agonizing pain he tolerated. This was not lost on me and I grew up with a belief that in order to achieve greatness one would have to go through immense pain. Later, when I was battling my own demons, I remember feeling a connection to my uncle Jack because of what he had endured and ultimately risen above in that room. I also derived some hope that I, too, might eventually triumph.

I loved this room not just because my uncle Jack had lived there but also for the privacy it afforded me. I could come and go as I pleased and, though entertaining one of the lovely local girls in the president's room promised to be a potent aphrodisiac, few actually wanted to be discovered coupling in the Kennedy manse. This proved frustrating to my surging eighteen-year-old hormones until one evening I was inspired to suggest a rendezvous in the ocean.

I grew up believing that the beach and ocean were sexy places. This may be true in movies or advertisements, but not in real life. Sand and salt water are not great lubricants no matter how hot and bothered you are—and there's also marine life to contend with. So I found myself fully aroused in the great Atlantic when a man-of-war jellyfish attached itself to my manhood. What are the chances? Maybe God was trying to tell me something.

Chapter 14

God is subtle but he is not malicious.
—ALBERT EINSTEIN

In 1993 I found myself on the show *Politically Incorrect* engaged in sound-bite competition with Ted Nugent, former heavy metal psycho; Nancy Glass, who does I don't know what; and a religious fundamentalist right-to-lifer. It was hell. I found myself in verbal conflict with the champion of the unborn about religion and choice. It got pretty heated. The fundamentalist said to me, "You of all people should understand the plight of the unborn—you're from a family of good Catholics." It floored me and I was speechless for a moment. I thought: don't fundamentalists hate Catholics? And I wasn't sure where he got his information that my family was full of good Catholics. Without missing a beat I replied with the only truly spontaneous sound bite of the show, "Excuse me, sir, but I'm a recovering Catholic." The audience loved it and we went to commercial.

SNAPSHOT:

I was thirteen and hell-bent on staying out of the stuffy Catholic church on Eighty-fourth Street and Park Avenue in New York City. The fact that my mom made it there just before the Gospel was read didn't matter. Religion wasn't working for me, and I had finally worked up the courage to let my mother know it.

Me:

I'm not going to church anymore.

Mom:

Why not, Christopher?

Me:

Because Uncle Bobby is saying all this stuff about poor
people and black people.

Mom:

I don't see what that has to do with giving thanks to God.

Me:

Well, everybody in that church is rich and white.

Mom:

Oh.

Me:

Getting spanked for original sin by the wrath of God all
wrapped up in a sea of sacramental mumbo jumbo just isn't
working for me anymore.

Mom:

I see.

Or something like that.

I was like most kids my age who didn't want to go to church on
Sunday. I didn't have a problem with God; I did have a problem with
institutional authority, nurtured by the anarchy of the sixties and by
being part of a family that was its own institution and seemingly im-
mune to the authority of others. It also struck me that there weren't
many people in my life who connected what they were doing in
church with the rest of their lives. My grandmother did and Uncle
Sarge, but most grown-ups I knew had a different voice when they
walked into church. I didn't trust it.

Catholicism was an important aspect of my Kennedy upbringing
although my parents had a much more relaxed practice than other
members of my family. My father never went to church or talked about
God. My mom had a minimalist approach to church, taking us each
Sunday but making sure we arrived right before the priest read the
Gospel and leaving before the host had dissolved in our mouths. My

mom was devoted to this practice. After she got sick I remember wheeling her up to Saint John's for a five o'clock Easter Mass. The priest was standing outside cheerily welcoming the parishioners. My mom began fidgeting in her wheelchair. She couldn't speak and was bundled against the cold under a mountain of blankets. I asked what time the service started and the priest replied, "Oh, you are just in time, we are just about to start." With that my mom's arm shot out from underneath the blankets, indicating that a few trips around the block were needed to ensure we arrived properly late.

I don't think my mother ever attended the first twenty minutes of a mass unless it was at my grandmother's house or at a funeral. I loved this about my mother. It was one of the things about her that spoke to her rebellious side.

There were three devout Catholics in the family: my grandmother, Uncle Sarge, and Aunt Ethel. They were each fiercely devoted to Catholicism; each had their own unique practice, and going to Mass with them was its own unique experience.

There was a gravity about going to Mass with my grandmother. We got there on time and it mattered how you were dressed. For my grandmother, going to Mass was as vital as breathing. There was no pomp or circumstance associated with it, no appearance; it was a holy ritual— one I often felt I was engaged in with a saint. Her piety was palpable, but humble; she would never proselytize but often quizzed me on the meaning of the Gospel we had just heard, quietly laughing when I couldn't recall. A quiet faith. Like most truly spiritual people she acted her faith, rarely talking about it. Her faith was her refuge; it was not something she shared with you. When walking into a church with her I felt as if she went somewhere I could not follow.

My grandmother wrote in her book, *Times to Remember*: "I find it interesting to reflect on what has made my life, even with its moments of pain, an essentially happy one. I have come to the conclusion that the most important element in human life is faith."

Going to church with Sarge was like jumping on a big noisy caravan of enthusiasm. There were kids all over my aunt Eunice's Thunderbird convertible as we careened down the back roads of Cape Cod on our way to Saint Francis. On the way home, we would take turns driving and get to stop at the news shop where Sarge would get us all ice cream. Sarge had an emotional and intellectual faith. He would get deeply excited about scripture, underlining his missal in a hundred places. He spoke about Christ as if he were walking around on the planet today. Sarge was always looking for a nexus between the spiritual and material worlds. He was convinced that the world would be a better place if we could find a way to live the words uttered by the Christian prophet two thousand years ago.

My aunt Ethel's brand of Catholicism was more desperate and explosive. She attended Mass every day with a vengeance. The kids were dragged along on Sunday and occasionally during the week if she thought someone's behavior needed an extra dose of God. It was a righteous obligation. There were always chaos and drama. Someone was inappropriately dressed (Ethel would have had us all in hair shirts, if available). There was often an altercation in the parking lot with an unreasonable parishioner. There might even be a spat with the good father. Dogs were always involved. It was always interesting.

HICKORY HILL was bought by my uncle Jack in 1954 after he and Jackie were married. After Jackie's miscarriage in 1956, the great house with its new nursery was too sad and echoing. In 1957 he sold it to my uncle Bobby for the same $125,000 he had paid three years earlier.

Hickory Hill was the perfect house for a big, wild brood. I loved being there when I was a kid. There was excitement and history, from my uncle Bobby's collection of letters of U.S. presidents to the powerful movers and shakers walking in and out of the front door, which never closed. It was also scary and unpredictable—like a big crazy hotel. Everyone who worked there seemed to be from Africa or Latin America, food came out of the kitchen all day long, there were fans in all the windows, phones ringing off the hook, somebody chasing somebody, guests galore, and always some dangerous activity to challenge one's courage. Someone was always going into the pool fully dressed and against their will. It was exciting, and because there were so many kids, there was an absence of control. Anarchy reigned. Our version of *Lord of the Flies*. This was all great, but after another shirt or pair of pants had been lost to the black hole that was the laundry room, another day spent not knowing what the plan was, or another stare-down on the field of "I dare you," I found myself thirsting for more structure and some nurturing.

The Shrivers' house had both. It was called Timberlawn and was in Rockville, Maryland, not twenty minutes from Hickory Hill but a world away in terms of temperament and structure. It was the most normal house in our family. There was an environment of activity, challenge, and guidance complete with a cast of characters: Rags, the chauffeur; the French cook, with his ever-present cigarette hanging from his lips. Bobby Shriver and I would keep an eye on him to see when his ash would fall into the soufflé until he chased us away, swearing at us in French. And there was always someone with a physical or mental disability visiting or working there. I spent a month at Timberlawn every summer working as a counselor to the busloads of mentally challenged and environmentally deprived kids my aunt Eunice bused in from Washington area institutions. The little day camp would eventually be transformed into the worldwide grassroots movement that became the Special Olympics.

I thought I would feel more comfortable in the relative normalcy of Timberlawn; I was wrong. There was only one place where I wanted to belong, and that was the kid-driven anarchy of Hickory Hill.

SNAPSHOT:

In 1968 Lyndon Johnson asked Sargent Shriver to be the U.S. ambassador to France. This act was full of political as well as familial repercussions, most of which I was oblivious to. I heard about the tension between RFK and Sarge over the appointment because of RFK's feud with Johnson and his own political aspirations. The upshot was that Sarge got dissed by the RFKs for putting his own agenda ahead of the family's. But enough about them . . .

What it meant to me was that I got to go to Paris and hang out at the ambassador's residence for a month over the summer. My cousin

Bobby Shriver and I were close friends. This was before my heavy descent into drugs. Once the drugs started and Bobby Jr. and Bobby Shriver were busted for pot in Hyannis Port, my aunt Eunice yanked Bobby Shriver away from us before you could say straight and narrow.

Paris was our last hurrah. We bombed around the city on mopeds, sampling "jambon avec fromage sandvitches" and trying to pick up young French girls. We played tennis on clay and wood courts. We had badminton marathons in the gardens of the residence. We had steak and eggs for breakfast. We played knee football on the plush carpets in the living room, which was as big as a football field, until in one particularly rough game I broke Bobby's shoulder. He was anxious about showing up at the Cape having had his shoulder broken by Chris Lawford. We were an unforgiving pack of fourteen-year-old boys. I told Bobby to tell everyone he was gored by a bull. They bought it, but his heart wasn't in the lie, so his deception was eventually sniffed out. I sent my mom a letter from the ambassador's residence:

> *Dear Mummy,*
> *I'm sorry I haven't written yet but I have been doing so much, I*
> *don't even have time to sleep. I'm having a lot of fun and I have*
> *seen where all the Louis xiii & xiv etc Napolean and Marie*
> *Antoinette stayed. I also saw the small peasant village Marie*
> *Antoinette built. The house we are staying in is big and nice,*
> *and you don't have to do anything, all the butlers do it all. The*
> *foods pretty good but they don't have any hamburgers. Oh I also*
> *saw the old town while Bobby and I were going around Paris on*
> *our mini bikes, because the driving age of motor scooters is*
> *fourteen. Well that's about it. Hope to see you soon.*
>
> > *Love*
> > *Christopher*
> *P.S. And as they say. Paris is OK to visit but I wouldn't want to*
> *live there.*

Who says they wouldn't want to live in Paris? It sounds pretty good to me. Except for the history part. I think that was my aunt Eunice's idea.

. . .

MY MOTHER sent me off to camp in the summer. The first was Camp Adirondack. I was so homesick. I sent my mom a letter begging her to come back from her vacation in Paris to spring me from my misery.

> *Dear Mom,*
> *Please send me a letter to tell me when you are coming up to*
> *take me home. I can't wait to see you. I have made a lot of*
> *things for you when you come up. I have talked to the girls and*
> *written them. How is everything up at the Cape? Has there been*
> *any dances yet? The weather has been pretty bad but otherwise*
> *it is okay. I miss you very much and I can't wait to see you.*
>
> > *Love,*
> > *Christopher*

When she arrived I said, "Hi, Mom. What are you doing here? I love Camp Adirondack. Can I stay an extra couple of weeks?" One of the great gifts of having children of your own is seeing what a pain in the ass you were as a child.

After that she sent me to camp with David, knowing that if there was drama, it wouldn't involve my wanting to come home. I went to a series of tennis camps in New England and then to the camp of all camps, Mayrhofen in Austria. It was the summer of Uncle Bobby's death and a change in our attitude toward everything having to do with being a Kennedy. It was like watching a big balloon lose its air. Things just didn't have much meaning anymore.

David and I packed our duffel bags and some Baggies stuffed with mescaline and pot. We transited through Munich, which was terrifying given our fear of the Germans. The Nazis might be gone, but we didn't want any part of what they'd left behind. Each of us carried our contraband in our underwear and tried to look like the innocent fifteen-year-olds we weren't. We touched down in the heart of the German Republic on a rainy morning in July with our troop of well-heeled, oblivious, aspiring tennis players. As we marched to customs David and I had visions of ending up in some gulag in front of a snarling German shepherd and a pair of Aryan-filled jackboots. Suddenly we became separated from the group. We were alone, but at least we had each other. Then suddenly David was gone. Vanished. One moment he was in line to show his papers to the not-so-nice immigration man and the next he wasn't. I made it through customs and onto the bus, which was when I volunteered to the head counselor, "Excuse me, Jeff, but I don't see my cousin David anywhere." Jeff initiated a search as I panicked. I was sure they had caught David, and I wasn't sure whether he would roll over. Forty-five minutes later Jeff appeared with David in tow. David slid into the seat next to me. "Where the fuck did you go, man?" I stammered. He gave me one of his looks of disappointment and said, "Thanks for leaving me alone with the Nazis, man!"

David could lose himself anywhere. One moment he would be next to you and the next he'd be gone. You'd find him lost in a book or magazine in the far corner of some store, his hair a mess flying in a hundred different directions, the shirttails of his Brooks Brothers button-down shirt hanging out, and the sleeves messily rolled to different lengths on his skinny arms. He would be completely oblivious to the fact that you might have been looking for him for the last hour or so and not apologetic in the slightest.

Mayrhofen was this quaint Austrian town tucked away in the Alps. In the morning we would ski in shorts and a T-shirt until the snow turned to water; then we'd head to the tennis courts. Not a bad life if you can get it. David and I were a perfect team. He was a great skier and terrible tennis player; I sucked on skis but was good with a racket. But winning didn't seem to matter anymore. I'd be in the middle of a match and just say the hell with it. Before Uncle Bobby's death I never would have done that. It wouldn't have been possible; you never gave up, never stopped trying to win. But those kinds of emotions didn't have much meaning anymore. David and I decided there really wasn't any reason to try to be good, so we might as well try to be bad.

We didn't win any sporting awards but we both got girlfriends. David lost his virginity to a girl who was "sorry about what happened to his father." I spent the summer trying to convince this one girl to "just let me put it in for a minute." No dice. My cries of anguish were not to be mistaken for bad yodeling.

Chapter 15

Good judgment is usually the result of experience. And experience is frequently the result of bad judgment.
— BARRY LEPATNER; QUOTATION SENT BY FORMER SECRETARY OF DEFENSE ROBERT LOVETT TO ROBERT KENNEDY DURING THE CUBAN MISSILE CRISIS

In the summer of 1969, a year after my uncle Bobby died, Neil Armstrong took a giant step for mankind and my uncle Teddy drove off a bridge at Chappaquiddick.

I watched it all on television in a house my mother rented on Carbon Beach in Malibu, California. I was only fourteen and knew the significance of walking on the moon, but had no idea of the repercussions that swirled around as a result of my uncle's misfortune that night.

There was a lot of talk about the moon.

Nobody said anything about Chappaquiddick.

From my vantage point it just looked like there was another dark cloud hanging over the family. Time to rally. I remember the images of family and friends gathering in Hyannis Port. My uncle Teddy in his neck brace. The crappy little bridge that to me didn't look like a bridge at all. Certainly not a bridge you could drive a car across. Anyway, this was another big family drama I didn't have a stake in. It was way too big. I knew it was big by the round-the-clock TV coverage and the fact that none of the grown-ups were talking about it. There was something different, though. This was the first time the attention focused was not all gushing greatness. Something bad had happened—that wasn't new. What was new—my uncle might have done something wrong. I don't remember giving that a lot of thought, but Chappaquiddick was the genesis of an onslaught of negativity directed toward the family in general and my uncle Teddy in particular, which made them all seem a little more human.

My mother got upset and hopped on a plane East. My sisters and I were left with Mademoiselle and the pleasures of Malibu beach. She had also left us with a local surfer she had hired to be our Sandy Eiler wannabe. The surfer kept us busy surfing, sailing, and playing volleyball. It was paradise, but I was bored and lonely. The upside to having three younger sisters is that you always have a slave; the downside is that it's impossible get up a game of football. I had been gone from California for five years and it had taken me a year to get over the move. But by the summer of '69, I was an East Coast boy who had lost touch with his friends in L.A., and what I wanted most was to be with my cousins on the Cape.

My mother returned from the family gathering in support of my uncle, stepping onto the deck of the house overlooking the Pacific Ocean and calling to me to come quick and see what she had brought me all the way from the East Coast. I came into the living room dripping wet from the ocean and the five hours of bodysurfing I did daily to keep me sane. On the couch was a blanket, which covered something that seemed to be moving. Suddenly, out from under it popped my best friend in the world and salvation from three more weeks of trying to convince my sisters to play with me—my cousin David. He had a cast on his arm from a break he had suffered a few weeks earlier, but casts were minor inconveniences and were usually shed before they were supposed to be. In the meantime we devised ingenious coverings for his cast so that he could bodysurf.

David and I convinced "Sandy the surfer" to take us fishing on a Malibu outrigger. It was a small sailboat, meant for one, but we were persistent, so Sandy finally relented and off we went into the deep blue Pacific with two fishing poles and some chopped-up squid. The Kennedys love the ocean. I grew up with everyone around me waxing eloquent about the sea. They had no fear of it. They sailed on it in the middle of hurricanes and dove into it from the backs of boats being dragged through huge waves on a rope. The actor Martin Sheen once came to spend a few quiet days at Hyannis Port after having a heart attack filming *Apocalypse Now*. I saw him return from an afternoon sail with my aunt Ethel, looking like he'd just spent the day with Colonel Kurtz. He told me later that he had thought the Kennedys would finish the job Coppola started and finally kill him. I will let you in on a little secret I've never revealed to any of my relatives for fear that I would be ostracized—the ocean scares the shit out of me.

I read a book when I was eleven, safely ensconced on the island of Manhattan, entitled *Danger, Shark!* The book chronicled shark attacks on navy soldiers whose boats were sunk in the Pacific during World War II. It terrified me. I actually would get out of swimming pools when I was a kid because of the fear I had of the Great White.

Wow, that's embarrassing.

So "Sandy the surfer" took David and me a mile out into the Pacific on a flimsy boat, two fishing lines hanging off the back with big hunks of squid on them, our legs dangling in the water. I kept my eye on the receding shoreline, saying things like "Maybe we should head in a little." David was looking to catch something big and figured the farther out we were the more likely it was that would happen.

He always thoroughly enjoyed my discomfort.

It's not difficult to determine the length of a thrasher shark. They have a dorsal fin as well as a fin on the tail. Add a foot or so for the head and teeth to the distance between the fins and you've got the size of the shark. The one I was looking at was twelve-feet long, and it was circling our boat. There are times when it pays to be the son of the parent that is paying the salary of the surfer who is sailing the boat. I told Sandy it was time to head back. I began reeling my line in with the urgency of a fourteen-year-old who didn't want to reprise the fate of those navy sailors I had read about bobbing in the South Pacific missing their lower halves. David was looking at things differently; he was going to catch the shark. He yelled at Sandy to sail toward the fins.

"Are you fucking crazy, catching a twelve-foot shark on this boat? If that fish hits your line we are going over."

David grinned his "I can't believe what a chicken you are" grin and said, "I don't know why you're getting all dramatic, Chris, it's just a shark."

He had me and he knew it. "Just a shark! What are you going to do if you catch it?"

"I'll reel it in!"

"Are you kidding me? Where would you put it if you got it up to the boat?"

David laughed. "We'll drag it into shore." Suddenly another fin appeared. Now there were two. Then the first shark disappeared. There were still two, but we didn't know where one of them was. I lost it. All I could imagine was being in the dark cold water at the mercy of something big and unseen below me.

David was thrilled. Now there were two targets. I demanded he bring in his line, losing all pretense of indifference and sounding a lot like one of our mothers. "David, if you don't reel that line in right now, you can forget about me being your best friend." He relented, but his disappointment at my cowardice was evident. We were headed into shore, the lines and bait almost out of the water, David using every tactic he could come up with to keep his line in the water as long as possible. It was annoying but expected. I was feeling a little less panicked, when out of the deep blue sea with squid and hook in mouth appeared the missing twelve foot thrasher. It was one of those slow-motion moments. I happened to be looking right at the spot where the fish broke the surface, six feet from our boat; and when it did, we got wet. I screamed, "Shit," at the top of my lungs. David shouted, "I got it." That brought another "Shit" from me. His duel was short-lived as the shark bit through his line and was gone. In the aftermath of such an encounter there is usually stunned silence followed by a rush of excitement and euphoria in the reliving of the event. So it was with the three of us, although my euphoria was somewhat tempered by the knowledge that I did not have the same penchant for engaging danger as my fearless cousin.

DAVID'S CAST had long since disintegrated in the waves of the Pacific Ocean and we had pretty much done all that could be done on the beach in Malibu when Ethel and Pat decided it would be a good idea for David and me to climb the second-tallest mountain in the continental United States, Mount Rainier, in Washington State. We were only fourteen, so we would need someone very accomplished at climbing mountains to help us. Enter Jim Whittaker, family friend and the first American to climb Mount Everest.

Climbing Mount Everest was one of those things that embodied all we had been conditioned to believe was noble and heroic. Man against nature, alone, facing death with only inner fortitude and outer strength to rely on. It was also pretty glamorous and sexy to climb the tallest mountain in the world. Jim Whittaker was very close to my uncle Bobby. They climbed Mount Kennedy in Alaska together. Climbing mountains became a family occupation and a litmus test for being a Kennedy.

After our adventure on the outrigger, climbing the second-tallest mountain in North America with the first American to climb Everest figured to be a walk in the park. It wasn't.

David and I flew into the rain of Seattle and were met by Jim, his brother, Lou, and Jim's two sons, Carl and Scott. We drove the two hours to Mount Rainier in the anticipation of doing something that would be difficult at best and life-threatening at worst. I had never seen Mount Rainier. It's huge, over fourteen thousand feet high. You know that's high because there's snow all over the top and it's the middle of summer. Looking at the mountain for the first time, I didn't see any way up that looked remotely like something I could do. I was beginning to feel the same panic I felt when I saw the first thrasher a mile off the coast of Malibu. The panic associated with the possibility of dying. The fact that Jim had survived Everest and Lou had been up and down Rainier over one hundred times as a guide eased my panic a little, but I was still hoping that I might come down with something that prevented climbing mountains. David was nervous but wouldn't show it. He had a whole association going on with his father's climb of Mount Kennedy fueling his determination. I was alone again in my ambivalence.

The first ten thousand feet of Rainier are not so much difficult as they are taxing and monotonous. This part of the climb is about trudging up an endless succession of snowfields with no end in sight. For an overweight, out-of-shape fourteen-year-old with forty pounds of camping shit on his back it's a prescription for an early heart attack. I huffed and puffed and whined about when we were going to get to base camp, but I made it. David just trudged with some kind of inner purpose.

Once at base camp, which took the entire day to get to, we got to rest in anticipation of a couple of days practicing the more serious aspects of mountaineering and acclimating to the altitude. I had heard of base camp before and always thought it would look like something out of M*A*S*H—you know, big tents, stuff to eat, maybe some electricity and a good-looking nurse. That's not it. Base camp is a frozen piece of ground between the ice and rocks where you put up your crappy little tent that is always in danger of blowing away because it's so fucking windy and cold. The only food is the freeze-dried stuff you carried up on your back, and the only entertainment comes in a book or from your imagination. David and I crawled into our tent, exhausted and cold. I was wondering why in the hell I had agreed to this and counting the minutes until I would be off this godforsaken mountain. David was thinking about the summit.

"The summit?" I said. "Are you fucking kiddin? Do you hear that wind out there? It will blow your skinny ass right off this mountain and leave me here all alone with the Whittakers."

"Shut up, Chris," David said. "I've got to get some sleep. We've got a big day tomorrow."

"A big day tomorrow"—this did not sound like the David Kennedy I knew, the David Kennedy who was negative about anything that could be classified as "a good thing to do." Shit, maybe this lack-of-oxygen-affecting-the-brain thing was for real.

When you are having a bad time, it's nice to have someone to commiserate with. David had always been the perfect companion for just these types of situations. He was cynical, disaffected, and funny. He had the ability to make any situation appear far worse than it was and make you laugh about it. There is comfort in that. But from the moment we stepped onto the mountain, he began acting weird.

For the next three days we were drilled in climbing techniques and stamina-building in anticipation of our assault on the summit.

David was focused and committed. He actually showed interest in learning how to do something he didn't know how to do for the first time in his life. I got through it keeping my eye on the eventual descent. The morning of the assault there were nerves all around as four boys and two giant mountaineers made their way in the dark before dawn to the first of the steep cliff faces we would navigate in our attempt to reach the summit. David and I were the youngest and tied to Jim. Carl and Scott, who were older and had more experience, went with Lou. We had been told that the youngest person to make the summit was sixteen. It wasn't clear if that was because nobody younger had attempted it or because they had tried and failed. If we made the summit, we would be the youngest group of climbers to accomplish this feat, and David would be the youngest individual to ever scale Mount Rainier. Quite an accomplishment, but still very uncertain.

Jim and Lou were giants in the world of mountaneering; they knew what they were doing. This was nice, but bad shit can happen on a frozen peak fourteen thousand feet above sea level, and being one of the youngest climbers to be this high up on the second-highest peak on the continental United States left me feeling a little vulnerable.

Watching the sun come up on a vertical wall of rock at six in the morning as you puke your guts out is an experience I never hope to have again. We had been advised by Jim Whittaker to get in shape before our trek. He had suggested a regimen of running and some strengthening exercises. He didn't suggest that we stop smoking cigarettes. I'm sure he didn't feel there was a need to, given our age. David had stopped for a month. I had trouble putting a few days together and was paying the price for it on the first real test of the climb. I was using every ounce of will I had not to be sick, but there was nothing I could do. I didn't want to be the one that didn't make it, the one who screwed up the climb for everybody else, but there was no way to stop the reflex vomiting that was splashing all over the rocks of Rainier as I struggled for oxygen at eleven thousand feet.

To climb the four thousand plus feet from base camp and get back again would take all day. There was no time to take me back and still make the summit. I was beginning to feel like an albatross, and although the boys were sympathetic, I could feel their "let's cut him loose" thoughts. I had been given what I had hoped for, an excuse for not putting my life in danger, and now that I had it I wished it would go away.

Be careful what you wish for.

They left me on a ledge not much wider than my sleeping bag at eleven thousand feet. With some lemonade and two chocolate bars. As they disappeared up the mountain, I felt a mixture of relief and longing not to be left behind—with a secret hope that they wouldn't make the summit, so I wouldn't be the only failure. I spent the nine hours of my isolation watching the clouds change shape below me as giant bees swarmed around me. I had had no idea there were bees that high up. I guessed they weren't the pollinating variety. I made pool shrines to the Mountain God with my lemonade, always looking off into the distance for a sign of the climbers' return. It was a very long nine hours. As the sun was sinking and I was getting nervous about freezing to death, alone, eleven thousand feet up on Mount Rainier, I heard their voices. They had made the summit and were approaching me with the weary success of the conqueror. My best friend in the world had become the youngest person to climb Mount Rainier—and I would never hear the end of it.

Chapter 16

I wanna die for something.
—THE PRETENDERS, "REVOLUTION"

The bridge at Concord, Massachusetts, and the events surrounding "the shot heard round the world" were well known to me. For as long as I can remember my grandmother made it her business to drill her grandchildren on grammar and the history of the American Revolution, particularly as it related to the great state of Massachusetts. I did well on the Revolutionary War but miserably on grammar. Despite my grandmother's urgings I remained sloppy in my speech, my rationale being that as long as I was intelligible, I would rather worry about emotional intent than structure. Typical son-of-an-actor shit, right? Now that I am older, I see the wisdom and power that come from precise articulation. Thank god my Kennedy genes balanced out my Lawford ones on that count.

When I arrived at Middlesex School in Concord, Massachusetts, the first place I visited, after asking the only student I knew where I might be able to find a tab of acid to take the edge off, was the woods around Concord. It wasn't to see the bridge where the war that birthed America began. My mom had decided that prep school would be good for me. These fine institutions of secondary education had helped form her brothers—and god knows I needed some forming.

The year was 1969, and we were near the end of the student uprisings at American colleges. All the students at our quaint, tranquil New

England prep school were well aware of the tumultuous ass-kicking that our brothers and sisters were engaged in just a few years north of us. We longed for the rebellion but had no stake. We were bent on finding one.

I had two major concerns my first year at Middlesex. The first was whether or not my cousin David was going to find a way to join me in my search for whatever struggle or trouble I might find. When I went to boarding school at Middlesex, David was going to the Potomac School in McLean, Virginia, and it was expected that he would continue there through high school. It didn't work out that way. David agreed to repeat ninth grade so we could be together at Middlesex. It surprised me that someone would like me enough to agree to repeat a whole year of school in order to be with me. It also made me a little uncomfortable—maybe because of the responsibility such a commitment implied.

By the time I entered high school I had learned that the only road to a pain-free existence was to be emotionally uncommitted. David was making a big commitment to our friendship. When it came time for me to do the same, I would bale. But this was way down the road—and still part of the great unknown. In this moment we were blissfully unaware and desperate for the feeling that there was someone in the world whose existence was enhanced by our life. We would reinforce our relationship by reminding each other that we were "best friends to the bitter end." David came up with our credo, and he loved it. It spoke to his need for an attachment to another and his need for permanence in that attachment. It was a lot to ask your buddy to stay back a grade, even if you were best friends, but that's what he did. We were in different grades, but it didn't matter—we were together.

I arrived at boarding school in the fall of 1969 to find that the students had the power. The offspring of America's ruling class benefited from the revolution occurring on college campuses. And if we couldn't find our own cause, we were at the very least going to take advantage. We were too young to be worried about going to Vietnam—it was not our war or our cause—but the spirit of revolt was intoxicating, and we wanted something of our own to die for. Or at the very least, a stake in the ancillary lifestyle benefits that resulted.

The pursuit of those ancillary lifestyle benefits proved time consuming, so I learned early in my first year the benefits of having a United States senator and his office as an academic resource. I sent my uncle Teddy a letter telling him how well I was doing and asking for help with some term papers.

> *Dear Chris:*
> *Thanks very much for your letter. And my congratulations on your grades. I'm sure that you can bring your average up those .5 points!*
> *I'm sending some material on Vietnam, crime and inflation. One thing you must remember, that there is debate <u>within</u> the Republican and Democratic parties on these issues, and therefore you cannot state a "Democratic" position or a "Republican" position. In other words, my positions on these issues are not necessarily shared by all of my Democratic colleagues here in the Senate.*
> *Good luck and let me know how you do.*
>
> > *Love,*
> > *Ted*

Then my uncle wrote a postscript in the hopes of steering me to other resources.

> *Congressional Quarterly has good information as well.*

MY FIRST year at Middlesex the students ruled the roost. The administration and our teachers were afraid. You could see it in their eyes. They were content to overlook everything but the most blatant infractions. We could get away with anything—and did. My freshman year nobody had disciplinary problems. Three years later, half the student body was booted out or on some kind of probation.

From the day I arrived on campus I was bent on pushing the envelope. Not in the classroom or on the athletic fields, but in the subculture of sixties experimentation. My friends and I created a community that spent as much time in the woods as it did in the classroom. We built hidden structures where we could meet and engage in our version of revolution—which centered on music, drugs, and figuring new ways to break the rules. It was far from a palace. We had managed to find enough wood to construct two large one-room rectangles, with roof and floor. Each was big enough for six fifteen-year-old boys wearing winter coats. We found some throw rugs and pillows to give them a bit of comfort. Our huts were built in a clearing a couple hundred feet off the beaten path, which ran from the back of the administration building into the Concord woods. We concealed the huts and the clearing with dead wood and brush so as to make our meeting place undetectable unless one knew where to look.

It was our intent to create an alternative campus, a utopia for those of us who had little interest in the corridor that was being prepared for us in the hallowed halls just down the garden path. We would flee to our sanctuary whenever we could, often sneaking out of our dormitories at night to ingest chemicals, listen to Led Zeppelin and James Taylor, and read Emerson and Hunter Thompson.

MR. KINGMAN HAD the demeanor and look of a United States marine. His hair was buzzed and he had that ramrod-straight thing going. His speech was always deliberate. He was everything we loathed and feared about the establishment, and as master of discipline at Middlesex he could suck the testosterone out of a sixteen-year-old boy with a glance. His ability to sniff out the slightest infraction of the rules was legendary, and once caught, the offending student usually rolled over before the interrogation began. Every boy at Middlesex was terrified of him.

When I arrived at school Brad Kingman made it his goal to mentor me. I don't know why he picked me. It was a little embarrassing. He tried to turn me from my chosen path of drugs and rebellion to a more traditional prep school experience. He became my faculty adviser, going the extra mile, seeking me out on the campus to see how things were going, inviting me to supper with him and his wife, even encouraging me to try out for the football team.

Brad Kingman's heart was in the right place, but he didn't have a clue about my messed-up sensibility and my commitment to an alternate lifestyle.

I stayed open to it though, knowing deep down that what he was trying to give me was what I needed, but my desire to blot out reality and kill the pain was more powerful than Brad Kingman's wisdom and good intentions.

SNAPSHOT:

On a bleak winter day in 1970 I stumbled out of Eliot Hall after a particularly dreadful performance on an early morning French exam and was making my way across the Commons of Middlesex School on my way back to my room in Peabody House when a pain came over me like nothing I had ever felt before in my short life. It seemed to materialize out of nowhere, hitting me in the solar plexus and psyche with vicious certainty. I was fifteen years old and within the first five minutes I knew that this pain would either kill me or make me crazy. Tears flowed from my eyes and my knees buckled. My chest seized with the weight of unrealized expectations and my gut descended into the pit of bottomless despair. The pain was both physical and emotional. It was the pain of knowing I couldn't measure up. Of knowing I was destined to be a failure. I would never equal those who came before and I was destined to spend the rest of my life trying. I could forget about having my own life. Looking back, I realize I was having a quintessential adolescent moment. Questions of identity and self-worth had mixed with raging teenage hormones to produce a toxic but somewhat normal stew of doubt and pain. I had no idea what to do with all this. I needed my father. Unfortunately, he was three thousand miles away and unavailable in California. The manhole cover would once again slide into place.

I had plenty of heroic representations of fatherhood, but no real human connection to any of them and I wasn't about to accept an outsider, who I figured would only be interested in me because of my family. In that moment, my relationship with chemicals moved from voluntary to necessary, and Mr. Kingman's continued attempts to sway me were utterly useless.

Football was a very important aspect of my young maleness. I had never played it in any organized way. My game was touch. It was the Kennedy game, and I identified myself with it any chance I got. Brad Kingman was the football coach, and he realized the sport might bring me back from the edge. He was relentless, constantly pushing me to try out for the team, until I finally caved and showed up for my first practice.

It was one of those brutally hot, stifling, late-summer New England days, and as soon as I put on my pads, the game was over. I was not used to playing under the weight and restriction of a uniform. There were drills and formations to learn. Grown men with whistles, and little patience, spewing abuse at hungry young men, eager to make a name for themselves on the gridiron.

This wasn't what I'd signed up for, and I didn't adapt well. I quit before I hit my first sled. It was way too hard, and I couldn't risk being bad at something I had so much identification with. So it was back to the JV soccer team, which went 0–9 for the season. Everyone on the team was a freak, and we took great pride in our perfect record. It was counter to what was expected and pissed the administration off. It was our version of taking over the administration building. Not quite as bold, but it fed the same need. An elite group of us called ourselves the Freon Gang because we sucked some Freon out of the air horns that signaled substitutions throughout the game, which kept us high enough so it didn't matter whether we won or lost. I scored half the goals for the season, a grand total of one, a source of great personal pride.

After football, there was one remaining life preserver that might have kept me from sinking below the surface of what was respectable and productive. It was drama—which I didn't know much about, but my father's notoriety as an actor provided the necessary context.

Hugh Fortmiller was the master of drama at Middlesex. He was a good man, and I'm told an excellent drama coach, although I wouldn't know because the only play I did was Shakespeare's *Twelfth*

Night. I had a very insignificant role—a shrub or spear carrier—but it didn't matter. The experience terrified me. Before my shrub experience my last performance was when I followed Marilyn Monroe and did the twist. I had no idea that all actors are terrified to walk onstage. Laurence Olivier used to blow chunks before he stepped onto the stage at the Old Vic.

I don't remember anyone telling me that courage is not the absence of fear but the ability to do what you need to do in spite of the fear. Well, maybe they told me, but I didn't hear them. I had my antidote for fear, failure, or just plain giving a shit—and it came in pill, herb, and powder form.

Or maybe it was that my relationship with these human characteristics was so out of whack that it was impossible for me to see things for what they really were. If someone had asked me what courage meant at this point in my life, I would have said pulling a wounded comrade through shark-infested waters in the South Pacific with a belt between your teeth, or running for president, knowing that someone out there wanted to blow your head off. Walking onstage in a high school production of *Twelfth Night* shouldn't be a big deal, and if it was, it meant this wasn't my gig or that there was something wrong with me.

After my failure at football and drama, my commitment to the counterculture was complete. I became a Dead Head, following the Grateful Dead all over the eastern seaboard. While at school, I spent most of my time smoking hashish in the woods or at our sister school, Concord Academy, trying to get my cousin Caroline's roommate, Cary Minot, to pay attention to me. Cary was the oldest of the Minot sisters and the most beautiful girl I had ever seen since my sister's friend Terry. I would have gladly given my left arm to do in real life what I did with her in daily fantasies. She was my high school obsession, along with Mrs. Brewster, who was the wife of my English teacher and the sexiest housemistress on the Middlesex campus.

I spent two years longing for and inventing ways to be in the same room as Cary Minot, but I don't think I ever talked to her until I was well into my thirties. I might have been this somewhat cool, fairly good-looking, famous-by-lineage drug addict, but I sucked with the girls. I was mesmerized, obsessed, and terrified all at the same time. It left me tongue-tied at best and more often than not sent me fleeing from whatever mixer I was at. During one of these particularly grizzly social inventions for repressed boarding-school adolescents, I found myself so uninterested or terrified by the offerings from the Dana Hall School for girls that I spent the entire evening petting the local campus dog. This seemed a valid choice considering the circumstances until one of the upperclass ladies' men decided to humiliate me for it. Oh, those adolescent males can be so cruel.

Mrs. Brewster was a different story. She was older and unattainable. This made her no less desirable, but more approachable. She was the perfect manifestation of the beautiful, sexy older woman obsession of the teenage boy, a bustier version of Jennifer O'Neil in *Summer of '42.*

David and I found out she was an accomplished potter. We thus developed a strong interest in molding clay. One day we summoned all our courage and asked if she would teach us. She said yes, and once a week we would make our way to the Brewster residence where Mrs. Brewster would guide our hands into and around the soft wet clay on her potter's wheel. It was glorious. This was the one class at Middlesex in which we had perfect attendance. We left inspired, hypnotized by our teacher's choice of wardrobe and arguing about which of us was the better potter.

My years at Middlesex were spent on the fringe. When I arrived in Concord for the forming I so badly needed, the fringe was in. Those of us on the fringe had a modicum of cachet thanks to our brothers and sisters smoking dope and flexing their political muscles on college campuses. The fringe suited me. I liked being different—outside the norm. It was what I was used to. There was only one place I really wanted to belong and that was with my family. That was my identity. I may have been in the second tier in the family, but as far as the world was concerned I was a Kennedy. I didn't need to join any group, society, or institution to give me my place in the world. Being on the fringe coupled with being a Kennedy meant I could get away with a lot of shit. The good masters at Middlesex winked for a few years, but the day came when the fringe lost its luster and even being a Kennedy wouldn't save me or our alternative society deep in the Concord woods.

Once it became clear to the powers-that-be that the outlaws weren't coming in from their hideouts voluntarily, they decided to come and get us. What we learned very quickly was that faux student revolutionaries get swept aside quicker than you can say spoiled rich kids. Once the administration decided they could move against us with impunity, they did. Our hideouts were demolished, and the manifesto declaring our commitment to freedom of thought and action was put on display in the entrance hall for all to see. It was humiliating. Overnight our revolutionary ranks were decimated by expulsions and suspensions; our cadre was sent packing in many different directions.

SNAPSHOT:

> Flash forward to the year 1986. I was thirty years old and newly sober. Ronald Reagan was in the White House and I was on my way back to Middlesex School to make amends to the teachers I had tormented there in the early nineteen-seventies. It was time to go back to all the people I had fucked over in my life and tell them I was sorry. Mr. Kingman was gone, as were many of the other teachers who endured my shenanigans, but David Sheldon, the headmaster, remained, and it was to him that I would apologize.

I walked across the Commons with the memories of my days as a student flooding through me. I remembered the deep despair I had carried across the same ground on that cold winter day fifteen years earlier. It occurred to me that the feelings I had at that time, though profound, needn't have dictated the years of subsequent misery. I had learned in recovery that feelings aren't facts. This is a hard lesson to learn as an adult; it is nearly impossible to learn as a teenager.

David Sheldon was a kind and forgiving man. He listened to my apology with appreciation and the amused detachment of a man who had long since moved on. "Chris, do you know who won the election for president among the students here?" he asked. I told him I had no idea. "Ronald Reagan, that's who. Most of the students here are preparing to go to business school."

"Things sure have changed," I observed.

The headmaster concurred. "Yeah, they have. You guys were a pain in the ass, but you were always interesting. I miss those times."

I had made my amends and been vindicated for my bad behavior at the same moment.

In 1971 my mother fled to Paris with my two younger sisters in another attempt to have *her* life away from the family. I was left at boarding school to be dealt with by the well-paid babysitters moonlighting as teachers of the offspring of the ruling class. Come summer the babysitters went to their cabins in Maine, and I was free to hop around the East Coast in my relentless quest for girls, drugs, and trouble. I found it all in New York City. Home sweet home. The Big Apple.

SNAPSHOT:

My mother had vacated her apartment on the corner of Eightieth Street and Fifth Avenue leaving only the rugs and a kitchen full of canned food and broken utensils. My cousin David and I had sleeping bags, which were all we needed to take up residence. We hung out in Central Park at a place called Dope Hill where the elite of the drug culture congregated. Heroin was four dollars a bag, and you could get high on three bags. That wasn't a lot of money, but we were high school kids on hiatus with very little cash.

The family office, Park Agency, was in the Pan Am Building on Forty-fourth Street and Park Avenue right above Grand Central Station.

David and I would head down to the office, and after unsuccessfully trying to convince the family accountant Gertrude Ball to give us an advance on monies we were supposed to get at twenty-one, we would head down to Grand Central for three hours of panhandling. We had a notion that we were living some kind of bohemian, hippy lifestyle, begging for quarters in our bare feet and then running out to our commune of junkies in Central Park. We were free from any authority, and it felt good. We had the illusion that we were living our own life. We had our own money, a crash pad, and some new friends.

One day we decided to have a party. It was our intention to invite every girl we could find in and around Dope Hill. We figured if we invited fifty good-looking girls and a few guys the odds that we might get lucky would be heavily in our favor. On the day, we spread out and invited fifty of the hottest young hippie chicks we could find in Central Park. We bought some soda and beer and waited for the influx of willing beauty that was sure to descend on 990 Fifth Avenue that evening.

They came. But they didn't come alone. They brought their junkie boyfriends with them and a bunch of other friends from neighborhoods far from the Upper East Side. Our guests showed up hungry, thirsty, and looking to steal anything that wasn't nailed down. The elevator men had never seen such an influx. They were nervous, and so were we when it became clear that the hundred or so party guests looked like they might want to stay awhile.

I was more nervous than David. It was my mother's apartment and her doormen, after all. My ass was on the line if she found out. David once again demonstrated contempt for my cries of alarm.

David:
Why are you getting so uptight?
Me:
Have you taken a good look at these people, man?
David:
What about them? You invited them.
Me:
We invited them. And we didn't invite *them*. We invited
the girls.
David:
The girls came. Did you see the one with the long brown hair
and the enormous breasts?

Me:
She's beautiful.
David:
She mine. I saw her first.
Me:
Fuck you. I saw her first.
David:
Chris, don't be an asshole. I saw her first.

There was no sense in arguing. Even if David was wrong he would argue until he wore you down and you gave him what he wanted.

Me:
Whatever, man. Just help me get all these junkies out of my mom's apartment.

FOR DAVID, any potential disaster was an inconvenience. The RFKs all slept with these big noisy fans in the windows of their bedrooms. I think it must have been a Skakel thing because no other Kennedys do it. This went on year-round. No matter how cold it got, the windows were open and the fans were on. I slept over at the RFKs' so much it became a habit with me, too, which continues to this day. One of those nights at Hickory Hill I woke to find that the fan had shorted out and set the window drapes on fire. I yelled to David, who was curled up under a pile of comforters, that the room was on fire. It always took David a while to wake up. This time was no different. His head popped up from the pile of blankets, he noticed the fire racing up the window treatments, looked at me, and said, "Have a little consideration and put it out, man. I'm trying to sleep."

WE FINALLY got all the junkies out by four o'clock in the morning. The drag was that they took all the girls with them. All except one—the one with the long brown hair. She needed a place to crash. There were only two sleeping bags. David tried his "I saw her first" routine, but at 4 A.M., after enduring the invasion of the junkie snatchers, I wasn't in

153

the mood. The competition was fierce if short-lived. She chose me, and I lost my virginity to a girl whose name I didn't know in a sleeping bag on the floor of my mother's abandoned Fifth Avenue apartment.

I didn't make too big a deal about this adolescent monumental accomplishment for two good reasons: like most teenage boys, I had been lying about sex for years, and I wasn't totally sure that I had actually had intercourse. See, I had a little trouble figuring out where my penis actually was supposed to go. It seemed to me that the opening should be somewhere higher up on the pelvis where all the hair was, not down between her legs. I searched long and hard for an opening in the wrong region. I may have been at the wrong destination, but the result was the same. You can't bump and grind like I did and not lose it, no matter how many times you recreate "the catch" by Willie Mays in your mind.

MY UNCLE Robert Kennedy had a political alliance and friendship with the activist and leader of the United Farm Workers, Caesar Chavez. My uncle's association with the farmworkers' movement defined him politically and humanistically for my cousins and me as much as anything he did in his career. Bobby Kennedy went through many political transformations, but when he died he left my generation with his commitment to civil rights and to the poor and disadvantaged. It is what my cousins and I were most proud of.

Later in the summer of 1971, David and I went to La Paz, California, to spend a month working for Caesar Chavez at his headquarters for the UFW. We had just turned sixteen. We appreciated our family's solidarity with the farmworkers, but it really didn't have anything to do with us, and nobody asked us if we wanted to spend our summer with them. It was pretty much a disaster from the start. We showed up smoking Marlboro cigarettes and drinking Coors beer—both of which were being boycotted by the UFW for unfair labor practices. The good people at the UFW thought we were coming out to work. We thought we were gonna hang out and rub shoulders with some frontline activists. We were more interested in our tans than in the nitty-gritty of social change. We spent our days assigned to a garbage collection detail, sneaking off when we could for an hour of sunbathing. Our nights were spent in the bunkhouse drinking beer, doing speed, staying up all night arguing about who was smarter, and fantasizing about all the fun we were gonna have when we got the hell out of La Paz.

It was clear that we were not yet ready to pick up the mantle.

I WAS suspended from Middlesex in my junior year for smoking cigarettes and drinking beer. A fairly inglorious end to my revolutionary struggle. I lied about this for years because I felt that the offense was so lame. I used to hint that I was kicked out for drinking and having an inappropriate relationship with one of the professors' wives. Even my failures had to be spectacular. My mother was living in Paris with Victoria and Robin, so she asked Peter Clifton, family friend and education specialist, to drive me around New England to see if there was a school that would take me. There weren't many. Peter was a good man with a family of his own and was between gigs after leaving his position as assistant headmaster at Saint David's. He was one of the men I looked to as a surrogate father because I liked him and because he seemed to care about me. As my mother wrote him: "Cherie, I have heard about how terrific you were about Christopher. I really appreciate it and I'm afraid he ended up with more than he deserved."

More than I deserved?

It turned out what I deserved was an obscure girls' school in Littleton, New Hampshire, called the White Mountain School. The school had sixty girls and had just recently started admitting boys. There were eight. I made it nine. The boys lived off campus, which was no real hardship considering the homely nature of the female majority. I spent four months there, finishing my junior year. In that time I instigated a student revolt. I can't remember what we were revolting against but we did manage to get rid of the headmaster, whom nobody really liked anyway. Before he was sacked he contributed his observations to my year-end report:

Academically, Chris has done very well with us. The confusion regarding lines of adult responsibility were in no way helpful to

CHRISTOPHER KENNEDY LAWFORD

*Chris over the past months. I do hope that the family and
school lines of responsibility in his last year of prep school can
be a great deal more firmly established than was the case with
us. Although Chris would on the surface object to greater direction for his life, I think that beneath the surface, he is pleading
for it. I hope he gets it. Basically, he is a fine young man and
could use any and all help which can be extended to him.*

After I got his report I felt bad about my complicity in his ouster.

I lived with the Walshes of Littleton, who had to be in their seventies. They had two sons, and treated me like their third. I would hitch-
hike to Boston every Thursday after class and come back on Sunday or
Monday. In Boston I would stay with my cousin Bobby, who was completing his senior year of high school at a day school in Cambridge, after having similar difficulties with the boarding school environment. I
spent the long weekends getting high, listening to the Grateful Dead,
and looking for girls. I had received word from Middlesex that they
would allow me to complete my senior year there as a day student, but
they wanted me off the campus by three o'clock in the afternoon. They
weren't taking any chances. My family was less than thrilled, as was
clear from a letter my mother wrote Peter Clifton:

*I have been advised by Sarge & Eunice that all is not well in the
Boston area. They seem to have a feeling that Christopher being
left at Middlesex might run into some trouble. As you and I have
been aware of for some time David seems to have an enormous
influence on Christopher (and it seems to me, none of it has
been good). This influence, of course, extends to Bobby. I think
therefore that probably Christopher should go to California and
let his father try to handle the problem. I think with his grades
so far he could survive another change in schooling.*

So in the spirit of letting "my father handle the problem," my mom
arranged for me to spend some quality time with my dad in the summer preceding my senior year to see if we could find a West Coast alternative to spending my senior year in Boston with Bobby and David.

156

SNAPSHOT:

They were making American movies in Vancouver back in the early seventies, though not at the level they are making them today. The unions were stronger then, and "Made in America" still had some relevance. I went there to spend a few days with my dad while he was making a movie of the week called *The Deadly Hunt* with Tony Franciosa — remember him? This was the first time I had visited him on location since I was a kid, when I went to watch the filming of *Sergeants 3* with Frank, Dean, and Sammy. I was enthralled watching grown men having a ball playing cowboys and Indians when I was five, but it was nothing compared with getting a taste of making movies on location at seventeen. What a gig. They fly you first class to a beautiful city, put you up in a five-star hotel, and actually give you money to live on, on top of the ridiculous amount they pay you to show up on a set every day and pretend you're someone way more interesting than who you really are. Who wouldn't want to do this for a living?

My dad's new girlfriend, Mary Rowan, picked me up at the airport. She was twenty-three and another of the most beautiful women I had ever seen. She was nice too. My dad had met her on the set of *Laugh-In*, the weekly TV comedy show Mary's dad hosted and my father guest starred on. Mary told me later that she didn't know what to expect picking me up. The only picture she had seen of me was when I was twelve. My dad was never current.

"I walked into the baggage claim and there is this six-foot-tall gorgeous seventeen-year-old, with hair down to your shoulders and a backpack. You had to be the cutest guy I'd ever seen!" That covers it!

At some point during my stay, Dad decided that it was cool to smoke a joint with his son. My dad's grass was better than anything I had seen in my short but experimental life. Well, if I wasn't completely co-opted before this visit, I sure was soon after. Good drugs, beautiful girls, and making movies: I was home. All I had to do was figure out how to move in permanently.

My mom must have had a sudden case of mother's intuition because she changed her tune on me spending time with Dad, deciding that another year in close proximity to David and Bobby would be preferable to completing high school on the West Coast with only my father to oversee me.

I sent her a letter in Paris indicating my disappointment.

> . . . I am sorry you did not think it a good idea that I go out to California but I suppose I will be able to wait. It was just that I finally had a new direction to head in and a chance to spend some time with daddy but I think it is better for me to finish at Middlesex. Daddy is still working on a job for this summer and I should be hearing from him soon. I don't believe there will be a problem.

Once again my mother's attempts to separate me from David and Bobby had been vanquished, and I returned to Middlesex for my senior year—with that stipulation that I leave campus by 3 P.M. every day. My mother's hope that I would go to California for an extended stay so that my father could "handle the problem" would be postponed for six months. It would prove to be an out-of-the-frying-pan-into-the-fire event.

Chapter 17

. . . if thou gaze too long into the abyss,
the abyss will gaze into thee.
— NIETZSCHE

I loved getting high. I was a pig from the gate. I took anything and everything. Opiates were my drug of choice, but whatever changed my consciousness was my friend. A bottle of Johnny Walker Black, a spliff of sinsemilla, a Quaalude, Benny, Valium — it didn't matter as long as it took the edge off. Drugs were my Wheaties. My breakfast of champions. They made me feel fortified. There wasn't anything I couldn't accomplish when my medicine cabinet was fully stocked. Of course, it was an illusion. I always ran out sooner than planned and the energy expended to keep the narcotics flowing was significant — but when they were flowing, watch out.

I took an extraordinary amount of drugs, seemingly to little effect. I was not the guy with the lampshade on my head. I was the guy who was ready to go out dancing when everybody else couldn't get up off the floor. I smoked PCP every day for two years and was more or less functional. There are folks who try PCP once and never put together another coherent sentence. It's either a miracle or a testament to my constitution that I'm not doing the Thorazine shuffle in an institution somewhere. One of the doctors who treated my addiction told me, "If you drank alcohol the way you did narcotics you'd be a wet brain chained to a bed somewhere." He never kept me sober, but he was right about the debilitating effects of the legal drug. I've often wondered what I might have accomplished in this life if I had made a different choice that autumn day when I was thirteen and first dropped acid.

NOTE TO READER:

I used drugs for seventeen years. I used pretty much every drug you have ever heard of and I used a lot of them. Just to illustrate: When I was in law school I routinely went to bed having consumed seven or more different chemicals. Uppers, downers, painkillers, antianxiety agents, cocaine, alcohol, pot, etc. I read a story about something called diapid nasal spray in *Time* magazine. It was for obesity but had shown signs of helping with depression and increasing memory. It was available by prescription for forty dollars for a small bottle. I took diapid for two years in the hope that it would help me memorize all those legal facts. It never occurred to me that I might do more for my memory by cutting down on all the other drugs I was taking. I fancied myself a cutting-edge pharmaceutical engineer.

The other thing you need to know about drug use is, it's not linear. It ebbs and flows. What I was taking and how much of it I was taking had as much to do with availability and circumstance as with desire. Throughout my using I attempted to remain somewhat functional. This meant I would not allow myself to lie around with a needle in my arm all day even if I might have liked to. I tried to amount to something by working, remaining physically active, and going to school. Hell, I managed to get three degrees and I was pretty much stoned through all of it. When it is the addict's intention to remain functional, then the addict's use becomes geared to keeping the addict in the game. Eventually, though, addiction *will* trump functionality. What you the reader need to know is that from the age of thirteen to thirty my primary purpose every day was to find whatever it was that I needed to get through the day. Some days it was a joint, some days a drink, some a pill; other days it was heroin or a methadone maintenance program.

In my senior year at Middlesex, students were allowed to do independent work-study in lieu of a regular academic schedule. I constructed a protocol that would bring me to Washington where I would work as an aide in my uncle Teddy's Senate office for the first half of the semester and at Universal Studios in the Independent Film Acquisition Unit for the second half. It was a perfect protocol for someone hopelessly stuck between two worlds but in search of recognition. But first I would get my first of many lessons in love and the opposite sex.

SNAPSHOT:

Lisa was the next most beautiful girl I had ever seen. She was a quirky-looking brunette with long stringy hair and a crooked nose. Her voice was soft and she spoke with an artist's hesitancy. There was only one thing wrong with her: she was off-limits. Lisa was Bobby's girlfriend. Well, one of Bobby's girlfriends. Kim, whom we had grown up with on the Cape, was in first position when it came to Bobby. He was currently holding her hostage in his first year at Harvard. Lisa lived with her family in Cambridge, Bobby and I lived with the Brodes, we rented a bedroom in their house while going to school. For both of us, they were the warm nurturing family that neither of us seemed to have had but were looking for. John and Joey Brode were the 1960s quintessential Cambridge academic couple. They had three kids with French names and seven cats that had the run of the place. The kids were sweet and I even liked their cats until one of them appeared to suddenly explode through its mouth and asshole simultaneously on the dining room table one night right in the middle of dinner. I never knew a cat could be capable of such a feat. The cat in question had lived way longer than it should have with an array of gastronomical issues. One night its ability to keep its insides inside dissipated along with its life force, and Bobby's and my compatriot Doug Spooner ended up with feline innards to go along with the pork chop Joey Brode had fixed for supper.

In the fall of my senior year at Middlesex I took a trip across the country looking at colleges. Lisa heard about my trek and asked if she could come. I said yes. That was my first mistake.

On the flight from Boston to Colorado I had a couple of rum and Cokes, looked into her big brown eyes, and it was over. This was my introduction to the narcotic that is unrequited love. By the time we touched down in Denver I had never wanted to put my hands on anyone more in my life. It was excruciating, the yearning coupled with the knowing that I was coveting my cousin's girl. Certainly I was going to burn in hell and probably have to go up against Bobby on my way there. I knew it was uncool to snake one of your friends' girls. It was unthinkable to do this to a member of the family.

By the time we arrived at my dad's house in Los Angeles, I had crumbled completely, convinced that I had found HER, the one that I could not live without, the female who awakened me and made me whole. I was eighteen years old, and this was my first foray into the magic and insanity of love. I would spend the next thirty years chasing the high, but first I would have to finesse the Bobby thing. My plan was to engage in every aspect of lovemaking with Lisa except the aspect where I actually put my penis inside. The Bill Clinton approach to sex before Bill Clinton became "Bill Clinton." How could Bobby be angry if I didn't actually have sex with his girlfriend? We headed back to Boston fully merged, with the knowledge that I was going up against the one peer I didn't really want to go up against and that once I did she would be mine entirely.

It was an exciting couple of days. It's funny, but I remember everything about Lisa going to tell Bobby and coming back to tell me how it went, but I don't remember anything about falling into her arms in bliss for the first time. I might have seen this for what it was and saved myself a boatload of pain. See, there is something in my nature that so desperately needs the feminine connection that my reality becomes blurred.

THIS DEFINITELY has something to do with my relationship with my mother. As a kid, I wanted to save my mom from her pain, but it was impossible. It would be years before I would understand she could only do that for herself. But by then the instinct to be a rescuer was firmly embeded in me. I wrote her letters and cards that were full of my love for her and how much she meant to me, but they were more a reflection of what I hoped for than what actually was.

> Dear Mummy,
> Staying with friends. Thanks for another terrific homecoming. I love you very much and hope you feel the same for me. It is important that we are friends. I hope I make you proud of me, despite what you may think I try very hard to give you the happiness and love you so richly deserve. See you at EMK's 50th.
> > Lots of Love. Your one and only
> > Xtopher

Bobby didn't take it very well. It didn't seem to matter that I hadn't had sex with his girlfriend or that he had Kim. The fact that a female was leaving him for me really pissed him off. We didn't speak for a year. He told me that Joe had said if it had been him he would have beaten the shit out of me. Bobby settled for a promise that he would sleep with my wife the day after I got married. A threat he didn't have a prayer or the inclination of carrying out.

Lisa and I settled into that uncomfortable place of getting what you think you want, only coming to realize that the drama of getting there was what was really interesting.

That Christmas I went to Paris to see my mother, who had moved there with Victoria and Robin in a fit of getting away from the family. While in Paris, I got a new wardrobe and visited a trendy Parisian hair salon.

> Henri:
> I think something . . . poofy and wild.
> Me:
> I was thinking just a trim.
> Henri:
> No, cherie, with your bone structure we need to make a
> statement.

> *Me:*
> What kind of a statement?
> *Henri:*
> I don't know—something that says, "I'm alive."

Be careful when your hairstylist says, "I don't know." I returned to Boston from the Eurozone looking very much like I belonged there. Lisa picked me up at Logan Airport and I knew before you could say gay Parisian haircut, it was over.

She left the next day for Mexico promising to write. I was left in Boston with no girlfriend and a pissed-off cousin. I was feeling pretty alone when I wrote my mom: "I am communicating with Bob now but not too much. I think things will get better. Still haven't heard from Lisa. It must be the mail or she's awful busy."

That wasn't it. I received a letter two weeks later telling me she was getting back together with the guy who used to tell her that "her pussy tasted like honey." Some guys will say anything. At the time, I wished I had thought of it. I didn't think it possible another man could adore this woman more than I, but apparently this guy did.

I THOUGHT I needed a big dick to run with the folks I had grown up around in Hollywood and Washington. I didn't buy into the idea that those who seek power and fame are often compensating for deficiencies in more fundamental areas. My problem was choosing which path to take. Both had their attractions and perks. Hollywood was my father: creativity, escape, a new world, fame, fun, girls, adulation. Washington was my grandfather: responsibility, importance, fame, my martyred uncles, and adulation.

I had no center and was as far from knowledge of self as one could be and still have a pulse. I vacillated between these two worlds like a whirling dervish with a split personality. I realized early on that I was more suited to a career in the arts; I just couldn't get over the accompanying feeling of frivolousness. Whenever I thought of my father or his world it paled in comparison to what my mother's side of the family had accomplished. I knew my soul would be nurtured more by the creative arts than by legislative government, but I was living my life from the outside in on a search for the elusive thing that would fill the hole in my center.

I had very little capacity at eighteen to hear the beat of my different drummer, much less march to it. It would be a long time before I would understand that it's an inside job and that, if I had moved from my head to my gut, I would have found all the answers I needed. This wasn't what was happening with me my senior year in high school. My thinking at the time was to find a way into these two worlds to see which might suit me and to add some pizzazz to my résumé.

On some levels I am well suited for a career in politics. I can kiss ass with the best of them, and I enjoy being the center of attention. I am pained by injustice and yearn for a better world. The problem has always been that I'm not very good with reality, compromise, or being accountable to someone else's agenda. I think this pretty much rules out a career in Washington.

Getting the gig with my uncle was easy. Hollywood was a little tougher. My father was no help. I don't think I even bothered asking him. I went to Uncle Steve. He was like the Robert Duvall character in *The Godfather*. He was the consigliere to the Kennedy family. He brokered the power of the family, worked for the family, and was in the family. He ran the family business, which basically amounted to trying not to screw up what my grandfather had created and keeping the beneficiaries happy. He asked people for favors, not just money and votes. It made him a pretty angry guy. He called up Lew Wasserman, who was the most powerful man in Hollywood, and asked if Lew had anything at Universal Studios for his eighteen-year-old nephew. Lew said yes, and off I went to engage the legislative process and the actresses of Hollywood.

Chapter 18

*Growing up is overrated. How many grown-ups do you know
that have anything you want?*
— ANONYMOUS

My uncle Teddy had this cool powder blue Pontiac GTO convertible. It was mint, and he looked like he belonged in it. I thought it was pretty hip that a United States senator and one of the most powerful men in the country would drive around our nation's capitol in a car that was so accessible and radical.

When I arrived at his house in McLean, Virginia, to begin my internship in his Senate office I had no idea what I would be doing or whom I would be doing it with. It was a shock when I found out that one of my jobs was to drive the then junior senator from the great state of Massachusetts to and from work in his souped-up Pontiac.

If you want to understand the craziness of my family, drive or sail with my uncle Teddy. You are always late, and there is always a better way to go. This is what I walked into that winter morning when I first slid behind the wheel of a car I prayed I wouldn't crack up. It was incredibly stressful, way more than anything I had to do on Capitol Hill. I was usually hungover, having crawled into bed only a few hours before, being dragged to consciousness by my uncle yelling downstairs that I had five minutes. It was a far cry from the should-I-go-to-class-this-morning-or-sleep-in world of prep school.

I sent a letter to my mother soon after I arrived at my uncle's house on Chain Bridge Road. I used his personal stationery so she would believe I had actually arrived.

> *Dear Mother,*
> *I have arrived at Teddy's. Today was my first day at work and I*
> *found it extremely interesting and a hell of a lot of fun, really.*
> *I am very happy and am getting along very well with Teddy*
> *and everyone else. . . . I met George McGovern today and he*
> *said he had a great time with you in London. He seems like a*
> *very nice man.*
>
> *xxoo*
> *Xtopher*

Teddy was mythic in my life. He was the link between the future and the past. His spirit and position were daily reminders of all that was great about our family. His energy and enthusiasm were boundless, but like most members of my family he had very little capacity for disappointment or things not going his way. Of everything he was, and all he represented, the biggest part of him was his heart. It was very important to me to get his approval.

I pretty much knew right away that Washington wasn't for me. The environment left me in need of No-Doz. I was a messenger, spending most of my time running up and down the miles of corridors on Capitol Hill. The atmosphere was stifling, and I yearned to be outside in the fresh air. The legislative process moves like molasses. If making movies is like watching paint dry, then following a bill through the legislative process is like watching paint dry in slow motion. I understood the importance of what was being done, but there was no excitement or vitality in it for me. I looked for what the payoff was for those engaged in minding the Republic's business. I had grown up with the ethic of public service firmly rooted in my psyche, but found that most of those doing time in Washington were driven by other motivations. This is not to say I didn't come across committed folk interested in doing good, but the system and the process have a way of perverting this intent into a game of power, money, and recognition.

I kept a journal of my time in Washington:

My Uncle Teddy often expresses his disappointment in the Nixon Administration. They listen to the voices of the few and overlook the voices of the many:

"It's very difficult to get anything worthwhile accomplished with an uncooperative president. Congress can't become a leader in the eyes of the people because there are so many voices and different opinions. Its very difficult for the Congress to collect the power necessary to override the President and present the country with a viable alternative."

It became evident to me that Teddy would very much like to be President but I believe him when he says he will not run. In his mind he cannot run and this is where a great deal of the frustration I see in him comes from.

In a closed door meeting with The Supreme Court Law Clerks he was asked if he would seek the presidency in 1976. My Uncle hesitated and became really nervous before saying "No."

SNAPSHOT:

After eight weeks driving my uncle Teddy to and from the Old Senate Office Building on Capitol Hill I was beginning to feel more or less comfortable sitting behind the wheel of the powder blue GTO. The senator was sifting through his nightly homework crammed into the oversized briefcase at the end of each day by his staff, which was acknowledged as the best and the brightest on the Hill. He found time between the dozens of letters he was signing to ride me good naturedly for finding the route home with the most traffic on it.

Teddy:
I knew we should have taken Chain Bridge! Ah, Chris, have you thought about what you might do with your life when you finish school?

Me:

Well, yeah, Teddy; I was gonna ask you if you could help me
find a job.

Teddy:

Get over into the left lane. Well, Chris, what kind of job
would you be interested in?

Me:

I've thought a bit about that, Teddy. I'm not sure if I want to
be in Washington or Hollywood but I want a job that pays me
a lot of money, where I don't have to work very hard and
where I might do some good in the world.

Teddy:

Well, Chris, I'll tell ya, I'll keep my eyes open, but the thing
is . . . if I find that job—*I'll* take it!

I left Washington for Hollywood figuring I might have more luck in the land of the locusts finding work where I at least had a chance of realizing my stated requirements.

Chapter 19

Happy families are all alike; every unhappy family is unhappy in its own way.
— LEO TOLSTOY

I arrived in L.A. in the spring of 1972 not having lived with my father since the age of eight. I was eighteen years old and had no idea what it would be like to live under the same roof with the man whom I had known more for his absence in my life than for his presence. But Vancouver had been fun and we had smoked pot together, so how bad could it be?

My father lived in a sprawling second-story apartment in a picturesque English-style complex on Cory Avenue just outside the Beverly Hills city line. He loved the place's understated elegance and the fact that "One block outside of Beverly Hills it was a thousand dollars less." He had recently moved from the Sierra Towers, a high-rise just across Sunset Boulevard, after the earthquake of February 9, 1971. He had been terrified by the way the building had swayed in the trembler: "Willie Shoemaker lived on the floor below me and he was thrown out of his bed, across his bedroom and almost out the window. The damn building was swaying twenty-five feet in both directions."

My dad loved the Towers but he wasn't taking any chances. The apartment on the twenty-eighth floor had already been the scene where his shot at becoming Johnny Carson's replacement on the *Tonight* show came to an abrupt end after he gave the late-night talk-show host a joint full of PCP by mistake, causing the star to threaten to jump from the balcony. My father didn't mean to do it, but Johnny was pissed and never forgave him. As far as I know he never sat on the couch or anywhere else on the *Tonight Show* set again. Hollywood can be a very unforgiving place. Anyway, his new pad was a very cozy, elegant bachelor pad with two bedrooms and a pool table.

I was ambitious when I arrived in Hollywood. If you could call sweaty panic ambition. I was ambitious about drugs and fame. I had grown up around fame; now I wanted some of my own. I wanted to be somebody. And I wanted to get high along the way. Well, there was no better place for it than California in the seventies. I spent my days at Universal Studios, learning the movie business, and my nights drinking and getting high with my dad and his movie star and rock star friends. That got to be pressure too. Being "somebody" in company like that can drain you.

I would drive over the hill every day to the black tower at Universal and service the VP in charge of independent film acquisition. At night I would come back to my father's house and party with Vic Morrow of *Combat!* fame, Al Lettieri, who played Sollozo in *The Godfather,* and some of the most beautiful girls on the planet. There were always women, but I was too young and inconsequential to have a chance with any of them.

SNAPSHOT:

It was Sunday, and everyone I knew was recovering from Saturday night. It was raining like a bitch in L.A. and I was driving down Sunset Boulevard on my way back to my father's, feeling really depressed about all the drugs I was doing, the women I wasn't sleeping with, and the fact that my nearest friend was three thousand miles away. Then I noticed a beautiful young soaking-wet creature hitchhiking. This was the early seventies, and kids still stuck their thumbs out. Dining on hitchhikers was not yet in vogue.

I stopped, she got in, and as she had no place she had to be for the next couple of years, I suggested we go to my movie-star dad's house. She said sure and off we went. I learned young and often that if you wanted someone to give you something or do something for you, celebrity worked wonders. I think what happens is transference. Our culture attaches so much importance to celebrity that if you fuck one or are otherwise associated with one, you become important. Anyway, I brought her to Dad's house and he was incredibly charming. She laughed and fawned. We got high. We got hungry. My father suggested chicken—and that I go get it. I got back with a bucket of crispy drumsticks to find my stepmother, Mary, standing at the top of the stairs holding a brassiere in her right hand as she glared at my father.

"Peter, whose is this?"

My father cleared his throat, indicating that he was annoyed by the question. My stepmother turned her attention to me.

"Christopher, does this brassiere belong to you?"

For one of the few times in my life I was speechless. I couldn't even manufacture a joke about cross-dressing.

My father was in his chair reading a script upside down, pretending to be engrossed in one of his favorite shows—*The Dating Game*. The other show he never missed was *The Newlywed Game*. The girl was cowering and acting indignant, my stepmother was pissed, and I was confused. This was a lot to digest. Your dad sends you out for chicken and seduces the only girl you might have had sex with in the last six months. Well, I took the rap for the bra.

"Yeah, Mary, I think it must belong to one of my girlfriends," I offered lamely.

I don't think she believed me, but it calmed her down. The girl scurried away. My father played oblivious indignation. I didn't get laid, but smoked another joint. I appreciated the grass, but it would have been nice to get a thanks and an explanation. I never did.

Despite Mary's incredulousness regarding the mystery brassiere she married my father in Puerto Vallarta, Mexico, and I was their best man. What I remember most about the wedding was the incredible villa we stayed in. I found two Tuinals on pillows in lieu of chocolates at night. It was truly a "lost wedding," but I was honored that my dad had asked me to stand up for him. The marriage imploded eight months later.

SNAPSHOT:

I was pretty certain Elizabeth Taylor was not trying to kill me, but I knew people died by accidental drowning and at this moment I wasn't sure that wouldn't be my fate. I had been underwater for over a minute, and my lungs felt like they were going to explode. We had gone swimming, and Elizabeth had asked me if I liked her new bathing suit. I made the mistake of saying something smart about it looking like something Cleopatra would wear. What I had yet to learn about movie stars was that if they have any sense of humor at all, it is rarely about themselves. And now, in the Beverly Hills pool, belonging to Edith Head, the costume designer, who had won thirteen Academy Awards for costume design and who had nothing to do with the swimsuit in question, I was about to be drowned by the biggest movie star in the world, presumably by accident.

I had just turned nineteen and had been living with my dad for a couple of months, doing my best to keep my bosses at Universal Studios from catching on that I was more interested in the considerable pleasures of Hollywood in the early seventies than in learning the picture business. My routine was simple if somewhat erratic. I woke up on weekday mornings at eight-thirty if the previous night's festivities didn't warrant an excuse to come in later, and showered the night's buzz away, helped by two blasts in each nostril of the pharmaceutical coke that came in little glass rocket ships and was in constant supply from Sid K, premier pharmacist to those in the know in Hollywood. Sid was an old friend of my father's who used to drive him and keep him company on the set until the late sixties and early seventies when he found a much more lucrative and vital way to service the A-list. I had heard about him, tasting his wares for months, but he wouldn't deal with me, given my age and all. It was a great day when my dad let me make the trip to the top of Mulholland to pick up some of the best coke in Hollywood from the man himself.

I liked Sid. He was this fat, really mellow, kind of spiritual drug dealer who, above all, seemed kind. My relationship with him didn't last long; he died of a drug overdose soon after my audience. His funeral was a three-day blackout attended by some very depressed movie stars. The casket was enormous and open; he was buried with a vial of his best and a blast in each nostril to hurry him along to his next destination.

Years later I found myself in the Boston Garden at a play-off game between the Celtics and the hated L.A. Lakers. Jack Nicholson was there, and everybody in the Garden was screaming at him. He ignored them all. I was there with a pretty girlfriend whom I was eager to impress. After unsuccessfully trying to get his attention, I yelled at Jack "Sid K" as loud as I could. He turned, zeroed in on me, and did the *Shining* smile, before he did *The Shining*, motioning me to come over. I did, got an autograph for the pretty girl, and, thanks to Sid and Jack, got lucky.

I treated my work in the Independent Film Acquisition Unit at Universal as something I did in between getting high and partying. My dad would get up at about 11 A.M. and hang out reading scripts, talking on the phone, sunning himself. Not much had changed since I was a kid. Mary was there with her infectious laugh, a group of young friends, and a willingness to indulge my father. She may have been in over her head, and I always felt she had a core disagreement with how my dad was living his life. After acquiescing to my father, she told Erma that she was beginning to worry that she was not a nice girl anymore. She was five years older than me and gorgeous. Unlike my old man who coveted most of my girlfriends, I never thought about sleeping with her.

Elizabeth Taylor called my father pretty much every day from Switzerland, becoming as much a part of his daily routine as his two pieces of sourdough toast and morning milk with a shot of brandy—which to my dad was being "on the wagon." She had been married and divorced from Richard Burton twice and was currently on her third Dance of Death. Elizabeth and my father had been child actors together. She had kissed him when they were young and fallen hopelessly in love. Nothing had ever developed but they had remained close friends. My father was the one she reached out to for comfort and guidance. He would always take her call and listen patiently as she described the latest drama involving Sir Richard, punctuating her long speeches with a strategic, "That's right, he needs to stop drinking," or "It's not your fault, Elizabeth." They talked for hours every day, and I would sit there impressed that my dad was helping the biggest movie star in the world through her difficulties.

Actors have a Herculean ability to maintain interest in themselves and their dramas. It's interesting that they seek guidance from those who have similar deficiencies in the very areas they wish help in. Why would Elizabeth talk to my father about her alcoholic marriage and not someone who had figured out how to stay married? Maybe she only liked getting married and getting divorced, not being married. There is quite a bit of drama in that. Maybe misery likes company. Maybe she still had a crush on my father. Anyway, after a month or two of this, my dad got bored, so one day he introduced the movie icon to his nineteen-year-old son over the phone.

"Elizabeth, I've got to run over to William Morris. Talk to Christopher."

Ms. Taylor hardly paused for breath, and before long, I became her Dear Abby.

ET:
Hi, Christopher.
Me:
Hi, Ms. Taylor.
ET:
Call me Elizabeth. Can you believe that son of a bitch is drinking again?
Me:
Uh, no. What son of a bitch is that?
ET:
Why Richard of course. I can't take it but I love him but I'm really sick of it but he needs me. What do you think?
Me:
Me?

175

ET:

Maybe I should give him another chance? He really is impossible but I love him. What do you think, Christopher?

Me:

Well . . .

ET:

Oh the hell with it, I'm going to divorce him—again. Life's too short. You know, Christopher, your father was my first crush and my first kiss.

Me:

No, I didn't know that.

ET:

Yep. You know, a girl never forgets her first crush. How old are you, Christopher?

Me:

Nineteen.

ET:

You're very wise for a nineteen-year-old.

I guess she needed someone to listen to her.

I got to know Elizabeth pretty well over the phone, so by the time she came to L.A. we were well enough acquainted to start hanging out.

One of the reasons we are so enamored with fame in general and movie stars in particular is that the closer we get to them, the more their specialness rubs off on us. Everybody wants to be special. For the average citizen, the more in the know they are about Brad and Jennifer, say, the more they participate in their rarefied existence vicariously. Well, when the biggest movie star in the world came to L.A., I was actually hanging out with her, so you can just imagine how special I was feeling. I saw so much of the biggest movie star in the world that people thought I was sleeping with her. Let's just say I didn't discourage the rumor.

One day I called up my friends who were hot rockers on the L.A. music scene and asked them if they wanted to go to Disneyland with me and Elizabeth Taylor.

I didn't have to ask twice.

We left by helicopter from the park on Coldwater Canyon in Beverly Hills. There were four helicopters in all: one for Elizabeth, Roddy McDowell, and the director George Cukor; one for hair and makeup; one for me and the boys in the band; and one for my dad and his new twenty-something girlfriend. My father didn't like being alone—it didn't take him long to find his next hostage. Elizabeth always seemed to be surrounded by gay men. Straight men were saved for necessary sex and drama.

The last time I had been to the Magic Kingdom was with David. We had trouble getting in because of our long hair and hippy wardrobe, the good people of Disney acquiescing after they found out we were Kennedys. There was long hair and inappropriate attire on this trip, but something told me we would not have a problem.

Our helicopters landed somewhere near the Matterhorn, and that's pretty much all I remember. See, I had brought a large supply of angel dust, which I smoked liberally. Angel dust, or PCP, is sprinkled on parsley leaves, giving off an odor most civilians assume belongs to some kind of fancy French cigarette. We were free to fry our synapses with impunity throughout the Kingdom.

One of the great benefits of going to Disneyland with the biggest movie star in the world is that you don't have to wait in line. We got to go on as many rides as we wanted, as many times as we wanted, and we did it all in under two hours. The great thing about going to Disney-land loaded on PCP is that even It's a Small World is a cool ride.

SOMETIME AFTER we returned from "the happiest place on earth" and I had recovered from all the angel dust consumed on Mr. Toad's Wild Ride, I decided to invite Elizabeth over to the Universal commis-sary for lunch. It was an innocent, albeit ill-conceived plan. There is nothing inappropriate about asking a friend to join you on your lunch hour for a ham sandwich in the company dining room. You run into problems when the friend is the biggest movie star in the world and the people you work for have egos the size of Texas.

My first mistake was not telling anybody. I just left her name at the front gate and went to meet her. She showed up more or less on time for an actress, and all hell broke loose. "Elizabeth Taylor is having a ham sandwich in the commissary" spread through the lot like wildfire. Soon Elizabeth and I were having lunch with pretty much everybody lucky enough to be on the Universal tour that day. The executives weren't happy because they couldn't get to their tables, and the bosses were pissed because there was a movie star on the lot walking around with an intern and not them. It was all kind of exciting and funny, but the result was that I lost the last little bit of goodwill I had left and soon after was dismissed. When I asked why I was being fired, the reason they gave me was that I had given an unescorted tour of the back lot to my cousin David, but I knew it was because I hadn't invited my boss to have lunch with the biggest movie star in the world.

SNAPSHOT:

> Henry was one of the many Hugh Hefner wannabes that populate L.A. He had a big house in the hills, good drugs, and great-looking girls hanging around his pool. I think he was a used-car mogul, but he saw himself differently. And so he worked very hard to create an environment that would attract the A-list to his faux mecca for sex and illicit substances.

I went to Henry's when nothing was happening at Hef's. On one of these excursions I brought the biggest movie star in the world with me. Henry loved me for it. He was smitten. I was clueless. The only thing I knew was that whenever I showed up anywhere with Elizabeth Taylor my stock went up, and Henry's playpen was no exception. At some point during the evening Henry sought me out and with his off-the-charts used-car-dealer smarm made a proposal:

Henry:
Chris, what do you think of my girlfriend?
Me:
I think she's hot, Henry, but she has a bit of a PCP problem.
Henry:
I know, but she gives great head.

Me:

What's your point, Henry?

Henry:

Well, I was thinking, maybe you can leave Elizabeth here
with me, and you can take my girl down the hill and do
whatever the hell you want with her.

Me:

Henry, are you suggesting I swap the biggest . . . movie
star . . . in . . . the . . . world for your PCP-addicted girlfriend?

Henry gave me his best used-car-dealer wink.

Now before you condemn me for being some form of low-life
white slaver, understand that I had no proprietary relationship with
Ms. Taylor. Hell, she had told some of the richest and most powerful
men on the planet what they could do with their plans and designs
concerning her. As far as I was concerned, the biggest movie star in the
world could make up her own mind about whether to stay with the
sleazy used-car dealer. As far as Angie was concerned, she might be ad-
dicted to PCP, but she was really hot and I kind of guessed she
wouldn't mind spending a little time with me. I was all for it, but I left
it up to Elizabeth.

Elizabeth thought about it for half a second and said yes. Say what
you will about actresses and their narcissistic preciousness, they sure
are spontaneous and fun. I poured Angie into my car and headed
down the hill to the lights of Hollywood. The next day Elizabeth told
me that five minutes after she had said yes she changed her mind, big
surprise, and went looking for me. She emerged from casa Henry just
in time to see my taillights leaving his driveway. She gave chase until
her ankle gave out, another big surprise, and was forced to hobble back
to face her decision.

Lest you think this deal only had to do with whom Elizabeth and I
were going to sleep with that night, you'd be wrong; it was nowhere
near so trivial. Elizabeth ended up staying with Henry for a couple of

years. It was the beginning of her descent into relationships with the Marginal Male. She got a good year or two of serious attention in the tabloids. After all, Henry was a used-car salesman, and she was the biggest movie star in the world. I got a two-year PCP habit and a threatened paternity suit, which necessitated another call to Uncle Steve.

SNAPSHOT:

I hadn't had a shot at twins since the Roach sisters in third grade. Like most sex-obsessed males of the seventies and eighties, the grail was sleeping with two females simultaneously, with a healthy supply of drugs to enhance the experience. I had spent a good deal of time lobbying my various girlfriends with limited success. It always got weird whenever we got close to actually doing it and it was never as good as I imagined. The two girls I met at the Whiskey on the Sunset Strip weren't really twins but they looked enough alike and were beautiful enough so that when they told me they were twins I didn't argue.

The Whiskey-A-Go-Go was a few blocks from my father's house on Cory Avenue and I used to hang out there listening to the great bands of the seventies, getting high, and trying to get girls to come home with me. Most nights all I got was good music and drunk enough to throw up in the parking lot, but tonight was different. This was one of those nights where everything seemed to be going my way. One of those nights when ease and grace combine to make anything possible. This can happen when all you have in mind are the more base pleasures in life. It's a waste of universal beneficence, but when it occurs, the drugs are good and free and every girl in the joint is checking you out.

For those of us with two grand trines in our astrological charts anything is possible—even twins. Bill Clinton has two grand trines in his chart and look what the universe gave him, Paula Jones notwithstanding.

From the moment I walked into the Whiskey they were on me. First with their eyes—then with more specific intent. We drank, danced, and snorted, the three of us, inseparable until the obvious movement to a place more private could not wait a moment longer.

My father had gone out of town and left me with the keys to the kingdom. He wouldn't be back for days, and the twins seemed willing to hang out as long as there were drugs available. The apartment on Cory Avenue was a treasure chest of illicit substances. The problem was that my dad had gotten pretty good at hiding them. I wasn't worried, it was a small apartment, and I had all weekend. If there was anything to be found, I'd find it.

I was standing in the middle of my father's bedroom, mirrors from floor to ceiling, with two gorgeous faux twins dancing around me in various stages of undress. I was rummaging through the medicine cabinet and thanking God for my good fortune when the phone rang. The little voice deep down inside of me that I never listened to was screaming, "So what, let it ring," but I have this compulsive relationship with the telephone. If there's a phone nearby I am compelled to use it, and if it rings, I'm toast. I think it has something to do with a fear that I might miss out on something. I had no idea what I could be missing out on that could compete with what was right in front of me, but I answered it anyway.

It was a musician friend. I had met him through my stepmother, Mary. I liked Mary's friends. They were musicians and actors close to me in age. He was a real talent who was writing his own ticket in the music business, but at this moment he was high on PCP, apparently getting the shit kicked out of him by four San Fernando Valley cops. This was pre–Rodney King, and this guy was white, so I had my doubts. I remembered being high on PCP at Lem's house in New York and watching the nuclear destruction of the city of Manhattan from his first-floor window. That drug can definitely fuck with your perception of reality.

"Chris, you've got to come get me. I'm in jail. I think these cops are going to kill me."

"Man, they're not going to kill you. They arrested you."

"Man, they kicked the shit out of me. I swear to God. They said the only way that I would leave this jail was in a body bag."

"Dude, are you sure? Because I'm just a little busy right now. Really busy right now."

"If you don't come and get me I'm going to die in a San Fernando Valley jail."

"Shit! I'll be there in an hour."

LEAVING THE twins and driving to a police station somewhere in the San Fernando Valley to pick up a potentially psychotic PCP addict was the last thing I wanted to do, but there is honor among thieves and loyalty between addicts, so off I went. I picked him up at a police station at the end of some road, and after making him swear to God and back again that he wouldn't smoke any more dust, I agreed to let him stay overnight at my dad's place. He was terrified the police were going to come to his house in the middle of the night and make good on their promise to kill him. I thought he might be a little delusional, but I took a chance. After all he was my friend.

I went to bed that night and I would like to believe I had the most amazing ménage à trois of my then twenty years but I don't remember. There are only three explanations for not being able to remember what happened that night. The first is I had taken so many drugs that I can't remember. Not likely. The second is nothing happened, and the memory of that would be too painful to allow. Also unlikely. The third and most probable reason I can't remember is the events of the following morning were so cataclysmic that all other recollection was blotted out.

I remember going out to breakfast, and all was good. I remember coming back to Cory Avenue after pancakes at Dupars and seeing the entire LAPD crawling on my dad's roof, and all was not good. I couldn't believe my eyes. It was like one of those scenes you see on the evening news of a massive law enforcement assault on a neighborhood crack house in South Central. But this was Beverly Hills. This kind of thing didn't happen here. There had to be some kind of mistake. Maybe they were visiting Lee Marvin's ex who lived downstairs. But wait, if they were visiting Michelle Marvin, why were they on my dad's balcony and in his living room. Shit! This was bad.

By the time I parked the car, the curious and indignant citizens of Beverly Hills had begun to gather. I assumed a curious posture covering my panic and blended in, asking one of the cops what all the commotion was about. He said some guy had gone crazy and climbed up on the roof and was threatening to jump off and kill himself. The cop couldn't be sure but he thought the house belonged to some famous Hollywood actor named Peter Lawford. Probably more information than he should have given me and definitely information I had no idea what to do with.

I made my way back to the car and the twins, who were on the edge of their seats and excited by all the men in uniform. I had lost interest. Shit gets real when you are looking at possible jail time for you and your old man. Girls don't seem quite as important. I drove to Sunset Boulevard, dropped the twins at a bus stop, and found a pay phone. I called my father's manager, Milt, who had been with my dad for twenty years and seen it all.

"Milt, there's a little problem at my dad's house."

"What's happening?"

"Well, there are about twenty Los Angeles police officers crawling all over the place right now."

"Shit!"

I could tell by the way he said "Shit" that he hadn't seen anything like this.

"Call Steve Smith."

"Do I have to?"

I REALLY did not want to call Uncle Steve. What was I going to tell him? He had just gotten me a job with the most influential man in Hollywood, and now I was going to ask him to extricate me from a potentially very public legal nightmare involving a drug-induced attempted suicide at my father's house, which at the moment was full of drugs and police.

I made the call.

Me:
Uncle Steve, it's your favorite nephew.
Uncle Steve:
What happened, Chris?

Me:
Well, I just got back from breakfast, and half of the LAPD is
crawling all over my dad's house.
Uncle Steve:
Why would they be doing that, Chris?
Me:
A friend of mine—well actually, more a friend of my
ex-stepmother's—was staying there. I have no idea what
he did.
Uncle Steve:
Are there any press there?
Me:
Not yet.
Uncle Steve:
Where's your father?
Me:
Out of town.
Uncle Steve:
Great! Give me a number where I can reach you. I'll get back
to you.

No wonder I never remember Uncle Steve answering the phone like
he was glad to hear from me.

I stood at that pay phone all day, fielding calls from Uncle Steve,
Milt, and finally my father, who was really not happy. The only silver
lining was that this PCP-impaired musician was first and foremost a
friend of Mary's, and this fact gave me some cover. My father called the
pay phone as the sun was setting.

Dad:
Christopher, what the hell happened?
Me:
I went out for breakfast, and when I came back there were
cops all over the house.
Dad:
We've got a problem! There's something in the back of my
closet that the cops cannot find.

Me:

What is it?

Dad:

A very big bag full of cocaine crammed into two of my boots.

Me:

What if they already found it?

Dad:

I don't even want to think about that possibility.

Me:

What do you want me to do?

Dad:

You and Erma should go in there tonight as if you are going
to clean up, and get rid of it.

Me:

How?

Dad:

Flush it down the toilet. And Christopher, don't do too much
of it before you flush! I called Erma. She'll meet you at the
apartment at eight P.M.

Me:

There's a cop guarding the place.

Dad:

Hopefully he'll be gone by then.

Me:

Shit. Okay. I'll call you when it's done.

Erma was used to cleaning up for my dad—but this was something
else. Each morning she would show up with my dad's dog Blackie,
who was an offspring of the Russian space dog Pushinka and my uncle
Jack's terrier, and clean up the mess from the night before. She had
seen it all, too. But tonight she was scared. I called my dad from the
corner to tell him the cop out front was still there. Did he still think we
should go? He said yes, but as I was about to hang up, he added, "Hey
buddy. If you can get the coke out of the house, do it! But only if you
think it's safe."

Erma and I arrived at the house after dark. She was more scared than I, but not by much. There was nobody out front. The cop had disappeared, which was good, but as soon as Erma's key hit the lock we were bathed in a bright spotlight and two of L.A.'s finest reappeared out of the darkness.

"What are you two doing here?"

Good question. Erma and I were stumped.

"Do you work here?" Stumped again.

And then Erma hit her stride. "I didn't come to work," she said. "It's Sunday. I got a call from Mr. Lawford's manager who said there had been some activity at the house, so I came by to fluff up the pillows."

Fluff up the pillows. Shit.

But the cops bought it, and we were left to do our fluffing. Those were the last words either of us spoke that night. We wrote notes to one another, in case the place had been bugged, as we went about our task of destroying incriminating evidence. I was twenty years old and wanted to earn my father's approval and to make amends for the situation I had created. But my instinct for survival told me that taking a pound of cocaine out of a house that was under surveillance by the LAPD was not a smart move. Still, as I flushed the coke down the toilet, snorting enough in the process to give me heart palpitations, it was tempting. Dad would have been happy.

But I wasn't about to accept the idea that the drugs were more important to him than I was.

That night I slept on my ex-stepmother's couch, uncertain whether I would be going to jail or back to Dad's after the cops finished their investigation. Mary had left my father because she couldn't take it anymore. My father's lifestyle—sex, drugs, and rock and roll—could be exhausting to watch except for the really committed and the very young. Fortunately, I was both. Mary was neither.

Once again the whole ugly mess was swept deep under someone's rug. I have no idea how it was done or who did it. It just got done.

My dad gave me a telephone credit card in high school with the admonishment not to use it very much "and whatever you do, don't give it to any of your cousins." Well, that didn't happen, and a few months later, people I knew started to get calls from the phone company. Soon after, I got a call from a very angry individual demanding one thousand dollars or threatening legal action for my fraudulent use of someone else's credit card. It turned out that I and a few of my friends had been reaching out to touch each other courtesy of Ed Sullivan. Somehow my dad had gotten hold of Ed's CBS calling card and I guess figured that since he had at one time worked for CBS, it was his calling card as well. I called Uncle Steve. It got handled and I didn't learn the lesson.

SNAPSHOT:

> I hadn't been to bed for days. My nineteen-year-old constitution coupled with the primo drugs enjoyed by Hollywood's A-list kept me running on empty far beyond what my precariously balanced psyche could endure. It was just a matter of time before I hit the wall. It happened on a Sunday. Bad shit always happened on Sunday. I hated Sunday. It was the seventh day, the day of rest, and all the liquor stores were closed. It was the day when those I ran with were recovering. As far as I was concerned, recovering was for wimps and amateurs. I would stop running when I was dead. Then I'd have plenty of time for recovering.

Hitting the wall feels more like walls crumbling. The demons I had kept at bay, unseen and unfelt since that winter day at Middlesex when the need for building the wall was revealed, suddenly came flooding into my consciousness. It was overwhelming. The dread and depression were enough to send me looking for a loaded shotgun. My father didn't have one and we were out of drugs.

I had no alternative but to give my father his shot at "handling the problem." I came out of my bedroom, catching my dad on his way out to dinner. "Dad, I've got to talk to you. Something is seriously wrong with me." At this point I lost it and tears streamed from my eyes as I struggled to continue. "What's the matter, Christopher?" My father never called me Christopher unless he was irritated with me or wanted to end the conversation. He usually called me Buddy. It was less intimate and satisfied his desire to keep our relationship on the "pal" plane.

After I had lived with him for a few months and we began exploring the intimate dimensions of the late night coke rap, he told me to call him Peter, something I was never able to do. My dad wished we were friends instead of father and son. It would have been easier for him.

"Dad, I can't take it anymore. I don't know what's the matter but I've got a hole in my gut and I feel like I want to die." Or some version of this.

I was asking for help. I was asking him to be my father.

"You've been taking too many drugs." My dad was good at stating the obvious.

No shit, I thought, as the snot dripped from my nose and I began to realize that I had revealed too much. This was one of those big-risk emotional moments. I had put my need out there because it felt like the only alternative. I had no idea what would come back. Now I knew. I frantically tried to reel it back in.

"Whatever, I'm sure I'll get over it."

"Take a sleeping pill and get some sleep. You'll feel better in the morning."

And he was gone.

The next day my dad tried to be helpful in his own way. Style and class, that was my old man's forte, so that's what I got.

Along with the Mongolian fold I was blessed with at birth, and which had proved helpful in the chick department, I was also given an abundance of body and facial hair. This was a mixed blessing. In my teens this hair gene had produced a rather pronounced unibrow, which kind of mitigated the whole bedroom eye thing. The day after my meltdown, my dad took it upon himself to identify my presentation flaw and offer a solution. He suggested I shave the middle, turning one eyebrow into two. It worked like a charm. My dad was pretty good at being a father in the style and presentation department.

SNAPSHOT:

Sunday night was movie night at the Playboy Mansion. My father was on the list, and by association so was I. In the 1970s, before the government went after The Man in the Pajamas for his contribution to America's moral turpitude, the Mansion, which sits off Sunset in Bel Air, was out of control. It was the place to party. Hef invited a hundred or so of his closest friends to watch the latest hot-off-the-movieola studio release, eat barbecue, get high on Hef's free booze and have orgy sex in the grotto. I kid you not, it was fantastic, but like all good things, it couldn't last. The rest of society can't tolerate it when a small segment is having this much fun. It had to come to an end, but before it did I got to taste what it might be like to live in Sodom and Gomorrah.

We would arrive at 7 P.M. for dinner and make our way into the library for the movie, which was always difficult to sit through, given the amount of chemicals I had ingested and the promise of what might come afterward. I was in my early twenties and just a little intimidated by the women I was rubbing up against. These were girls that the rest of the world was admiring only in pictures in Hef's magazine. I was out of my league, but that didn't stop me from trying. After the movie, I would follow Hef, the girls, and the movie stars into the grotto. The grotto was this huge cave with a dozen Jacuzzis, lit by candles, sur-rounded by luxurious little nooks with giant pillows—perfect for hav-ing sex with multiple partners. I would sit in the Jacuzzis and swim through the canals of water that went in and out of the grotto while the elders played their version of spin the bottle. I was out of the loop, but it was kind of cool watching Hugh Hefner getting a blow job from two of the most beautiful girls in the world. Still, there's only so much vi-carious sex a twenty-year-old can have without getting dreaded semen backup and the anxious depression that usually accompanies it.

One night I met a girl who seemed to like me. She was beautiful and didn't have that radar for the rich and powerful most of the women walking around Hef's house had. I made a date with her for the next Sunday at the Mansion. I showed up with flowers and first-date jitters. Her name was Tiffany, and she was waiting for me in a red dress and with a glass of vodka. Perfect. We talked and strolled the grounds, played the pinball machines in the game room, finally finding our way to one of the bedrooms connected to one of the little cottages tucked away on the property. Tiffany kissed me like she was on fire. It was a little scary. I had never had a romantic encounter with a girl who was acting more like the guy. After about twenty minutes of intense foreplay she broke it off suddenly and said she couldn't go any further. It turned out she had a boyfriend who was in the porn business and had a nasty temper. His name was John Holmes. She said his name like she thought I would know it. But I had never seen a porno film. I had never heard of John Holmes and didn't understand why the girlfriend of a guy who spent his days having sex with a lot of different girls on camera would think he would mind if his girlfriend had sex with a desperate twenty-year-old at the Playboy Mansion.

I never saw Tiffany again. L.A. is a transient town, especially in the circles I was traveling. People disappeared right after I met them, phone numbers were good for a month, good friends and long relationships lasted weeks. I wasn't too upset that Tiffany had disappeared. I knew John Holmes was a porn star because Tiffany had told me and I was a little intimidated. If I had known his cock was thirteen inches long I would have fled before she did. My brief encounter with John Holmes's girlfriend gave me reason to hope, though, that I might actually get laid at the Playboy Mansion. I had finally hit a single, when all I had been doing was whiffing.

A couple weeks later I was walking around Hef's pad on movie night, and I bumped into two girls who weren't looking for a bigger, better deal. We had a great time all night, finally ending up in the grotto naked and really high. I was too intimidated to make a move — there were two of them; one was the most beautiful girl I had ever seen and the other was probably the fourth most beautiful girl I had ever seen. I certainly never thought I would see girls this hot, naked, in such close proximity. It was more than I could handle at twenty. They were a little disappointed. When we left the grotto to get dressed and leave, they were looking at me as if they had picked the wrong guy. I left that night feeling like a putz and wondering whether the Mansion was doing anything for my self-esteem. I was beginning to think I should take a break. Than I came to my senses, realizing I had just spent the evening with two playmates, eating, drinking, and getting high while we sat in Hef's Jacuzzi naked. Get back on the horse, I thought. Next Sunday meant another new movie, another bevy of beauties, and another shot at getting laid.

It was not to be. The following Sunday, when I called the Mansion to put my name on the list for movie night, I was told I would not be welcome that Sunday or any Sunday in the foreseeable future. I panicked. What was going on? What had I done? No! This can't be happening. What am I going to do on Sunday night in L.A. if I can't go up to Hef's?

Hef had two secretaries who handled movie night and probably a lot of other shit. They were former playmates who had seen their day. One was a bitch and wouldn't tell me anything; the other liked me and took pity. Apparently, the incredibly gorgeous girl that I didn't make a move on in the grotto was on Hef's rotation. Meaning she was off-limits, and Hefner thought I had fucked her. I told the nice secretary nothing had happened, but it didn't matter. Hef probably didn't believe me. I mean I was in the grotto naked with the girl for an hour and a half. Who's gonna believe nothing happened? Even if he did believe me, he probably couldn't let me back. It's a pride thing, you know, like with gangsters. Hef is like the Don of sex. He can't be made to look bad. Somebody has to take a hit. So I was barred from the Playboy Mansion for having sex with one of Hef's girls whom I didn't even have sex with. Talk about bad luck.

Chapter 20

None of us can help the things life has done to us. They're done
before you realize it, and once they're done they make you do
other things until at last everything comes between you and
what you'd like to be, and you have lost yourself forever.
— EUGENE O'NEILL

After an exhausting year trying to keep up with the heavyweights in Hollywood, I moved back East to attend college.

I wanted to go to Harvard. I had grown up with that as part of the plan. Bobby and David were both there, and I had the ultimate recommendation: Robert Coles, a Harvard icon.

> *I write to recommend strongly Christopher Lawford, a sensitive,*
> *thoughtful, idealistic and thoroughly honorable young man,*
> *who possesses an unusual mix of analytic skill and*
> *compassion. He has lived an interesting life; has worked on*
> *behalf of others, less fortunate; is a decent and generous*
> *person; and will become, I believe, a valuable person, indeed,*
> *in the coming years.*

Robert Coles was one of the premier social historians in the country, having written the influential series of books entitled *Children of Crisis*. He taught one of the most popular courses at the college. He was also a great admirer of my uncle Bobby, which I think is why he overlooked my shortcomings. It was common knowledge that if he wrote you a recommendation you'd get in. He wrote one for Bobby, one for David, and one for me. They got in. I didn't.

I got into Tufts University, which is located in the town of Medford, Massachusetts—right next to Cambridge. I wasn't at Harvard with Bobby and David, but I was right next door. I spent more time at Harvard than I did at Tufts, which didn't do much for my academic or social performance.

Tufts University was the college that P. T. Barnum made famous by donating a stuffed elephant named Jumbo. Jumbo burned up in a huge fire, which occurred while I was a student at Tufts, a fire I was oblivious to. Years later, when I brought my son David to look at the school, I asked the nice student guide who was showing us around, "What ever happened to Jumbo?" You either have to be very stoned or not around much to miss the biggest fire in the school's history, which destroyed the nationally recognized school mascot. I was both.

I arrived in 1973 at the college as a drama major but quickly changed majors after coming face-to-face with the incestuous nature of university drama departments and how terrified I still was of acting. I had convinced Dr. Coles to write a letter to the dean documenting my imagined social phobias, making it impossible for me to honor the requirement that all freshmen live on campus their first year. I was serious about hanging with my cousins. This unfortunate choice meant I never really got to know any of my classmates. The only instinct I had to socialize with other Jumbos (what Tufts students are called) was when exam time rolled around and I needed to borrow someone's notes from all the classes I hadn't bothered to attend.

Years later, when I was doing press for the film I produced and acted in—*Kiss Me, Guido*—I went on *The View*, the daytime talk show with all those well-informed women, Barbara Walters et al. Meredith Vieira, who is well informed and well formed, came up to me before air and said, "You don't remember me, do you?"

I panicked, quickly scanning my damaged memory banks for a clue as to who this woman was who was about to interview me on national TV. Nothing.

Then she said, "We went to school together."

Still nothing.

"At Tufts."

Nada, zippo, not a clue. I was beginning to sweat.

Then, "We took Sol Gittleman's Yiddish Lit class together."

Now we were getting somewhere. Sol Gittleman I remember. He was the best teacher at Tufts and maybe on the planet. He taught the Holocaust and Yiddish literature and made the history and mysticism of Judaism come to life. If I could have gotten off my ass in college, I would have converted and become a Jew—that's how powerful Sol Gittleman was as a teacher. Him I remember, but on Meredith I was still drawing a blank.

"You borrowed my notes for the final and said we were going to go out."

"Oh!"

"I never saw you again after the final." Oops!

"Sorry. I was a little fucked-up in college."

"Yeah, I guessed that."

"Hey, Meredith, you're not gonna tell that story on the air, are you?"

She smiled impassively. "No, I wouldn't do that to you. After all, you are a guest on my show."

The first words out of Meredith Vieira's mouth as I walked out onto *The View*'s set at ABC Studios in front of a live audience were, "Chris and I go way back, all the way to college, where he stood me up after I gave him my notes. . . ."

Hell hath no fury. . . .

PETER KAPLAN was Bobby's roommate at Harvard. He was smart and a great writer. So was his brother Jimmy. Neither one of them had been west of New York, so when they sold a pitch to *Harper's Magazine* to cover the 1973 Academy Awards, they needed someone to keep them from getting lost in Hollywood. They invited me along to open some doors and take a few photographs to go along with their words.

The three of us landed in L.A., checked into a shitty motel off the Sunset Strip, and called my father. My dad was kinda glad to hear from me. I mean he was glad that I was in L.A. and wanted to see me, but he was less than thrilled when I asked him if he could introduce me to some of his celebrity friends as some background color for our article on the 1973 Academy Awards.

The next day he called and told me to be at his house at 7 P.M. Some friends were going to drop by and he thought they might work for the article.

Peter, Jimmy, and I had some tuxedos to rent, so off we went to Sol's Tuxedo Rentals. The Kaplans ordered up two of Sol's cheapest tuxes; I found a gray number with a ruffled shirt and some style for a bit more money. That night we showed up at my father's house on Cory Avenue. There was a party going on.

My dad was entertaining some mates from England—John Lennon, Ringo Starr, and Mick Jagger. Yeah, this will work. The rock stars had brought their women, so the Kaplan brothers and I spent the evening ogling Bianca, getting high, and playing pool with the boys. Peter and Jimmy had a few beers and stayed away from the drugs but I had whatever the fellas were having. We played eight ball. My dad and I against Lennon and Starr. My father and I won. I don't remember saying much that night, except, "It's your shot, Ringo," or "You want some of this joint, Mick?" I tried to be casual about it all, but I spent the night in disbelief. I was hanging with icons, and my old man had actually delivered. It was a good night. Later we all went out to some clubs. We stopped by my dad's club in Beverly Hills called the Candy Store and from there made our way to see Tommy Smothers at the Troubador. Mick took off with Bianca—wouldn't you?—leaving Lennon and Ringo behind. Lennon got drunk and surly with a waitress during Tommy's act; he was enduring one of his forced exiles from Yoko. His rudeness pissed my father off, words were exchanged, they shoved each other, and both marched off in righteous indignation.

The next day my dad got a big basket of flowers and a note:

Dear Peter,
I have no words to express how sorry I am for my bad manners.
I hope you can find it in your heart to forgive me. I can only

say I am not usually so rude or so drunk. Actually, I'm a quiet
neurotic, who took a little bit too much "Dutch Courage"!
Again, I humbly apologize,

John Lennon

P.S. Please accept these flowers as a peace token.

After the Troubador fiasco, we all went back to my dad's where he entranced the Kaplan brothers with stories of old Hollywood. The day L. B. Mayer had my father into his office and accused him of being a homosexual. Mr. Mayer told my father not to worry because he was going to "send him to a doctor who would cure him with a series of shots." My father told Mr. Mayer that he wasn't homosexual and that if he didn't believe him he could talk to Lana Turner.

My old man went out with some of the most beautiful women who had ever lit up the silver screen. Ava Gardner, Rita Hayworth, and Betty Grable to name a few. I asked him one day who was the best lover. Without hesitation he said Lana Turner. When he was under contract to MGM, Lana Turner used to come pick him up and take him to the studio. She did this every morning for eight months without fail until one day when she didn't show up. She disappeared for a week. My dad was dying inside, but he would never show it. My father never showed his feelings unless he wanted you to see them. He was an actor, after all. One day he got a call at the studio. It was Lana.

My dad picked up the phone and said, "Hey, baby, how are you?" as if nothing was amiss. "Where are you?"

Lana said, "Boston. I'm with Gene Krupa," and that was the end of Miss Turner.

It took a year for my dad to get over it.

I asked him about Marilyn Monroe, and he told me he never slept with her because she had bad hygiene. My dad was real particular about clothing and hygiene.

I went to bed that night with the knowledge that my dad had done something big for me, and that felt better than getting high and shooting pool with rock stars.

The night of the Academy Awards, the Kaplan brothers and I

showed up in our tuxedos with press credentials, eager to soak up all that is Oscar. Peter and Jimmy were the writers and therefore had better seating. I was stuck in the balcony, where I discovered, to my horror, that all the ushers in the Dorothy Chandler Pavilion were wearing *my tuxedo*.

I spent the evening explaining to people that "I don't work here." And "No, I have no idea where your seat is."

Sometimes the more expensive tuxedo is not the better tuxedo.

Sitting in the upper balcony and being mistaken for an usher all night definitely dampened the Oscar experience for me. The Kaplans loved it and headed off to the official parties after the show. I didn't have a ticket, but my dad came to the rescue again and invited me to tag along with him to Sammy Davis's house for an after-Oscar party.

Sammy Davis and my dad stayed buddies throughout their lives. Frank and my dad never recovered from the Bing Crosby fiasco, and Dean Martin stayed pissed at my old man for disappearing with a cute little actress that Dean had spent the night wooing at a party in Paris, lamenting, "Whatever happened to all for one and one for all?" Sammy and my dad were different. Their friendship survived the rigors of show business and fame. They did the Rat Pack thing, made two buddy movies about two guys named Charles Salt and Christopher Pepper—*Salt and Pepper* and *One More Time*—and remained friends to the bitter end. Sammy sent my dad a telegram during his last stint at Betty Ford promising a third Salt and Pepper movie.

MY DAD was one of the only people I have ever known who was truly oblivious to a person's skin color. His upbringing, traveling the world, had exposed him to dozens of races. Despite the racism and anti-Semitism of his own mother, my dad had learned from a young age to judge a person by who they were and not to stereotype. I had heard the story about the time he crossed paths with my grandfather, Joseph P., while parking cars in Palm Beach as a kid. According to legend, he and his two African American coworkers would have their lunch under a tree at the side of the unpaved lot and play penny-ante poker. This was put to an end one day when my grandfather saw the three boys and complained to the owner that this kind of interracial fraternizing was bad for business.

My dad called me one day in Boston after Richard Pryor had blown himself up smoking cocaine. Richard was in the hospital dying from third-degree burns and my dad wanted me to call my uncle Teddy to see if he would call Richard in the hospital. My father figured that a call from my uncle would mean a great deal to the comedian, and my dad wanted to do something meaningful for his friend. I vetoed the idea, thinking that my uncle wouldn't want to become embroiled in a drama involving the controversial drug-addicted entertainer. At the time I didn't know why I thought this way, but the thought of passing along my father's request to my uncle filled me with unease. It had to do with perception and respectability. The shenanigans of Hollywood would never be dignified enough to be brought to the Washington table. In time I came to see that the players from these two worlds were feeding at the same trough, with similar deficiencies in integrity. My dad was just trying to do something for a friend. I couldn't see it. I wish I had.

I THOUGHT there might be something happening at Sammy's that would be good for our article, so I brought my notebook and camera. Wrong. All we did was watch Sammy on some late-night talk show, listen to Sammy's new record, and watch a rough cut of Sammy's new film. It was a Sammy fest, which isn't a bad thing. Sammy Davis was one talented motherfucker. My dad told me that Sammy was the best tap dancer he had ever seen; but tap was a bitch, and Sammy didn't want to work that hard. So I sat on my ass and watched Sammy Davis perform in three different mediums while the Kaplans painted the town with the more current movie stars of Hollywood.

I'M A starfucker—just like the rest of America. You'd think that, having grown up in America's royal family, I wouldn't be enamored of fame. You'd be wrong.

My mom dragged me to all sorts of wonderful musical theater in New York when I was growing up. The stuff the whole country wanted to see: *Hello, Dolly!* with Carol Channing; Philip Schofield playing *Doctor Doolittle; The Nutcracker;* all the classic shit—and I hated every minute of it. The worst part was, after the curtain dropped, we had to follow my mother backstage to say hello to the performers I had just endured for two and one half hours. These were particularly mortifying moments for me. It elongated the experience by forty-five minutes, which was bad enough, but on top of that, the whole saying-hello-to-the-stars-in-their-dressing-rooms routine made me nervous, and I had to bow and scrape as my mother gushed all over whoever it was who had just "entertained" us.

People act differently around the famous, and my family was no exception. We are conditioned from an early age to understand that fame makes you special and being special gets you a lot of extra stuff. It's crazy that people would want to be around actors and fawn on them if they didn't have any real affinity for the work they did. Most of the ones I've met aren't that interesting. They are famous, though, and for most of us, that's enough. To my family it was more than that. Like everything else, it came down to power.

In 1961 my father was asked by my grandfather and the newly elected president to produce the gala that takes place the evening following the inauguration of the new president. Together with Frank Sinatra, my old man put together the most star-studded gala to date. Along with the Rat Pack there were over thirty of the biggest stars from the world of entertainment, including Laurence Olivier, Anthony Quinn, Sidney Poitier, Frederic March, Ella Fitzgerald, Ethel Merman, Nat King Cole, Tony Curtis, Janet Leigh, Milton Berle, and Harry Belafonte. Never before had such an invasion of talent landed on the shores of the Potomac. On the night, my uncle Jack said, "The happy relationship between arts and politics which has characterized our long history I think reached a culmination tonight. . . . I know we are all indebted to a great friend—Frank Sinatra. . . . And I want him and my sister Pat's husband, Peter Lawford, to know that we're all indebted to them, and we're proud to have them with us."

A few months later my uncle decided Frank was a political liability and left it to my father to give him the bad news. So much for indebtedness.

My grandfather hired an NBC crew to film the evening, and my father was supposed to bring the footage back to L.A. and put together some kind of show. Shortly after the event, my grandfather had a stroke, leaving the fate of the gala footage very much up in the air. My uncle's death in 1963 killed any interest in the material on the part of my family and it languished in a film vault in Hollywood until my father's death.

I wanted to complete the work, but I needed to get the family's okay to do a film on the synergistic relationship between Hollywood and Washington—with the centerpiece being the footage of President Kennedy's inaugural gala. The okay was hard to get.

My family doesn't fuck around when it come to maintaining The Image. Even if you're in the family, it's not easy. I jumped through hoops, finally getting a letter from my aunt Eunice.

Dear Chris,
I believe you spoke with Jay Emmet about the possibility of making a film on President Kennedy's inauguration, specifically on the evening events.
I understand from Jay that the Foundation will have veto power over the film in case it does not give correct impressions of President Kennedy.
With that veto power in mind, I think that you could go ahead and develop the film as you see fit.

Kind regards,
Eunice Kennedy Shriver

SNAPSHOT:

In 1974 I was wading through my sophomore year at Tufts and Richard Nixon was drowning in Watergate. William Simon was Nixon's treasury secretary. I didn't know it at the time, but the secretary of the treasury can order Secret Service protection for those in need of it. I suppose the president can order it too, but given Richard Nixon's preoccupation with Woodward and Bernstein and his hostile relationship with my family, I would not have wanted to rely on him making the call if a member of my family were in need of protection.

It turned out that sometime in the fall of 1974 the FBI got a tip from one of their informants, who happened to be a Hell's Angel, that a particularly nasty chapter of the motorcycle gang was planning to kidnap a Kennedy. The informant didn't know which Kennedy, so on a crisp fall day in Boston, my cousins Joe, Bobby, and David got their very own Secret Service details. What these motorcycle geniuses thought they were going to get by kidnapping one of my cousins I have no idea, but I knew that if they took Joe, Bobby, or David they were going to get a handful. Getting Secret Service protection meant that three guys with earpieces and no-nonsense attitudes would follow them everywhere they went until the threat dissipated.

Hey, wait a minute, I'm a Kennedy. Why didn't I get a detail of guys with earpieces and interesting little code medallions on their lapels?

I didn't dare speak my thought out loud for fear that my feeling of second-class status would be revealed to my cousins. It didn't make it easier when David offered to have "one of my guys drop you off at school, if you want."

"No thanks, man, I can drive myself."

Then, "Hey man, it's too bad you didn't get a detail of your own. We could have a football game. Me and my guys against you and your guys."

David was a master at rubbing your nose in it.

"Yeah, man, too bad."

So it went for a couple days until one day I was sitting in Professor Senelick's Modern American Playwrights class. There was a knock on the door. Professor Senelick, who was very serious and dramatic about the drama he taught, answered with the irritation of the knower having to endure the petty distractions of the unknown.

He opened the classroom door to one of those tall, serious-looking white guys with the earpiece and secret button on his lapel, who motioned him out into the hallway. When Professor Senelick returned, he no longer had the smug look of an academic god, but instead the look of someone whose reality had been invaded by the bigger forces of real-world good and evil. He motioned for me to come out into the hallway, where I was introduced to Secret Service Agent Hess.

I was living with my cousin Bobby in an apartment just outside of Harvard Square, equidistant between Tufts and Harvard. I scurried back to the apartment with my very own Secret Service detail, eager to serve notice that I was enough of a Kennedy for the Hell's Angels to want to kidnap me.

The apartment was a two-bedroom with a porch (where we used to practice our knife-throwing), hardly big enough to accommodate Bobby and me, our girlfriends, and six big guys with earpieces. Anyway we didn't really want the guys in the house. They weren't cops, but they probably could and would arrest us for some of the shit that was going down in the apartment on Concord Avenue.

It turned out that the reason for my tardy detail was that the brain-surgeon bikers who were going to kidnap a Kennedy thought that Ethel Kennedy was married to Peter Lawford.

My cousins and I figured if these Hell's Angels idiots couldn't get who was married to whom right, we weren't in much danger. So we just enjoyed the attention and the extra bodies for touch football. Bobby and I had a party one night to celebrate his birthday. All the nefarious characters in Cambridge showed up, having to pass through the gauntlet of earpieces stationed out front. The party raged into the wee hours and somebody took a leak out one of the upstairs windows, soaking one of the agents posted outside. We didn't hear about it until we read it in a Jack Anderson column a few weeks later. We didn't believe it actually happened. Not that the partygoers weren't capable of urinating out a window, but we knew how fast those Secret Service agents were. We had been playing football with them for a week. There was no way one of them would get doused by urine from a second-story window. By the time the article appeared, our guys had been reassigned to targets under more imminent threat, so we had no way of checking the veracity of Mr. Anderson's information. We figured it was just another tactic used by the Republicans to discredit our family.

I TRANSFERRED to Georgetown University from Tufts in my junior year to take advantage of one of the finest American Studies programs in the country. I moved into an apartment in Georgetown that happened to be in the same neighborhood as a commune of heroin addicts, kind of a junkie's "welcome wagon." I fit right into the neighborhood. Say good-bye to Jefferson and Fitzgerald and hello to oblivion and emergency rooms. I was hanging out with people who I thought were colorful, but later came to realize they were just lower companions.

There were two profound occurrences that year in the nation's capitol as I scrambled to fulfill the academic requirements of the Jesuits and the increasing demands of my drug addiction. The first I realized the implications of right away, but the other's effects remained hidden for twenty years.

Snapshot:

Daniel and Philip Berrigan were Catholic priests who became activists for nonviolence in opposition to the Vietnam War. Like everyone else in America I had seen the Berrigan brothers on the cover of *Time* magazine. In spite of the activism in my family and the social and political anarchy of the time, they scared me. As a young white boy growing up in American affluence I was afraid of those in the society who were advocating radical change. Malcolm X and Martin Luther King were black and scary. I remember the evening newspaper announcing Dr. King's assassination arriving at my mother's comfortable and safe Fifth Avenue apartment and being confused as to whether his murder was a good or a bad thing.

This seems insane to me now, but at the time all I knew about Dr. King was that he was black and he was making a lot of white people uneasy. The Berrigans were priests, more familiar and therefore not as threatening, but equally difficult to comprehend for a thirteen-year-old. Looking back I understand that although my family was perceived to be a force for the disenfranchised and dispossessed, those of us growing up in the family were living with all the trappings of the ruling class.

I took a class with Philip Berrigan at Georgetown, on nonviolent civil disobedience. In it the good father would provoke us with questions like, "If you were walking down the street with your girlfriend and a mugger attacked you, would you kill him to protect your girlfriend's life?" Heavy shit like that.

Berrigan challenged our ideas about justifiable force and what responsibility those of us in a society have when governments move beyond the will of the people. The teachings weren't restricted to classroom theory. Those who were willing went on field trips to air shows and other gatherings where military hardware was on display. Berrigan believed that Vietnam was "a war run to show the world, and particularly the Third World, where exactly it stands in relation to our technology." The students would hold signs advocating peace and nonviolence while the good father and some of the more committed would throw cups of their collected blood onto the machines of war. I opted for holding a sign. I rationalized that my resulting arrest from pouring my blood into the cockpit of an F-14 fighter would be a public embarrassment that I didn't have the right to inflict on my family.

This came up a lot for me—balancing my public persona with that of my family. Nobody ever said I couldn't be a radical, but I didn't feel like I had the right. The truth was that I was scared and would never let myself go enough to find out whether I had the soul of someone who would take drastic action for a belief. There just seemed to be too much at stake. I guess this is what anyone who makes a stand outside the norm must confront. I would choose instead to follow a more destructive and secretive path. A path that would bring public embarrassment for no higher purpose.

My political indoctrination began at my birth. My introduction to the political process was initiated at the highest level. There was never any question that I was a liberal Democrat, and my expectation was that one day I could be president. This was America—any kid could grow up to be president—and because of the family I grew up in, I had a bit of a head start. It was normal to think that anybody in my family could hold high elective office if they wanted to. It's what we did.

Snapshot:

My first glimpse of my political truth came when I went to work for Ramsey Clark in his unsuccessful bid for a Senate seat from New York. Ramsey had been assistant attorney general under my uncle Bobby and attorney general under LBJ. Ramsey Clark was as different as you could get from a Kennedy and still be on the same ideological planet. He was a tall lanky Texan, not particularly good-looking, with an awkward propensity for telling the truth. He spoke with the gentleness and hesitancy of a man who knew he didn't have all the answers. He was unapologetically liberal bordering on radical. He never had a chance of getting elected—it didn't seem to bother him.

My mother contributed money to the Clark campaign and suggested her son go to work on the campaign to see how the other half runs. I had only known Kennedy campaigns, where people were paying attention and the lifeblood of American politics—money— flowed freely and often. Nobody paid attention to Ramsey and fewer contributed. I was an all-purpose campaign worker. I helped with position papers, did advance, traveled with the candidate, and got coffee for the campaign director, Mark Green. My favorite job was traveling with Ramsey. My least favorite job was getting coffee for Mark.

What struck me was that for the first time I was seeing a political candidate who seemed to have a life and identity outside of politics. Good thing, because he got creamed. The other thing that struck me was the humility with which he approached running for office and his alternating pain at injustice and anger at the arrogance of the powerful. He was an outsider. All I had ever known were insiders.

Ramsey Clark wasn't even a blip on the political radar screen, but his influence on me was profound. I learned that it is possible to be who you are when you are an outsider. I also learned that my politics were more radical than my family's politics.

. . .

THE SECOND epiphany occurred when I awoke in the small studio apartment in Georgetown with a heroin habit and the frightening realization that I could no longer "just say no." For the first time in the seven years since taking that first tab of LSD at thirteen, I couldn't walk away from the drugs.

The fellas who lived nearby had an inexhaustible supply of some really good heroin and it was cheap. There is no mystery to heroin addiction. Heroin makes you feel like you are floating on infinite promise. Moving from this world to the next on a cloud, in the absence of pain. To quote Ewan McGregor's character, Renton, in *Trainspotting*, "imagine the best orgasm you have ever had and multiply it by a thousand and you're still nowhere near it." Once you have done heroin, it is very difficult not to do it again. Do it enough and it owns you.

I've heard addiction described as like dancing with an 800-pound gorilla. You keep dancing until the gorilla stops dancing. Well, my 800-pound gorilla went into full Macarena. I didn't know what to do. I called my doctor in Boston.

Me:
Doctor, it's Chris, I'm having a little problem down here.
Doctor:
What's the problem?
Me:
Well, I'm not really sure. I don't feel good. I've been doing a lot of heroin and I woke up this morning feeling like I had the flu and there were ants crawling in my bones.
Doctor:
That doesn't sound good. Maybe you should stop doing the heroin.
Me:
Yeah, but in the meantime I think I need something to stop the ants from crawling.

Doctor:
Well, I'm not sure that's the best solution.
Me:
Look, Doc, I'm coming out of my skin here. You've got to
help me out.
Doctor:
I'll call something in for you this time, but you are going to
have to find a more permanent solution to your problem.
Me:
Yeah, yeah, I will. Thanks, Doc. I'll have the pharmacy call
you.

I would spend the next ten years convincing doctors to medicate my addiction.

I left Georgetown with a drug habit and returned to finish out my college career at Tufts. The Jesuits were tougher than I thought, and their robes gave me the heebie-jeebies. Tufts would let me graduate in three and a half years with a work-study at the end of my senior year. Tufts would have the honor of handing me a diploma. After that, it was time for this young man to go west again.

Chapter 21

People are slaves to what they see, not what they know.
— ANONYMOUS

Although I prayed for an intervening miracle that would illuminate another path, I figured I'd end up in law school like everyone else in my family. So, in the summer of 1977 I decided that having a little legal experience under my belt couldn't hurt. I had no idea when I applied for a summer internship in the Los Angeles District Attorney's Office that they would stick me in the Organized Crime and Narcotics Division. I felt a bit awkward about it but thought that my real-life experience might actually give me a leg up. I was also eager to gain insight into how law enforcement was dealing with the drug problem. It might come in handy.

BUT FIRST I had some fun planned with my cousin Steve Smith and longtime friend Peter Emerson in Cabo San Lucas. I hopped on a plane at Kennedy Airport headed for L.A. and settled comfortably in first class. I didn't have a first-class ticket but that didn't matter. I sat up front all the time and when they asked me if I belonged there I said yes with so much conviction they usually believed me. If they wanted to see my ticket, I told them I lost it. Before computers, this worked like a charm. It wasn't working on this flight. The first-class flight attendant somehow knew I wasn't suppose to be in seat 3A and she wanted me to acknowledge it by moving to 24B.

"Mr. Lawford, I think you may be in the wrong seat."

"No, I'm sure this is the seat they gave me at the gate. If I could just find my ticket . . ."

"Mr. Lawford, I believe you are suppose to be sitting in seat 24B."

"That's not possible. I'm certain the travel agent booked me a first-class ticket."

"I don't think so, sir."

"Let's call her."

"The door has already been closed."

"Well, I guess we'll have to call her when we get to L.A."

My charm was lost on this woman but I wasn't moving. I had already consumed three rum and Cokes and there was a girl sitting in 2A who had shown some interest in joining the mile-high club. I held my seat but never made it into the bathroom with the girl in 2A because the flight attendant never stopped glaring at me.

I was met at the gate of LAX by six of L.A.'s finest. They offered me a choice: jail or pay the first-class fare. I paid and headed out to meet my boys for our road trip to Mexico. I found Emerson blending in with the terminal crowd, trying to look inconspicuous. "I was making my way to your gate when I saw the LAPD welcoming party. Somehow I knew they were going to meet your plane."

Cabo was uneventful. We tipped some cows on the way down and assumed alter egos. Mine was a version of Elvis Presley and a Hare Krishna guy. Emerson's was a secret agent guy, and Steve was a smarter version of Hunter Thompson. We dressed the parts and I had enough drugs for me to keep it real.

It was all becoming less and less interesting to me, but I didn't know how to get off the merry-go-round. I had made it through college. Now life was going to get a bit more serious. I didn't want to be serious—I'd rather be Elvis. The thing about drug addiction is that all the good intentions and willpower in the world don't mean shit. I wanted to get my life together and move down a road of purpose and accomplishment, but once the monkey climbs on your back it's tough to get him off.

I returned to L.A. and showed up for my summer job at the D.A.'s office with the enthusiasm of the condemned.

My job turned out to be keeping track of the drug arrests in L.A. County. Hardly the insight I was looking for.

After work I would head home to the house I was renting in Beverly Glenn with my sister Sydney, my girlfriend Gina, and our friends John and Mitch in the hope that I would not become one of the statistics I was keeping track of for the Los Angeles district attorney.

The job was monotonous but the house was another story. We had the who-gets-which-room? drama, and John and Mitch were in a catfight all summer. John is gay and Mitch is straight but anal. Mitch became convinced early on that John was stealing his clothes: "You know *they* love giving clothes and presents to their boyfriends." I had no idea how Mitch knew this or how he could have known if any of his shit was missing—he showed up with two trunks, six hang-up bags, and a suitcase of toiletries for a month in L.A.—but you know those anal types, they sure can keep track of their shit. All this drama was making me antsy. I needed something strong to take the edge off. I had been staying relatively clean. Spending my days with D.A.s and sheriffs' deputies helped, as did living with my girlfriend and sister. If I was going to dance with the gorilla, I was going to have to do it alone.

I found a connection for heroin in the South Bay. I took a trip with some surfer dudes who knew a guy who was selling the brown Mexican heroin that came in a balloon and was as good as anything that had been on the West Coast for a while. The dudes drove a VW bus that had seen better days. It did forty miles per hour going downhill. We found the guy with the tattoos who sold smack out of a knapsack while cruising around Manhattan Beach on a skateboard. The ride back to Beverly Glenn was excruciatingly long, with the Mexican brown talking shit to me as we crawled along the 405: "I'm waiting, dude. What's taking so long? I really want out of this balloon and into a cooker." The surfers dropped me off at my house. I made my way through a chorus of questions about where I'd been, to the bathroom and peace. The last thing I remember was pushing down the plunger. I came to with two

EMS guys working on me while my sister and girlfriend cried in the background.

They were right about it being kick-ass heroin. I was out before I hit the floor. John and Mitch put aside their differences long enough to break down the bathroom door, where I was revealed in all my glory, needle in arm and frothing from the mouth. I was laid up for a couple of days and had to dance around some uncomfortable questions, but as soon as I was vertical I was back on the horse.

Most people think addicts are lazy and weak with serious moral deficiencies. To all those who have this impression I would suggest they ask themselves how long they might function in this world carrying an 800-pound gorilla on their back that punches you in the face all day. Most alcoholics and addicts I have come across have enormous will and fortitude. Their addiction has more to do with a physical allergy than with morality. For much of my active addiction I was more or less functional and ethical. There was the occasional overdose, arrest, or unexplained outburst, but after a flurry of concerned activity the veil of denial descended and we all went about our lives until the next crisis. Addiction also demands that the occasional crisis occur with ever-increasing frequency and severity.

An addict's pat answer for dealing with these crises is the geographic. Things will always be better "over there." I had a doozy of a geographic up my sleeve. I tried to sell it to my mother in a letter I wrote to her while she was cruising the Mediterranean on a rich guy's yacht. After setting her up with oblique references to a summer of insanity and madness, I assured her that "This insanity has nothing whatsoever to do with me wanting to depart L.A. early and head for the Amazon with all it's snakes, bugs, diseases and head-hunters. . . . California is beginning to grate on the old nerves. It's not anything that can't be swept under the rug with relative ease but. . . ."

I didn't break with the fact that what needed to be swept under the rug was that I had almost killed myself with some off-the-charts Mexican Brown. Instead I followed the family tradition of focusing on the positive and trying to get her to lend me the money.

*I think of the two options I have i.e staying in California or go
to the Amazon, the latter seems more exciting and worthwhile.
If you decide you do not wish to support me than I can take
out a loan.*

xxoo

Xtopher

In white-water rafting my cousins and I had a way to prove our mettle
that had an important link to our legacy. Big Bobby had given us the
thrill of white-water river rafting when we were young. The thrill of
bouncing off the rocks and waves as we barreled down the pristine
canyons of the American West on thirty-foot rafts made of rubber was
in our veins. It had been nearly six years since the debacle on the Snake
River with Uncle Teddy and the nasty grown-ups, but in the summer of
1975 my cousins and I finally found our way back to the river.

Thinking back on it now I realize that our preoccupation with the
white water was a way of negotiating and living up to the expectations
of our greatest role model—Uncle Bobby. If Robert Kennedy was what
the family would have become, the river was a connection to that for
us. It was also a way of escaping civilization. A way of postponing the
contract and obligations we were born to. What we needed was a way
to make it our own. We would have to come up with a wrinkle. The
jungles and unexplored rivers of South America would take care of
that.

The trips with Uncle Bobby were exciting, but cushy. We were
well taken care of by Hatch River Expeditions. Tents were set up,
meals were as good as anything one is likely to get in the great outdoors, and real danger to life or limb was minimized. River rafting in
South America was different. It's not cushy and your life and limbs are
always in danger.

Rio Apurímac in Peru, which was known as "The Great Speaker"
by the Incas, probably because of its loud and ferocious rapids, is a trib-
utary of the Amazon and although not known at the time—because
nobody had rafted it—one of the great white-water rivers in the world.

The expedition included myself, Bobby Jr., David, Lem, Doug
Spooner, a college friend from Cambridge, Morris Stroud, who was

one of Lem's friends' kids, and a journalist/travel agent named Harvey, who was one of Bobby's admirers. Harvey not only owned a travel agency, but his mother was a doctor who got us the drugs that were essential to survival for travel in these countries. This being our first expedition without the resources and largesse of the older generation, we arrived in Lima, Peru, lean and completely disorganized.

I was looking forward to chewing coca to deal with the altitude.

We made our way over the Andes to the town of San Francisco on the banks of the Apurímac. Our plan was to find a guide in San Francisco to help navigate the three hundred miles of unexplored river and to hire or build some rafts out of balsa wood. Bobby was the only one who had bothered to learn Spanish. This put him in a position of power and kept the rest of us at his mercy. This was fine with him. We hopped a plane to Cuzco, the Rome of the Inca Empire, bought supplies, and I bought more coca, and we threw our shit into the back of a dump truck we hired to drive the hundred and fifty miles to San Francisco. We arrived nine hours later in the middle of the night at a town with a few huts and no lights. We found level ground, pitched our tents, and spent the entire night evacuating our bowels all over the field we had set up camp on, diarrhea being a chronic aspect of life for gringos in this part of the world. We were awakened when the sun rose by the inhabitants of San Francisco, all thirty of them, looking into our tents as we slept. They were confused and a little angry at the visitors who were camped and had shit all over their soccer field.

We made peace and cleaned up our mess. We spent three days in town, built a couple rafts, and hired the town drunk as our guide. His name was Epifinio. He drank the moonshine they made locally, which was strong enough to run a car. He rubbed his urine all over his body to keep the mosquitoes away, which was disgusting but worked. Whenever he did this, Lem would shout to Bobby, "Make him stop, Bobby. Look what he's doing now. Please make him *stop!*" There are giant persistent mosquitos in the Amazon basin. After a while, rubbing urine all over oneself seemed like a bargain.

We were on the river for ten days. We caught a 100-pound catfish, which we dragged behind one of the rafts until it was decimated by piranha when we hit some still water. We brought ten live chickens. We killed one a day for food. There is an art to killing a chicken by putting its neck between two fingers and snapping. Bobby was best at it. I was the worst. I have never had the stomach for killing anything, but I appreciated the chicken salad.

We floated by Indian villages, once having to avoid the arrows being shot in our direction by a drunken tribe on the shore. The Indians made this stuff called cheecha which looked like Pepto-Bismol and had the alcoholic content of beer. Everyone in the village would sit around chewing yucca and spit the juice into a large vat where it would ferment. It tasted like shit but it gave you a buzz. When we went into their villages to trade the sneakers and T-shirts we had brought for food, they would present us with a cup of the stuff as a gesture of friendship. If you refused to drink they wouldn't deal with you.

The Indian women we ran into in the Amazon basin were beautiful, but their men were extremely jealous and possessive. No free love in the Amazonian jungle. During one of our visits I found myself transfixed by the girl pouring the alcoholic Pepto-Bismol for the visitors. She was dark and wild with exquisite features. She seemed curious about the twenty-four-year-old boy from another world who stood before her mesmerized. Just as I was about to try communicating, one of the village males came between us, interrupting the moment with a look that could kill. It was time to go.

We had brought a bag of drugs along just in case we ran into trouble. Morphine in case of pain. Tincture of opium in case of diarrhea. Someone had convinced Harvey's doctor-mom that there was a good chance we might have a need for them given that we would be spending three weeks in one of the most isolated, inaccessible, and dangerous places on the planet. What she didn't know was that even in the absence of a legitimate need, the drugs would be unlikely to return to the United States. Bobby was in charge of the bag, along with everything else. This didn't sit well with David and me. We had to accept that being the only one to speak Spanish had all sorts of tangential advantages. David and I kept wondering when we were going to get to break open the goody bag, but every time we asked Bobby he would say, "Not yet, man. We're in the middle of nowhere, a week from civilization. You never know, we might really need them." We didn't buy it, but the bags were still sealed so it was hard to argue. After four days of this we couldn't take it anymore and managed a closer examination of the bags in question. It seemed that though the bags were sealed the drugs were dwindling, but we didn't know how or who was dipping into the stash. Someone had figured out how to get the cookies without opening the cookie jar. David and I were pissed. What had happened? This was the first salvo in a new proprietary and more territorial approach to fear and loathing in Camelot.

It took us ten days to navigate the roughly three hundred miles of river. When we finally reached the prearranged location where the truck was waiting that would take us back to civilization, we were ready. The great thing about spending two weeks in the jungle is the shower and the burger you have when you finally get back to civilization. We spent a few days in Lima, where we woke up to military tanks in the streets indicating a coup had taken place overnight and where I fell in love with a beautiful Peruvian girl named Blanqui Boza. I met her the night before we were to board a plane for the Dutch Antilles and two days of luxurious R&R before heading back to New York. Another female-inspired dilemma: stay in Lima with another girl of my dreams or get on a plane with my homeboys. I chose my boys. Regrets? Like my uncle Frank used to say, I had a few.

We arrived in New York just in time to make an entrance into the annual Robert F. Kennedy Memorial Tennis Tournament Dinner at the Plaza Hotel. The entire family was there along with the best and brightest from the worlds of sports, government, and entertainment. Nobody in the family had heard from us for close to three weeks and there was great concern as to whether we were still alive. We loved creating this sort of drama. Bobby, David, Lem, and I made our entrance into the Grand Ballroom like the conquering heroes we felt we were. It was quite dramatic, and for the moment we were adored.

But only for a moment . . .

Chapter 22

I chose not to choose life. I chose something else. And the reasons? There are no reasons. Who needs reasons when you've got heroin?
—"Mark Renton," *Trainspotting*

So you want to be a tough guy?

I grew up thinking Kennedys were tough. It was part of our myth. I grew up hearing that "Kennedys don't cry" and with stories reveling in the mettle of those who came before me. My grandfather was the toughest businessman this side of Myer Lansky. He stole the Merchandise Mart from Marshall Field for a song, causing the retail magnate to exclaim to a gathering of associates, "How did a bunch of Jews let an Irishman steal the second biggest building in America out from under their noses?" He hoodwinked the feds when he was running booze with Seagrams. My uncle Joe, who was supposed to be the first Catholic president, flew a suicide mission over Germany in a plane packed with explosives when he didn't have to. The plane blew up. My aunt Kathleen also died in an air crash, after the war. My uncle Jack's PT boat was cut in half by a Japanese destroyer, and he swam through shark-infested waters dragging a buddy by a belt clenched between his teeth. He lived with a back that would have left anyone else incapacitated. My uncle Bobby was the smallest kid on the Harvard football team and so tough I never doubted the story that he played a full half against Yale with a broken leg. He ran for president knowing somebody might blow his head off.

This was the backdrop against which I would grow to measure just what kind of backbone I had. I have no way of knowing how much of the lore I grew up with was fact or fiction, but I bought it all. It provided a historical context for our swagger. Of course, my generation was blessed with a much more genteel playing field. We had none of the tests that faced those who came before us, so we settled for football, acts of reckless daring, and pushing the envelope when it came to the ingesting of chemicals.

I knew I wasn't tough. I had one fight in my life. Armando was a really fat Puerto Rican kid who was the only example of ethnic diversity in Mr. Nappoli's seventh-grade class at Saint David's. He wasn't one of those tough Puerto Rican street kids. His family had money. But I had to believe he knew more about fighting than I did. The only time my fist had gone anywhere near someone's head was when I lunged with futility at David as he did his irritating mosquito thing in our makeshift Hyannis Port boxing ring and Aunt Ethel broke my thumb.

Armando and I squared off in the loading dock of the Guggenheim Museum. Both of us had our posses. They were meant to encourage and to keep us from running home to Mommy. Armando and I stood in the shadow of Frank Lloyd Wright's architectural masterpiece looking at each other, not knowing what to do next. When the anticipation got to be too much, he lunged, catching my shoulder. I followed with a desperate right to the chest, and from there we dissolved into a muddle of wrestling meatballs. It was pretty pathetic, but I was the best wrestler at Saint David's in the heavyweight class. So despite Armando's superior girth, I got the best of him. I walked the eight blocks to 990, my tie askew and drenched with Armando's sweat and spittle, feeling not at all like a conqueror. I cried like a baby all the way home. I didn't like fighting; it didn't feel good unleashing all that anger. I decided I was more comfortable being a lover, and better at it. Kennedys were lovers, too.

I had a friend named Jack Weeks who really was tough. He was born in the projects of South Boston, was a Golden Gloves fighter, and went to Harvard courtesy of the GI Bill. His brother Kevin was the enforcer for the infamous Irish mob boss Whitey Bulger. I met Jack in the early seventies when I was running around Boston with my cousins, impervious to danger or consequence. Jack was our enforcer; we made sure everybody knew his history. I became tough by association.

Jack didn't have the heart to tell me then, but years later he confided that my cousins and I "thought we were tough guys but in truth we were pussies." This didn't stop us from trying to prove him wrong by putting ourselves in all sorts of ridiculous and dangerous situations.

With the exception of John Phillips of Mamas and Papas fame, I never bought heroin from a Caucasian. John had some of the best heroin around, but it was pricey and you sometime had to deal with his woman, who was a glassy-eyed zombie he kept wrapped in Saran Wrap to prevent her from sticking the used syringes that decorated his Park Avenue apartment into her tiny transparent arms. My favorite heroin dealers were black or Hispanic. They were way less complicated and a better value. I loved venturing into the heart of the inner city where I would stick out like a sore thumb in one of the corner drug bazaars or shooting galleries in Harlem or Roxbury. To me it represented the pinnacle of dangerous drug behavior. The Mount Everest of drug daring. None of my contemporaries would consider it. I thought, What pussies. I loved the thrill of finding my guy in a sea of dangerous faces looking to rip off "whitey."

I loved the little cellophane packages full of white powder with the catchy names like Lightning, Midnight, XXX. I loved playing hide-and-seek with the cops and finding a shooting gallery where I didn't have to share the needles. I loved the whole dangerous ritual, but most of all I loved the cooker, the boil and the cotton ball, the needle piercing my skin, my blood mixing with the diluted heroin, and the plunger pushing it into my vein. There was something perversely heroic in it all. I suppose the unattainable expectations I was born to, coupled with my withdrawal from the normal fare of adolescence, made it inevitable that I would find a darker path to construct my own heroic archetypes. There was also the pain of this existence. I held on to it like a badge or a ticket. This pain would be my ticket to greatness. My uncle Jack had his back. The dark side of addiction would be my cross.

There is nothing like the rush of good heroin. As the great junkie writer William Burroughs observed, "Junk is the ideal product . . . the ultimate merchandise. No sales talk necessary. The client will crawl through a sewer and beg to buy." I crawled through my share of sewers and had my share of close calls north of Ninety-sixth Street.

SNAPSHOT:

> I didn't want to be in this stairwell in a crumbling brownstone on 101st Street on a dark night, talking to a dealer I didn't know but had to deal with because my guy wasn't around; that is, had died or been arrested. This dealer was a skinny, pissed-off Puerto Rican kid whose eyes never settled. We were having words in the tenement stairwell.
>
> "This is bullshit, man. This isn't heroin, it's baking soda."
>
> "What do you mean, man, this is good stuff—the best."
>
> "It doesn't taste that way to me."
>
> "You calling me a liar, man?"
>
> I never understood why these wannabe dealers wouldn't just fold the scam when I was hip to the rip-off. Instead, they became indignant, getting all insulted that I was accusing them of doing what they were doing—trying to beat me out of my hard-inherited money.
>
> "No. I just want what I'm paying for."
>
> "Fuck you, white boy."
>
> And out of nowhere he punched me in the face and put a knife to my throat. "I can stick you and let you bleed to death or you can give me the money."

These are the moments in life when you know whether you are tough or not. I bought the baking soda, trying not to shit my pants while I dug for my wallet. I beat it back to the safety of the Upper East Side with a good war story, pissed that I lost the money and was still in need of a fix.

I spent more time running from irate dealers than from the police. I liked to think of myself as the White Phantom when it came to 110th Street and Broadway. I was part James Bond, part ghost as I made my way around the hood, staying off the cops' radar. They knew I was there; they just weren't interested—most of the time. They had bigger problems, but that didn't stop them from teaching me a lesson now and again.

My using had passed the point of no return—the die had been cast. Whatever control I'd had had been decimated after years of being pummeled by the gorilla. My primary purpose was to find oblivion, and the cops or my family didn't have a prayer of intervening.

SOME OF the beat cops in the drug-infested neighborhoods of New York City had a practice called "rolling," which they demonstrated in part to me one night in front of a burned-out shooting gallery on the Upper West Side. It consisted of spread-eagling the suspect on the hood of the patrol car and beating him with their nightsticks for half an hour, being careful not to leave bruises. More than a practice—an art, marked by the absence of evidence, like an artist who paints negative space. It required four cops, but it was fun for them so they never had a problem getting a quorum. They only gave me the appetizer, putting me in "the spread" with one shot to the kidney. It was enough to convince me I didn't want the main course, which was promised if "We ever see you north of Ninety-sixth Street again."

Getting rolled convinced me that I needed to find a better way to access the fine heroin of the Upper West Side. Enter Carlos and Joyce, junkies with an apartment. I would go there, give Carlos the money, and talk to Joyce about what was on "the stories" that day while Carlos went about town looking for the best of the best. When he returned we would all get high. It was safe, clean, and reliable and worked for me until Carlos ended up in Riker's Island for a stretch.

I took pride in my apparent fearlessness when it came to all this, but looking back, I see it for what it was, a pathetic, misappropriated use of testosterone fueled by addictive necessity.

The moment of truth is always revealed. We may not choose to recognize it, but it's there. My moment of truth concerning me being a tough guy came in a girlfriend's brand-new BMW on the streets of Cambridge on a sunny fall day in 1974 when I was nineteen years old. I had just returned from another cushy summer getaway and was looking forward to a year chasing girls and drugs around the student capital of the world.

On arriving in Boston I saw an advertisement that read, "There are over a million students in Boston. If you're not getting laid, there's something seriously wrong with you." I don't remember what the ad was for, but it doesn't matter. The ad told the truth. There were all sorts of girls in Bean Town.

My friend AK and I were driving around Harvard Square eating lunch and minding our own business. AK had the best arm I had ever seen. He could throw a football farther and with more accuracy than anyone I had ever played football with. We were in a long line of traffic, finishing up our to-go order from Bartley's Burger Cottage, heading out of the square on Brattle Street. Next to us were two guys in a beat-up Chevy convertible who were dissing us with their eyes. You know, looking us up and down in our yuppie car like we were a couple of rich mama's boys. It was obvious they had just gotten out of prison, so we kept our mouths shut. When they had moved up ahead in the traffic fifty yards or so and there were plenty of cars between us—and we had a back door escape down an alley—I looked at AK and said, "Throw the milk container at them, man." So much for minding my own business.

"Are you fucking nuts, Chris? Those guys are killers."

"They'll never get out of the traffic, man. Do it."

"Bad idea, man."

"Pussy."

That did it.

Andy heaved his half-empty milk carton as far as any human could heave a half-empty container of milk. It was one of those slow-motion moments, the milk carton sailing through the air over the ten cars between the target and us. It came down in a perfect trajectory, hitting the top of their front windshield and splattering all over the ex-cons. We saw the results of AK's miracle throw and hauled ass down the alley to a secluded spot behind one of Harvard's dormitories. I stopped the car as Andy and I reveled in our heroics.

We showed those convict townies just what kind of rich mama's boys we were.

I looked up from our revelry and saw in my rearview mirror what I didn't want to see and what, having seen, I didn't think was possible: the beat-up Chevy convertible with the two pissed-off convicts, covered in milk, bearing down on Andy and me in my girlfriend's brand-new *stationary* BMW.

How the fuck did they get out of traffic, double back, and find our secret alley and our even more secret hiding place? This was my moment of truth, and it wasn't even close to heroic. I called out for my mommy. I knew we were dead if they caught us, so I drove that car faster than I had ever driven any car in my life through the streets of Cambridge, trying to lose the Chevy, which stayed glued to my tail. AK was whimpering, "We're gonna die, man. Those guys are going to kill us."

It's a drag when you know you are going to die and your wingman continuously reminds you.

I yelled at him, "Shut up, man. Do something." He didn't.

"What are they doing? Where are they?" I kept asking. He didn't know.

After ten minutes of trying to lose these psychos in traffic and one-way streets with no luck, I decided to try and outrun them on Memorial Drive, a four-lane thoroughfare along the Charles River.

Bad idea. They overtook us going 100 miles per hour and the really mean-looking one in the passenger seat leaned out his window so that fully half his body was outside the car. He had a huge chain in his right hand, which he snapped once, totally obliterating my windshield. His proficiency indicated he had done this sort of thing before. There was an explosion of glass, much of which became embedded in my face. I hit the brakes, sending us into a 360. Hearing the explosion and seeing the blood pouring from my face, AK thought I had been shot. Our car came to a stop, both of us knowing we were way out of our depth. The convicts were twenty-five yards ahead. Facing us. Two cars alone in the middle of Memorial Drive. A perfect setup for chicken. The cons wanted to play. We didn't. I turned the BMW around and ran away, praying to God they wouldn't follow. They didn't, and I was left with my life and the certainty that there were a lot of people in the world much tougher than me.

Snapshot:

My last river trip was almost my *last* river trip. The Caroní
River in Venuzuela is a monster river that runs for three hundred and fifty miles from the Venezuelan/Brazilian border
across Venezuela. According to legend, when Sir Walter
Raleigh was searching for the City of Gold he spent some
time near the Caroní looking for it. Whenever anybody in his
party misbehaved, they were put in a canoe and sent down the
Caroní to their death. It was a very dangerous river. I had arrived in Caracas with Lem, Bobby, Michael, and a dozen
friends to make an attempt on the Caroní in fourteen-foot
rubber rafts. This time I brought my own drugs. I had everything I needed for three weeks in the jungle in my knapsack,
which I put down for a second in the Caracas baggage claim.
It was gone before you could say stupid gringo. There are few
things more unpleasant than rafting and camping in the
South American outback while experiencing narcotic with-
drawl.

Well, there is one thing: Being thrown from your raft into a class-five
rapid full of rocks, and then being sucked into a giant whirlpool that
pulls you down into the murky darkness of the river where you will
drown because there is no air in your lungs. Being fully present as you
struggle vainly against the power of the river, as the light fades, as you
are pulled deeper into the darkness with the realization that you really
are not ready to die on this godforsaken river. But you don't die because the river spits you back into the rapid full of rocks just before you
pass out, so you can begin the whole process over again.

When you miraculously escape this torture you find that the im-
passable rapid on the river you should never have attempted in such
shitty little rafts has destroyed 85 percent of your supplies and equipment, leaving you with little shelter and food for a week in some very
rainy and inhospitable jungle. Well, at least it took my mind off being
dope-sick for a while. As one of Bobby's friends from Alabama who was
unlucky enough to have been invited along said, "I did two stints in

Vietnam, I've been shot down four times, I've seen a two-legged dog and a kangaroo that could dance, but I've never seen anything like that."

After the Caroní I decided to hang up my paddle and test my mettle in areas where I had a little more control and where, if I was going to die, at least I wouldn't be conscious.

Chapter 23

Excess is the road to recovery.
— Eric Clapton

After graduating from college I found myself further adrift in the sea of uncertainty. The call of my addiction was becoming more incessant with each passing day. There were choices to make and I had no idea what to do. The paths followed by those that went before me were clear: Write a Pulitzer Prize–winning book. Go to law school. Fight in a war. Get a high-profile job in Washington. Run for public office.

I was beginning to have second thoughts. Bobby wasn't. He went to London to wrestle with the London School of Economics and cement another brick in his path to becoming the heir apparent.

I headed to New York to check on my finances. Things weren't looking too good on that front. My mother wasn't cooperating with my wait-and-see approach to my future. It seemed like a good time to leave the country and spend some time in the city of my dad's ancestors, London. I tried to convince my mom that the fact that Bobby was there was mere coincidence. She didn't buy it.

Dear Christopher,
I am sorry you had to leave under such circumstances.
However I must make my feelings plain. Bobby is over there in
school, and taking a vacation. On the other hand you are

again delaying the day that you must face the fact that you must find something to do with your life. You must <u>at least</u> <u>start</u> to look to your future. It is all very well to say you don't need the office and I am sure that if a bank will take care of your overdue or bounced checks and budget something could be arranged. I know this letter sounds very tough but I think you must realize that the world and all of us in it don't necessarily owe you anything. I love you very much but I also think you know I am disappointed.

Much Love,
Mummy

Time for another geographic. Geographics don't work, because the place may be new, but the person doing the traveling is the same old addict. Things didn't get better for me in London; in fact, they got worse. I had nothing to do but (1) watch Bobby try to go to school and (2) attempt to get drugs out of British doctors who were way more hip to my game than their American counterparts.

What I learned in London was that making drugs legal does not make them easier to get!

One night I found myself in a men's-room stall with Keith Moon, the drummer of The Who. I never liked The Who, but Keith had promised to give me some of his cocaine after much badgering, so at this moment I was loving Keith Moon. The drummer put the mound of white powder in the indentation on the top of his right hand, where practiced cocaine aficionados snort from. I bent down in the crowded little stall in the trendy London disco, eager to receive my reward for an evening of groveling, but when I went to inhale, the rock icon spitefully blew the powder into the air, muttered an unintelligible expletive, and stumbled out of the stall. I was shocked and pissed. Briefly considered collecting the powder from the urine-drenched floor beneath the toilet. Thought better of it and headed back to my table to tell everybody what an asshole Keith Moon was. Rock stars suck, and so did London.

I know. . . . I'll go to the Middle East.

It was Christmas, and Eric, a friend and fellow drug addict, was going to Israel to do an article on Menachem Begin for *Rolling Stone*. I decided to tag along and spend Christmas in the birthplace of our savior Jesus Christ—Bethlehem. It might do some good. We got to Jerusalem the day before Christmas. Eric came down with hepatitis, turned yellow, and had to be evacuated to a hospital in Tel Aviv. I spent Christmas Eve alone in Bethlehem, trying to avoid the Israeli soldiers, and said a quiet prayer asking God to please find my file and straighten my life out. On Christmas Day I headed to the Sinai on a bus destined for Elat. I had been told that Elat was a hot vacation spot in the desert with great diving. What I wasn't told is that it's freezing in the Sinai at Christmastime. I spent four days in a-one room trailer—it was all I could afford. I spent my time reading *Trinity* by Leon Uris and kicking the legal heroin I had finagled out of the doctors in London. The words of Leon Uris were inspiring. They awakened the Irish fighter and romantic in me: "When all of this was done, a republic eventually came to pass but the sorrows and the troubles have never left that tragic, lovely land. For you see, in Ireland there is no future, only the past happening over and over."

There would be a future for me. I vowed that I would go back to my world and change my life. I sent myself a postcard as a reminder of my new commitment.

I had a prescription in my hand before the postcard ever arrived. My past was indeed happening over and over.

Law school has got to be better than this.

SNAPSHOT:

The guy who figured out that if you put velvet ropes up outside a nightclub and make regular people wait while celebrities breeze in, thus increasing their desire to come in rather than making them want to burn the place down, was a fucking genius. Studio 54 had the biggest and baddest velvet ropes on the island of Manhattan. Steve Rubell, the owner, could smell celebrity no matter how faint and he was on the ropes pretty much every night. I had enough of a scent to breeze in with the rest of the New York glitterati. I have no idea what Studio 54 really looked like on the inside. It was just another big, noisy disco with obnoxious lighting. Getting in was the whole thing. Once Steve waved me through the anonymous masses huddled before his ropes, my mission was to find a girl, score some coke, and find someplace to play hide the salami.

I had more luck scoring coke from the 54 bartenders than I did finding a girl. The thing about hanging out at the hottest disco in the world is that there's lots of competition when it comes to finding someone to have sex with. Every mover and shaker, movie star, rock star, artist, fashion guru, you name it, they were all there with the same agenda—to find that special someone to party with. It's Darwinian. One night I got lucky and met a Brazilian who was the most beautiful girl my inebriated eyes had seen since the last most beautiful girl I had ever seen. I pounced and was on my way out the door and through the velvet ropes before any of the guys higher up on the New York food chain got a whiff of my prey.

As the velvet ropes parted, Steve Rubell appeared with a warning, "Chris, things are not always as they appear."

Now, before you think that Steve Rubell was some sort of metaphysical guru, he wasn't. Steve was a guru of sorts—of people, their station in life, and their anatomy. What he was saying was that the girl I had found was not a girl at all, and though I wasn't 100 percent convinced he was right—he had created enough doubt for me to abandon my catch and begin the hunt anew. I spent the rest of the night in a futile search for a true female replacement, hampered by the continuous onslaught of the Brazilian, who was desperately trying to prove her feminine gender by following me around showing me different parts of her/his anatomy.

When Bianca Jagger married Mick, she was *really* one of the most beautiful women in the world. When she separated from Mick she still was, and she was looking to get even. She picked me. We danced seductively amid the noise and light of 54 and when it was time to leave, she surprised me by agreeing to follow me home. The ropes parted, and once again Steve appeared, this time with no admonishment but a simple, "So where are we going?"

Now before you think Steve Rubell was some sort of buddy whom I invited to come along after hours, he wasn't. I had never gone anywhere with him but into the pulsating disco on Fifty-fourth Street and I hadn't given a hint that he was welcome to come along, but that didn't seem to matter, he was coming, and no amount of facial displeasure on my part could dissuade him.

We arrived at my mom's apartment on Sutton Place, where I spent the next two hours trying to get some alone time with Mrs. Jagger. It proved impossible. Steve Rubell could not be ditched. He was everywhere. It was really annoying. At 4:30 A.M. I gave up and ushered Rubell and Bianca into the elevator and went off to bed to dream of what might have been and await the chirping of the damn birds. The next night when I arrived in front of Steve Rubell's velvet ropes he told me, "Sorry about last night, man, but Mick asked me to keep an eye on Bianca. I did you a favor. He would have been really pissed if he had known you were with her."

A couple weeks later the *National Enquirer* ran a two-page color spread of me, in my stupid-looking cream-colored suit, and Bianca dancing provocatively in Steve Rubell's disco. I never found out what Mick thought about that, but I'm sure Steve didn't mind the publicity.

My evenings out at Studio 54 usually meant getting in bed just in time to play deny the dawn, necessitating a flurry of notes to my mother justifying my nocturnal habits:

Mummy,
Due to a very long and tiresome evening conducted with
relentless energy and vigor in the pursuit of FUN but
nevertheless produced nothing more than a throbbing head
and an upset tummy I (your loving son) do respectfully request
SLEEP until the hour of 12:00 noon.

All my Love
Xtopher
(your son in one of his many hours of need)

And on another occasion:

> Mummy,
> Had a very late night. Please wake me at 12:00. Lets meet at
> the theater to get a bite after the show.
>
>

XXOO

Love from your hard working son
Xtopher
>

What sort of hard work I was doing at four o'clock in the morning I can only imagine. No wonder my mother rolled her eyes whenever I proclaimed how hard I was working.

And then there were the evenings when I had done so many drugs that my notes became theatrically incoherent.

> Mummy,
> This evenings encore performance of the new hit musical, "The
> nocturnal exploits and other assorted goings-on of the infamous,
> gifted and talented son of PKL" (written, directed and acted by
> yours truly, CKL) was a smashing success! Unfortunately for
> our hero the price of success is high. Consequently he is near
> death due to physical exhaustion. His body has threatened to
> leave for Costa Rica if, our hero does not sleep until at least
> 12:00 noon! Mummy, please wake me at 12:00. Not before
> unless you don't mind having a Costa Rican son!
>
> Love,
> Xtopher
> PS Andy will call me for football at 1:00 tommorrow. Please
> wake me if he calls before 12:00.
> Xxoo

My mom never let on that my notes, although becoming more creative, were also becoming less coherent. I guess she figured that as long as I was still playing football, things couldn't have gotten too bad.

She left me a note and a check sometime around my birthday:

Dearest Christopher
Happy Happy Birthday!

I had to go to bed for at least two days after looking, looking, searching for a present for my wonderful son. So to no avail, here it is <u>only</u> to be spent on <u>yourself.</u> I hope you will have a happy day although it cannot be as happy as I was the day you were born March 29th 1955 at 2:00 P.M. St. John's Hospital all 6 lbs 13 ozs, 20" in length and a head 13 3/4. (What is it now?)

You have made my life truly fulfilling, joyous and I love you very much. Come back soon so we can walk the streets of NY.

> *Xxxooo*
> *Always,*
> *Mummy*

My dad used to send me postcards on his travels around the world but I only got one letter from him. It was in December of 1978. My father had done one of his disappearing acts. My sisters and I were used to it but this time he felt compelled to explain himself.

Dear Christopher,
As Elton John would say; "The bitch is back."
This form letter if you will, is to enlighten you all, as to where the hell your father has been for these many past few weeks, which at times, must have confused you and taken on the air of the bizarre to say the least.

My dad went on to explain that he was injured on a movie when "that dumb girl Carol Lynley hit me in my 'jambe' with a crystal glass during the making of that never to be forgotten film, 'Fantasy Island,' seen only by the producer and some close relatives who were accompanied by their seeing eye dogs."

He recovered in UCLA Medical Center and from there he went to an Indian reservation with

*marvelous mineral waters, bubbling out of the ground. I've
never felt better or been in a better place in my entire life.*

    *The one thing I feel terrible about and, I stand corrected,
is the total lack of communication between us, which by the
way included the entire outside world. It may sound selfish,
but it was the only way I could hope to accomplish the end
result, all started by these mysterious red men!!! As Frank
Sinatra would say, "I did it my way."*

    *Please try to understand and please know that you four,
take precedence over everything in my life.*

    I love you all more than you know.

Always,
Daddy
D.O.M.

It felt good to get a letter from my dad but I had no idea what he was
talking about. I still don't know what D.O.M. means. My father would
do that a lot. He spoke as if I knew him and was privy to what was going on in his life, but I didn't, so when he reached out to me in moments of inclusion I was just confused.

    Today I know he was just trying to save his life; and much of what
was happening to him he couldn't share with his children. I also know
that in those moments of euphoria brought on by chemicals or brief recovery, he wanted his children to be a priority in his life, but history
and circumstance would not allow it.

Chapter 24

The needle is not important. Whether you sniff it smoke it eat it or shove it up your ass the result is the same: addiction.
—WILLIAM BURROUGHS

I was having some credibility issues. Lawyers are credible—well, some are: I'll become a lawyer. I aimed at something I could hit—Fordham Law School in New York City. I got a recommendation from Ramsey Clark, who attested to the fact that I was, "an unusually imaginative, sensitive and venturesome young man. His wide ranging interests, deep concern and disciplined perseverance give him qualities the legal profession badly needs. He will make an outstanding law student and a real contribution to justice."

I enrolled in the fall of 1978. It was a disaster from day one. I arrived for my first day of Torts with a nasty Percodan habit, big hair, and a psychotic Siberian husky who was cute but spent all day sitting on his ass doing 360s. We were perfect for each other. I named him AW, short for Ass-Wipe, and after two months of his twirling I was tempted to open the big glass door on the top floor of my West Eighty-Fourth Street apartment and play fetch. I gave him to someone in New Jersey instead.

I went to one of those Upper East Side docs who tried to wean me off; but it didn't work. He had an office just on Lexington and he was one of the Dr. Feelgoods. He was an old Eastern European with a big red puffy face and long white hair. He sat behind a mahogany desk I never saw him get up from, in a long white coat. The coat was the only real indication that he was a doctor. I suspected he was so stoned he couldn't stand up without the help of one of the beautiful alleged nurses who serviced him. Or maybe one of the nurses was under the desk giving him head, because he always had this stupid smile on his face. I would arrive at his office every day with the other well-to-do junkies who could afford his fee and wait . . . and wait . . . and wait. Eventually I would be ushered into the inner sanctum where I would get one of the good doctor's "special shots," vitamin B12 with some speed and narcotic mixed in. He would swear to me, "Dis vill cure your drog problem."

Then he would ask, "Vat else I can do for you?"

"Well, Doctor, I'm having trouble sleeping, which means I'm having trouble getting up in the morning. My back hurts, and all this pressure is making me anxious."

He would scratch out four prescriptions: Seconal, Dexedrine, Dilaudid, and Quaaludes. "Dat vill be two hundred dollars." I paid him in cash and hurried up to the pharmacy on Madison Avenue the doctor had a special relationship with.

It was a junkie's dream, but not great if you had any intention of making it through law school, so I ended up on the New York City Methadone Maintenance Program, which went something like this: You show up on the first day and have to prove you are an addict with dirty urine, after which they give you 40 milligrams of methadone, which gets you pretty high for twenty hours. If you show up with drugs in your urine the next day, they increase your dose by 10 milligrams. They continue this protocol until you max out at the legal limit of what they can dispense, which is 100 milligrams. Guess where I ended up? That's right—100 milligrams. I never understood why they would think that any self-respecting junkie would ever settle for less of a drug than they were *legally* allowed. The other drawback to methadone besides the withdrawal, which is like having ants crawling in your bones with an Asian flu kicker, is that after you've been on it awhile you don't get high anymore and it prevents you from getting high on any other opiate-based narcotic.

This is, of course, the point. Methadone allows criminal-minded junkies who would otherwise lie around all day with needles in their arms to become semifunctional members of society. What society doesn't realize is that most of these folks are there for the refuge and still have the junkie mind—which dictates getting high and killing the pain whatever the cost. So I found myself in Constitutional Law 101 on the nod and unable to read the textbook. See, I was supplementing my 100 legal milligrams with street methadone, which made the words all blurry, because I still had a junkie mind, and although I liked the idea of getting clean and being able to read my Con Law textbook, I didn't, yet, have the requisite willingness or capacity.

THERE ARE moments in our lives when we are asked to choose between our head and our heart. Sometime these moments are a big deal. Sometimes they aren't. I've learned in my life that whether big or small, it doesn't pay to bet against your heart. If you win, it feels like shit, and if you lose, you'll never forget the pain.

Muhammad Ali was my hero. It wasn't just his skill as a boxer and talker that appealed to me. It was that he saw the world differently and had the courage to risk everything to honor that vision.

I didn't know it at the time, but Ali had done in his life what I needed to do in mine but had yet to find the courage for. He had taken a stand and risked everything for what he believed in, defining himself as an individual and transcending the environment that had formed him.

Ali embodied in his fists and in his heart the belief that anything could be overcome. I knew one of the guys in Ali's entourage, Gene Kilroy. Gene became a friend to David and me, which meant we got to go to all of Ali's fights and I even got to hang out with my hero once in a while.

When Ali fought George Foreman in Zaire, I knew Foreman would kill him. All the smart people in the boxing world knew it. It was a mismatch, David vs. Goliath. I wanted Ali to beat Foreman more than I wanted anything but I bet against him. I bet against him because I had no faith that someone could overcome what seemed impossible to overcome. I gave in to fear and the inevitable. I played it safe, betting against my hero, rationalizing that if he was going to lose, I might as well make a dollar on it.

SNAPSHOT:

I listened to the broadcast alone in the apartment Bobby and I shared on Concord Avenue just outside of Harvard Square. Bobby and David had gone to the Boston Garden to see the closed-circuit broadcast. I had stayed behind not wanting to see the slaughter. I sat in the beaten-up leather chair in the center of our living room, my certainty reinforced by round after round of rope-a-dope. When Ali came out from behind his wall of leather and put the invincible Foreman on his back, I let out a scream of joy that could be heard all the way to the Garden. I jumped up and down yelling "Booma Ali" for fifteen minutes, alone in my living room. After my joy subsided, something else welled up; a feeling of betrayal, of not deserving to celebrate Ali's victory because I had not stood with him in his defining moment. I had allowed the expediency of my mind to overrule the truth of my heart and it felt like shit. I had done it to minimize the hurt of a loss I thought inevitable, and it cost me a piece of my spirit. I swore I would never do it again.

LIFE IS funny when it comes to lessons learned. I was sure after playing Judas in Ali's "rumble in the jungle" back in 1974 that I would never again betray my heart or the people in my life who inspire my heart or spirit. I soon realized that it's never that simple.

Alcoholism and drug addiction are progressive diseases. Those who suffer from it get worse, never better. Some get worse more quickly than others. My experience has shown me that a person's ability to withstand the inevitable debilitating effects of drug addiction and alcoholism has to do with luck, their physical constitution, and genetics. My cousin

My cousins Teddy, Kara, me, Patrick, and Uncle Teddy applaud Kennedy for Senate campaign director and political heir apparent, my cousin Kathleen. PHOTOGRAPH BY FRANK TETI

On the set of my first movie, Impulse, *after moving back to Hollywood in the late 1980s.*

Posing for a family photo while trying to keep my eyes open after a wild night in Palm Beach.
PHOTOGRAPH BY KEN REGAN

My grandmother showing pleasure with my knowledge of the Mayflower and Plymouth Rock.

My mom and me tripping the light fantastic at Club A in New York City for my engagement party.

Uncle Teddy with my new bride Jeannie and me on the island of Bequia in the West Indies. PHOTOGRAPH BY JOHN OLSSON

Our official wedding photograph, which we sent as a gift to the attendees with the inscription "A portrait of too much rum punch."

My dad and me at my sister Sydney's wedding in Hyannis Port. PHOTOGRAPH BY BRIAN QUIGLEY

My dad and friend at Hef's in one of my father's favorite photos. PHOTOGRAPH BY DAVID L. FONT

My young family, circa 1999: Little Matthew and David help their sister, Savannah, celebrate her birthday with mom and dad.

Savannah with me on the beach in South Hampton.

Matty and me at our family house in South Hampton.

My eldest son, David, with me in front of the Paramount studio. PHOTOGRAPH BY HARRY BENSON

Sailing off Hyannis Port with the "Grande Fromage" on his boat The Mya, *with my cousin Bobby Kennedy, Jr.*

Hanging out in the Hamptons with Arnold.

I wish it were me playing quarterback instead of my cousin John. I'm the one with the hat.
PHOTOGRAPH BY KEN REGAN

Me and my cousin Bobby at President Bill Clinton's 1992 inaugural parade. I was serenaded with chants from the crowd of "Charlie! Charlie!" by viewers of All My Children, *the daytime soap opera I was on back then.*

In search of votes and fun: Savannah and me getting wet on one of Uncle Teddy's family camping trips in western Massachusetts. PHOTOGRAPH BY KEN REGAN

David and Matty looking tough.

Matty trying hard to meditate while I try hard to catch a breath.

Me and the great dictator: Fidel Castro in Cuba.

Fidel and me leaving the screening of the film Thirteen Days, *a dramatic re-creation of the Cuban Missile Crisis in which I played the part of a real-life Navy flier.*

Me and Arnold moments after his surprising election as governor of California.
PHOTOGRAPH BY SYLVIA MAUTNER

Me, Teddy, and my son David in front of "The Big House"—my grandparents' house in Hyannis Port.

Me with Lana and
Angel: Two great
ladies!

Alec Baldwin; Bobby, Jr.; and me skiing in Canada and in need of a hairdresser.

Peter Emerson, Lana Antonova, David Black, me, and Richard Dreyfuss at Richard's opening of Sly Fox *in Boston.*

Tony Hopkins and me on the set of The World's Fastest Indian. PHOTOGRAPH BY TODD CHERRY

The Kennedys doing their daring lemmings impersonation on another one of Uncle Teddy's camping trips in western Massachusetts. PHOTOGRAPH BY KEN REGAN

Watching the sun rise over my favorite city—Havana, Cuba.

Me in front of the apartment where I finally got sober in 1986. My life was transformed.

David had the gene, which runs in our family, that allows incredible abuse to body and mind to little effect, but he was physically frail and his luck wasn't Irish.

David got his assed kicked by his disease before the rest of us.

The by-products of addiction—getting arrested, overdosing, being physically attacked, and having chronic health problems—began manifesting in his life while Bobby and I were still partying. It was a problem.

SNAPSHOT:

It was becoming increasingly difficult to manage the unman-ageability of my life. The leaves of autumn had already lit the city, providing the illusion of optimism. The gloom of winter was around the corner, and I was facing it chained to a beast I was powerless to say no to. Bobby had left for Alabama to write his book on the federal judge Frank Johnson Jr., one of the good white guys in the civil rights movement. David was becoming increasingly distant and preoccupied by his own dance with death. The camaraderie of shared experience and resources had given way to a proprietary need to make sure each of us got what we needed to make the gorilla happy. There was little to look forward to in the late fall of 1978 as I sat contemplating the mountain of law books required for my freshman year at Fordham.

The phone rang. It was Bobby.

Bobby:
Hey, man, What's happening?
Me:
Nothing, man, I'm just sitting here wondering how the fuck I'm going to read all these books and lose all this weight.
Bobby:
Get Cliffs Notes and go to the gym.

Me:
They don't have Cliffs Notes for law books.
Bobby:
That sucks.
Me:
Yeah, it does. What's up?
Bobby:
I'm worried about David. He's getting his ass kicked. We
need to help him.
Me:
How the hell are we going to help him, man?
Bobby:
I don't know, but we have to.
Me:
We could stop getting high with him.
Bobby:
Maybe that's what we need to do.

This was the first time anyone had ever tried to intervene in one of our lives in an attempt to stop the downward spiral—and it was someone in the spiral. Our parents were uncomfortably ensconced in the role of crisis management. My mom was afraid and maybe she didn't want to deal. The Big E was pissed off and didn't want to hear about it. Teddy was busy with his own problems and the expectations of half the country. Sarge and Eunice wanted to be helpful but had their own family and their versions of saving the world. At this point we were on our own except for the shrinks and Lem. Neither were much help.

I knew that if I were to stop getting high with David it would be tantamount to cutting my best friend out of my life. I felt the pain of that but I was incapable of making another choice. At this point in my life the drugs had become my best friend. My friendship with David would just be another casualty.

I also had finally achieved the proximity to Bobby I always wanted. That was the gain. The cost would be to turn my back on my best friend.

"It's for his own good," I rationalized. "He can't handle it. I'm not going to stop using. And if I can't get high with him, the only thing to do is stop hanging out with him. There's no other way." So once again I ignored what had been in my heart since that day David and I met on the great lawn in Glen Cove, and I said good-bye to my best friend in the world so I could have what I thought I wanted—my drugs and the confidence of the cousin I most admired. The plan didn't work. Instead of helping my friend, the isolation hastened his slide into the abyss. Later I realized that I never wanted to look at this for what it was. David was becoming the version of me that I did not want to see. The version of me that I never believed was possible. So I turned my back, looked away, and left my best friend to figure it out for himself.

I never told David what I decided or why, but I think he knew—and it hurt him.

After that day I never again had the same relationship with David. And my pride that Bobby had trusted me felt like what it was: just pride, the worst of the seven deadly sins. It was indeed "the bitter end."

One of the other downsides to methadone maintenance is diet. My diet consisted of Reggie bars—Reggie Jackson's attempt to usurp The Babe's share of the chocolate bar market—and Pepperidge Farm cookies. By the time December rolled around and I accepted the inevitable and withdrew from Fordham, I was tipping the scales at 240 pounds and there wasn't a store within ten blocks of where I lived that had any Reggie bars or Brussels cookies in stock. The words in my Constitutional Law textbook were a blur and I could no longer squeeze into my size 40 corduroys. From here on out it would have to be sweatpants. The writing was on the wall—although I couldn't read it—but I withdrew from Fordham Law School just the same.

Sarge Shriver helped me get a job at an agency that provided free legal services to the poor. That didn't work out too well either. It turns out you have to be able to read to help the poor get legal services. My health began deteriorating to a dangerous point. One morning I came to in my apartment with a pain in my chest. As usual, I ignored it. I staggered around my bedroom searching for something to wear. I found the pair of extra large sweatpants where I had dropped them. As I struggled to get my overfleshed legs into the pair of dirty sweats, it occurred to me that somehow my life had gone terribly askew. How the fuck did I end up like this? With that thought came a stab of pain like nothing I had felt in my twenty-four years. I fell to the floor and could not get up. It felt like an elephant was sitting on my chest. I thought I was having a heart attack. I crawled to the phone and called my mom. Things were as desperate as they could be for me to bring my mother into the mess I had made of my life.

My mom couldn't handle it when I got sick. It drove her up a wall if I had a stomachache, a bad back, or pneumonia. To her it was an irritating sign of my weakness. Her contempt obliterated any compassion she might have had for me. This confused me. I used to think it was because her life had been so full of real sickness and death that was involuntary. She saw what I was going through as a cry for attention and as something I had brought on myself. She wasn't always wrong. Later I realized that her reaction came from the fear a parent feels for a child who might not make it in life.

She walked into my apartment and her disappointment was written all over her face. It covered the fear that her only son had one and a half feet in the grave. I was lying on the floor unable to move and barely breathing. She stepped over my bloated, immobile body, picked up the phone, and called an ambulance.

It turned out I had pleurisy and pneumonia. After recovering for ten days at New York Hospital, I accepted the doctors' and my family's recommendation that I go to Mclean Hospital to get help for my drug addiction. I agreed to go to rehab because I was out of money and out of moves.

I showed up at McLean willing to address my addiction to narcotics, but I wasn't taking any chances. I brought an assortment of other drugs to relax me, help me sleep, and help me wake up. The doctors weren't amused. I was incredulous. I didn't understand what sleeping pills had to do with heroin addiction. It was clear I didn't have a clue.

My mother visited me on the locked ward at Mclean's and we actually did some therapy together for the first time ever. It was difficult for both of us. My mom wasn't big on therapy. She didn't think that our secrets were our business, much less anybody else's.

After a couple months of walking around in slippers and answering questions about my family of origin I was beginning to feel a little better. Time to get back in the game. I decided to apply to law school again. Addicts keep going back to the same wells even if they are dry. The shrinks suggested I stay out of New York so I applied to Boston College Law School.

I vowed that it would be different this time. This time I secured recommendations from Arthur Schlesinger and Senator Edward Kennedy. I wasn't taking any chances.

Arthur stuck to history, rambling on about my connection to Camelot lore.

My uncle stuck to whatever it is that he does. It usually works, especially in Massachusetts.

He spoke to the dean on my behalf. I had no idea what my uncle said to the dean about me, but I was granted an interview to plead my case. I agonized for days over whether I should tell the truth about where I had spent the last two months—in case it came up. I had decided to tell the truth, not out of any virtue but because I just couldn't be sure that my uncle hadn't already dropped the dime on me.

I walked into the dean's office, and pretty much the first thing out of his mouth was, "So what have you been doing with yourself lately?"

For a second I considered giving him some bullshit, but something inside told me, "Tell the truth, asshole."

And I did.

"I'm in rehab, getting clean and trying to get my life together."

"I know you are. That's why I agreed to see you. I think what you are doing is very admirable."

What? Knew where I was? Admirable? Now I'm really confused.

"I've had people close to me who have had similar struggles and I know how difficult it is. You deserve a chance to succeed. I will help you any way that I can."

Wow. This telling-the-truth stuff really pays dividends. I left the meeting sky-high. The only legal high I'd had in years. Or ever. As I made my way back to the locked ward at McLean's, I knew I would be accepted for the fall semester and there was someone at the school who knew what I was and was pulling for me.

Chapter 25

*The whole world is strewn with snares, traps, gins and pitfalls
for the capture of men by women.*
—G. B. SHAW

I met her at the Fan Club in Boston when I was thirty days out of
Mclean Hospital. They finally opened the door to the locked ward and
let me out. I had a drink in my hand and drugs up my nose a week
after I walked out the door. The Fan Club was the place I went to look
for a hostage. It was not a pretty picture. I still weighed 240 pounds
and there were five or six different chemicals swimming through my
bloodstream. I was frantic, always running from the certain truth that
whatever it was wasn't working. I didn't even know what *it* was that
wasn't working.

I would career through the sea of eager singles, looking for that
connection, that moment of understanding, that mutual desire. Oh, to
be transported out of this reality, however briefly, into that orbit of sex-
fueled obsessive love. To quote Saint Augustine, "I was in love with loving." Having Jackie Kennedy and Marilyn Monroe as benchmarks has
never made finding *her* very easy.

ON THIS night, I had settled on Bonnie, a blonde with great tits and a
mouth that never stopped moving. I knew what Bonnie should do with
her mouth, and it had nothing to do with talking, but *that* was reserved
for the future Mr. Meal Ticket.

Anyway, she was hot and so was her friend, a dark beauty who rarely spoke. My cousin Steven and I had nothing to do that weekend but take a couple of girls down to the family "compound" in Hyannis Port. I learned early in life the mythic as well as the real value of my family homestead. This could be a time when I might say, "Wanna go to the compound?" instead of "Wanna go to the Cape?"

I was not above using my lineage for sex.

We drove the seventy miles from Boston to the Port with Bonnie yakking at me in the front seat while Steve tried to impress her friend in the back. I didn't hear a word Bonnie was saying. I was looking in the rearview mirror at the one Steve was talking to. This is another one of my problems, never looking at what I have but always at what I don't have—yet.

What the hell was she—Asian, Polynesian, American Indian?

I didn't have a clue, but she sure was beautiful, and when she put on her bathing suit I was convinced that I had found *her*—again. Her name was Jeannie.

JEANNIE AND I spent five years hanging out before we were married. I had taken one of the suggestions of the good doctors at McLean's and stayed in Boston. I would be starting law school in the fall of 1980. I had a year to kill. I tried driving a cab but I didn't know my way around Boston, so after two days of listening to angry dispatchers and getting lost I decided to hang up the ole medallion. I was sitting in my apartment in Brookline when I got the call. My uncle Teddy had come to the rescue again. He had announced his candidacy for president of the United States, which meant I would be working on the campaign and not as a waiter or a car salesman. I guess the nervousness I had seen in him with the Supreme Court law clerks *was* an indication of things to come. My job on the campaign would be as a surrogate speaker for the candidate, which would mean a lot of traveling. When not on the road, I was in Boston with Jeannie, trying unsuccessfully to keep my medicine cabinet fully stocked.

Jeannie and I spent a lot of time making love, making war, and making mischief. It was very volatile and very dramatic. We'd stay up all night doing drugs and playing floor hockey in our apartment in Brookline with anybody who was awake and full of cocaine at 3 A.M. Or I might choose night basketball with my favorite drug dealer Ron and the other drug addicts we considered our close friends. If we weren't burning off the coke in some frantic physical activity, we would reorganize every photograph, document, or piece of memorabilia in our possession. The good thing about cocaine is that you get organized. You don't remember it the next day, but for a night, your life is totally organized. So after the activity came the sex. Good, hot, long drug-induced sex. When that was finished I waited the five minutes it would take for Jeannie to start messing with me.

"What did you mean when you said she was nice?"

"What?" I like to pretend I don't hear the question when I intuit there is something disagreeable around the corner.

"Why did you think she was nice?" Jeannie was really good at getting to the point.

"I don't know. Jesus, she just seemed nice," I said, in the hope that by invoking the Lord's name, it would put an end to the conversation.

It didn't.

"She was trying to pick you up." Now we were getting to the meat of it.

"I didn't notice." Defensive tactic number one—feigning to be oblivious.

"You were flirting with her all night." Fire one.

"You're projecting." Defensive tactic number two—psychological judo. I'm a master at obscuring inappropriate behavior by making it your problem. I guess all those years of therapy weren't a complete waste.

"Well you could have fooled me. You never took your eyes off her tits." Fire two.

"Why are you doing this to me?" Defensive tactic number three— victimization. This was my go-to tactic. I felt comfortable as a victim and I was pretty darn good at it. After a while I could usually get her to feel sorry for all the shit she was giving me, even though she was probably right about whatever it was she was giving me shit about.

Our fights usually had something to do with other women or

245

something I said I was going to do but hadn't gotten around to . . . yet. She may have been right about whatever it was, but why now? Why at the moment when I had just achieved my maximum level of intimacy, when I'm feeling pretty good about myself and pretty good about her, and the only problem I have at this moment is the cocaine that's still coursing through my veins and won't let me sleep, and the birds are going to be doing their thing in about a half hour. That's what made me crazy, sending me into a rage, which sent her into a rage, which meant we'd both be in a rage when the birds got up.

Jeannie knew how to tussle. Good thing.

This was something new to me. I may have come from a big, noisy Irish family, but I never saw anybody fight. I had seen people leave or turn cold and silent but never fight. Fighting scared the shit out of me, and Jeannie was a much better fighter than I was. I would either capitulate, asking over and over in my best victim voice, "Why are you doing this to me now?" or I would leave.

Once every six months or so I would lose it and punch a wall, or threaten to jump out the window, but usually I just took it, feeling bad that I had disappointed another woman. It's what I learned to do living with my mom in a household of women.

When my mom got angry she would walk around the apartment seething for days. My sisters and I would walk on eggshells until I finally got up the nerve to ask her what was wrong. She would smile and say, "Nothing is wrong, Christopher." Then she'd turn on her heel, march into her bedroom, slam the door, and burst into tears. There were a lot of mixed messages flying around 990 Fifth Avenue when I was a kid. It left me feeling like I had done something terribly wrong. So wrong, in fact, that it was unspeakable and unfixable, leaving me feeling trapped, and as if I would never have the freedom of my own life. Because nothing was ever confronted, I never learned how to fight. I only had two speeds, rage and victimization. Not very useful or healthy in navigating a relationship.

Jeannie and I broke up a million times but we always found our way back to each other. I never understood why Jeannie kept coming back. I was sure that life with me, while glamorous, was no picnic. I guess at my core I never believed anyone could love me. When we met in the Fan Club she was thinking of becoming a flight attendant. Then she met me. Let's see, travel the world on 747s or hitch your wagon to a train wreck waiting to happen. She must have seen something in me I wasn't aware I possessed.

Chapter 26

Nobody told me there'd be days like these.
— JOHN LENNON

In 1980 I was a vital, vibrant fixture on the family toasting circuit. I would always stand up and raise my glass, especially if Doug Spooner was in the room and got on his feet first. Doug was like Zelig. If there was a Kennedy or a Kennedy event, he was there. It was guaranteed that if there were toasts to be given, Doug would give one and it would be awful. My cousins and I would allow Doug to do his worst and compete to be the first one on our feet after he had finished. There was no possibility of not looking good when you followed Doug Spooner giving a toast.

Giving a funny, smart, or passionate toast was pretty much a prerequisite for any sort of base-level credibility in the public speaking and charisma department. Getting on one's feet in a room full of people was a proving ground for anybody aspiring to distinguish themselves. Teddy was the master, with the rest of us trying to make an impression in some very tough rooms. We all developed our own styles. The Shrivers were loud and combative, with brevity never a characteristic. Joe was uncomfortably demonstrative; Bobby went for humor, which was often off-color, and if that didn't work, tried to inspire. David hated the whole process.

He was the only one of us who was free from the ambition and delusion. By the time 1980 rolled around, David had sunk below the waves. He had developed endocarditis from his IV drug use and was the first of us to get arrested in Harlem for possession. There was a group of family and friends who kept tabs on him, including Teddy, Steve Smith, Dick Goodwin, Bob Coles, his brother Joe, and his sister Kathleen. David referred to them as the Committee to Keep David Out of the Picture. After his bust in Harlem, the committee gave David a choice: Mclean's or a rehab in Sacramento run by a guy named Don Juhl, which specialized in "therapy by humiliation." David chose Sacramento. I think primarily to get as far away from the family as he could. He spent that year in his room in Sacramento watching Uncle Teddy's campaign unravel on his black-and-white TV. Nobody in the family went to see him. He wasn't toasting anyone and nobody was toasting him.

My approach to the cannibalistic ritual was to go for the heart, which usually elicited a response of "very nice toast, very heartfelt," hardly what I was looking for. The two cousins who were the best on their feet were Steven Smith and Douglas Kennedy. They both were hilarious, with wit and pacing that was thoroughly their own. They were often outrageous, speaking truths that some of those present wished not to be shared in public.

SNAPSHOT:

My toasting career came crashing down one night in 1980 at a dinner at Hickory Hill. Ethel was giving Teddy a major fundraiser for his presidential campaign. The dinner was held in the living room, and there had to be five hundred of the richest and most powerful contributors to the Democratic Party along with the customary complement of famous and powerful window dressing that usually attended big Kennedy events.

As the toasting began, my nerves got the better of me and for the first time in my life I got toasting block. I couldn't think of anything to say. Now before you think, so what, just don't stand up, that wouldn't work. Not having anything to say was worse than giving a bad toast. See, part of the whole cannibalistic ritual included the calling of people to their feet.

Even if I didn't want to speak, my cousins would heckle me until I got up. The only way not to give a toast at one of these events was to hide in the bathroom, which I was considering, when Bobby came to my rescue—or so I thought.

Bobby:
Chris, have you noticed that all the waiters look Iranian?
Me:
Come on, Bobby, this is serious. I don't have a toast.
Bobby:
Seriously, they look like they just got off a plane from Tehran.
Me:
Okay, man, you're right, they all look like Merdad [our
Iranian friend]. So what!
Bobby:
Give a toast saying if everybody in the room doesn't make the
maximum contribution to Teddy's campaign, the waiters,
who are Iranian Shiites, will take them hostage.
Me:
I don't know, Bobby, I can't be sure, but I don't think that's
funny.
Bobby:
Man, you have no sense of humor.

We were in the middle of the Iranian hostage crisis, so the toast made sense, but was it funny? I thought it might be, but had ingested enough chemicals to sedate an elephant, so my humor meter was a little impaired. I sat in my seat in the midst of the best and the brightest hoping something better would come. I was contemplating an extended stay in Ethel's bathroom when the crowd started calling for the next gladiator— Chris Lawford. Ethel's bathroom was no longer an option. I got to my feet and delivered Bobby's toast with all the conviction I could muster. There was stunned silence. Well, that's not entirely true, there were a few derisive snickers and gasps at my inappropriateness.

My toast horrified everyone in the room and I was utterly humiliated. I replaced Doug Spooner as the person you most wanted to follow when making a toast. It would be a long time before I would get to my feet again at a family function to toast anyone or anything. Let's just say I spent a lot of time in the bathroom. I'm not at all certain this wasn't Bobby's intention.

I ARRIVED in Aspen, Colorado, for the Christmas holidays tired and haggard from two months on the campaign trail. I have no idea why my uncle decided to challenge Jimmy Carter; I guess it seemed like a good idea at the time. I liked Jimmy Carter, appreciated his honesty and willingness to tell us what we Americans didn't like hearing, but as soon as EMK threw his hat into the ring, the peanut farmer became the enemy—and there was no more good in the Carter presidency.

Being a surrogate speaker for a candidate running for president of the United States is no picnic. You freeze your ass off in places like Iowa and New Hampshire, making speeches and shaking hands with voters who would much rather be listening to or shaking hands with the actual candidate. In order to minimize expenses, you stay with a family of supporters in whatever town you happen to be in, usually bunking in little Scotty or Susie's bed, which is always six inches too short. The family is grateful to entertain anybody from anywhere and eager to grill you 24/7 about what's happening in the world or in your family. Because all campaigns are always running out of money, you get to pay your own expenses but are admonished to "keep your receipts," which you dutifully send to national headquarters where they get lost and are never seen again.

We had no shortage of surrogates in our family. Most of us were eager to heed the call. We competed furiously to be the best public speaker of our generation. I loved giving speeches. I usually opened with a promise that the candidate would make it to see the folks I was addressing soon, which was a lie. From there I went to the story about campaigning with my grandmother, when she told me the secret to winning campaigns: "Christopher, get married soon and have as many children as you can; in a campaign you can cover a lot of territory."

This got a lot of laughs but was also untrue. I never campaigned with my grandmother, and she might have said it but she never said it to me. It was probably made up by a speechwriter and I bet my other cousins used the same story. After the introductory bullshit I got to the meat of my uncle's record, which wasn't bullshit but was packaged for the widest possible audience. It didn't work—he was still way too liberal.

I practiced my oratory in Ted Kennedy's Senate campaigns as well as his presidential run, in Sarge Shriver's VP bid, and in my cousin Joe's congressional campaigns. I was honored to be asked, and always felt as though I was doing something important for my family and, in the bigger picture, for participatory democracy. When you get beyond the bullshit, there is a lot of integrity at the core of electoral politics. Those that participate bring with their need and hope an honesty that is often lost after the votes are counted. I met thousands of people across the country who believed in our system and those that run it.

SNAPSHOT:

I had made my way to Aspen after spending three weeks traveling by bus all over the Midwest. Sometimes I was with The Candidate, sometimes I was alone but always I was in search of votes. One day I found myself on the press bus playing cards with the fellas keeping track of the Kennedy campaign for the national press. We were making our way to another appearance in the frigid heartland, I was forty dollars down and needed to, as they say in Beantown, "take a wicked piss." I asked the bus driver to pull over and made a beeline for the only tree within a hundred miles. It was freezing cold, the wind making it difficult to keep my coat out of the projected line of fire. I pulled my manhood from the warmth of my pants and waited for relief. It didn't come. The midwestern chill coupled with my awareness of the curious and prying natures of those on the bus shriveled me as well as my intent. Were they watching? How long would they wait before calling out or taking a look? Would my diminished member develop frostbite if I didn't go in the next instant?

The harder I tried the less likely it became that I would be successful. I've always been pee shy and this was one of those quintessential pee-shy moments. I couldn't go and I couldn't get back on the bus without going. I was screwed. What a wonderful metaphor for my life. The expectation I might walk the path to greatness but when it came to actually doing it, I couldn't. The pressure of producing greatness, and the pressure of taking a piss. I couldn't do what I had told myself, and them, I needed to do—what they expected me to do. I was left ice cold, with my dick in my hands looking over my shoulder.

One of the tricks to being a drug addict is maintaining a supply of whatever it is you need while you're on the road. I had developed the talent of forging doctors' BNDD numbers—numbers assigned by the FDA to make sure that only those with medical licenses prescribe drugs. When I arrived in town, I would scour the phone book for a generic local doc's name, construct a BNDD number, call a local pharmacy, order a class-three painkiller under one of my aliases, and head down to pick it up. This worked well in Boston, New York, and other large urban areas, but it was a little trickier in small towns. Aspen is a small town, but I didn't have a choice. I had just arrived for a week of skiing and partying with my cousins, and I wasn't going to do it straight.

There is no name more generic than Smith, so I chose Dr. John Smith as my mark and went through the ritual. It was New Year's Eve, and Peppo Vanini, the owner of Xenon, our nightclub of choice in New York City since Steve Rubell had been indicted for tax evasion and Studio 54 had died, was having a bash in Aspen. I was planning to be flush. Everything went perfectly, the pharmacy took the script, and sixty Darvocet-Ns were waiting for Chris West at his convenience. I had learned that Darvocet-Ns were similar to methadone in their chemical structure and effect. It was a good maintenance drug, with not much kick, but long lasting and easy on the stomach. The sixty tablets courtesy of Dr. Smith would last me six days until I got back to Boston and the safety of the Dr. Feelgoods I had cultivated over the years.

I felt optimistic as I headed out the door in my new leather coat into the promise of New Year's Eve. I grabbed a cab and headed first to the pharmacy on my way to the party. I told the cabbie to leave it running and left my new coat as security as I ran into Aspen Drugs. They were about to close, but the pharmacist seemed glad to see me, cheerfully saying, "Yes, Mr. West, we've been waiting for you. We have your prescription right here." I stepped up to the register to pay, and as I did the Aspen police officer who'd also been waiting for me stepped up behind me, threw some handcuffs on me, and read me my rights.

To add insult to injury, the pharmacist confided to me, as I waited for the squad car that would transport me to the Aspen police station, that Dr. John Smith was one of the most well-known doctors in the area with a booming distinctive voice. They saw me coming a mile away.

That New Year's Eve I never made it to Peppo's party and an Aspen cabbie inherited a hot new leather coat. I got my one phone call and called Uncle Steve, who was not happy to hear from me but arranged bail and a lawyer. I spent the night in jail and had to endure the contempt of my family for the remaining five days of what proved to be a horrific holiday. I ran into my aunt Jean the next day on top of Ajax Mountain. She had no interest in skiing with me. I thought, What's her problem? She was very close to Teddy. This was her campaign as much as his. And my antics weren't a positive development in what was already proving to be an uphill fight. I was no longer anyone's favorite nephew.

My arrest in Aspen was one of those signposts they talk about in addiction. I could have seen it for what it was: a public humiliation and indictment of a way of life that had been suspected but never proved. It was another indication that the elevator had descended yet again, but it never occurred to me that I might want to get off.

I headed back to Boston with a February court date in Colorado and some media-fueled notoriety that made all those Dr. Feelgoods very nervous. This did not bode well for future prescriptions.

These were desperate times in need of desperate measures.

I arrived in Bean Town to a changed landscape. Nobody was calling from the Kennedy campaign to sign me up for surrogate gigs anytime soon. This surprised me. Now do you understand how far I was from having a clue? Jeannie seemed glad to see me, but she was working for the head coach of the USFL's Boston Breakers football team, which kept her busy. My aunt Eunice would drop in periodically to keep tabs on me. She sent my mom a letter filling her in and trying to lift her spirits concerning her wayward son.

> *Dear Patty*
>
> *. . . I called Christopher to ask if he would like to have lunch with me. We had a lovely time. He is really an extraodinary boy. I have spent a lot of time over the years working with young people & I have not met any boy who has less malice or meanness or unkindness. He is so kind, so positive, so sensitive. I think he is more like you in character than the girls. He looked wonderful. . . . He is working hard, he seems determined and he loves you. I admire him and love him. I just thought you would like to know this. I would like as a mother to find someone who thought as highly of my son as I do of your Chris.*
>
>
>
> *Love & hugs*
> *Diamondless Eunice!!*
>
>

The one thing that hadn't changed back in Boston was my habit, which still needed to be fed. With doors closing all around me, the only path open seemed to be the illegal one. I resisted for a time, but the gorilla wanted to dance and I was powerless to resist, so one night in March, a few weeks before the Massachusetts primary, I became Dr. Whoever and phoned it in.

What I learned from my Aspen fiasco was that if I hadn't gone to the pharmacy, I wouldn't have been arrested. This suggested that I should have someone else pick up the goods. My roommate was tempting, but I wasn't all bad, so I called Brookline cab and told them to pick up a prescription for Chris Schwartz and deliver it to the house three doors down from mine. I figured I would meet the cab in front of the house and make my way back to the safety of my unimplicated address. Who says junkies aren't creative?

I felt pretty confident as I walked the half block to the rendezvous.

The big black sedan that cruised by gave me pause, but it passed — and so did the little voice deep down inside me that was screaming,

"Danger, Will Robinson or Chris Schwartz." The cabby showed as planned but he seemed nervous. I grabbed the package, threw him some cash, and started back to safety. I could see the door to my house a few yards away. Oblivion was just on the other side of it. The big black sedan turned the corner ever so slowly. The headlights hit me, and I was that proverbial deer, frozen. The sedan was on me before I could think. I only had time for one involuntary reaction toward self-preservation: I threw the package farther than I had thrown any object in my life. It took the two undercover police officers two hours to find it, and when they did, the contents were pretty much obliterated. This wasn't going to save me. They still had evidence and I was on probation in Colorado.

I told them who I was.

"Officer, I need to tell you something."

"Yeah, what is it, asshole?" He wasn't happy that he'd had to crawl through a lot of bushes looking for the drugs I had heaved.

"My uncle is Senator Kennedy."

"Shit! You're kidding me. Why didn't you tell us sooner? We already called it in. I guess you're screwed."

Guess again.

They say that addicts stay active in their disease longer because of those who enable them. That night I was enabled by two cops from Brookline, Massachusettes, who let me out the back door of their precinct because my uncle was the United States senator from their state. I guess the fact that they had "called it in" wasn't such a big deal. At the time I was grateful. Now I'm not so sure.

If I had been arrested that night, I would surely have been forced to deal with my addiction either in jail or out. As it turned out I got another six years of self-inflicted misery.

The next day I got a call from the lieutenant governor of Massachusetts. He wasn't happy:

Lt. Gov.:
What the fuck is the matter with you?
Me:
Sorry.

256

Lt. Gov.:
Do you think you might be able to stay out of trouble until
the primary?
Me:
When's that?
Lt. Gov:
In a month.
Me:
I can do that.
Lt. Gov.:
Because if you can't, I'm gonna send over a really nasty state
police officer to babysit you!
Me:
Tommy, I swear to God I'll never do another illegal thing as
long as I live.
Lt. Gov:
Behave yourself.

And he hung up.

Needless to say, this was all interfering with my political aspirations. World leader didn't look like a career option for me after all. The family was concerned, but a little too tied up to do an alcoholic intervention. I've heard of families hiring therapists. I would just get a threatening phone call from the lieutenant governor . . .

I sent my mother a letter in March, after they had let me back on the campaign.

Dear Mummy,
Just a note to let you know all is going well and I am back on
the campaign trail knocking em dead for "our Candidate."
I hope all is well with you. From what I hear we should be
running "you" for president! I love you and miss you and
please don't worry about me. After all I was brought up by you,
how can I not be the greatest.

All my love
Xtopher

A month later I received a note from my uncle Teddy signaling that all was forgiven.

> *Chris*
> *A note to thank you for being a part of our effort in this campaign. I think what we are doing is important and I am honored to have you as part of the team.*
> *My thanks & love*
>
> *Ted*

I was back on track . . .

Chapter 27

The bottom is where things worsen quicker than you can lower your standards.
— ANONYMOUS

I showed up for my second go-round with those massive legal text-books they dump on you the first day of law school, with the best of intentions and the goodwill of Dean Huber. As usual it meant nothing once the 800-pound gorilla started dancing. They say the road to hell is paved with good intentions.

Sometime in the fall of 1980, Steely Dan released *Gaucho*. I fell in love with one of the songs on it: "Time Out of Mind." It was a won-derfully produced ditty about chasing the dragon, aka smoking heroin.

Tonight when I chase the dragon
The water will change to cherry wine.

The more I listened to the harmonies of Donald Fagen and Walter Becker, the more compelled I became to try the only method of con-sumption that had eluded me. I was halfway through my first year of law school and living in the same house in Brookline where the two cops had jumped out of their big black sedan. I asked the friend I was with—I can't remember his name; we'll call him Henry—if he was up for a little adventure. Henry was usually up for anything, especially if I was paying, so we piled into my red 280 ZX and headed into the

Roxbury ghetto to see if we could find some brothers with heroin pure enough to smoke.

I had heard that the streets were flowing with heroin that was 70 percent pure. Much stronger heroin than what I had cut my teeth on on Dope Hill in the seventies. Chasing the dragon was the answer for heroin that was too pure to shoot. When smack is smoked there's less chance of overdose. Once again the hype proved to be bullshit. Not only were the streets not flowing with smokable junk, Henry and I were having trouble finding anyone holding anything. One of the things that happens when you are on the hunt for drugs is that you lose sight of what you are looking for and become fevered to the point that you'll do anything in a glassine bag. I never thought I would end up in some of the places I ended up in, doing the things I was doing.

I just wanted to chase the dragon.

I ended up in a shooting gallery with a bag of baking soda, a needle, and a spoon. I got mine, Henry was out of luck. But being the good wingman I am, we kept looking. Enter a five-foot-one-inch brother with knowledge of a shooting gallery across town where there might be some dope and clean works. So the three of us piled into my two-seat, very noticeable sports car and headed off on another wild goose chase so Henry could get high. The brother had been right. We copped and headed out to drop our guide back where he came from.

If I were a cop and saw a bright red Datsun 280 ZX with two white guys sandwiching a tiny twitching brother driving around the drug-infested inner city, I'd pull them over. That must have been what the cop who just pulled up behind us thought. I don't know why I was holding Henry's bag of heroin and why I didn't give it to him as soon as I saw the flashing lights in my rearview mirror.

I remember thinking, Put it in your boot; no, keep it close in case you have to get rid of it. They won't search me. I'm the driver. They'll search Henry and the brother—not me.

This is what went through my mind, which I admit was slightly fogged by the little bit of heroin and large amount of baking soda I'd ingested. I took my time pulling over. Henry was frantic—"Get rid of it, man"—which I couldn't figure out because it was his dope. I wouldn't have considered getting rid of a bag of heroin if it was mine. Shit, I wouldn't get rid of it, and it was Henry's—but that had more to do with the fact that I had always felt beyond the consequences of breaking the law. Hell, two cops had just let me out the back door of their station house in Brookline; these bozos in Roxbury weren't gonna touch me. The brother just kept saying, "Be cool, man. Be cool."

As the car rolled to a stop, I kept my eyes on the rearview mirror to catch a glimpse of just whom I would be dealing with. I slipped the glassine bag full of god knows what in the left pocket of my ski parka and waited to see what would happen next. The cops made their way to either side of the car and told us to get out. It was all very casual as they zeroed in on me and asked me where the drugs were. I was a little surprised.

Why are they picking on me? I thought. It was Henry's dope. And there's a brother from the neighborhood standing here. Certainly these are more appropriate targets than yours truly.

Maybe. But the officers had been watching us for a while, and from their vantage point I was the guy who had the most to do with the drugs in question.

I had the dope clutched tightly in my left hand, which was buried deep in my pocket. I played it with cool indignation as they began digging in my clothes. I backed away, threw both arms in the air, indicating surrender and letting the glassine bag fly into the night. I should have learned from my experience with the cops in Brookline that throwing your drugs into the night may buy you some time but they always find them in the end. And it makes them angry when you make them work that hard. These guys didn't have to work that hard because I had parked under a streetlight. Everything that went down on that corner in Roxbury was fully illuminated. The officers had no trouble finding the bag.

"What have we got here?"—and out came the handcuffs. Only one pair—for me. Henry and the brother were free to go, but first they offered us a deal. Henry and the brother could go back to the shooting gallery where we bought the dope and make another buy, giving the cops the dealer, and I would be free to go. I saw a slim ray of hope. Henry indicated a halfhearted willingness but only because I was pleading like a man who was on his way to the gallows. The brother didn't look like he thought he had a choice and would go along for the ride, looking for his opportunity to bolt. As Henry and the brother headed off to entrap the dealer—followed by one officer in the cruiser—I felt as if my life hung in the balance.

Addicts are plagued by fanciful thinking. We trust in the long shot and are convinced a miracle is just around the next corner. As I stood on that frozen street, hands bound behind my back, watched over by a disinterested cop, my life in the hands of two individuals in whom I had absolutely no faith—I hoped for a miracle.

It didn't happen.

Henry returned and told me they couldn't find the guy.

"What about the brother?" I asked.

"He left," Henry offered lamely.

"Where did he go?"

"I don't know, Chris, I guess he went to do whatever it is drug dealers do at two o'clock in the morning." Henry was beginning to piss me off.

"You should have kept an eye on him."

I was beginning to panic.

"I did but he disappeared," Henry pleaded.

"Disappeared. That's just great, Henry."

The cops began moving me to the cruiser. Henry was looking a little like Judas—which in my mind, I guess, made me feel a little like Christ. Paying for everybody's sins. As they sat me in the back of their patrol car I took my last shot.

"Why not let me try? I know what he looks like and I'm good at finding drug dealers." They weren't buying, and off we went to the Roxbury police station.

They put me in my own holding cell. I was the only Caucasian being incarcerated in the Roxbury jail at 2 A.M. that night. There were four or five real-looking criminals of color in the other cell. I was grateful for my own space. My fellow inmates took notice of me and at first thought I might be an Italian mobster from the North End worthy of respect. But after a short time they surmised that I was just a rich white doctor's son from the suburbs, looking for drugs. From the moment they came to this spontaneous and unanimous conclusion, respect went out the window, and I was treated to a barrage of threats and in-sults.

"Don't go to sleep, white boy, or we'll piss in your mouth."

"We can't wait to get your ass in the van that takes us all to court."

"You're all mine, pretty boy."

Shit like that. Fuck! Who do I have to blow to get out of here!

It turned out to be my cousin Joe. He gave me the good news and the bad. They weren't going to let me out the back door, but I could make bail that night and miss spending the weekend in my new digs and the van ride to court on Monday.

The papers got hold of my latest exploit. Within a few days, my fel-low students at BC Law were discussing the suitability of having a first-year student who had just been arrested for possession of heroin enrolled in their law school. I was hurt and angry that there were those with so little compassion. Not seeing for a moment any legitimacy in their concerns. I did feel bad about Dean Huber. He had gone out on a limb for me and trusted me when I said I intended to turn my life around. I meant it at the time, but you know that gorilla. Addicts sure can break your heart.

My aunt Eunice came to Boston to hold my hand through the meetings with lawyers and my arraignment. I was given another slap on the wrist—probation. Everybody else in the family was keeping their heads down.

I don't know where my mother was and why she wasn't there. She had moved back from Paris in 1979, buying an apartment on Sutton Place in New York City. Eunice had been a surrogate mother during the Paris years and I think my mother thought Eunice and I were more comfortable with this arrangement.

My dramas were too much for my mom. She was worn out from battling her demons and my demons at the same time. Whenever some misfortune befell me, it was as if I had punched my mother in the stomach.

Eunice had the Kennedy ambition to save the world and was fully equipped to do it. For the time being I was the world. And she was go-ing to save me. She had the energy and desire. Hell, she had almost single-handedly transformed the way the world viewed mental retardation; straightening me out shouldn't be that difficult. I remember her saying to me in a fit of frustration as we sat in my lawyer's office, "We're so goddamned good at taking care of everybody else's problems, but absolutely lousy at looking after our own." But saving the world in some ways was easier than saving me from myself. Still she was determined to try.

It was common knowledge in our family that if Eunice had been born male she would have been president of the United States. There wasn't anything Eunice couldn't do if she wanted to. She had a mighty will. Eunice also had a genuine soft spot for those who needed help. This drew her to my mother. Eunice always demonstrated a belief that whatever the challenges a person faced, they could be overcome through the exercise of will.

I think my mom proved to be her most complicated and heartbreaking project. My mother may have been less accomplished than her siblings in the real world, and she had her difficulties with the slings and arrows of life, but she didn't want any help. As a matter of fact she preferred that the do-gooders mind their own fucking business, thank you very much. Her will to live her own life was just as strong as the wills of any of those who were looking to meddle. I loved this about her. She was tough.

You MIGHT think that my experience in law school would have provided a clue that I was not meant to be a lawyer. It didn't. I just figured I wasn't suited for academic environments. I learned that a career in the law would not be my path by spending the summer as an associate in a large entertainment law firm in Los Angeles.

In the summer between one's first and second years in law school it is customary for the law student to get a summer job with a firm that practices the kind of law the student may want to work in. I wasn't really looking forward to going to work and was dreading going to work as a lawyer.

My experience as a summer associate at the large entertainment law firm confirmed for me two important facts: One, it is impossible to do good legal work in the real world when you are high on Percodans all day. The lawyers at the firm might as well have been speaking Chinese. They would hand me an assignment I didn't understand, and when I went back for clarification they were speaking Chinese and Greek.

I really should have gone to class more often.

My solution was to prepare briefs with as much information as I could find, hoping that somewhere in the mountain of paper I dumped on the lawyer's desk would be what he needed. The shotgun approach to legal brief writing. This was not useful to my employers.

The second epiphany I had was that being a lawyer is a lot of work. I realized this one beautiful Saturday afternoon while working at my desk on Jaclyn Smith's Max Factor contract, which called for multi-million-dollar payments for a few days work. I didn't want to be a lawyer, I wanted to be Jaclyn Smith.

At the end of one's summer associate internship it is customary for the firm to make the associate an offer of full-time employment upon completion of law school. I did not get a job offer. I felt terrible and worthless when I got the news, but later realized the lawyers had done me a favor. If they had offered me a job, I would have taken it. I would have become a lawyer and missed out on all the exciting adventures I've had "not knowing what to do with the rest of my life." I left that big entertainment law firm taking the mountains of briefs I had written with me. There might have been too much information, but I was proud of my work. I stayed at the Holiday Inn on Sunset and the 405 for a few days as I waited for the plane to take me east. One day I ran into a girl at the pool and invited her up to my room for room service. When the food and sex were done I told her I had a dinner engagement, politely suggesting she should go. She didn't take the hint and basically said that since she had slept with me, my room was her room for the night.

And here I thought I was this hot failed summer associate, and all she was looking for was a room for the night. Shit!

Thus began our war of the roses.

I started by pleading with her to leave. From there I went to disbelief. Then contempt.

None of it worked. She wasn't going anywhere.

Soon we were hurling insults at each other across the divide that separated the two double beds we had each staked out. I must have crossed a line, because she got up from her bed and marched over to the desk where my temple of briefs sat. Only a couple of hours ago I had regaled her with the story of their production. She picked up my summer's work, walked to the balcony, and heaved them off to the parking lot twenty stories below. I didn't believe she would do it, that's why I didn't get off my bed to stop her until it was too late. I had never been involved with a person who wouldn't leave or who would throw a person's flawed but prized legal briefs off a twenty-story balcony.

It was scary. Probably what it feels like when you are being stalked. But once I saw the papers leave her hands, something in me snapped and I came very close to being the guy who is being led away in handcuffs saying, "I don't know, Officer, one minute we were having dinner and the next I was heaving her off my balcony."

I did grab her. I did lift her up, but I moved away from the balcony and toward the elevator, where I deposited her amid a torrent of verbal and physical abuse. She took the hint—and the elevator.

What I got from all this was a confirmation that I really wasn't meant to be a lawyer. If I had had the capacity to go a little deeper, I might have realized that holding on to a mountain of not very good legal briefs as some sort of trophy was pretty clear evidence that I was not in touch with what was really going on. And being a hairbreadth away from tossing a girl I didn't know but had just slept with off my twentieth-story balcony was pretty clear evidence that my life was capable of going from summer associate to prison inmate in a New York minute.

AFTER MY close call on the Holiday Inn balcony, I headed back to Boston to complete my senior year of law school. In September of 1982, I moved into my cousin Joe's house in Brighton. Jeannie came with me to the crappy little place on the top of a hill in the middle of a working-class neighborhood. Things were getting serious on all fronts. Having Joe as a landlord was no picnic. We had to mind our p's and q's when it came to taking care of the place, which wasn't easy given the considerable effort it took just to get through the day dancing with the 800-pound gorilla.

Joe was particularly concerned with the trees he had planted in front of the house to keep the neighbors from seeing what the Kennedys were up to. After every snowstorm, he would call to make sure that I had taken a broom to the trees to prevent the snow from building up and breaking the branches. You have to understand, I didn't do winter very well, being from California and all. Snowstorms sent me into a drug-induced hibernation for weeks. The last thing I was thinking about was Joe Kennedy's trees. The winter of '82 was particularly nasty. I was sedated for much of it. Joe's trees turned into popsicles. And Joe was pissed. He called me one day after driving by for a look-see.

The conversation went something like this.

"Chris Lawford, have you seen my trees?" I don't know why he always used my first and last name when he was mad. I think it was his way of documenting the seriousness of what was going down and making sure he had my full attention.

"No, Joe, I haven't been outside today; it's freezing," I replied, hoping Joe might let it go. He didn't.

"My fucking trees are ice cubes. They didn't get that way in one day." Joe was beginning to ramp up.

"I don't know how that could be, Joe," I said. "I whacked them with a broom a while ago."

"'A while ago,' you asshole; it's been snowing for two weeks."

"Joe, take it easy. I'll go whack them now."

"That's the point, you loser, you can't whack them now. They'll break."

And so it went, Joe getting madder and madder until he hung up. I had been making Joe mad for years and would usually just tune the tirade out, but this time he said something that got through.

"Do you know what character is, Chris?"

"Joe, I don't see what character has to do with your trees."

"Think about it, asshole."

I did. And Joe was right. I was seriously lacking in character. But it was winter, and it was cold outside. I would have to deal with my character later. In the meantime I would need something to take my mind off just what a dirtball I was. Let's see . . .

SNAPSHOT:

> Ted Kennedy was having a big fund-raiser in Boston for his "You can bet the farm on it" reelection to the Senate, and Robert Redford was coming. I had made one of my bimonthly pilgrimages to pick up some methadone from my New York homeboys for the weekend. I'd hop on the Eastern shuttle in the morning, take a cab to Ninety-sixth Street and Lexington Avenue, and wait for the junkies to show up with the weekend doses they sold so they could buy the drugs they really wanted.

One of the drawbacks to buying methadone on the street is you that can't tell if it's been cut. Let's say a junkie gets 90 milligrams from the clinic. He might drink half and fill it back up with water. The only way to tell what you are getting on the street is by taste. Cut methadone is less bitter. Or by the representations of the seller. Neither method is very reliable. I always assumed whoever I bought methadone from was a lying junkie, so I would take more than I should, figuring what was in the bottle was less than represented. This can be a recipe for disaster; you never know when you might run into an honest junkie.

Methadone releases in your system slowly, so you may get high and seem fine, then go to sleep and never wake up. That's what almost happened to me the night I met Robert Redford at the Park Plaza Hotel and coaxed him to sign an autograph for Jeannie who was back home nursing a resentment.

Me:
Excuse me, Mr. Redford, I'm Chris Lawford, Ted's nephew.
Could I get an autograph for my girlfriend?
Bob:
Sure. Got a pen?
Me:
Uh. No.

Ted:

Oh Bob, there you are. I'd like you to meet my niece
Caroline. . . . Oh Chris . . . Chris isn't bothering you, is he,
Bob?

Bob:

No. We just need a pen.

Me:

Got a pen, Teddy?

Teddy:

Ah. No. The thing is, we need Bob over here with the
contributors.

Me:

I'm just trying to get his autograph, Teddy.

Teddy:

Chris, this *is* a fund-raiser.

Me:

Geez, Teddy, after all the time I spent in Lowell and
Worcester for *the campaign,* I think the least you could do is
let me get Robert Redford's autograph.

Ted:

(to his assistant)
Rainy, give me a goddamn pen!

Me:

Bob, could you make it out to Jeannie, with a J?

Bob:

Sure.

I hustled back to the Brighton manse with the Popsicle trees, gave Jeannie Redford's autograph, and nodded off.

I woke up in the intensive care unit of St. Elizabeth's Hospital with a big hose in my side. It was put there to reinflate the lung that had collapsed as a result of me aspirating vomit, which I had choked on as a result of the coma I was in, caused by the junkie scumbag who had decided to tell the truth when he sold me his 90 mg take-homes.

When I came to, I didn't follow his example. The doctors brought me back to life uncertain if I would ever be able to comprehend *People* magazine again, much less be on the cover, and the first words out of my mouth were a lie.

"I didn't take anything." Nobody called me a liar, so I figured they'd bought it. A few days later when some of the tubes that were keeping me alive had been removed, I was forced to have a conversation with my cousin Joe. I guessed Uncle Steve wasn't available. I told Joe what I had told the docs about not taking anything. He laughed and said, "You're full of shit. They did a blood screen and there was methadone, Valium, alcohol, cocaine, and Quaaludes. Is there anything you didn't take?"

You always knew where you stood with Joe.

I figured I was pretty well committed to the "I don't know what you're talking about" approach, but a slight embellishment was needed. "Well, they must have gotten it wrong, I just had a couple of beers at Teddy's fund-raiser." I hung up the phone wondering whom I might call to bring me some drugs to ease the pain while I convalesced at Saint E's.

When I got home there was a manila envelope containing a photograph of Robert Redford giving a very high Chris Lawford an autograph, with an irritated Ted Kennedy looking on. I figured Teddy was a little more irritated now.

A couple days after I received the photo I got some more bad news from the New York family office.

> Dear Chris:
> I regret having to write this letter. However, your level of spending has deteriorated your financial situation to the point that your running out of funds is imminent. Although the facts may be unpleasant to deal with, they are rather straightforward. As a result of your over spending during the past six years, you have gone from a net worth of $179,000 in 1976 to $2,000 as of today. . . . You have pretty much used up your capital.

Things were definitely looking grim. Time for action, something bold. I know, I'll get married.

I proposed to Jeannie in the upstairs bedroom of Joe's crappy little house in the middle of a wicked snowstorm. My life wasn't working on any level. I figured getting married might straighten a few things out. Jeannie was a good woman. We complemented each other, but the clincher was that for the four years we had been together we had good sex every day. At least it was good for me, I can't speak for Jeannie. With all my previous girlfriends I had lost interest in sex after two years.

SNAPSHOT:

The night I asked Jeannie to marry me, she had already gone to bed: I was chasing the dragon in the den at three in the morning and woke her up with my big impulsive idea. She was groggy, incredulous, but willing. Jeannie had hitched her wagon to mine three years earlier. We had been in a ditch for much of that time, but hey, we were in the ditch together. I didn't have a ring, given the fact that the idea had just come to me and it was 3 A.M., so the next morning I ran down to Shreve, Crump & Low and got one — on credit.

It was $27,000, way too expensive for someone with only $2,000 to his name, so later that night when I asked her to marry me again and gave her the ring, I explained that we would have to return that ring and get something a little more affordable. I couldn't find anything in Boston, so I decided to get the ring in L.A.

I was headed there in search of a summer job at a law firm and was certain to find the time to pick up a nice little bobble in Beverly Hills. I found a job and a ring: a beautiful sapphire and diamond number that set me back $10,000. I'm not cheap, just noncommittal. I had the ring forwarded on to Palm Beach where I was supposed to rendezvous with Jeannie for a little R&R. I was beginning to have some doubts about the whole marriage thing. It wasn't Jeannie. I was just terrified of getting married. I didn't know it at the time but my parents' divorce had left me with a psychic scar so profound that Marriage = Pain. My plan was to see how well we got along on our vacation. This would be my sign. If we weren't at each others throats, she'd get the ring. If we were, that would be my excuse and I'd send the ring back. We were walking on the beach in front of my grandparents' house and I couldn't find a reason not to give her the ring. I pretended to find a shell in the sea, gave it to her, and when she opened it the ring was revealed. I was once again adored. It would be a very long engagement.

SNAPSHOT:

At first I had no idea why my uncle Teddy wanted to fight me. Sure we both had a little too much to drink in the Edelweis Café deep in the Swiss Alps in Saint-Moritz, and I had been a bit of a smart-ass, egged on by my cousins John Kennedy and Willy Smith, but it still seemed like having a fistfight with your twenty-seven-year-old nephew was a bit of an overreaction. We were in the midst of a family holiday. Teddy's family, the JFKs, the Lawfords, and the Smiths. The RFKs and Shrivers weren't invited. The RFKs, due to numbers and bad temperaments, and the Shrivers were doing their own thing. We had spent the week skiing and hobnobbing with the likes of Johnny Agnelli and the well-heeled Eurotrash that skied and discoed in one of the most famous ski resorts in the world. At this moment my uncle was standing unsteadily on a patch of ice, his fists raised, and he was calling me out: "Come on, Chris Lawford, I'm gonna fight you here and now. I've had enough of your crap. Come on."

I looked at my uncle and I had one of those brief moments of clarity. I caught a glimpse of just how infuriating carrying the entire weight of the Kennedy legacy could be. If I had sacrificed my life for a bunch of bratty kids who didn't give a shit, I'd want to punch me in the face too.

I just stood there. I didn't know what to do or what to say. For a second I thought about accepting, but then I remembered Armando and the hole in my gut as I walked down Fifth Avenue after our fisticuffs at the Guggenheim. I was pretty sure that if I went toe-to-toe with my uncle Teddy, the hole would be significantly greater. Then I wondered who would win, and in that moment I realized I was in one of those coming-of-age moments. Teddy had moved from the mythic to the human. I was looking at the main man in my life and wondering if I could take him. I decided to walk away. I wasn't ready yet to assert myself.

I HAD a great drug dealer in Boston named Floyd. He was a white-collar dealer, one of those guys who ran a legit business, had a straight wife and a mortgage, balanced a checkbook, and sold drugs out the back door. It was a mystery to me how he managed it. He took Perco-dans, Quaaludes, and cocaine just like me—not as many, but few did—and he still managed to function in the real world. That was extraordinary—but what really amazed me was that he could make money selling drugs when he was using them himself. I was the type of drug addict who would procure a stash that was supposed to last a week and within twenty hours everything would be gone. I had no capacity for parceling or saving for a rainy day. I liked the idea of a business where others would pay for my consumption, but I was cursed with the personality of a consumer. I financed a good deal of Floyd's life and chemical intake.

Floyd was plugged into some drugstore cowboys, who robbed pharmacies up and down the eastern seaboard. He never knew what he was going to get or when he was going to get it. One day I'd call and he'd be flush with morphine sulfate and pharmaceutical coke, the next it would be methadone "biscuits" and Dilaudid. I got as much of a rush from the call as anything. I would try to gauge by the tone of his voice what he was holding and when I might get my hands on it. Like most dealers Floyd loved the power he held over those of us who would chew our hands off to be allowed to pay him twice what he had paid for what he was holding.

Floyd loved racquetball. He would play a couple times a week. I liked squash and felt that racquetball was an idiot sport for those who couldn't manage the finesse of squash or tennis, but I would rush over to the Newton racquetball club to sample Floyd's new shipment of co-caine and buzz around the court with my heart pounding out of my chest. It was during one of these exercises in heart attack simulation that I first heard about LAM, or long-acting methadone.

The government had developed a methadone that apparently lasted three days. It was totally experimental but apparently the cow-boys had stumbled on some during one of their robberies and were go-ing to be making a delivery to the starving junkies of Boston. I couldn't wait. A narcotic that lasted three days sounded really good to me, no matter how much it cost.

Since LAM was classified as an experimental drug and was only being used in very controlled environments, nobody knew much about it. Most good druggies claim to know anything and everything about any drug on the street and are more than willing to act as guinea pigs, if it promises a good high. I was no exception. I showed up at Floyd's office after the cowboys had dropped off the suitcase, eager to do my bit of research.

LAM tastes like crap, but its effect was as promised. Three days on a pain-free methadone nod. There was a problem. Although I knew intellectually that the stuff would last three days, I guess I didn't really believe it. I certainly didn't fully realize that three days after I took it, I would be as high as I was the first day. If I had, I never would have agreed to be the bowman for my cousin Joe in a canoe race down a river full of giant rapids in the annual River Rats Race on Millers River just outside Athol, Massachusetts. That's right— Athol.

I was a little shaky, as Joe, Bobby, the ever-present Doug Spooner, and I piled into Joe's truck for the trek out to Worcester County. Joe had been tapped by my uncle Teddy to run his Senate campaign. This elevated him to that lofty position of future Kennedy political entity. This meant our canoe race, along with all other events from that point on, was a political appearance and as such had conse-quences for Joe. All of us had spent a fair amount of time in white water, but that was on rafts. Canoes are different. And this was a big race full of canoers who knew what they were doing, but we were

Kennedys and figured we should win. This was a Massachusetts river after all.

I have no idea how I ended up in Joe's canoe, probably through process of elimination. Doug Spooner didn't know which end of the paddle went in the water. Bobby and Joe were incapable of being in that close proximity for five minutes, much less a whole race. I would do what Joe told me to do and knew how to paddle. So I was chosen to help the future political icon navigate the treacherous rapids on Millers River.

Joe had no idea, as we strapped on our life vests and helmets and headed into the current, that I had enough LAM in me to kill any normal person. A couple of things became immediately evident as we headed into our first rapid and the good people of Worcester County screamed, "Way to go, Joe." LAM does not enhance one's reflexes, vision is a problem, strength dissipates quickly, and seasickness—or river sickness in this case—is almost instantaneous.

From the moment Joe and I hit the first five-foot standing wave, I began losing my lunch—and it seemed like everything else I had eaten in the past week. It's not easy paddling a canoe through rapids while you're throwing up. This was a fast river, full of big waves, and something bad could happen at any moment. There wasn't a moment's respite from trying to stay on course and out of harm's way. It's also impossible not to vomit in your canoe no matter how hard you try to do it over the side as you bounce off of rocks and waves in a class-four rapid. By the time we got to our first portage, Joe was knee deep in regurgitated LAM and tacos, and the only canoe behind us was Bobby and Doug's.

I had never seen Joe so mad, but it didn't faze me since I was certain that I was going to die on this river, and pissing Joe off in the process was the only bright spot. I kept saying, "I'm sorry, Joe. I don't know what's the matter with me," as he hurled insults at me about my character: "What the fuck's a matter with you, man?" "Paddle harder." "God, you are so lazy." "Nice time to get sick, Chris."

Halfway through the race, Joe decided I should be in the stern of the canoe, where you steer. I guess his thinking was that because I was so ineffectual in the bow and we were hitting every rock, log, and wave on the river, if he was in front he might be able to avoid these things and paddle. He put me in the stern on my knees, my legs under the seat, and told me just to keep my paddle in the water and attempt to steer us down the middle of the river. Seemed like a good plan; but the river didn't cooperate, pushing us toward the bank and those nasty-looking low-hanging branches that were whizzing by head-high. My paddle limply hanging from our stern had no effect, and all of Joe's will and anger could not alter our direction from the bow.

A branch caught me under my chin and ripped me and the seat out of the canoe, landing me in the icy water. That got my attention and stopped the projectile vomiting. I know God was watching out for me because there is no other explanation for my not being decapitated and drowning. I popped up right next to the canoe, and Joe hauled me back, saying shit like "Jesus, man, what's the matter with you? Stop fucking around!" but saving my life in the process.

The only bright side was that by the time we reached the finish line all the voters had long since vanished and those still waiting to catch a glimpse of the Kennedys couldn't see us because it was too dark.

I GRADUATED from Boston College Law School in June of 1983. My mother, sisters, Mademoiselle, and Jeannie watched me accept my juris doctorate from Dean Huber in cap and gown on a sweltering day in Boston. I had no intention of pursuing a career in law but took the bar exam anyway. I didn't pass. The Boston press had a field day. I was ridiculed along with my cousin John Kennedy, who failed to pass the New York bar exam. My sister Sydney came to my defense in a letter to the editor:

I am very angered by Ms. Nathan's Monday article entitled "Chris Trips Over Bar Exam." Law School consists of 3 years of extremely hard work, followed by a grueling 2 day examina-

tion. For those who fail to pass the bar exam, feelings of great personal disappointment are experienced. Ms. Nathan's insinuation that failure runs in our family was cruel, unnecessary and certainly unjustified! Neither my brother, my cousin, nor anyone in our family is a failure!

You tell her, Syd!

Chapter 28

For everything you have missed, you have gained something
else; and for everything you gain, you lose something.
— RALPH WALDO EMERSON

My sister Sydney married Peter McKelvy in 1983. It was a big
Kennedy wedding at "the compound" in Hyannis Port. Sydney is one
of those people everybody loves, so it didn't inconvenience anyone to
come.

My mother gave the wedding, and my father made the trip from L.A.
It wasn't easy for him. But he did it so he could walk his oldest
daughter down the aisle. He was on his last alcoholic legs, which were
pretty wobbly, and he was coming back to Kennedy country for the
first time since it all blew up twenty years before.

My dad's arrival into the life that became mine when my parents
split was huge for me. In a family where lineage was a big deal, my dad
always provided a counterbalance to the Kennedy strain. His celebrity
and life were banners that I flew with pride. Now he was here in the
flesh. Very few of my cousins or friends had ever met my father. I was
eager and proud to walk with him through the eastern form of my life
in spite of his humbled condition and mine. Or maybe because of it.

The night before the wedding, my dad, some of the guys, and I
pulled an all-nighter in my dad's suite. As usual, booze and coke fueled
the festivities—with my dad doing his best to keep up with a younger
and stronger generation.

David showed up looking a lot like the beat-up Pontiac he had driven down from the rehab he had just been kicked out of in New Hampshire. The fact he had no license didn't bother him in the slightest. When I asked how he managed it, he looked at me with the quizzical contempt he had elevated to an art form and said, "Man, you don't need a license to drive." It was pure David. I sat with my best friend and my father that night, knowing we were far from what we could be. David's bravado was still evident, but he had changed. I could see in his eyes that he was beaten, and although there was a thirty-plus age difference between my dad and him, they both looked like club fighters at the end of a punishing fifteen rounds—powerless to dodge the inevitable outcome. David regaled us with the story of how he got me fired at Universal Studios and we continued our ancient argument as to who was smarter while we waited for the birds. I had the feeling I was seeing him for the last time.

My father told his stories of Hollywood. Everyone was riveted. As the sun came up and the birds began to sing, I hardly noticed. I was riding high, feeling the rush of being the one with the father everybody was paying attention to.

I wrote my mother a letter after the wedding:

Dear Mummy,
Well, you did it again. The wedding which you gave Sydney
will not soon be forgotten by those that were fortunate enough
to attend. The words that are often used to describe the wedding
are: beauty, taste, warmth, joy and class. These are the same
words I would use to describe my mother. As Eunice said in her
toast at the rehearsal dinner, you have spent much of your life
giving love, guidance, security and friendship to your children.
She left out the word patience, which you have shown more of
with me than anyone could hope for. I am so grateful for the
love, patience and friendship which you have shown me.

I cannot possibly express my love and respect which I have
for you. I only hope that I will be half the person that you are.
I am the luckiest son to have had you as my mother. I love you
more than you can know.

Love,
Xtopher

I wrote this letter in 1983. I got sober in 1986. My perception about women has always been a little off. This perception problem began with my mom. Emerson said, "Men are what their mothers made them." I was made to try and please women. The theory goes like this: My mom adored her father and brothers. They were forever enshrined in that place of perfection reserved for saints and martyrs. The pain in my mother's life was a result of the loss of these men. It would be different if they were around. I was the male in her life. It was up to me to fill the void and make it all right. This could never happen, but it wouldn't stop me from trying. I had the additional handicap of being my father's son. My father was on the other side of the spectrum from the saints. I reminded my mom of my dad. It put me at a slight disadvantage.

SNAPSHOT:

I was invited back to movie night at the Playboy Mansion four months after my dad's Herculean effort to attend Sydney's wedding at Hyannis Port. I had forgotten about movie night and the night I picked the wrong girl, blowing an invite to the place where just about every straight male on the planet would lose a testicle to hang out, when I got a call from the man in the pajamas himself:

Hef:
Chris. Hef here. We're having a problem with your dad.
Me:
What's the problem, Hef?
Hef:
Well, we don't really know. He stays in the guesthouse all day talking to squirrels.
Me:
That doesn't sound good.
Hef:
No. We found a trash can full of vodka bottles. I don't think he's taking any drugs.

Me:

How would you know?

Hef:

I wouldn't, but he hasn't been out of there in a month, and
nobody's visiting.

Me:

I'll fly out and see what I can do.

Hef:

Thanks.

Hugh Hefner had been a good friend to my father. When my dad really hit the skids, he bailed him out or enabled him—depending on
how much you understand the disease of alcoholism. He lent him
money and let my dad stay on the property. I was invited back to movie
night because my dad was killing himself in Hef's guesthouse, and the
man in the silk pajamas didn't know what to do about it. My father was
in bad shape. He was rail thin, his liver was distended, and his speech
was so slurred it was difficult understanding him, unless you were one
of the squirrels that he spent much of his day in discourse with, while
feeding them Hef's peanuts. He hadn't shaved for months and had a
long white flowing beard to show for it. He bore little resemblance to
the Peter Lawford everyone knew.

I arrived at the place I had been banished from five years earlier to
collect a parent who was so ravaged I hardly recognized him. My father did his best to clean himself up and engage me. It must have taken
every ounce of strength and courage he had. He walked the hundred
or so yards to the main house to have dinner with me and the other
guests, who were looking at him like he was a pariah. I remember sitting on the porch with my father when Bill Cosby walked by us with a
look of utter disdain and said to the woman he was with, "Look, that's
Peter Lawford. Can you believe it? How pathetic is that?" It broke my
heart, and I'm sure my old man's.

The next day I met with Hefner, and he had no idea what to do.
He felt terrible for my dad but said Dad had to leave. He wanted me to
tell him. I made plans to take my father to Saint John's hospital, the
hospital I was born in, for detox and treatment.

We had come full circle.

When we arrived at Saint John's, I had to carry my father into the hospital because he was so debilitated he couldn't walk. I also had to sign his name on the admissions sheet. It was not an easy day. My dad drank and used all sorts of drugs in his life, but at the end it was booze that brought him to his bottom. It was a powerful lesson for me. I had always considered alcohol less damaging because it was legal. I looked at alcoholics as lightweights, compared with the heavyweight dope slammers I proudly identified with. I saw in the progression of my father's disease and that of my cousin David the debilitating and deadly power of alcohol.

My dad dried out for a few days and at first seemed grateful for my intervention and the prospect of getting sober. Tony Hopkins and other friends went to see him and encouraged him to stay in treatment and bite the bullet of sobriety. One day I came to see him, and I saw in his eyes and demeanor that he wasn't going to make it.

"Are you telling me that I can't have a glass of white wine with dinner?" he asked.

The next day he walked out of Saint John's, against the advice of his doctors and those of us in his life who still gave a shit. He was off and running—again.

After his close call with sobriety, my dad and I lost touch with each other. I was back East fighting my own demons. If alcoholism is a descending elevator, my dad's elevator crashed through the bottom floor and reached depths no one should have to endure. I would hear from him when there was either a financial or medical emergency. There were usually one or two a year, and at first I responded like a dutiful son, marshaling whatever resources I could to help bail him out. Soon, though, his drama got old, and I was having enough trouble keeping my own shit together.

SNAPSHOT:

In 1984 I moved to the South End of Boston—just on the other side of the tracks. The neighborhood was in the process of gentrification, but our block—Chandler Street—still had enough sleaze to make me feel comfortable. We lived in the bottom two floors of an old brownstone. When I say bottom two floors, I mean the bottom. I'm talking bunker. Both floors were below street level. I had a great view of people's legs as they walked by.

It was perfect if you were concerned about having a place to survive an aerial bombardment or needed a nice cozy place to engage in deviant behavior. It appealed to me on a variety of levels. It was safe. There was an outdoor patio that opened up onto the back alley. The drawbacks were the Massachusetts Turnpike, a six-lane highway abutting our patio, and a deck the owners of our brownstone had built themselves that sat squarely over our patio, leaving just enough headroom so we didn't have to duck when going outside to barbecue.

When I found this rental, I thought I had stumbled upon one of the great apartments in the city. I was so excited. I called my friend Jack and told him to hurry over to take a look at my new gem. His expression as I showed him around fluctuated between that of a guy bearing witness to his best friend losing his mind and relief that he'd get to leave after the tour.

I remember for the first time thinking that my judgment might be impaired. I quickly dismissed the thought, realizing that Jack was just jealous of my good fortune, but I'll never forget the way he looked at me. Drug addiction and alcoholism necessitate living a life of diminishing expectations. "It's not so bad" becomes one's mantra. I'm an optimist and love fantasy, so "Isn't it great!" suited me better.

I took the apartment on Chandler Street and it lived up to all my expectations. The City of Boston decided to build the tallest building in Back Bay and installed a four-story jackhammer outside my bedroom window the day I moved in. It wasn't so bad, I thought at the time. Looking back it sucked big-time, and I should have tried to break my lease. I'm healthier today.

I called it the bunker—and that's what it was. A fortified cave where I could isolate myself from the world and engage in the neurotic and compulsive behavior that complemented the massive daily ingestion of whatever chemicals I could get my hands on.

Some of my favorite behavior: Rearranging the contents of storage containers. Identifying and labeling every single photograph in the apartment and in the storage containers. Making lists of "things to do" for the next twenty years. You get the idea.

I loved strippers and strip bars. The red-light district in Boston was called the Combat Zone and was five minutes from my apartment on Chandler Street. I spent a lot of time in a classy place called the Naked Eye where I would try to get real and establish an emotional connection with one of the girls working the pole. It wasn't the sex that drew me. I don't remember getting any. I was looking for love and someone to rescue.

The way I figured it was that since I couldn't save my mom from the onslaught of her life, I looked for relationships that re-create that dynamic. Usually this means that I pick women who need saving—where I have all the power.

I spent a lot of time seeking out women who either needed me enough or adored me enough to let me try to save them.

Okay, it's not original and I never found any strippers to save, but I had a good time looking. In between my jaunts to the Zone, I tried to do something about my drug problem.

You know that thing you read about or see in movies where someone gets some unforeseen really tragic news and they have this involuntary, completely unconscious physical reaction to it. Well I never believed in that. I mean I had seen it in movies and read about it and I wasn't sure it couldn't happen to regular folk, but I was certain it couldn't happen to me. After all, I had been privy to a couple of the most shocking and surprising tragedies in history and I hadn't had anything close to an involuntary, unconscious physical response. I had kept my wits about me and stayed resolutely in my head, which I had learned was the only safe place to react and respond to anything emotional or cataclysmic. You would never catch this puppy losing control of his tear ducts, motor skills, or anything else as a result of emotional surprise. God only knows it could be my bowels next.

SNAPSHOT:

I had just returned from trying to engage the world. Every day I would dress myself, stuff the briefcase, which I had been given as a gift for graduating from law school, and head out to some sort of bullshit meeting that would make me feel like I was doing something. It was terrifying, and I was not very good at it. I was convinced as I watched all the other humans participate in the hustle and bustle of daily existence that whoever was in charge had forgotten to give me the manual. I had no idea how to function in the world of getting things done. All I could do was fake it and run back home to the refuge of addiction.

I saw this therapist at Harvard for ten years and the only thing I learned was that my drug addiction had as much to do with regulating dis-ease as it did with the quest for euphoria. An addict controls his world through regulating his chemical intake, thereby controlling his emotional being. This is kind of smart information to have, but it doesn't mean squat when it comes to putting that 800-pound gorilla back in the cage.

So I had just come back from the outside—where I had no control and very little aptitude—to the inside, where I had total control and the only aptitude required was knowing how to get my next fix. Jeannie was sitting on the corner of my bed, and it was obvious she had been crying. She looked up at me and said, "David is dead."

For the first time in my life, I had one of those involuntary, unconscious, physical reactions. The briefcase stuffed with all the bullshit papers for the bullshit meetings hit the floor, and I had no idea how it got there because I didn't open my hand to drop it. It was like the instant before you get hit. I cringed in an attempt to soften the blow. Then I began to shrink, becoming small and hidden in the middle of my physical body. Retreating to a place where the pain couldn't find me. This was way too big for the manhole cover. The moments passed, I thawed, and the awful realization that one of us had died was inescapable. David had been dying for years but I never thought he would pull it off. I stood at the corner of the bed looking at Jeannie and at the briefcase lying on the floor thinking about what it might have been like for him at the end. Did he just nod off or was there the fear of knowing he wasn't coming back? How could he do this to me? Leaving me alone in my sinking boat no longer with someone closer to the edge than me. What a son of a bitch!

The day was August 25, 1984, and although I did not realize it at the time, David's death was his gift to me that led me to get sober eighteen months later.

I learned later that David had died because he was trying to get sober. David had gone to treatment in Minneapolis, and, for the first time in a while, his system was clean. This is a dangerous time for an addict. We go back to doing what we were doing before treatment at the same dosage and it's sayonara amigo. He came out of treatment to face the publication of some interviews he had given for a book, which were less than favorable to the family. It was more than his fragile sobriety could tolerate.

DAVID MAY have been way outside the family, he may have known before any of us what a cruel joke it was to have such an illustrious legacy, but he loved his family and hurting or disappointing them was not something he could live through. There was no place for David in the family, and he could not go away to honor his authentic self. He had been in a purgatory of pain pretty much his entire life. So he did what he had always done to stop the hurt. He got high, and it killed him. He died on the floor of a shitty hotel room in Florida, crammed between the wall and his bed, alone with the pain of knowing that he had disappointed the family that meant everything to him, but he could not be a part of. He was finally free. I was happy for him.

I never thought of the decision I had made six years earlier that resulted in the end of our friendship until two years after his death. I was six months sober and thinking of those I owed amends to for the pain I had caused them as a result of my addiction. My cousin David was at the top of my list.

Chapter 29

Every woman should marry — and no man.
— BENJAMIN DISRAELI

It took me two years to get married after my proposal in the upstairs bedroom in Joe's crappy house in Brighton. My problem was never with Jeannie. She was everything I could hope for in a wife: beautiful, loyal, honest, and organized. Plus she loved me and I was not easy to love.

What I needed was a great place to get married. A place that would make a statement, and was remote enough to keep the guest list to a minimum. It took a while to find.

We had a good friend named Charlene who was an heiress and lived in Cambridge. Her father made his money in South African diamonds. He made so much money on diamonds that his friend Ian Fleming modeled the character Goldfinger in the James Bond series on him. I guess Goldfinger is a better title than Diamondfinger. Charlene knew the great spots of the world that only the very rich have access to. She had been going down to an island in the Grenadines called Bequia and was building a house there, which was called The Palace. The name was appropriate.

An advertising executive from Chicago had dropped out of society and settled on the island of Bequia twenty-five years earlier with his twenty-year-old wife, buying an eighth of the island and calling it Moonhole. He built seventeen homes for friends into the landscape of the island. Each house was unique and spectacular. It was rustic luxury at its finest. Nobody had ever heard of it, and to get there you had to take two planes, a boat, a truck, and then walk two miles. It would definitely cut down on the guest list. It was the perfect place for my wedding.

Only the most adventurous or truly obligated showed up. My mother and sisters made it. My father baled three weeks before, but my uncle Teddy did what he always did and showed up for the absent father. David was supposed to be my best man but he died before either one of us stumbled down the aisle. Bastard. Jack Weeks, my buddy from Boston with the golden gloves and discriminating taste in apartments, watched my back in David's place. Jeannie and I engraved "To the bitter end" on the inside of our wedding bands as a tribute to my fallen friend. He wasn't there but his sardonic spirit was.

We spent the first week in paradise recovering from the trip to get there. We drank rum punch until our livers hurt. There were no drugs to speak of, as we had been warned, by our hosts, about the consequences: "Please tell all guests that laws governing Saint Vincent, Grenadines, are severe concerning drugs and are enforced with great vigor. Guests of Moonhole should know that in view of this situation we have no choice but to ask guests to leave immediately if any drug use is observed. We will do this in their interest as penalties are very steep."

Alcohol was the drug de jour.

We invented a new sport: drunken night scuba diving. Uncle Teddy sailed us all over the Caribbean basin on Bob Dylan's yawl. Jeannie and I got married.

I sat with my uncle the day before I got married. We were sipping rum punches in paradise, looking out at the sea. I was trying not to listen to the voices in my head: Man, are you sure you want to do this? You don't *have* to. If you do this—it's for life. That's a long fucking time! You should have brought that vial of coke. You could have gotten your ass thrown off this island.

My plan had always been that when things got bad or old enough in the real world, I would flee to a place like this and drink myself to death. Faced with a lifetime of monogamy and commitment I was beginning to think that day had come.

Uncle Teddy put things in perspective:

Me:

I just have the feeling that there may be someone better out there for me.

Teddy:

Well the thing is, the thing is, there isn't. I mean the thing is that every guy thinks that the day, ya know, the day he gets married.

Me:

But what if I'm making a mistake? Maybe I'm not ready.

Teddy:

Well, Chris, the thing is that you're ready. You've done the thing, the thing with women, and it was more than most of us, ya know, see in a lifetime. The thing is it's time to grow up.

Me:

I don't know, I haven't seen a lot of happy endings in the marriage department.

Teddy:

You can say that again. Well the thing is, it's hard. The other thing is, it's work. Jeannie's a great girl, and good on the work thing.

Me:

It feels like the end of my life.

Teddy:

Well being on this island feels like the end of *my* life, so get married and we can all get the hell out of here.

The great thing about my uncle Teddy is that he can be emotional and pragmatic at the same time. Just having him around made me feel better. There was something in the fearless lust with which he embraced his own struggles that was inclusive and inspiring. He made me feel that no matter how crazy it got I could keep moving forward.

Me:
Okay. I can do this. Let's get married!

Jeannie and I were married the next day by a Grenadian priest who was six foot eight, black as night, with a beard and manner that were as substantial as God himself. We were serenaded by a group of Grenadian voodoo priestesses and, the moment we said our vows, were showered by soft Caribbean rain. It was all very auspicious.

After the ceremony we had a feast and the required toasts. I didn't know it at the time but Teddy wrote my mom's for her. She had an aversion similar to mine to the whole toasting ordeal.

There is an old saying on an occasion like this, which expresses an appropriate feeling. I haven't lost a son but have gained a daughter. However, today I am saying, Jeannie, you can have him, he's all yours.

Seriously, I want to say something serious about my son Chris. PAUSE . . . PAUSE.

One last thought. No son cared about his sisters as much as Chris. Sydney, Victoria, and Robin's lives have been enriched invaluably by his caring, love, and thoughtfulness. Chris has always realized how much this meant to me and our family. I am proud of him, love him, and wish Jeannie and him the happiness which they have given to all who they have called friend, sister, and mother.

The best they could come up with was that my mom was glad to finally be unloading me on another woman—poor Jeannie. There was nothing serious to say about me, but I was a good brother. This was hardly the declaration of inspiration and greatness I was hoping for but I couldn't argue with its veracity. My mother had a lifetime of good reasons for not being overly thrilled with her "number one son." Can I get another rum punch, please?

The festivities were brought to a close with a group toast, which pretty much summed up the collective feelings about their week in paradise.

Oh what a beautiful morning,
Oh what a beautiful day,
We have a wonderful feeling
We only have one more day.

There's no bright shining light in the evening,
There's no hot water in the morning,
The rocks are as high as an elephant's eye,
And the mud reaches up to your thigh.

Oh what a beautiful morning etc.
There's rooms on the mountains of Bequia,
There's rooms overlooking the bay,
There are people all over the island,
But you sure as hell won't see them all day.

Oh what a beautiful morning etc.

There's ice on Saint Vincent, Barbados,
There's champagne on Grenada they say,
There's coconut drinks that can fill up your sinks
But not on Bequia today.

We know this is a small island,
We know it is far far away,
But if you ask us if we are returning
We will answer we hope another day.

Our wonderful odyssey is ending,
Their happy voyage starts today,
You couldn't have given us a better time on this island,
And we're with you all of the way.

Jeannie and I had an official wedding picture taken. Me in my white linen suit with bolo, something that Humphrey Bogart might have worn in *Casablanca*. Jeannie was in her wedding dress. The only wrinkle was that we had our backs to the camera. We sent the picture out to all those who braved the trip with a note explaining:

> *Dear Bequia Survivor,*
> *We thought you would like a copy of our "official" wedding portrait as a remembrance of Bequia. We call it "a portrait in too much rum punch."*
>
> > *Love,*
> > *Xtopher & Jeannie*

I returned from my wedding in paradise to a stack of telegrams. The best telegram was from the Shrivers:

> CONGRATULATIONS. ESPECIALLY TO JEANNIE THAT SHE FINALLY GOT YOU TO CHURCH ON TIME.
> LOVE, THE SHRIVER FAMILY

I also returned to a mountain of the same problems I had before I left.

Some additional action was necessary. Something even bolder than getting married.

I know, I'll have a baby.

Unfortunately for me but fortunately for the baby, Jeannie couldn't get pregnant no matter how hard we tried, and boy, did we try. I tried for a year and a half, figuring it was a good way to get people off my back.

I was still under the misguided assumption that if I changed the outside circumstances of my life, I would change what I was.

Having a kid would fix everything, plus my family might even throw me some much-needed cash. A lot of children get to have really shitty childhoods as a result of this kind of thinking. I guess I wanted to have a baby but, like most guys, hadn't spent a whole lot of time thinking about it and had more or less abdicated my responsibility in that decision to Jeannie. My experience has shown me that women are more invested and thoughtful about the whole kid thing. Some of it is biological, some socialization, and some of it security. Men acquiesce unless they make a stand on the finances. I remember feeling I was beginning a walk down a road I wasn't fully convinced I wanted to walk down. It would take us a year and a half. By then, my life would have changed completely.

Chapter 30

Death is not the greatest loss in life. The greatest loss is what dies inside us while we live.

— NORMAN COUSINS

In December of 1983 my dad had his last and best chance to get sober. Elizabeth Taylor checked into the Betty Ford Center, and my father followed her in. I guess he figured if Betty Ford was good enough for the former biggest movie star in the world it was good enough for him. I received the daily logs of the man who helped him get admitted and kept tabs on him during his stay. These are his notes.

> 12/23/83 P. Lawford went from Eisenhower to BFC. Reports are o.k. Liz Taylor spent time with him on Thursday.

> 1/5/84 I stopped at BFC to visit Pete Lawford. He's really a nice guy. I think he's getting well, despite liver damage (distended). The staffers are encouraged. They like him. They want him to win.

> 1/6/84 Peter was more relaxed, more at ease . . . was carrying a telegram from Sammy Davis: a warm message about doing a sequel to "Salt and Pepper" someday. Pete seems to appreciate the support he's getting. Vulnerable.

1/20/84 Peter was elusive, a bit rude; he couldn't find his coffee cup which had his name on it. Situation became ridiculous. His manner was quite condescending. . . .

. . . on my last visit, Peter had checked out, apparently a bit earlier than expected. I never saw him again.

I spoke with my father by telephone while he was at Betty Ford. I had never heard him sound as good. He was sober, talking about doing it a day at a time, and going to meetings. I really thought he might make it. Then he disappeared. I got a phone call from him sometime in late October of 1984, a couple of weeks before my marriage in the Grenadines, telling me he couldn't make it. That was the last time I spoke with him.

12/25/84 Peter Lawford died yesterday.

SNAPSHOT:

My father had been threatening to die for at least five years. Unlike with David I knew he would pull it off—I just never knew when. He finally made good on Christmas Eve of 1984. I was in New York City with Jeannie visiting my mother for the holidays. We were gathered with my sisters at her apartment to engage in the American holiday family ritual of gluttonous, conditional, alcohol-fueled gift-giving. My mom loved playing Santa Claus. Her apartment looked like the North Pole with a giant spruce and a living room full of presents. There were always parties full of relatives and friends. We had had our yuletide grab-fest, stuffed ourselves with roast beef and Yorkshire pudding, and fueled our merriment with daiquiris and wine.

It was now time to immerse myself in the anonymity of the New York night, but first there was "the call" to be dealt with. It was from another

California doctor. There had been so many over the previous five years. They had called to apprise us of this condition or that. The calls would usually include a warning and a plea for cash. I answered the phone with the detachment and irritation reserved for calls from the dry cleaners about a piece of dry cleaning they thought had been delivered but wasn't. Dr. So and So told me my dad was going to die, and he was going to die sooner rather than later.

My response was "Are you sure, because I don't want to get my sisters and me on a plane to come all the way out to California if he really isn't going to die this time." This is what it had come to.

I guess there are only so many times you can go to the emotional well before it's dry. So when the bell finally tolled, I no longer gave a shit. Or the well had been dry from the get-go because my dad had never put any water in. Maybe the pain of it all was so great that ambivalence and anger were my only recourse. Whichever it was, the result was the same. I got on a plane to L.A. on Christmas Eve with the certainty that my dad was once again fucking up my life and with ambivalence about whether he lived or died.

He died while we were in the air.

I spent four days in L.A. attending to my father's death with the awful feeling that I hadn't seen him before he died. The last time we were together was in a hospital, where he apologized to me in tears for marrying shortly before his death the woman who would become his fourth and final wife. My father was terrified of being alone, and she was all he had left. He said we had everything and would he take care of. He wanted to take care of her. But there was probably another reason. In the long stages of alcoholism, he just had to have some one to take care of him.

I don't know why at the end of his life my dad felt compelled to justify to me why he felt he didn't have to worry about his children's welfare. He had never shown any inclination to do so when he was young and healthy. I'd like to believe it was his way of making amends for never being able to show us the love and care he had for us in his heart. This last interaction with my father showed me his greatest asset, his heart. My dad was a softy. He was an artist, a little boy. A beach guy who would have been happy surfing all day. He was not built emotionally for this world or the life he would be fortunate enough to get. I believe today that all that he did and what he became were in reaction to his inability to emotionally tolerate this world.

I remember standing in the baggage claim of LAX wishing my last encounter with my father had been something different, though. I didn't know what at the time; I just didn't feel right about what had happened. Today I know that what I was yearning for was some kind of closure, a resolution or understanding of what we had and what we didn't have. I wanted forgiveness so both of us could move on. That didn't happen, and I never saw him again, which means I get to struggle with the genetic and social predisposition to behave like my old man until the day I die and he gets to come back and try it again.

Los Angeles is a really fun town if you are the center of attention, money is no object, your ride is styling, and the booze and drugs have no end in sight. So it was for me in the days following my father's death. Stan Kamen, who was the head of the motion picture group at the William Morris Agency and had been my father's agent early in his career and his loyal friend long after it was profitable, pretty much took care of everything but the drugs. That wasn't a problem. There isn't a doctor, dentist, or shrink on the planet who wouldn't be good for at least one prescription for painkillers when presented with these circumstances. The extended family rallied. My uncle Teddy released a statement:

> *The death of Peter Lawford is a special loss to all of us in the Kennedy family, my heart goes out to his children. . . . We take comfort from the fact that we know that he will also be missed by all the people who enjoyed his many roles in films and on television. He was a dedicated and creative actor as well as a loving father and loyal friend to all of us, especially in the challenging days of The New Frontier. The legacy of his love and his fine performances will be a cherished treasure for his family, his friends and his many admirers.*

Once again there was a different picture to be painted in death.

My cousins, Bobby Jr., Caroline, Maria and Timmy Shriver, and

Courtney Kennedy showed up to support us. We went to the funeral home to make arrangements and to view the body. I had never seen a dead person before. It's true what they say about dead people—they don't seem real once the soul is gone. My father looked like he was something they were getting ready for Madame Tussaud's. I remember kissing him on the forehead. I didn't want to. I just did it because I didn't know what else to do and this is one of those times in your life where you want to do something.

The thing I remember most is that I didn't feel anything. I stood there looking down at my father's yellow sclerotic lifeless body and I couldn't have manufactured a tear if my life depended on it. What's that about? I mean this was a man I had a lot of history and a shitload of unfinished business with. I should have felt something—anger, pity, sadness, relief, something—but it wasn't there. You have to understand that when my father died I was at the end of my active alcoholism although I didn't know it.

Standing there in the funeral home I had the conscious and emotional awareness of a rock. I didn't feel anything because I wasn't capable of feeling. I had perfected the junkie's manhole cover response to anything emotional. I wasn't aware that I was capable of emotion. We are not talking underdeveloped muscle here; we're talking no clue that there was such a muscle. One of the tragedies of alcoholism is that when an alcoholic dies he leaves those behind with only the transparency of a relationship. There's nothing there. The alcoholic never develops emotionally beyond the moment he picks up the first drink, and he spends the rest of his life trying to conceal that fact. I never got to know my father because he never got to know himself.

WE HAD a big dinner on Christmas Day at a restaurant in Beverly Hills. A hard rain pelted the streets as we gathered to celebrate and mourn my old man. It's weird when one's life becomes a caricature. Here we all were, brought together by the death of a movie star whose life had followed a path that even those who don't know it know. Only child, overbearing alcoholic crazy mother, child actor, star, marries royalty. Too much booze and too many women destroy it all. Long slow decline to death, survived by a wife half his age with the integrity of a desperate Hollywood producer, and the children who never really knew him. We've all seen the movie. As I sat there in the middle of the restaurant feeling empty and awkward, it struck me that at the end of my dad's life there was hardly anyone around who loved him. My three sisters were grieving the loss of a relationship they were never allowed to have. I was confused and conflicted. There were few friends left— that weird hybrid found in abundance in Hollywood, the friends who also makes their living off you. Of all the people who were still around at my father's death, these people seemed to have the most authentic and appropriate reactions.

My father died too young. He never got to see his grandkids. He never got to get sober. He never got to see his life for what it was. He never got to be free from his shit for one sober moment. He never knew peace. My father died on Christmas Eve, 1984. I got sober a year and a half later. Coincidence? I don't think so. I believe he died so I could do the things he never could. I love him and thank him for that.

My mom didn't make the funeral, but when my sisters and Jeannie and I were done in L.A., she bundled us up and delivered us to a beautiful beach house in Jamaica so we could all grieve and tan together. She put aside whatever was going on for her with my dad's passing and was totally focused on and present with her kids. It felt good to know that the circumstances of my life and how they were affecting me were her priority.

After taking care of her kids, my mother went back, alone, to her apartment in New York and fell apart. My father's death may have left me cold, but I think it did a number on her. She had been battling her own drinking demons for years. In the winter following my dad's demise, her condition turned critical.

MY SISTERS and I organized a family get-together. We met with our mother on a cold day in January in the living room of her New York apartment. Teddy, Eunice, and Jean were there with us to convince Mom to get some help.

One of the cornerstones of a family meeting is that you confront a person who is an addict/alcoholic with consequences that make getting help look like a bargain. It was suggested that my sisters and I threaten to cut off all contact with my mom if she didn't agree with our recommendations. Because of their emotional attachment, my sisters wouldn't do it. I was on the fence. We came up with a compromise: our position was that we would go to rehab even if she didn't. Quite a threat, huh? We sweetened the deal with a private plane to fly her out there. When we presented all this to my mom, she looked at us, raised her hand, waved good-bye, and walked right out of the room.

So my sisters and I ended up at a rehab in the middle of a frozen Minnesota winter for family week without my mother. At the time, I was pissed. Looking back, I have to admire her chutzpah. It takes a lot of guts to tell a room full of family to go to hell. My mom was an original who always did it her way.

You might think that going to a rehab for family week without a patient would be a waste of time. It wasn't. While there, the staff asks you not to drink for the four days. I couldn't do it. Another nail was hammered into my coffin of alcoholic denial.

When we returned, my mom had pulled herself together, and I received a letter from her.

Dear Children:
In the future, I think it will be better if we work within the
family on our own problems without importing Eunice, Jean
and Ted, various offspring, private planes, etc.
   I find this repugnant.
   I do not wish to discuss the matter further.

Love,
Mommie

Chapter 31

I was living a life of silent tears, broken dreams,
and unresolved relationships.
— ANONYMOUS

At the end of my active addiction pretty much everything and everybody was gone. But I was finally somebody. I was somebody that nobody wanted to be with. The money, movie star girlfriends, wild nights at Studio 54, and getting high with rock stars were all faded memories. I had been born with every conceivable advantage. I had failed to take advantage of any of them. This was not due to a lack of effort. I had managed to graduate from college and law school. I had traveled extensively and put together an impressive albeit abbreviated employment history. I had even gotten married. None of this mattered, because I could not put the 800-pound gorilla back in its cage.

My last days as an active addict were spent bicycling from my therapist's office after my daily appointment to Brown's Steakhouse, where I drank because they made their rum drinks in vats, alcohol to the top, a splash of grenadine for color, and an umbrella to make it festive. It reminded me of the Islands. I liked to say I was spending half my day at Brown's because I liked their steaks.

SNAPSHOT:

Cambridge City Hospital is not a very luxurious place as far as inner-city hospitals go. After fifteen years of drug addiction, I didn't have a whole lot of options left. In the beginning of one's descent into the physical ravages of chemical dependency they send you to the best medical institutions. For me it was McLean's and New York Hospital. But after the third or fourth emergency, the insurance had run out, and as the revolving-door nature of the disease became known, I started getting shipped to less-swell digs.

The hospital with the worn gray and brown exterior that sits just outside Central Square in Cambridge was my home away from home. I spent five to seven days there every six months to detox. I would check in with my pillow and my toothbrush. The nurse would escort me to a private room on the sixth floor with the contempt reserved for those who are stealing resources from the truly needy because of some inner weakness.

During one of these detoxes, the one doctor I had never been able to con suggested I stop drinking and go to a Twelve-Step program.

"Are you nuts?" I said to him. "I'm not an alcoholic," I protested. "My problem is narcotics, not booze."

"Yeah," he said, "I understand that. But when you drink, you do coke, which inevitably leads to your drug of choice, heroin."

This bit of reasoning made sense, and the knowledge that my insurance was no longer going to subsidize these little respites forced my hand. A few days after I was discharged, I called my aunt Joan and asked her to take me to one of those meetings she went to.

MY AUNT Joan Kennedy was married to Uncle Teddy, but didn't have whatever gene it is that runs on the Kennedy side of my family, enabling those who have it to remain functioning and stay alive far longer than they should, no matter how badly they abuse themselves. I never really had much to do with her except trying to avoid her whenever she had too much to drink. Joan was sweet and sensitive, not the qualities needed to successfully navigate our family. Those qualities, coupled with active alcoholism, were a recipe for disaster. I always liked Joan, and I am forever grateful to her for being the person who brought me to a new life.

I had been battling the 800-pound gorilla for fifteen years and I was not winning. Joan did for me what no doctor, therapist, priest, or guru could do. She brought me to a church basement full of a diverse group of apparent losers who would teach me how to live without drugs and alcohol a day at a time, and a whole lot more.

The first basement she brought me to was not a basement at all but a cafeteria and it was located in the very hospital I had detoxed in for the past couple of years—a place that would now only accommodate me if I showed up with cold hard cash. I heard a guy tell my story about his addiction to booze and drugs. The meeting was a lot like an orgy: after it was over I felt really good but I didn't know who to thank. I knew I had found a home—but I still had more research to do.

In 1984 Joan sent me a postcard from the People's Republic of China with an image of the Great Wall and a message that joked,

Dear Chris,
The only meetings over here are political indoctrination
meetings in the thoughts of Mao!

Love,
Joan K.

Joan Kennedy had brought me to a place that ruined my terminal uniqueness. I became aware that there was a whole world of people like me—not exactly like me, but close enough—and they were staying sober. This blew my mind and wrecked my using. No longer could I act with the arrogance of being special that had given permission to my willful and destructive behavior. I believe my addiction is in my genes. But I also believe the circumstances of my birth and life allowed me to excuse behavior and refuse to acknowledge any of the paths to salvation that were readily available to me. This awareness was the first step in my recovery.

In the meantime I had no place to go to clean up and dry out. My solution was to have Jeannie lock me in the apartment on Chandler

Street when she left for work. She was still working then as the assistant to the head coach for the Boston Breakers football team. I would spend the day writhing on a mattress in the den, watching reruns of *Buck Rogers* and staring out the window at the legs of the people walking by in wonder at how they managed their lives. They passed by the window of my first-floor den in their suits and dresses, carrying briefcases and pocketbooks, with an ease and intention I could never find. I envied them and wanted whatever it was they had that allowed them to engage and function in the world. My manual for the successful navigation of life had obviously been lost in the mail. The anonymous legs marching back and forth by my window had undoubtedly received their copies. I nursed my misfortune as I twisted and turned, full of aches and sweat, struggling to unravel the mysteries of Buck Rogers. At night I would lie awake in bed as Jeannie slept soundly next to me, and wonder: if I ran full speed down the hallway outside my bedroom headfirst into the wall would it successfully end my life.

After five or six days, the worst of the withdrawal passed. I realized years later when I finally got sober that there was a key to the back door. But I never let myself realize it. A testament to how badly I wanted to get clean.

Desire didn't much matter, though, because once I started to feel a little stronger and was confronted with the reality of living life on life's terms clean and sober, I called Dr. So-and-So and hightailed it back to the sanctuary of chemical dependency.

Cambridge City Hospital is one of six teaching hospitals at Harvard University. It's probably the least prestigious; it's where you find most of the doctors and shrinks who are interested in the field of addiction. My therapist was there.

One day I had my therapist send a letter to the last remaining Dr. Feelgood:

Dear Dr. So-and-So,
I'm writing to you at the suggestion of Chris Lawford who has been working with increasing success towards establishing a drug free life.

Chris has made me aware that you have continued to treat his medical illnesses and will probably continue to do so in the future. It is very important to him that no matter what his illness, that hereafter you will not provide him with any medication whether it be narcotics, antianxiety agents or sleeping pills without first consulting me.

Chris has related to me the important role that you have played in his struggle over the past years. However, it is his feeling that he must begin a new phase in his treatment which calls for total and complete abstinence from psychoactive drugs. He is aware how difficult it is for you, as a doctor, not to treat a legitimate medical illness as you see fit. However, as we are all aware, Chris occupies a special category of patient where physical discomfort must give way to his most important goal of remaining drug free and learning to bear his distress, whatever its sources, in other ways. If you are confronted with a request by him for medication, he would prefer that you provide him with a copy of this letter instead of a prescription.

That should cover it! It didn't. If a drug addict wants to get high he will find a way. There is no human power that can relieve us of our addictions.

Snapshot:

At the end I had a job at the Cambridge City Hospital when I wasn't using it to detox. The job was ingenious. I was working with one of the therapists, who also happened to be a professor at Harvard Medical School, to start a division on addiction. It was the perfect job for me. After all, if there was one thing I knew about it was drug addiction. I raised a small stipend from friends and family, went through a training process, ministered to the heroin addicts in the program, and went out into the world to try and raise more money for Harvard University, whose endowment was greater than the economies of 75 percent of the world's countries. All of this was done for the honor of putting the Harvard name on addiction. I was given an academic appointment as a lecturer in psychiatry at Harvard Medical School to add to my credibility. Just what the world needs—a credible junkie.

I received a letter from the president of Harvard, Derek Bok, giving his blessing to the center as a "timely address to addictive behaviors" and encouraging me to raise a ton of cash for the medical school.

It *always* comes down to the money.

The scheme was inspired and took some effort, but it left me with a hole in my gut. See, I was still using. This level of dishonesty is exhausting and debilitating.

My uncle Teddy sent me a contribution and a note indicating "both my confidence in the objectives of the program, and more importantly, my confidence in you."

I had finally hit bottom. I would stay there for another year.

NOTE TO READER:

Okay. So I just want to make sure you've got it. In a nutshell: I was born with the American dream fulfilled. I blew it all, drowning in a sea of alcohol and drugs. My best friend and father died. I was alone and bankrupt in all categories.

For those of you who bought this book for stories about my descent into darkness, the Rat Pack, and the Kennedys— you can stop reading now. For the rest, I'm here to tell you the most interesting part of my story is not what happened in the dark alley but what has happened in the sunlit room.

Chapter 32

In our adversity, God shouts to us.
— C. S. LEWIS

God it was cold. I remember it being the coldest day ever recorded in the City of Boston, well maybe the coldest day in my lifetime, or maybe it was the coldest day in the twentieth century. Whatever it was, it was fucking cold, and I had finally run out of options. I awoke on the morning of February 17, 1986, with a dread so great the best I could do was move. I had always been able to move, that was my strength. To keep going no matter what I had done or not done, no matter how many chemicals I had ingested, no matter whom I had hurt or how badly. The way I saw it, it was a gift from the family I grew up in. We were a family that moved fast. It's hard to hit a moving target, and where I come from, if you hit us and we don't die, we move even faster.

I was standing in my living room in front of massive floor-to-ceiling windows looking out over Commonwealth Avenue, trying to figure out my next move. I had moved from the South End to Back Bay in a fit of changing circumstances. Winston Churchill had called this boulevard that runs through the heart of Boston's Back Bay one of the most beautiful streets in the world. He was right—but not today. Today, all I could see was gloom and doom.

It's funny how at certain critical times in our lives the universe, or God, depending on your sensibilities, orchestrates a perfect alignment

of people, place, and circumstance to illuminate a course of action undeniable to even the most obstinate and fanciful character. I was out of
money and out of luck. My family had realized the inevitable outcome
of my chosen life path and were resigned to waiting for my turn to die.
The doctors had finally learned how to say no, my wife couldn't manufacture a baby or any other drama to deflect attention or elicit sympathy; even the dealers were bored with my rap.

I stood there looking out over the city I had played for the past ten
years knowing there were no more games I could buy into. It was in
this moment that the universal confluence of events mercifully delivered me to that state that I have come to recognize as the greatest in all
the human condition — surrender.

I think my grandfather just turned over in his grave.

Let's get something straight. I come from a long line of very willful
and successful people. The family credo was "every man can make a
difference, and every man should try." *Surrender* was not in anyone's
vocabulary — unless it was a tactic by which you lulled your enemies
into a false sense of security, after which you would turn the tables on
them and win. The grace that descended on me was neither immediately recognized nor appreciated. What I got that morning looking out
at the frozen streets of Boston was that the jig was up and the only answer for the pain that was coursing through my being was to put a gun
in my mouth.

The problem was I *still* didn't have a gun.

Plan B was to give up. There's always a Plan B. I'm not talking
throwing your hands up in the air or waving a white flag so that you
can live to fight another day. I'm talking falling prostrate on the
ground, a heaving, critical, open wound of humanity with so much
desperation that you become willing to accept anything, death, torture, celibacy, even turning your will and your life over to the care of
one of your relatives.

My cousin Bobby Kennedy had gotten sober the year before, after
getting busted on a plane to South Dakota. The media got a whiff and
pounced. Once sober, he never looked back and did his best to share his
new path with me. I wasn't buying. I still had some back doors to slip

out of. When David died, Bobby called me into the bunker looking for solidarity in getting through the pain of it without using. I remember saying to him, "You do it your way, man, and I'll do it mine." I had no intention of dealing with David's death without my other best friends— chemicals—at my side.

It's funny. I had spent much of my life idolizing Bobby and would have followed him anywhere, but by the time sobriety rolled around there was a lot of water under the bridge, and he was the last person on the planet I wanted to give up my power to. This is the wonderful thing about total desperation: you become willing to do things that a moment ago you wouldn't have even considered.

Bobby's previous attempts to share his newfound path with me had fallen on deaf and resentful ears. I would have none of it. Sometimes there is a resistance that comes up with vehemence whenever someone we are close to encourages us to do something that may be good for us.

Like most alcoholics, I only like advice I agree with.

Before the moment grace descended upon me and I was delivered to that exalted state of surrender, I had plenty of pride. My pride did not stand up and shout, "I'm a drug addict and have made a mess of my life for twenty years." No, my pride is craftier than that.

Pride:

Chris, you did this to yourself. Only *you* can get *you* out of it.

Me:

Yeah. I know.

Pride:

Don't listen to these assholes. They just want to tell you what
to do.

Me:

Yeah. Bastards.

Pride:

Nobody knows addiction better than you, my friend. You are
a genius at this shit. You know what needs to be done.

Me:

Yeah. Right.

Pride:
You have some pretty unique circumstances, buddy. Some of
the most unique circumstances in the whole world. Nobody
could possibly understand what you have gone through.
Me:
That's right. Nobody understands me!
Pride:
That's right, my friend. How about another cocktail?
Me:
Sure. What the hell. I deserve it.

Well, things changed on the morning of February 17, 1986, and I
called the one guy on the planet I didn't want to bow to, my cousin
Bobby, and asked him to tell me what to do. This was my first experience with humility, and although I didn't know it at the time, it
demonstrated to me one of the keys to living a life guided by spiritual
principles.

In case there is any confusion, let me point out that there is a big
difference between humility and humiliation. I had humiliated myself
many times over the previous twenty years, but I had never humbled
myself. My pride had convinced me that humbling myself meant weakness and would ultimately lead to my death. My pride allowed me to
endure my humiliation by convincing me things would be different "if
only they would understand and stop fucking with me." Are you confused? Good, welcome to the club. The point is that on the morning of
February 17, 1986, my pride abandoned me—and my life was saved.

This was the first of many spiritual paradoxes that I would learn to
endure.

I believe that what happened that morning twenty years ago was
the only hope for someone like me. A moment of grace, which humbled me, allowing me to surrender and find the key of willingness. My
spiritual journey began—and the keys to my recovery were revealed:
trust God, serve others, and clean house.

Why do some alcoholics and addicts get sober while others die?
I have no idea. It's a mystery, but I know in my heart there's a con-

nection. The grace that came into my life the morning of February 17, 1986, was a gift from David and from my father. I have carried my sobriety for twenty years in their memory and with their help. The life I have been so freely given for the past twenty years is an expression of their lives and my relationship with them. I think of them often and continue to learn about myself as a result of their influence in my life.

Chapter 33

*. . . faith is a faculty of the spirit. It is just the same as talent,
one must be born with it.*
— ANTON CHEKHOV

Carl Jung said that he had never seen an alcoholic recover unless there was some sort of spiritual experience involved. That's what happened that cold day in Boston. I had a spiritual experience and I didn't even know it. God sure is tricky sometimes, but I think I always knew, deep down inside, all that God stuff I got from my family as a kid would come in handy.

I was sixty days sober, and I hadn't thought of God since the day I walked out of Saint Ignatius Loyola when I was thirteen years old. Emerson said, "Self-reliance, the height and perfection of man, is reliance on God." I had foxhole spirituality like every other addict I know: "Please, God, get me out of this, and I'll never ever, ever, ever do it again." But a conscious contact with a power greater than myself that I could rely on to do things for me that I couldn't do myself—like stay sober a day at a time—forget it.

MY WAR had always been with God and the human condition. I never really trusted God and looked on the human condition as his cruel joke. But now I had been delivered to a level of desperation where I became willing to crawl on my belly over broken glass if that was what I needed to do to change. The problem was I wasn't strong enough to do it alone. I would need a lot of help!

THE DOCTORS at McLean's knew what they were doing when they recommended I stay out of New York City. It was Pavlovian. When I was there I had to party. Just the act of getting on a shuttle flight bound for the Big Apple was enough to start the frothing. I had prescriptions at pharmacies up and down the West Side and a familiar drink waiting for me at every East Side bar.

I would walk the streets of the city with my overstuffed briefcase slung over my shoulder going from go-see to audition. I felt like Robert DeNiro in *The Mission*, carrying his bundle of belongings up the mountain as penance for his sins. The bars and drugstores screamed at me with their blinking neon signs, "Hey, Chris, remember us? We're waiting for you. All you have to do is walk in the door. Come on! We miss you." Shit like that—all in neon.

It was a bitch not taking a wrong turn. I needed a God badly.

A guy I met in New York named Brian, who had drunk himself out of the seminary, suggested I throw my shoes under the bed as a way to get on my knees and ask a God of my own understanding to remove the obsession to use drugs and alcohol. I did it on the eighth floor of my mother's Sutton Place apartment, convinced that everyone in New York City was watching me.

Within thirty days the daily obsession to drink and use drugs that had vanquished me for seventeen years vanished and it has not returned for twenty years and counting. This would be the first great change. To me it was nothing short of miraculous. There is no level of difficulty when it comes to miracles, and there would be many more miracles yet to come. These miracles would lead to a life beyond my wildest dreams.

I had found a God to help me change. I had found a God I could trust.

One of the great gifts of having a spiritual awakening is that you come to realize that the world can operate in more than one way. When a human being is firmly rooted in the material plane, there is a logic and order to their existence that most of us accept as "the way it is." If you do A, you get B.

Once a person has a spiritual experience, no matter what form it comes in, everything changes. A new set of laws becomes applicable, and often this new order seems to contradict everything a person knew about the way the world works.

It can be very disconcerting. For instance: *pain*. In the world where most of us live, pain is to be avoided. We are taught on a personal and societal level that pain, although a reality, has no value in and of itself and is only an aspect of life to be endured so you can ultimately reach a place where there is an absence of pain.

Anyone can tell you that no such place exists, but most of us cling to the hope of such a place with childlike zeal. When attempting to live one's life according to spiritual principles, we come to the understanding that pain in and of itself is a great blessing.

A wise man told me when I was newly sober, "Be grateful for the pain. It's God given, just like the good stuff." This does not mean we come to enjoy pain. I whine as much as anyone, but today I am filled with a certainty that whatever pain I have in my life is there to give me a gift. On the other side of my ordeal will come new understanding and blessings. My drug use had enabled me to emotionally detach from the normal pain of life. I always thought my pain was of the extraordinary variety. It wasn't. It was just pain. Pain is like a fever—an indication that something is not right and an opportunity to correct whatever is wrong. I came to know that some of life's greatest gifts come in very ugly wrappings.

You probably think that my family was thrilled with my newfound sobriety. Well . . . when a family member gets sober, it's like holding up a giant mirror to the others. Sometimes they don't like what they see in the mirror. The sober person also gets a whole new group of really important sober friends—a new family—which further pisses the relatives off. My mom was happy I wasn't ending up in emergency rooms and on the front pages of the newspapers, but she hated that I wouldn't make the daiquiris anymore.

"I don't understand why you can't have a cocktail once in a while," she lamented.

My sobriety kind of put a damper on the cocktail hour. It changed the family dynamic. Everyone had a little trouble dealing with the new me.

I think what also happens is, a schism develops between the drinkers and nondrinkers. Those that drink feel self-conscious around the newly sober. What they don't understand is that the newly sober person is way too self-obsessed to judge or even notice what anybody else in the family is up to.

Chapter 34

The family you come from isn't as important as the family you are going to have.
— RING LARDNER

We are our parents. Accept it, forgive them, make peace, and then get on with the business of change. This is one hell of a notion. There are few people I know who, faced with this realization, would not start looking for a bridge to jump off. My dad was somewhat handicapped in the fatherhood department. I've come to believe that you are what you get when it comes to parenting. My father wasn't given a lot, and as his son, neither was I. So I had to make it up as I went along—mostly by counterexample: I did whatever he didn't.

SNAPSHOT:

> Jeannie came out of the bathroom holding the early pregnancy test, and there was little doubt from her expression or the color of the liquid in her hand that our relentless quest for impregnation had finally been realized.

The die was cast and my first child was conceived. God gives you what you can handle at the exact moment you can handle it. I was terrified of becoming a father. I had no idea how to do it. My experience with my father had centered on good drugs and the Playboy Mansion.

I walked into a sober meeting after we got the news, raised my hand, and blurted out to a room full of strangers, "My name is Chris and I'm an addict. I found out this morning that I am going to be a father and it scared the hell out of me because I have no idea how to be a father, because mine was totally incompetent."

It felt good to get this off my chest, and I got a lot of "Thanks for sharing that, man" from the people there, but I still had the fear in my gut. A friend of mine named Dennis, who had a South Boston twang and looked like Ratso Rizzo with a goatee, walked up to me and delivered me to one of those wonderful moments of clarity when he said, "There's one major difference between you and your father and it's the only one that matters—you are sober and he died drunk."

Wow! What a concept.

I might actually be able to do it better than my old man if I kept the plug in the jug.

Dennis died of a drug overdose in 2003. He knew the difference between living sober and living drunk, but the disease killed him anyway. Before he died, he passed the knowledge of the difference on to me. He saved my life by screaming at me every day, "You can't think your way into right action—you have to act your way into right thinking."

Up until that moment I had lived in that magical place where my thoughts were my reality. If I could think it, then it must be real. My thinking stank, and it had a very fleeting relationship with reality. *Thinking* I wanted to be a good father wasn't enough. I would have to *act* like a good father—and that would take a lot of hard work, something else I didn't have much familiarity with. My first problem was even more fundamental: I had very little idea how a good father would act. The only example of being a good father I had growing up was my uncle Bobby. His dynamic lust for life coupled with the controlled anarchy that pulsed through his brood offered an attractive example of family life in general and fatherhood in particular. But was this me?

My son was supposed to be born sometime in the middle of June. He decided to come early, on Memorial Day weekend, when every doctor in Boston is on Cape Cod getting their clubs out of storage. It was cold and rainy. I was panicked as I raced Jeannie to Beth Israel Hospital, try-ing to get any doctor on the phone. A national holiday is a good time to have a baby. It's quiet, with even the severely pregnant out of town. Our guy wasn't around, but somebody is always covering. Doctors are far less important than nurses anyway, and ours seemed glad to have some-thing to do on these slow days. Jeannie was in labor for twenty hours, and though the baby had no interest in coming out, everything else did.

I was there for it all.

It was a hell of a difference from Chinese chicken salad with Cary Grant at Madame Wu's in Tinsletown.

There were three major decisions faced in the birth of my first child. The first was whether Jeannie would take drugs to numb the in-evitable or opt for natural childbirth or not. That was settled in the af-firmative in the first few hours. Nobody can prepare you for the pain of childbirth, and I was only watching. I remember telling my aunt Jean when I was younger about the incredible pain I had felt in having a plantar wart removed from the bottom of my foot. She listened politely before saying, "Men are lucky. You'll never know real pain. Try having a baby. It's like having your top lip stretched over your head."

The second decision was how long to allow the baby to try and cram his big head through Jeannie's small pelvic opening. After twenty or so hours of intense labor, cutting open her stomach seemed like a good idea—so off we wheeled to the OR, where she got more drugs and I donned my greens and stood holding her hand, awaiting the mir-acle of modern birth. My first son was born at 9:43 P.M. I counted his toes and fingers. All were there and, with the exception of the shape of his head, which was conelike and black-and-blue from his twenty hours of banging against his mother's pelvic girdle, he was a healthy, beautiful boy. The doctor handed him to me and said, "Congratula-tions, it's a boy."

When Jeannie and I arrived back at our apartment on Common-wealth Avenue with our yet unnamed son, reality hit me like a ton of bricks. I was a father. Now what do I do?

I spent the first two days washing every window in our apartment building. I did not have the option of opening a bottle of J&B or stop-ping by the Beachcomber. Too bad. Windows are a lot less fun, but they served the same purpose—to take my mind off the one dominant feeling I was having—fear!

The third question to be faced was what to name my son. I had always felt slighted by having an original name. I wished I had been named Peter after my father, but my mother didn't want a Junior. One Peter was enough. All my cousins who were my contemporaries were named after their fathers. The Juniors in our family had greater visibility in the world and therefore greater currency in the family. I struggled mightily with this when naming my first son. There was a strong pull to name him Christopher, even though I don't care for the name and hate the whole Junior thing. In my heart I wanted to name him David after my cousin. The struggle went on for days as I scrubbed the dirt from all those panes of glass while having a conversation with my cousin David in my head:

Me:
I hate my name, always have. Why on earth would I inflict it
on my son?
David:
Because that's what we do in our family.
Me:
I want to name him after you.
David:
Why don't you, then?
Me:
Because I'm a chickenshit and remain bound to the bullshit
traditions I don't really believe in.
David:
Well, if you want my opinion, those traditions never served
me and I don't think they serve you either. Besides, you owe
me, man. You should name him David, after me. It's a way
cooler name than Chris.
Me:
Fuck you, man!

In the end, I did the right thing and named my first son David. It turned out honoring our friendship and making amends for turning my back on my best friend all those years ago was more important than honoring tradition. Whenever I look at my son, I can see the twinkle and crooked smile that was my cousin and best friend to the bitter end. He was right—David is a way cooler name than Chris.

AT THE risk of stating the obvious, many of the great insights into self occur when somebody close to us is born or dies. If you are an addict, these opportunities are often lost in a haze of inebriation. I no longer had the option of drowning my fear, joy, or sadness in a sea of chemicals. When my son was born I confronted my self-centeredness by washing windows instead of opening a bottle of J&B. It's still avoidance but at least I was conscious. I experienced an enormous relief with the birth of my children—the relief brought on through the realization that there was suddenly someone in the world more important than me.

I have had equally profound revelations in my experience of death being sober.

All my life I've had a strange relationship with death. The assassinations of my uncles Jack and Bobby were extraordinary events that colored the way I experienced death. It seemed that whenever someone I knew died, it was newsworthy. That changed on a spring day in 1989.

My mother had let Mademoiselle go when she moved to Paris with Victoria and Robin in 1972. I guess she figured, why bring a Mademoiselle to a country full of mademoiselles? My grandmother gave her work in Palm Beach, and although Mammy never revealed the signs of age on the outside, her health began to fail. I would see her once or twice a year when visiting my grandmother. She never chastised me for not staying in touch, though I knew she wanted to hear from me more. In the fall of 1984 she sent me a note explaining why she could not attend my wedding. It was classic Mademoiselle.

. . . It breaks my heart to have to tell you that I don't think I will be able to take that trip. My doctor is very firm in telling me that by doing so I will only jeopardize my state of health. The emotion and excitement of this beautiful event is not what

he recommends at the present, and I would never disrupt the joy of such a beautiful day and I believe that it would be an imposition on you and your beautiful bride. I will miss it tremendously. I will be with you both with all my heart and if I may say, my blessings will be with you. I love you both and always will. May God bless you and guard you.

Your Mademoiselle

I never saw her again.

SNAPSHOT:

Mademoiselle lived out the last years of her life in a crappy retirement village in West Palm Beach. She didn't much care for her neighbors. "Christofere, everybody here is Jewish." I didn't know what she had against Jews. I think she felt outnumbered. It was just Mademoiselle and her sister, Janine. Two old French ladies in a sea of matzo. She didn't have much of a social life. Mademoiselle had spent her life mothering someone else's children.

All children grow up and leave home. Some will return to visit their blood. Less return to visit the woman who raised them. My sisters were more conscientious than I, but the woman who showed me unconditional love from the age of two was lonely at the end of her life. She never complained. Mademoiselle died in the spring of 1989. Her funeral was held in West Palm Beach in a small church just outside the retirement village where she had lived. It was a significant death for me, and the first I experienced sober. I sat in the cramped wooden pew, self-conscious and unable to get comfortable. I listened to the priest, who didn't know Mademoiselle, struggle through the platitudes. When the priest asked if anyone wanted to say something I couldn't get to my feet. The woman who raised me, gave me my gentleness, and loved me unconditionally would get no words from her charge. There were no scripts or television cameras at this funeral. Only my sisters and I, in an unimpressive little church on the Florida coast. It was far from Saint Patrick's Cathedral. I didn't know what to do with the simplicity of it.

SNAPSHOT:

When I heard my aunt Jackie was sick, I sent her a note. She replied promptly, despite her illness, thanking me for taking the time to write. She said she was well and looking forward to summer, when we would all be together. She drew a little heart at its conclusion. It was her way.

Jackie died less than a month later. I went to 1040 Fifth to say good-bye. Jackie was in a coma and would die twenty-four hours later. I stood in her bedroom with her family and many of mine. My mother was there doing what I had seen her and my other relatives do my whole life, avoiding the reality of death by acting out the charade of life unchanged. She was sitting on the side of Jackie's bed, holding her almost lifeless hand, and talking about her day: getting her hair done, what the kids were doing, what was happening in the news, and what they might do when Jackie rose from her deathbed. It was touching, my mom fending off the reality of death by recalling the activity of life. I had witnessed this many times with my grandfather and grandmother. My mother, along with her brother and sisters, bringing life to the dying. It was an act of will and selflessness. The will to cheat the inevitable through activity and effort. Selfless because there is nothing coming back from the dying. I never understood what the payoff was. Maybe that's the point. There wasn't one. Just the unconditional loving act.

My mom was talking Jackie through the events of her day when from the back of the group surrounding her bed came, "Jesus Christ, Pat, shut up, she's dying."

It was one of the in-laws not practiced in the art of denying impending death and it hit everybody like a blast of cold water. It was so un-Kennedy-like and a completely appropriate moment for Jackie.

The survivors in my mother's generation hold on to life with a vengeance. After losing three brothers and a sister to violent deaths, there is a strong instinct to grasp life no matter how diminished it might be. This often leads to people living longer than they should.

Jackie Kennedy epitomized our family, yet had her own ways of doing things. She stayed connected to the family but she did it on her terms. She was vigilant about maintaining her independent identity and that of her children, separate from the family. It was appropriate that she should die differently.

Her funeral was a national production, done as much for the country as the family. My cousins and I were once again actors in the drama, along with heads of state and other notables. It's difficult to get in touch with your personal grief when you are standing next to Bill Clinton, when television cameras are recording every nuance, when the Upper East Side of New York City is cordoned off by police, and you travel by motorcade and presidential jet to the burial. I found my-self on the steps of Saint Ignatius Loyola near Eighty-fourth Street on Park Avenue, the same church I walked out of at thirteen with a resentment toward God, thinking more about my surroundings than why I was there.

My cousins and I were pallbearers. We were lined up on the steps leading into the church, six feet apart in orchestrated perfect symmetry, forming a gauntlet through which Jackie's casket would pass. I was across from Jack Walsh. The news media of the world were encamped all over Park Avenue, capturing the events. As we waited for the hearse bringing my aunt's body to the church, I found myself increasingly aware that I was on camera.

Voice:
Hey, Chris, look at all those cameras over there.
Me:
Yeah. What about them?
Voice:
There must be a thousand, and they're all taking pictures of
you.

Me:
Yeah, I know.
Voice:
No, wait a minute, I'm not sure they can see you. I mean it's
like a sea of big-teethed Kennedys on these steps. I'm not
sure they'll be able to find you.
Me:
Leave me alone.
Voice:
No, I'm serious. Those cameras will definitely find John and
Caroline and Uncle Teddy, but as far as everybody else goes
it's up for grabs.
Me:
What's your point, Voice?
Voice:
Well, if you stepped up to a higher step, you'd be a head
taller than everybody else and the cameras would definitely
find you.

It was a completely inappropriate and narcissistic thought, with little regard for the situation or my place in the family; but after years in the rabid search to distinguish myself, a part of me had learned how to identify opportunities—and this was one of them.

When Jacqueline Kennedy Onassis died I was eight years sober and therefore cannot claim that chemicals swimming in my bloodstream perverted my thought process on the steps of Saint Ignatius Loyola. What was at work that day was the narcotic of attention. It had entered my bloodstream at an early age and I had struggled for my fix in an environment in which I often came up short. Fame is intoxicating, even if it's fame by association. There are those who thrive on the attention and those who recoil. I love the attention. Like a drug, it fills the emptiness inside and gives the illusion for the moment that I know who I am. I may have been eight years sober when my aunt died, but my identity was still very much wrapped up in my family of origin. That day on those steps as I waited for Aunt Jackie's hearse to arrive, I still needed the attention.

Jack Walsh noticed I was out of place and a head taller than everyone else and motioned me back to my assigned spot, but I had gotten my five minutes of fame, distinguishing me from "all those big-teethed Kennedys on TV."

I had put down the drugs, but there was still a great deal of work to do on me as a person. It would be a long road.

Chapter 35

If you have not seen the devil, look at yourself.
— RUMI

One of the great fictions of recovery is that once you sober up, your work is done. Not true. This is just the beginning. Bill Wilson, the co-founder of Alcoholics Anonymous, said, "When you sober up a horse thief, you've got a sober horse thief." The truth is that many of us who stop our active addictions remain just as despicable sober as we were when using. We just aren't as obvious. When I got sober, I was told I would get to do sober everything I did drunk. It scared me to death, and I didn't believe the guy who said it, but I understood what he was saying. Alcohol and drugs are merely symptoms of a more pervasive fundamental disease, a disease of attitudes and perception. Said more simply, my windshield gets dirty on the inside. This is why it is critical for addicts to find a basis for living that will allow them to change who they are on the inside. Mahatma Gandhi, who knew a thing or two about self-change, said that the man who changes himself is greater than the man who conquers ten thousand armies. He said it with more humility and eloquence, but you get the idea. This is cleaning house, and it is very difficult to do.

For me, it has always been a short trip from Gandhi to Donald Trump.

Many of us choose instead to throw ourselves into other

obsessions—work, sex, food, gambling, shopping, you name it. If it can be abused and used as a way to avoid facing the demons, I'll find it. I've tried some of them. None were as good as heroin, plus all of them only work for a little while. In my experience there is only one road that offers lasting peace—and that's the spiritual path.

It's easier to judge one's life using the outside stuff as the measure. Money, property, and prestige are easily quantifiable. If, instead, you find yourself trudging a path that brings you to an inner journey, the quantifying is more difficult. Most humans need to think they know who they are and where they belong. This is easier to do if one can attach oneself to attaining jobs, substances, sex, money, and fame. If on the other hand one is on a spiritual path, there is little to attach to but the journey and one's reliance on a higher power. I'll take door number one, thank you.

> Awakening begins when a man realizes that he is going
> nowhere and does not know where to go.
> —GURDJIEFF

I spent twenty years trying to be somebody, then got sober and realized that I wanted to entirely change who I was. This realization did not occur right away. I woke up one day and realized I hated who I had become. This was a disconcerting revelation because I was my own construct. Love for myself or others had never been a priority. I came from this amazing family where ambition and achievement were more highly thought of than love for oneself.

Love and hate cannot coexist simultaneously. They are the opposite sides of the same coin. You have to pick one or the other. And it's not like, "Well, today I think I will love myself," and love just fills up inside of you. No, we all have love and hate in us, but the process, circumstances, and individual predisposition of each of us individually conspire to allow one of these states to be dominant.

I pick my cuticles. It hurts like hell when you tear skin off the side of your fingers and draw blood. I've been doing it as long as I can remember. It's a form of self-flagellation, not as extreme as what the Shiites do, but just as effective. The problem is: I don't do it with any spiritual intent, I do it unconsciously. I do it because I don't like myself very much.

It is said that the root cause of addiction is "our defective relations with others." I would add to that "and a healthy dose of self-hatred."

I think my dose comes from *knowing* I could never be good enough and the choices I made along the way that supported this conclusion.

All human beings are blessed with the ability to consciously struggle to live a life based on love or one based on hate. An addict continually makes choices and takes actions in his life that support his self-hatred. This is what allows him to keep using. For the addict who hasn't stopped, the drug provides all he needs to manufacture the necessary amount of self-loathing to allow him to continue on his road to oblivion. For the sober alcoholic or addict, it's a little trickier. The sober guy has a choice. He no longer has John Barleycorn to serve as his hate minion. He needs to act in a way that will cause him to feel bad enough about himself that he will have no choice. Going hand in hand with this willful descent into despicable behavior is the necessary removal of God from the picture.

An addict is always moving toward or away from the drug.

THERE IS another great fiction of recovery—that is, once you stop using, your life becomes a bed of roses. Anybody who has stayed sober for any length of time knows that living sober is about learning to live life on life's terms and a good part of life is painful. When I got sober someone said to me that I would get to realize all my greatest fears in sobriety. Wow! Realize all my fears. That sounds great. Where do I sign up? You know what? He was right, and it's not half as bad as I imagined.

Running out of money. Not being a big movie star. Getting sick. Getting divorced. . . .

And the answer is: "What are Chris's biggest fears?"

. . .

I'VE GONE broke in sobriety. I had money my entire life. I didn't think I could survive if I ran out. Guess what? I did.

Thanks to my grandfather we grew up in the upper economic class of America. Everyone in my family got the best of what this country had to offer and never had to really work to earn it. It surprised me that none of us became Republicans. I remember saying to my uncle Teddy once during the Reagan era, "You know, if half of the legislation you are sponsoring is passed, it's going to cost us a lot of money." He laughed and said sadly, "Unfortunately, there's not much chance of the Republicans letting that happen."

My grandfather took care of everything even after he got sick and died. The money, the deals, the path; he was the wizard behind the curtain. Growing up I was aware that Kennedys rarely carried money on them. They relied on those around them to have cash if it was needed. They knew very little about it and didn't have to. My uncle Jack borrowed a hundred dollars from my dad one night before they went into a restaurant for dinner—my dad never got it back. It didn't matter to my dad. It went with the territory. When you are in the saving-the-world business, money is somebody else's responsibility. My grandfather used to lunch at La Grenouille in New York, where he was never presented with a bill—it was sent to the office. I heard about this growing up. This was my legacy and I aspired to carry it on.

I never got there. It turns out that in order to have money, you have to pay attention to money. You have to work for it and care for it. I was used to calling "the office" in a panic about all the money that was no longer in my checking account. This behavior will not get the maître d' at La Grenouille to send the check to the office.

Because I inherited money, I was terrified of going broke because I had very little confidence in my ability to replace it. This was not an unreasonable fear, given my lack of attention to managing the green stuff and my aversion to hard work.

I ran out of money, so I learned how to make it and how to live with less. I learned the value of money, how to take care of it and manage it. I wouldn't trade these lessons for a million bucks. . . . Well . . .

MY CHOSEN career as an actor also didn't turn out the way I had planned. I wanted to be Tom Cruise. Instead I ended up as— Christopher Lawford.

Chapter 36

You really are the actor schmuck of this family.
—ALEC BALDWIN TO CHRIS LAWFORD

M y uncle Sarge told me that everything he wanted and tried hard to get in his life never brought him the happiness or satisfaction he thought it would, and all the stuff in his life that came to him freely and unexpectedly brought true meaning and joy. He looked at those things as God given and figures that God knows best what we humans want and need. Whenever I spent time with Sarge he made me feel as if I had been seen—and as if I mattered. This was not usually the case with some of my other relatives.

I used to go to him for advice. Sarge actually connected his advice to who I was as a person. To do this you have to care enough to take the time to figure out who the person is you are giving advice to.

Sarge wrote me a long letter in response to the note I sent him requesting contributions for the work I was doing on the Center for Addictions at Harvard. He sent me five hundred dollars and these words:

> *I think what you are doing in your work is truly important. I*
> *am guessing, moreover, that you will do it very well. You have*
> *a very gentle and understanding and effective way of dealing*
> *with people, and I am hoping you have found exactly the right*
> *niche in which your many attributes can flourish.*

I never liked Sarge's advice.

I didn't see myself the same way he saw me. He saw my heart and my aptitude to engage other people. I saw myself as a star, as an unrecognized talent. He always steered me toward service. I was looking for my throne. I would leave our conversations feeling frustrated but knowing that he had spoken a truth I wasn't ready to accept.

When I decided to become an actor, Sarge was surprised, saying, "You don't strike me as having the temperament of an actor. The ones I've met are pretty self-involved and always *on*, always performing."

It pissed me off. He might be right that I didn't have the actors' all-consuming need to perform. But I could be as self-involved as any of them.

SNAPSHOT:

I was six months sober. I hadn't stopped shaking yet, and had no idea how I was going to make a living. A photographer in Boston asked me to come down to her studio and hold a glass for a product shot. She paid me a hundred dollars to take a picture of my hand. This was easy money. A lightbulb went off in my head. Thus began my modeling career. I got an agent, a modeling book to collect my pictures, a new haircut, and a diet. Nobody in my family had ever been a model, so it was all mine.

I was way too big to be a model and I felt ridiculous when I went on go-sees, which is what they call auditions in the modeling world. I would show up in a room with twenty of the best-looking hard-bodied twenty-year-olds on the planet, where some big-haired, pissed-off hermaphrodite would ask me to walk up and down like I was on a runway. It was pretty humiliating. I liked the money, though. One day I was hired by Bruce Weber to shoot an ad for Polo in L.A. I knew my days as a model were numbered when I couldn't squeeze into the size 32 jeans and Bruce kept telling me to "kneel behind the couch" in an attempt to hide my big fat ass.

I was thirty years old. I had a law degree from Boston College and a Master's Certification in clinical psychiatry from Harvard Medical School. I had tried a bunch of things, but nothing had stuck. There was something empowering about getting paid for showing up as me, no matter how shallow the work was.

And there were lots of pretty girls.

I was married and faithful, with all that energy that was no longer being dissipated through my use of chemicals flooding my loins. It was a constant struggle. During one shoot in Manhattan, I had to lie in a bed all day in my boxer shorts making faux love to another one of the most beautiful girls in the world. My first major quandary in recovery. I wanted this girl more than I wanted anything—even more than a drink. I also wanted to remain faithful to Jeannie. I was between the devil and the deep blue sea. I called my cousin Bobby.

"If you have sex with that girl, you'll feel so guilty that you'll probably get high," he said.

"But man, she's gorgeous!"

"Are you willing to give up your career to stay sober?" he asked me. I couldn't believe my response.

"Yes," I said. "I'm willing to give up my dream of being an actor and making faux love to beautiful models all day to stay sober."

My response was miraculous for someone like me. Remember, I don't take direction or ultimatums well. Especially from the guy I had competed with for most of my life. I was also not very good at denying myself pleasure. But I was willing to do both these things to stay sober, and the paradox was that, in being willing to give it up, I didn't have to. I went back the next day and made more faux love without any attachment to doing it for real. I have little doubt that if I had been unwilling to surrender my right to do what I wanted to do, I would have doomed myself to a very different outcome. Amazing.

I survived the pitfalls of modeling and made a little money along my way to the more illustrious career of actor. I never really planned on becoming an actor, but the flow moved me from the still camera to moving pictures.

My dad never encouraged me toward his line of work. I think that though he loved being an actor and took pride in his work, it's a painful life and he didn't want me to have to endure all the bullshit. I also think he didn't want the competition. Well, when I became an actor my father was dead so there were no worries on that score. I was free to act out all the unconscious paternal identification dramas I had the energy for.

I thought of acting as a silly profession for which I had neither the patience nor the talent. I pursued it initially because I liked the idea of being famous and getting paid a boatload of money for doing very little work. It was the job I had described to my uncle Teddy that day in his GTO. A lot of money for not very much work, and I could do some good with all that fame—or so I thought. The further I got into it, the more I found a real love and appreciation for the work. It isn't easy to do well, but it is a joy. I'd do it for free. Looking for work is a nightmare. Waiting to work, excruciating. It's what you get paid for. Being famous is a pain in the ass. It feeds the ego, which causes lots of other problems. What is good for the ego is bad for the character and vice versa. Getting recognized for your work feels good. So does getting bumped up to first class.

MY FIRST movie was the last film written by John Huston, to be directed by his son Danny. The movie was called *Mr. North* and starred Robert Mitchum, Lauren Bacall, Angelica Huston, Anthony Edwards, and Virginia Madsen. I was to play Ms. Madsen's love interest. My agent told me that when they were considering whether to cast me, John Huston rose up from his deathbed and asked, "Is he tall, dark, and handsome?" When Danny nodded in the affirmative, Mr. Huston shrugged and said, "That's all you need. Cast him." That pretty much sums up why I got roles and why I didn't.

The only acting job I was ever fired from was the pilot for *Sex and the City*. I was fired for being too good-looking. I had landed the role of the first guy to have sex and dump Sarah Jessica Parker's character. I showed up for the readthrough and introduced myself to the head of HBO, who had flown in from L.A. to have a look-see, saying. "Hi, I'm a friend of So&So and just wanted to say hello." He was gracious, asked me if I wanted a bagel, and we got down to the business of reading the script. Later that day I was lounging by the pool in Westchester with my family when I got the call:

> Producer:
> Chris, I'm sorry to have to tell you this but you won't be playing the role of the guy who has sex and dumps Sarah Jessica Parker.
> Me:
> Why not?
> Producer:
> Well, the brass at HBO thought you were too damn handsome.
> Me:
> So what? I'm an actor. I can look like shit if that's what you want.
> Producer:
> We need a shlubby guy to play the part to make her getting dumped really outrageous. If you dumped her it wouldn't be such a big deal—being you're so good-looking and all.
> Me:
> Oh. Do I still get paid?
> Producer:
> The check's in the mail.

I was crushed but managed to write the head of HBO a note saying that if I had known bringing up So&So's name would have had such disastrous consequences, I never would have done it. I learned my political lessons well. You never know when the head of a cable giant might come in handy. A few years later I was in L.A. pitching the same head of HBO an idea for a series and asked if he received the letter I had sent him. He laughed, saying he had but had not understood what I meant by "disastrous consequences" because he didn't know that I wasn't in the pilot until he actually saw it. Later I heard that it was the producer's idea to get rid of the too-damn-handsome actor having sex with Sarah Jessica Parker in the bathtub in favor of a Calvin Klein model the producer wanted. He was much better looking than I am. Go figure. Big surprise—a producer who's a dog.

MY SCENES were filmed in one of the large mansions in Newport, Rhode Island. I arrived full of excitement and nerves and was promptly informed that Miss Madsen wanted to see me to get acquainted. Having no idea what that meant I headed over to her bungalow. I spent the next three days falling in love with Virginia Madsen, and I thought she was falling in love with me. I wasn't going to do anything—I was married. But it sure was nice being adored by a beautiful movie star. On our last night of shooting, after the lights and cameras were shut down and everyone had wrapped and said their good-byes, I looked around for Virginia. She was gone and I would not see her again for fifteen years. It was my first lesson in the power of illusion in making movies.

It took a long time for me to actually own being an actor. In those early days if someone asked me what I did I would say, "I'm an actor but I went to law school and I've got a clinical psych degree . . . blah, blah, blah."

One night I went to a party at my cousin Maria Shriver's house. Maria had married the bodybuilder Arnold Schwarzenegger, who had become the biggest movie star in the world. Hollywood's movers and shakers were paying homage to the biggest movie star of the moment. Joel Silver, the producer of *Predator,* was in attendance, and Maria was eager for me to meet him. She introduced me. Joel shook my hand and said, "So you're an actor?"

I said, "Yes, but it's not the only thing I do in my life. I'm a father, a lawyer . . . blah, blah, blah."

Halfway through my declaration of how well rounded I was, Joel turned his head, dropped my hand, and completely lost interest in me. I would never get his attention again. It was my first lesson in the importance of first impressions in Hollywood.

To be noticed at all, you must convince whoever holds the power that you would literally die to give them what they want.

Those who look at Hollywood from the outside are shocked to

learn that there are people in this town who will actually have sex with someone for a role or to get ahead. I heard a story about a major movie star—and one of the great ladies' men in history—offering to let Tennessee Williams give him a blow job for the lead role in the movie version of one of his plays. I was incredulous.

"That's impossible," I said. "So-and-so is the most hetero guy I know. He likes pussy way too much to suck somebody's cock for a role. I don't believe it." Tennessee's friend looked at me with the sympathy reserved for those who have no idea how the world really works and said, "Christopher, that role would completely change his life, bottom to top, for the rest of his life. It would make him a star. He would have done anything for it. Sucking a cock was getting off easy."

I'm not sure I was prepared for this.

I grew up in that rarified environment that was rarely penetrated by the ugly realities of existence on this planet.

Having to scratch and claw to get people's attention and get ahead was not part of my experience. I remember my cousin John telling me about the moment he realized that someone was trying to screw him in a business deal. John couldn't believe this relationship had turned into something where this guy was figuratively trying to kill him, and John was being forced to kill him first. I never learned about this growing up. When my generation came along, there was so much stuff and collective goodwill, we just had to learn how to graciously accept all the good shit folks were willing to give us. When I moved to Hollywood, I got a wake-up call in the way things really work.

A few days after I alienated the biggest producer in Hollywood, Maria called me to inform me that Joel was doing a big movie with Patrick Swayze and that she had talked to him about a role, and he was expecting my call. I thanked her, and called Joel. He didn't call back. I called Maria to let her know Mr. Silver hadn't returned my call. She asked me how many times I had called him. I said once. She laughed and said, "Christopher, one phone call isn't going to do it. Not in this town. Call him every five minutes until he picks up the phone."

She had obviously already begun her education.

CHRISTOPHER KENNEDY LAWFORD

When I first got to Hollywood, an out-of-work screenwriter I played basketball with pulled me aside on the court one day and whispered the Hollywood version of the famous Gore Vidal edict that "It is not enough to succeed. Others must fail." In Hollywood, "It's not enough to succeed. Your best friend must fail."

I wondered who could even think up such a thing.

Chapter 37

It's easy to see without looking too far
That not much
Is really sacred.
— BOB DYLAN

After my parents divorced and I was assimilated into the Kennedy family, I forgot how much I loved movies and wanted to be involved in their creation. That all changed again in a dark movie theater on West Fifty-eighth Street in New York when I was twenty-four.

Kramer vs. Kramer starred Dustin Hoffman and Meryl Streep playing two divorcing parents fighting over custody of their young son. It hit close to home and moved me like nothing I had read or seen in my life up to that point. I walked out of the theater determined to be a part of a creative effort that could have that kind of effect on a human soul.

After a short time in Hollywood, I came to realize that not much of the movie business is about creating a product with as much integrity as the film I saw when I was twenty-four. It's a business, after all, a big business—which along with armaments accounts for a large portion of the dollars the United States earns from exports. But I knew there were those in the movie business who were driven more by content than bottom line. I figured Oliver Stone to be one of them.

Oliver was one of my heroes. His movies, politics, patterns of consumption, and irreverence were an inspiration. Soon after I got to town, I landed a small role in Stone's *The Doors*. I was thrilled to be able to work with him, even if the role was less than significant. There *are* small parts, and this was one of them. He wouldn't give me a start date, saying, "You'll work sometime in March." It was December, for Christ's sake. Well, as things usually go in the movie business, as soon as you book one job, you can be certain you'll book a better job that you can't do because of the first piece-of-shit job you were grateful for before you booked the second job that would change your life—if you could do it.

Well, that's what happened to me. I got a big role in a high-profile movie at Disney, only it conflicted with my tiny, insignificant, one-step-above-extra role in Oliver's movie. No problem, right? Oliver will understand. He wouldn't wreck someone's career if he didn't have to. Think again. He called me personally at home that weekend and said, "Your scene is vital to my film. I expect you to honor your commitment to me and show up to shoot this scene—whenever that might be!" Say hello to the out-of-control Hollywood ego.

As it turned out, this was much ado about nothing, which is usually the case in Hollywood. I was able to shoot both movies, and after Oliver had finally assembled his rock-and-roll homage, I received a note from the great auteur informing me that I had been largely cut out of his film. He assured me that it had nothing to do with my performance, said he was sorry and hoped we could do it again real soon.

Why do people in Hollywood send notes like that? They don't have to. The contents are a lie. It's not because they are nice people, because they aren't. My theory is that the landscape in Tinseltown can change in a New York minute and one never knows which lowly assistant will be running a major studio and what wannabe actor will become a major studio star. You can't take any chances pissing people off. Nice note, but full of shit. I never worked for Oliver Stone again.

SNAPSHOT:

Anthony Hopkins is a great actor. He is also a great human being. I had been in L.A. for a few months when I ran into him. I introduced myself and thanked him for trying to help my dad in a time of need. I asked him if he would have coffee with me so I could talk to him about acting. To my surprise he said yes. We sat in a coffee shop in the Pacific Palisades as I grilled him about his preparation for the role of Hannibal Lecter in the film *Silence of the Lambs,* which had just been released.

Me:

How did you find the voice, the walk?

Tony:

I don't know. It just came.

Me:

Come on. The way you walk away at the end of the film. It was brilliant. What physical condition were you playing.

Tony:

I wasn't playing anything. I prepare for every role the same way. Its really quite simple.

I couldn't believe my good fortune. I was about to get the secret that would make me a great actor! But dare I ask? Ah, fuck it.

Me:

Can you tell me how you prepare?

Tony:

Sure. I read the script out loud one hundred times. I make little wagon wheels to keep track of how many times I've read it. Each wagon wheel represents five times. At the end I have twenty little wagon wheels at the top of my script.

Me:

That's it?

Tony:

That's it. After reading *Silence of the Lambs* a hundred times I went to a read-through in Salt Lake City with Jonathan Demme and Jodie Foster, after which I drove back to L.A. By the time I got to town, Hannibal Lecter was screaming to get out of me.

Tony Hopkins taught me that genius is simple. Unfortunately, not all of us can be geniuses. He also taught me something else when he said, "All my life I wanted to drive down Sunset Boulevard and look up and see one of those giant billboards advertising a movie with my name above the title. I did that this morning, Chris, and you know what? It doesn't really change anything."

Tony Hopkins taught me that it is possible to achieve greatness in this world without losing one's humility or one's self.

OCEAN'S 11 was my favorite of all my dad's movies. Ever since that day in Vegas when I was six years old and found myself at my first craft service table watching the Rat Pack steal all that casino money, I wanted to make a movie like that. My dad had found the original script, bought it with my mom, and brought it to Frank Sinatra to get it made. After I had been in Hollywood for a while, I went to see my friend Lorenzo di Boneventura who was head of production at Warner Bros. about acquiring the rights to remake *Ocean's 11*. Lorenzo was one of my cousin Michael's best friends and had survived the Caroní River with us, and though I had no illusions, I figured I might have a shot.

"Lorenzo," I said, "I want to remake *Ocean's 11*, what do you think?"

He laughed and said, "God, Chris, I wish you had come in four months ago. I just gave the remake rights to Jerry Weintraub!"

They say timing is everything, and mine sucked. I tracked the movie through development and when Steven Soderbergh was attached to direct, I wrote him a letter telling him how important this movie was to me and how I would love to be involved in the remake. I had the same agent as Steven when we were both starting out. When he was casting *Sex, Lies, and Videotape*, Peter Gallagher and I were Steven's top two choices for the role of John. Peter got the role and I got a one-way ticket to palookaville. A month after I sent the letter, I got a call from the casting director and read for a small role.

Steven Soderbergh offered me the role of "the 3rd FBI guy from the left" in his remake of *Ocean's 11*.

As an actor my requirement for taking any job had always been one of three things: good money, a great role, or someone I wanted to work with. There was no real money for the actor lucky enough to play "the 3rd FBI guy from the left," and the part sucked, but I wanted to work with Steven Soderbergh, and I would have liked to be in the remake of my favorite of my old man's movies—so my gut said I should take the part. But my ego was bruised and my manager advised that I pass—so I passed.

I figured this was the end of it, but when money and egos are as out of control as they are in Hollywood, it's never that simple.

Four years later HBO was doing a show set in Washington, a blend of fiction and reality entitled *K Street*. The show was being produced by Steven Soderbergh and George Clooney. I went to Clooney's house for a party and to see if there might be a job available for me in *K Street*. Clooney was gracious, but I should have known something was amiss when he said, "What happened with *Ocean's 11*, man? We tried to get you in it." Later that evening I met the producer who had brought *K Street* to George and Steven. He was excited about my potential involvement and suggested I think of "how Chistopher Kennedy Lawford could be in the show." I came up with a plot line where I would hire the political consulting firm at the center of *K Street* to help *me* run for president of the United States. Of course, I didn't want to be president. I wanted to be a movie star. But this stunt would create the notoriety needed to get what I really wanted, which was a career in Hollywood. The guy loved it. It was the perfect blend of reality and fiction with a nice twist on the actor-becoming-politician theme.

Two days later a friend was having lunch with the head of the company that was producing *K Street*, and when my name came up, he said, "Chris Lawford doesn't have a very good reputation around here." She asked why, and he said, "Because he turned down a role in *Ocean's 11*."

People have long memories in Hollywood, and no matter how successful or powerful they become, they never forget. I wrote Steven and George a letter apologizing for turning their offer down. I realized that if you ask someone for something and they give it to you, you should take it even if it's not what you had in mind. I never heard back from either of them.

Hollywood is pretty democratic despite the elephants who never forget. There are all sorts of different people doing all kinds of different jobs. The only requirement for success is some talent and a lot of perseverance. Nepotism doesn't really work. There are too many chiefs and way too much money involved to give someone a job because they know someone.

Arnold Schwarzenegger sent me a note after I worked with him in the film *The 6th Day*, assuring me that nepotism had nothing to do with my getting the part: "I hope you know that while I may have opened a couple of doors for you, if you were not such a good actor, nobody, including myself, could have landed you the job!"

This was the first time I had ever heard the Terminator admit he couldn't get something done, but I took him at his word.

My first film after arriving in Los Angeles was a movie starring Theresa Russell called *Impulse*. It was a forgettable film about cops in the LAPD. I worked on it for six weeks, shooting nights with Ms. Russell and five actors and the producer Al Ruddy, who produced and won Academy Awards for *The Godfather* and *Million Dollar Baby*. We had a ball playing cops and robbers in between poker games and listening to one of the producer's strategies for getting Ms. Russell to show her tits on camera, which would mean hundreds of thousands more dollars in foreign sales. What a business!

Al Ruddy is a great old-school Hollywood producer who loves movies, knows how a set works, and enjoys hanging out with his cast. One night during a game of Texas Holdem, he passed along, in a voice that resembles churning gravel, the secret to success in the movie business: "Everybody I've ever met who has been successful in the movie business has one similarity. Some are rich, some poor, some smart, some dumb, some beautiful, some ugly, but any actor, writer, director, or producer who makes it has one common trait—perseverance. You throw them out the door they come in the window, you throw them out the window they come down the chimney. They refuse to take no for an answer. They refuse not to be successful."

This is what you need to make it in Hollywood: perseverance—and a little bit of luck. At the age of thirty-five I was going to have to let go of the "how many people I knew" thing. Even when I realized that all the big shots I could get on the phone didn't mean shit, it was hard to let go of.

Nobody wanted me to get a job more than my uncle Teddy. He was always offering to help and was kind of frustrated, I think, that he couldn't. He was always sending off notes to people he knew introducing his struggling actor nephew.

Mr. Robert Redford
Sundance, Utah 84604
Dear Bob:
I've been in close touch with my nephew, Christopher
Lawford, who is very excited about his budding acting career.
He has just finished a Warner Brothers film, Impulse, and will
be appearing in three other films as well. I do hope that Chris
might be given the great priviledge of participating in the
Sundance June workshop.

As ever,
Ted

Hope you are well. He really is very special — my thanks.

Dear Ted,
The actors program is already filled for this summer, but we
would love to consider your nephew, Christopher Lawford, for
next year's program. . . .

Regards,
Robert

June 20, 1989
Dear Bob:
Many thanks for your personal response to my inquiry in
behalf of my nephew, Chris Lawford. . . .
From what Chris tells me, I can certainly understand why
your excellent program fills up early in the year. I just hope
that things work out for Chris next summer.

Warm best,
Ted

He sent a letter to producer and friend Mike Medavoy asking if Mike would meet with me. Mike sent him back a note agreeing to meet me and asked my uncle to meet with his three-year-old grandson—as a joke.

None of this was very good!

I WAS in acting class one day and in walked Bill Hurt. He was a hero of mine. I loved his work and the fact that he refused to travel to Hollywood without a return-trip airline ticket on him at all times, guaranteeing he would be able to flee. He had also attended both Middlesex and Tufts four years before me. I had never met him but was aware of his legacy and it inspired me. I introduced myself to him in class and later wrote him a letter asking for his wisdom concerning the craft of acting. He wrote me a three-page letter telling me he didn't want to meddle in my process. "Acting is about truth," he wrote. "About people being worth more than their functions." It's "about mystery and conflict and transcendence" and that if "it's compromised fundamentally, it dies." He urged me to be specific and serve the play, my fellow actors, and the writer. "The play's the thing wherein I'll catch the conscience of the king."

He ended with a quote from *A River Runs Through It* by Norman Maclean, which Robert Redford had yet to make into a film: "all good things—trout as well as eternal salvation—come by grace and grace comes by art and art does not come easy."

I knew about grace and I knew it didn't come easy. I was learning that art didn't either.

AFTER TOILING in Hollywood for five years, I saw the light at the end of the tunnel. I hoped it wasn't another train. It looked like I was finally going to get my big break in the Eddy Murphy movie *The Distinguished Gentleman*. It was the second movie directed by Jonathan Lynn, who did *My Cousin Vinny*. It promised to be a big movie. I was the favorite for the lead bad guy, who was a sleazy lobbyist—and a perfect breakout role for me. It was a Disney movie, and they made me jump through hoops for two months, reading and screen testing over and over. At the end of the day, Jeffrey Katzenberg overruled the director and cast the actor Kevin McCarthy, who was thirty years my senior, in the role. As consolation I received a note from the director assuring me that the reason I did not get the role had nothing to do with my "undoubted talent" and an expression of his hope that we would work together in the future.

Don't these people realize that if an actor doesn't get the role they will *always* think it's because they suck and the act of reassuring them only confirms it? That's how insecure actors are. By the way, I never worked with Jonathan Lynn again, and his follow-up to *My Cousin Vinnie* came and went after Eddie Murphy got pulled over by the cops on Santa Monica Boulevard for picking up a woman—"Call me Shalomar"—who turned out to be a transvestite.

The *Distinguished Gentleman* ordeal was the straw that broke this actor's back. The ABC daytime soap opera *All My Children* had been after me for a year to do a role but I had said no. Soaps weren't interesting to me. I thought they were stupid and that I would be embarrassed to say some of the words actors have to say on those shows. After my last disappointment in Hollywood I figured saying stupid words couldn't be as bad as getting fucked by the likes of Jeffrey Katzenberg.

I moved my family back to New York and spent three years as the character Charlie Brent in the fictitious soap town of Pine Valley saying stupid words I swore I would never say. I made a bunch of money, lived in a great New York apartment, bought a house in Westchester, and learned what it would be like to have a regular acting gig. I received a letter from my uncle Teddy congratulating me. I'm sure he was relieved he didn't have to write letters to all his Hollywood supporters trying to get his nephew a job.

Dear Chris:
Now that you're such a big star, I hope you won't forget us!!!
Seriously, I just read the TV Guide story, and I've heard very
good things about your performance on All My Children.
Keep up the good work!

Love,
Uncle Ted

CHRISTOPHER KENNEDY LAWFORD

I learned a couple of things during my stay in Pine Valley. I learned that I like getting a regular paycheck. I learned that as stupid as I thought soap opera was, a large segment of the America public gets its education on social issues from them, and because most of the writers and producers are more liberal than conservative, the point of view expressed in storylines about AIDS, addiction, interracial marriage, abortion, gay rights, etc., is often of a liberal persuasion. As Agnes Nixon, one of the creating divas of daytime, told me, "Soaps are often the only education on social issues that the underbelly of America ever gets." They do it pretty well, too, because they have six months to tell a story so they get to explore all the aspects of an issue in detail.

I learned just how profound soap operas can be in people's lives when I received a letter from one of the fans of the show: In it she told me the story of trying to save a fifteen-year-old girl from spending the rest of her life in a wheelchair. For years she had fought with the hope that this little girl would walk. The day came when they learned this would never happen. She had just come home from the hospital, and "I couldn't stop crying, couldn't stop screaming. . . . I was losing it. In the deepest depression over this child I had ever had." She had taped a week's worth of *All My Children*. She decided to watch them. I came on, and she had never seen me but I reminded her of an actor she was in love with when she was sixteen and seeing me brought her back to a time of happiness and hope in her life. The actor was Peter Lawford. She watched the credits and saw my name. "I just knew at that moment that everything would be alright. I knew that life continued, life goes on. Life would get better again. Peter Lawford had continued on in you, in your lovely face and kind eyes."

I LEARNED that I am never far away from being my father's son and that God can make me useful in ways that are far from the ways I might expect.

WHEN YOU join the cast of a soap opera you quickly realize that it's a woman's medium. The women drive the story lines; the men merely service the women. I was servicing Kelly Ripa, who played Haley and was the last virgin of daytime. The big day came when Haley was to lose her virginity and Charlie was the lucky guy. I'm a method actor. I had spent years studying with teachers who had impressed on me the need to keep it real by staying sensorially connected and not be "one of those light switch actors who turns it on and off at will." Jack Nicholson was one of my acting heroes and I had reveled in the story of him showing up in nothing but a pair of cowboy boots to coax a very nervous Sally Struthers from her trailer to shoot their sex scene in *Five Easy Pieces*.

What's good enough for Jack . . .

That's right, I showed up on the set of *All My Children* to shoot the scene where Haley loses her virginity to Charlie with nothing on. Yes . . . stark naked . . . the full Monty. It was cool with Kelly, but the executives at ABC began looking at me with a little alarm after that. A short time later I wasn't working with Kelly anymore, and a short time after that my contract wasn't renewed.

Coincidence? I don't know, but from now on I will take the advice of the flamboyant director of that memorable episode where Charlie had Haley in the raw. He strongly suggested that in my future professional endeavors, it would probably be wise if I "do not shit where I eat."

SNAPSHOT:

In January of 1992 Bill Clinton became president and Chris Lawford, aka Charlie Brent, was invited to walk in his inaugural parade. I was accompanied by some of my cousins who held or aspired to hold elective office. I had just joined the cast of *All My Children*. I was having some self-esteem issues walking with my cousins, who were a lieutenant governor, a congressman, and a well-known activist. Being the newest cast member on a daytime soap opera was not a very substantial calling card. My cousins were mildly amused that I was included in the parade to begin with. We started walking down Pennsylvania Avenue through the throngs of ordinary Americans lining the road to the White House. Suddenly people started to call out "Charlie!" All the way to the White House people were yelling "Charlie!" I was a star. My cousins were anonymous and a little annoyed.

In 1994 my Uncle Teddy had another reelection campaign for the U.S. Senate seat he had held since 1962. It was usually a cakewalk, but this year was a little different. He was running against a guy named Mitt Romney who had political pedigree, good looks, and lots of money. The only thing he didn't have going for him was his name. What the hell kind of name is Mitt? Anyway, Teddy was vulnerable and my cousin Michael was running the campaign, which meant Michael had been tapped as heir apparent. But Teddy would have to win in order for Michael to get all the cool stuff that goes along with being heir apparent, which meant that all Michael's cousins were pressed into heavy political service. I brought a bus full of soap stars from *All My Children* to western Massachusetts to scour the malls in search of votes for the embattled senior senator.

It's not easy to get a soap star up to speed on the importance of keeping Ted Kennedy on the Senate Judiciary Committee, but soap stars are good at delivering their lines, so we stuck with that. I wrote the scripts, and my divas and hunks delivered them to the good people of Worcester County, Mass. I don't know if we changed any voters' minds, but there were crowds in the malls and stories in the press. The campaign was rejuvenated, Michael was appreciative, and it felt good helping him out.

I received a letter from my uncle after his reelection:

Nov '94
Dear Chris,
You made a real difference in my campaign.
* It was your win too.*

*   Love you,*
*   Uncle Teddy*

Michael never got to get all the good stuff that comes from being heir apparent. His rising star crashed and burned after it was found out that he had inappropriate relations with his underage babysitter while he was married to Frank Gifford's daughter. He died two years after the triumph of the 1994 election when he hit a tree on Aspen Mountain playing football on a pair of skis. To many, it didn't make sense—he was way too good at both sports to die like this—but to me it made perfect sense. If I hadn't had drugs to alleviate my internal angst, the emotional pain would have sent me looking for a hot babysitter to fuck or a giant tree I could slam into going seventy miles an hour on skis.

Before Michael found his tree, my cousins and I got to have our greatest football game ever in Hyannis Port on my grandparents' lawn. It was the summer of 1996, and though I didn't know it, it would be our final game and the last time we would all be together in the place that I loved.

SNAPSHOT:

I was in the best shape of my life. Being on national television, even if it's a daytime soap opera, is a great motivator to lose weight and get to the gym—I never knew when I might be asked to take my shirt off and make faux love to one of my beautiful costars. My cousins and I had been squabbling for years over who would best whom on the family field of honor. Today we were going to settle the football question once and for all. On one side of the line of scrimmage were myself, Steve Smith, and Bobby and Michael Kennedy. On the other side of the ball were my cousin John with Bobby, Timmy, and Anthony Shriver.

It wasn't even close.

Our team won 5–2. I threw three touchdowns to Michael and one to Steve; Bobby ran for another. Michael proved himself the undisputed best athlete in the family with his speed and acrobatic catches. I ran circles around Bobby Shriver, which surprised me and left him gasping in frustration, "Come back here, you bastard." I became the undisputed best quarterback in the family. All of this would stand for eternity, as Michael and John are now gone and the rest of us are too old and tired to give a shit.

JOHN WASN'T like the rest of us when it came to many of our tribal rituals. His independence always showed. He liked football but it didn't matter to him the same way it mattered to us. He had managed to find a certain detachment when it came to the unconscious yardsticks of how much of a Kennedy you were, but he still had a power, which his death meant he would never fully grow into. John had the soul and talent to be an actor, but that choice would never do. He had the weight of "the path" on him more than any of us but somehow managed an aloofness and humanity that allowed him not to get eaten up by it.

John was like David in that he understood what a dreadful, dreary burden the legacy had become, but unlike David he was capable of escaping it, creating distance, which allowed him to come to it on his own terms. David once said to me that he knew the family's idea of reality was different than his but it had a hold on him nevertheless. John knew he was different and he lived it.

AS AN actor, I have been privileged to look at life from the perspective of an artist. As an artist I am given permission to transcend the reality of the given. Encouraged to look beyond the boundaries that are defined by our society. Sometimes work blends with reality to provide an experience that transcends the boundaries of what we know, delivering us to who we are and what might be possible.

When I signed up to play a real-life navy flier in the film *Thirteen Days* —a dramatic recreation of what happened in the Kennedy White House during the Cuban Missile Crisis—I had no idea that the experience would transform me politically and change the way I saw the world. We shot the film in L.A. and the Philippines. The movie turned out to be something I was proud to be a part of—in spite of Kevin Costner's unfortunate Boston accent. My family was less than thrilled.

They were particularly appalled by the elevation of Kenny O'Donnell, played by Kevin, to equal billing with my uncles in the orchestration of what would be the finest foreign policy achievement of the Kennedy administration.

My Aunt Ethel has made it a yearly habit to send out funny, highly produced Valentine's Day cards to friends and family. The year that *Thirteen Days* was released, her card showed Ethel sitting in the oval office behind the president's desk, gesturing toward the camera, with an inscription reading, "Roses are red, violets are blue, you've got 13 Days, Valentine, to figure out what Kenny O'Donnell would do."

When I was six years old I was in a presidential motorcade. My mom and I were in one of the cars with Kenny O'Donnell following the president. Kenny was not pleased to be in the car with the president's sister and her six-year-old son. I got carsick and blew lunch all over the appointment secretary to the president of the United States. He never liked me after that, and my mother never liked him.

Kevin Costner was invited to travel to Cuba and screen *Thirteen Days* for Fidel Castro and the Cuban people. I called the producers and asked if I could come along. They agreed. Having a Kennedy along probably wouldn't hurt.

We flew to Havana on Kevin's G4 and were greeted at the Hotel National by a mob of fans, thirsting for proximity to a Hollywood icon. Not what I expected. I, like my family, like most Americans, viewed Cuba as a totalitarian dictatorship, isolated from the world, stubbornly clinging to the defeated Communist ideology, for years a real threat but now just an irritant to American liberty. From the Missile Crisis in 1962 onward, I believed the island to be surrounded by barbed wire and decimated by Communism, populated by bearded revolutionaries with evil intent and miserable dupes who were constantly trying to flee to the promised land in boats that couldn't make the ninety-mile journey to Miami's prosperity and freedom. The culture was Soviet gray and the big-finned cars were testament that Cuba would be forever stuck in the golden era of the fifties—their last great hope to participate in the American dream. Stepping into the vibrant life and cultural confidence of the Hotel National as part of an American movie star's entourage told me right away I had some very large misconceptions I'd have to overcome.

IN THE center of Havana is the Palace of the Revolution. Built by Batista to house the Cuban Supreme Court but appropriated by Castro after he put Batista on a plane for Miami. There's a screening room in the basement of the Palace of the Revolution. It's not Disney, but the seats are plush. My first night in Havana I sat in one of them next to Fidel Castro, the man my uncles tried to kill, to watch a movie about the thirteen days when the wisest men in the world almost blew all of us to radioactive smithereens. Ain't life strange?

A few months after I returned from Havana, I learned that my uncle Teddy had been invited to the White House shortly after the inauguration to screen *Thirteen Days* for the new American president, George W. Bush. My relatives in the government were invited. I was not. I chalked this up to appearance. My family knows how to manipulate the Kennedy currency. My name is Lawford, and I am an actor. On the Kennedy playing field of politics, it's not always a plus. When I saw my uncle after the screening, I said nothing. Neither did he.

WHAT I found in Havana was not dissimilar to what I have grown to cherish in my recovery: a sense of interdependence and a reliance on something bigger than the individual, fueled by a certainty that if you don't get it right, it means death.

My trips to Cuba inspired a growing distrust of authority, whether it's your government or your family. To me now the only thing you can trust is your own experience, and even that is a little tricky.

I learned that I was more liberal than where I came from and I became more realistic about the way I view the political dynamic. Once politics becomes systemic, it's all about power—those who are feeding at the trough and those who want to be.

Ultimately, I learned that no matter how hard I tried, I would never be a first-string Kennedy. And that was just fine with me.

WHAT I thought would be my last job in Hollywood wasn't in Hollywood at all but in New York. A friend of mine, David Black, one of the few people I met in show business who actually does what he says he is going to do, had been telling me for years that he was going to create a show and only hire people that he wanted to work with, and I was one of those people. I didn't believe him; lots of people have said they would give me a job when their project got made and few of them did. David Black was one of the exceptions. By the time I slogged through four feet of fresh snow to show up for my first day of work at a church on the Upper West Side, I had finally come to a place in my life where I didn't care if I was an actor anymore. These moments are dangerous in one's life. This is when the universe finally gives you what you thought you always wanted. It's like God asking you if you are sure.

The show I had been freely given by David Black, *Copshop*, was a dream job. It was like a play. It was about the drama between human beings, smart, funny, and not very commercial. It was being produced by PBS for peanuts, and the actors Richard Dreyfuss, Rita Moreno, and Rosie Perez were working for nothing. It was independent and a little subversive. I had a good role. It was perfect and I didn't care if I did it. That's how I knew I had finally made peace with the demons and was now free to find my own path. God had one more little teaser for me, though. At the end of shooting, Richard Dreyfuss pulled me aside.

RD:
Can I tell you something?
Me:
Sure. As long as I can use it in my book.
RD:
Okay. I hope this doesn't offend you.
Me:
I can take it.

RD:
You know, you are much more compelling to watch than your father.

Hey wait a minute, maybe I should be an actor! Nine months later. . . . the phone rang and it was my agent with an audition for a movie.

Agent:
Chris, we have a meeting for you on a film called *The World's Fastest Indian.*
Me:
I'm not an actor anymore. Call someone else.
Agent:
Roger Donaldson, who directed *Thirteen Days,* is directing and requested you.
Me:
Shit. I guess I have to go.
Agent:
Yeah. I guess so.

They sent me the script, about an old guy from New Zealand, named Burt Monroe, who realizes his lifelong dream by racing his Indian motorcycle on the Bonneville Salt Flats at over two hundred miles per hour. I was to play the part of Jim Moffet, a jet car driver who attempts to break the land speed record. Jim befriends the old Kiwi and helps him realize his dream. I arrived for my meeting with Roger Donaldson with the enthusiasm of the obligated and disinterested.

RD:
Hey, Chris. Nice to see you.
Me:
Hey, Roger. Nice to see you too. You know I don't do this acting thing anymore.
RD:
Yeah, I know. It was a bitch finding you.

Me:

I've been locked in my house writing my book. The last time
I acted was nine months ago with Richard Dreyfuss in a
series for PBS.

RD:

That must have been fun.

Me:

Yeah. Dreyfuss told me I was more compelling to watch than
my old man. A fitting end to a mediocre career.

RD:

You're a good actor, mate. I want you in my movie.

Me:

Thanks. By the way, who's playing Burt Monroe?

RD:

Anthony Hopkins.

Me:

You don't say.

My disinterest evaporated. My audition was inspired. I got the part. I
was number two on the call sheet, starring in a movie with Anthony
Hopkins. I spent a month on the Salt Flats laughing and working with
Roger and Tony, two very successful and talented individuals who were
glad to have Chris Lawford working with them.

Chapter 38

They call me Superman,
I'm here to rescue you . . .
— EMINEM

An alcoholic in a relationship is like flies on a screen door. Those on the outside want to get in and those on the inside want to get out.

What do you do when you realize at the age of forty-five that you have been dealing with women your entire life from a lack that had its genesis when you were three months old? I have a need to be loved by women beyond what is reasonable or sustainable. As I mentioned earlier, I think it probably has something to do with not being breast-fed. I end up resenting them and searching for another. It has propelled me through the world looking for a succession of great loves and allowed me to walk out of a marriage of seventeen years.

Growing up in a female-dominated house has given me a good deal of insight into the female psyche and an ability to run my game on the fairer sex; it has also left me susceptible to them. It has been impossible for me to say no, to disappoint, to put my own needs out there in an open, honest way. I had no idea how to not acquiesce to a woman's needs when in a relationship. I would give them what they wanted, stuff the resentment, and keep my eye out for the perfect woman on the horizon. I never found her, but I found a few who were powerless enough to let me get away with a lot of shit. I have always cheated and rebelled in response to any demand. Acquiesced, and then did what I pleased. This is a chicken-shit approach and not very grown-up.

People will tell you that marriage and relationship are about compromise. Fuck that. My experience is that women will try to form a man. The ones who are looking for nuclear security surrounded by a white picket fence will stop at nothing to turn you into the guy who brings home the bacon and runs to the 7-Eleven for a carton of milk. Sorry! Not interested!

WHEN I was newly sober I was told, whenever I fought with my wife, "You are wrong. Now go apologize for your part in it." Fuck that too. I stayed married, but the man has to surface somewhere. Joseph Campbell says that the man has to capitulate in a marriage in order for it to work. Joseph Campbell is a whole lot smarter and more enlightened than I am, but fuck that too. I think the only way to engage a woman is to be true to yourself, go to war, and let the chips fall where they may.

I once said to a therapist that there were only two things I absolutely could not do in my life. The first was to drink or drug again and the second was to be unfaithful. My thinking at the time was that if I drank, I would die and that if I were unfaithful, it would be the end of my marriage and, I thought, the end of my life. The therapist looked at me and said, "You can do both of those things today if you choose to." This was my first glimpse into creating my own life, although I didn't realize it at the time. In creating absolutes we limit choice. This isn't necessarily a bad thing; it all depends on what kind of life you want to live. I have come to the understanding that to impose absolutes out of fear or conditioning doesn't work for me.

My life has been in constant reaction from the beginning. First as the beneficiary of a profound family legacy and later as a drug addict. It became imperative for me that if I was ever going to find out who I was, all bets had to be off and everything had to be up for grabs. I would have to let go of the absolutes and the identifications I had clung to. Okay, I know you're thinking most people do this in their teens, or maybe the truly underdeveloped may not get to it until their twenties, but to do this when you are in your late thirties and forties is not only selfish but ridiculous.

Point taken and I can't say you are wrong, but this is my life and this is how it worked out. Anyone who knows anything about addiction will tell you that when the addict starts using, emotional and psychological growth stops. Addiction is like driving through life in a giant station wagon at a hundred miles an hour and every time something fundamental and emotional comes up, you just heave it in the back of the wagon and forget about it. When you get sober the wagon comes to a screeching halt and all the stuff you threw in the back lands in your lap. I may have been in my forties, but developmentally I was still in my late teens or early twenties at best.

See, the truth is that I started to look around, and what I saw were a lot of miserable people in relationships who were lying to themselves and to others. Very few, if any, had anything I wanted in their entanglements, but more importantly I knew on a deep level that the road I was on would only deliver me to a one-dimensional facsimile of what I had been programmed to become. When I gave myself permission to do the two things that I could never do, and then chose not to do them, I was taking some of the power away from them and providing a safer, more realistic relationship with these taboos. I was also giving myself permission to create my life as I saw fit, making conscious choices about what that life would look like. The therapist was right; I could choose to be unfaithful. I chose not to for a while, but guess what? If you leave the door open long enough, chances are you are going to walk through it. As of this writing I am separated from my wife and I have chosen not to drink or drug one day at a time. As to the latter, I have little doubt that if I did it, it would mean my death.

BEFORE I decided to really tell the truth, I had pretty much decided to spend the rest of my life married, leaving the question of fidelity open. I felt justified doing this because (1) I was conditioned to do whatever I wanted, (2) my wife was happy and didn't know what I was doing, and (3) I had crafted an airtight fiction that went something like this: "I have a really good marriage, but I can't get everything I need or want from one woman and refuse to put parameters around any relationship." Pretty good, right? The key to the success of this type of thinking is that you discuss it only with those who similarly rationalize dishonest behavior and never breathe a word of it to someone who may disagree. Delusional thinking is best done alone or in sympathetic environs. One day as I was running this shit up the flagpole, the woman-of-the-moment looked up at me and said, "If you have such a good marriage, what are you doing here?" Thus began the crumbling of my house of cards.

Chapter 39

Madness need not be all breakdown. It may also be breakthrough.
— R. D. Laing

There is an old Sufi saying that goes something like this: Tie two birds together, and they will be unable to fly even though they have twice the number of wings.

I left my marriage in sobriety because I was being dishonest and after seventeen years wasn't sure I wanted to be married anymore. I looked around my life and saw a lot of people lying to themselves and I was one of them. To tell lies to others is foolish; to tell lies to yourself is a disaster. I have always had a certain ambivalence about marriage. This may come from the fact that my role models were so fucked up or maybe it was me; but as I said, the white picket fence doesn't suit me. When we lived in the suburbs, I always wondered what I was doing there. Something about that life didn't feel right to me. It wasn't Jeannie or my kids. It was me. My behavior in my marriage masked deeper problems in me. It was not just about the relationship.

MANY OF the people in my life, including my kids, thought I was crazy to break up my marriage and got very angry with me. At the time, it was something I felt like I had to do. I could not lie anymore to others or myself. I thought we would all acclimate to the change and go on in the new circumstances. I seriously underestimated the pain my leaving caused and how difficult it would be for Jeannie and my kids to adjust. I never again want to be the cause of that kind of pain to another. When I was thinking of leaving Jeannie and the kids, a good friend of mine said to me, "You better back away from that thinking, man. You're going to lose yourself without your family." He was almost right.

I had agonized for five months about what to do. It had all come to a critical mass. I spent much of that time making the case that my life was as yet unrealized. I felt like a fraud—as if I had spent all my time living someone else's design. Nobody had ever told me to do anything. I had always been free to choose my own path and had been given every opportunity to do so. The problem was I could never let go of what I had been born to. I had rebelled mightily but only on the most superficial level. I had made quite a show of trying to destroy myself, and now, after years of reconstruction, I was left with the knowledge that if you took away my sobriety, the only thing that I knew how to do was take advantage of the circumstances I was born into.

I believed I needed to leave home to find out who I was.

After five months of this talk, the therapist I was seeing looked at me and said, "What about your children?" It was in this moment that I realized that throughout my whole messy process, I had not really considered my precious kids. The horror of this realization brought with it the knowledge that I had in fact become the aspect of my father that had damaged me most as a child: the aspect of a man's nature that allows him to behave as though his children do not exist.

This is when the therapist said to me, "It is vital that you do not re-create unconsciously what was done to you by your father. You can re-create it consciously. You can choose to turn away from your family, or not. It's your life, but you must make a conscious choice."

I think it was at that moment that I understood how to take responsibility for my own life. It was also at that moment that I decided that having my kids in my life was not negotiable. I was determined to be the father I never had and the father they deserved.

. . .

DURING THIS time I had a recurring dream. In it I saw the house Jeannie and the kids were living in. I was coming and going but wasn't living there. Jeannie and the kids were happy, vibrant, and alive. Everyone seemed better off to me than when I was living there. I took this as a sign that what I was doing was not only for me but for all of us. I considered that this might be an elaborate subconscious rationalization but I didn't think so.

What I failed to consider fully at the time was that my kids would also make a conscious choice—and it might not be compatible with mine.

Me:
This is something I have to do for me.
My son David:
It's your choice. I don't agree with it.
Me:
It doesn't mean I'm leaving you. I love you and I'm still here
for you.
My son David:
I don't understand how you can say that when you are not
living with us anymore.
Me:
I really believe that this will be good for all of us.
My son David:
You keep saying this is going to be good for us. It's not good
for me. As far as I can tell, it's only good for you.

The way I see it is, after seventeen years of marriage I decided to change the rules and not live up to my side of the bargain. This makes me an asshole but does not invalidate all that came before. My decision to leave didn't just change the future, it also changed the past. My experience has been that even if a woman gets everything she wants in a marriage, if a man leaves, past history is rewritten and suddenly it is she who sacrificed her life so he could live his dream. The reality is that in many of the marriages I've known, the males are definitely in "second" position when it comes to having their dreams fulfilled. Or maybe all of this was just the ghost of my father making himself known.

The truth is, I have behaved in all sorts of different ways than my father did. My father never saw the inside of a delivery room. I was there when my three kids were pulled from Jeannie's womb and I was home with them pretty much full time for the first ten years of their lives. My kids were a priority and I acted as if they were. My old man never did with us. I struggled ferociously with the issue of fidelity. I can't say for sure, but I'd lay odds that my old man never gave his infidelity a second thought. I once took my kids to Fenway Park to see a baseball game. I vowed I would stay with them until the end of the game, unlike my parents, who usually left early. My kids got bored and wanted to leave. I had a choice: force them to stay or be there for my kids in whatever way they chose. It was not just about changing the past. I didn't have to make everybody stay at the game to be a good father and put the past to rest.

THE THING that's so weird about all of this is that I have behaved in all sorts of different ways than my old man yet I am only a hairbreadth away from being him. James Baldwin said, "Children have never been very good at listening to their elders, but they have never failed to imitate them. They must, they have no other models."

Yes siree, it's a bitch to change who we are—and not give to our children what we were given by our parents.

> *Nothing can bring you peace but yourself.*
> —Ralph Waldo Emerson

Snapshot:

I knew I had to go. I was just afraid to do it. I wanted to go in honor of my journey toward finding myself and not merely to run to a piece of ass. Both were true. I wouldn't be doing one without the other. So the decision had been made. I would be spending the next week or two at the Hotel Oceana in Santa Monica while I looked for a place. I had come home the previous night to find Jeannie huddled with David, explaining to him that she had asked me to leave the house, something she would never do "unless he had done something really, really bad." I figured it was a good time for a road trip. My daughter, Savannah, came bounding up the stairs, mercifully oblivious to it all. In one of the greatest moments of pain and anger I have witnessed in my life, my wife screamed at me to tell Savannah that I wasn't coming back home.

Savannah was stricken. She started to cry. Jeannie was crying. I was standing there with my bag and pillow. If there were any way not to leave, to do it a different way, I would have chosen it in that moment.

It had to be about something bigger.

I LEFT my family in the spring of 2001, five months before the attacks of September 11. My kids were left to feel very unsafe from these two events.

Savannah sent me a poem she wrote while I waited to get home from New York City two days after the Towers fell:

The 11th day of the 9th month and there is yet to be silence
But then again all I hear is silence
My ears hear nothing will my eyes can't do anything but stare
With my own two eyes I stare at scene that will never be forgotten
The scene of two towers collapse after being hit by two large metal birds
Now my ears don't hear anything but the chaos in the city of New York
While my eyes are shut tight

SNAPSHOT:

My daughter, Savannah Rose, was born on February 13, 1990. She was scheduled to be born by C-section on Valentine's Day but she has her parents' willfulness and decided to come early. I watched her being pulled from Jeannie's belly in the same hospital where I was born thirty-five years earlier. Ten years earlier the singer Jimmy Buffet had named his daughter Savannah and Jeannie fell in love with the name. Rose was for my grandmother. I was nervous that Savannah Rose was a lot of name to carry. My beautiful daughter carries it with ease.

Savannah had colic. She screamed her lungs out from 6 P.M. to 11 P.M. every night. She sucked on a pacifier and didn't use words until she was three. She had her own language of sounds. I never had a problem understanding what she was saying to me. She was my little girl. She adored me until the day I left. After that, she didn't like me, or trust me very much. It's been a long road back.

One day recently she came to me after a very bad day at school. Some kids had made fun of her and the teacher was being a pain in the ass. I listened to her woes and then I did something that surprised the hell out of me. I said to her, "Savannah, I'm sorry you had a bad day at school; it's hard being fourteen." And that's all I did. I didn't try to fix it or diminish it. I was just there for her. I validated her experience and it floored her. I had been looking for this my whole life, and I was able to give it to my daughter because I'm sober and had done the work I've done on myself. And because I have the patience of a part-time dad.

SNAPSHOT:

My youngest son is named Matthew Peter Valentine Lawford. Valentine was Jeannie's father's middle name and a pretty darn cool name. It is a name that makes a statement, as he is a boy who has never failed to live up to that promise. He was born in the hamlet of Mount Kisco, New York, deep in the sleepy woods of Westchester County. From the moment he was pulled feetfirst from Jeannie's body he has besieged me with his boundless energy, unceasing capacity for surprise, and an uncanny knack for pushing every button I have. When I left him to go out into the world, he tearfully and with great fear asked me what was going to happen as a result of my leaving. He was six at the time. I told him that he could look at it as instead of having one house he would now have two. He thought that was cool and I thought at least with him I would have a chance. It was not meant to be.

One night we were doing homework together, an incredibly stressful parent-child activity. Mattie was showing typical disregard for his finished work. He crumples his finished assignments and smears them with all sorts of grossness to the point that it really does look like the dog ate them. I seized on the obvious parenting opportunity and began to talk to him about respecting his work. I said that by keeping it neat and orderly he would be showing respect for what he had done. I shared my experience with him, telling him that I used to not show respect for the money I carried, by always having it here and there and all crumpled up in my pockets. I told him that when I began to treat my money with respect, by keeping it neat and in my wallet, I miraculously found that more money came to me. He thought about this for a moment and said, "That's great, Dad, but I don't want any more homework."

Matty sent me a poem shortly after I left. It sustained me:

My Dad
My dad loves me so much
And also loves nuts.
I like to play catch with him
And he doesn't live in a cabin.
My dad is the greatest
He never drives me to school
And is never a fool.
He likes pie
And he can't fly.
My dad is the greatest
He likes to eat fish
And he hasn't eaten a dish.
He makes me happy when I'm sad
And he is very glad
My dad is the greatest
LOVE MATTHEW

In having children I learned gratitude. . . . In being a parent I learned acceptance.

My kids have seen me insane but never drunk or stoned. They can read about it in the newspapers of the late seventies and early eighties, or in this book if they ever come out from behind the computer games . . . but reading old stories hardly has the same impact as active alcoholism on the psyche of a little kid. For me as a child, the most terrifying and damaging aspect of active alcoholism was the inconsistency. As a father I have been crazy and wrong, but always constant.

I had a fantasy ever since I visited my father on the set of *Ocean's 11* that one day my dad and I would work together and be able to have what I saw those guys have on that set. That never happened. The closest we got to that kind of intimate collaborative camaraderie was when he gave me a vial of cocaine for my twenty-first birthday. It was the best either of us could do at the time.

Today, I'm making a political documentary with my son David on the state of democracy in America. We attended the 2004 Democratic and Republican conventions—neither one of us got high. A 180-degree difference from what went down between me and my dad. After overdosing on Republicans in the Big Apple we spent four days on the road looking at colleges. I don't know where my parents were when I was trying to decide where to spend my four years of college life, but I can tell you they weren't on the road with me.

I have learned that I can act like a caring, loving father, realizing my dreams, even if they look a little different from what I had imagined.

SNAPSHOT:

I walked into a party for HBO at Sundance three years ago. I was shooting behind-the-scenes footage, asking the celebrities if the ideals envisioned by Robert Redford when he started the film festival all those years ago had been perverted beyond recognition by the Hollywood influx. In the middle of this narcissistic sea of fame and beauty was the latest in the parade of the most beautiful girl I had ever seen. The first thought that came into my head as I gasped was, "I'll never fuck her as long as I live, she's way too beautiful." This was kind of an odd thought to have and atypical for me. I pretty much think I can sleep with anyone. Nevertheless, I put my camera in the gorgeous ingenue's face and asked her some questions about the state of independent film and then for her phone number. Her name was Lana and she gave me her number. I've been living with her for two and a half years. She is the only woman I have ever told the whole truth to. It's not easy. There are days I wish I could be duplicitous but the road has gotten narrower. It's worth it.

Chapter 40

If you want to make God laugh, just tell Him your plans.
— ANONYMOUS

The doctor in Mount Kisco told me that my test for hepatitus C had come back negative. It was a relief. Most of us who survive drug addiction show positive for either AIDS or hep C. When I showed up for a routine physical at my doctor's office in Beverly Hills I was under the assumption that I had dodged both. I was mistaken.

I can't be sure, but I think the last time I shared a needle with anyone was 1981, maybe 1982. It had been almost twenty years, and it was a hell of a shock when my doctor called with the news.

"Chris I've got some good news and some bad news." What is it about doctors in L.A.? They all want to be comedians. "You don't have AIDS, but you showed positive for hepatitus C. I'm sure there's nothing, but you should have a biopsy and see if anything's going on in your liver."

Fuck! I was seventeen years sober and the wreckage of my past decides to stop by for a little visit.

I'm not sure where I got the hep C but I'd lay odds it was from Papa John Phillips. John and I had a significant intravenous association. His hep C forced him to get a new liver in 1992 and ultimately killed him.

This is not good.

I had just left my family. I was living in a $2 million teardown next to the Terminator, dating an actress whose self-obsession was matched only by her irrationality. Now I get to put my name on a liver recipient list.

I went to see one of the liver doctor gurus in L.A. for my biopsy. I didn't hear from him for a month so I figured everybody was right: there was nothing to worry about. I called his office one day just to make sure.

Receptionist:
Oh. Mr. Lawford, I'm glad you called. We need to schedule you for treatment right away.
Me:
What are you talking about?
Receptionist:
Your biopsy came back and your liver is on its way to looking like a piece of cardboard.
Me:
Are you kidding?
Receptionist:
No, sir. We don't kid.

Where the fuck was my doctor guru, I wondered? Was he ever going to call me? Or was he out playing golf too? When I finally got in to see him, I was informed that my liver was presclerotic with bridging fibrosis, too close to cardboard for comfort. I had to be treated and went on the interferon protocol. Interferon is similar to chemotherapy. I injected myself once a week, taking another antiviral, riboviron, twice a day orally. The medicine caused me to lose twenty pounds, feel like I had a really bad flu 24/7, and become so depressed that I often thought about killing myself. The fact that I went through this after having just left my family made the hopelessness almost unbearable. It was suggested that I take antidepressants. Most of those I know who have endured this treatment took some kind of mood elevator. I told them to take their happy pills and shove them. I am serious about feeling every bit of pain and joy I can in this life. I was numb for too long. From here on out I want to be fully awake.

THE HOUSE my cousin Maria was letting me stay in was free but it was a wreck. I was grateful to be close to family even though I never saw them. My first night a mouse appeared in my bedroom. I opened the door so he could escape to the outside. He left but he came back. We became friends, kind of like my dad and his pal the squirrel at Hef's Playboy Mansion. I'd sit in the large empty living room, think about all the pain I was causing to my wife and kids. I'd feel the pain of illness. I obsessed about women. I talked to the mouse. I felt like I was becoming my father without the booze. It was terrifying.

Joan Didion asked if there was "ever in anyone's lifespan a point free in time, devoid of memory, a night when choice was any more than the sum of all the choices gone before." I had a few as I writhed and wrestled with the choices I was making. When you truly act outside of any memory it doesn't feel good. It feels like you are doing it wrong.

SNAPSHOT:

My kids hated my new digs. They were used to warm and cozy. This place was cold and cavernous. Even the mouse and the close proximity to the Terminator didn't win them over. They would have been happy if I had disappeared from their lives forever. That wasn't going to happen. I may have left their mother's house but I would be their father until hell freezes over. I would sit outside their mom's house in the green Jag and wait in futility for them to come out and spend time with me. Back when we had moved to the Westside of L.A. from the innocent woods of Westchester, before the upheaval, Jeannie was driving Savannah and a couple of friends to school:

Friend:
When I am eighteen I am going to have enough money to pay for college and buy myself a Jaguar.
Savannah:
I didn't know you could have a jaguar for a pet!

After four years in L.A. Savannah knew what a Jaguar was and she wanted no part of mine. I decided to have the dad's Thanksgiving dinner in the new digs. I don't know how to cook so I got Gelson's Market to do it. I worked on the ambience and tried not to fuck up the heating instructions. My kids hated all of it. They blamed it on all the spices the cooks at Gelson's put in their food, but they would have hated anything I served. They hardly ate, but it wasn't about the food.

Nietzsche said, "The thought of suicide is a great consolation: by means of it one gets successfully through many a bad night." It worked for me on many of my bad nights during those eleven months.

My war cry was, "Don't drink, don't drug, don't kill myself or anybody else—just for today." It was the thought that sustained me. I was firmly convinced that nothing short of my life was at stake. I was walking a razor's edge. There was no going back. I would transform or die. I took my medicine as prescribed for eleven months and I beat the hep C. Moving through the pain with Jeannie and my kids would be more complicated.

Chapter 41

In skating over thin ice our safety is in our speed.
— RALPH WALDO EMERSON

One of the great gifts I was given by my family was an appreciation for life, a passion for living each moment fully. My uncle Bobby was my first inspiration for this. He embodied the ethic of activity and of sucking the marrow out of life. My grandmother told the historian Doris Kearns Goodwin that if given a choice, her children who died would still choose to be who they were, despite the shortness of the years they were allowed to live because they had "such adventure, such richness in their lives."

In pursuit of this richness, taking risks goes along with the territory. Everybody took risks. My grandfather in business. Jack in the war in the Pacific. Joe and Kathleen in the war in Europe.

Uncle Bobby kicked it up a few notches. Family history coupled with the volatility of the times combined to foster a fatalism about running in 1968—but he ran anyway. Big Bobby believed in having faith, taking the risk, and proving yourself. I appreciate this dynamic that Robert Kennedy epitomized and that runs through my family. There is an honesty and vitality to sucking the marrow out of life that is exhilarating. It is also dangerous.

SNAPSHOT:

John got around pretty good on crutches. We had cruised the West Village the night before, having dinner and checking out some parties. It always amazed me when I went places with my cousin John how any room would just tilt toward him when he walked in. Everyone's conversation and attention narrowed to the vortex where he stood. He handled it all with a lot of grace. John had all his mother's grace.

I bumped into John the following morning in the Lobby of 500 Fifth Avenue. He had just come from our family office on the seventeenth floor. I was on my way there to try and make sense of my quarterly financial report, with the hope that the accountants had gotten it wrong. He had lost the crutches and was dragging his broken foot with the heavy cast behind him like Quasimodo.

John:
Hey, man. What's up?
Me:
Hey. Nothing. Just going to do battle with the accountants.
John:
Make sure they don't put any of my money in your account.
Me:
Not a bad idea. When are you going to Rory's wedding?
John:
I'm flying up this afternoon. Do you want to come with us?
Me:
I would, but I left Jeannie on the Island with my mother and sisters. We're going to fly up tomorrow.
John:
Okay, man. I'll see you at the Cape.
Me:
Yeah. I'll see you up there, man.

The following morning I was awakened by my cousin Kerry Kennedy telling me that John's plane was missing. It never occurred to me, and I'm sure it never occurred to John, that flying a plane with a cast on his foot might be a problem. I knew he would show up, he always did. Then they found his plane at the bottom of the ocean.

I DON'T know how much this dynamic of sucking the marrow out of life contributed to my cousin Michael killing himself playing football on skis on Aspen Mountain, and my cousin John flying a plane at dusk with a broken leg. What I do know is that I grew up believing that life is enhanced by challenge or danger. The imperative had always been to experience everything and never stop moving. Now I realize the challenge is to live each moment of my life as deeply as possible, being fully present with the genius to stop and smell the flowers. As Gandhi said, "There's more to life than increasing its speed."

I think that the reason people run is because they are far away from themselves. The closer I get to myself the more I don't have to run. One of my great fears is that when I stop running, I will die.

Chapter 42

I been double-crossed now for the very last time
and I think I finally see.
— BOB DYLAN

Many people have asked me what it was like growing up in my family. I tell them that it was the only family I knew and therefore I had no idea how extraordinary it was. I didn't deserve the circumstances I was born to and never realized how lucky I was to have them—until now.

I wonder how my life would have changed if I'd had a clue. I probably would have made more friends in Washington; you never know when friends in high places might come in handy. I might be running a Hollywood studio instead of begging for acting jobs. But then I'd be on the inside, feeding at the trough like all the other guys who did have a clue. I spent a lot of time wishing I had something different than what I had. It took a long time to realize that happiness is not getting what you want but wanting what you have.

SNAPSHOT:

My uncle Teddy was relaxed and at ease. This was not a state I often found him in unless he was sailing his sailboat, *Mya*. He wasn't. We were sitting in the kitchen of my mother's New York apartment, having just returned from an evening honoring someone for something or trying to get money out of them for something else. It usually came down to recognition or cash. Recognition + cash = power. The recipe for success in America. The family had become very good at this equation. The event was over and my sisters and I were talking to the head of our family about life and family.

"If I hadn't gone into politics I would have been an opera singer." My uncle Teddy loves to sing. "Can you imagine going up into those little Italian villages, learning those songs, and having pasta every day for lunch?" My uncle Teddy loves pasta. "Singing at la Scala in front of three thousand people throwing flowers at you. Then going out for dinner and having more pasta." My uncle Teddy loves an adoring crowd. "But I went into politics—now I can't eat and I don't sing!"

My sisters and I were doubled over with laughter, not unusual when hanging out with The Grande Fromage, which is what we affectionately call my uncle. My uncle Teddy loves to laugh.

THE BIG Cheese took a long, slow gulp of his vodka and tonic, thought for a moment, and changed tack, "I'm glad I'm not going to be around when you guys are my age."

I asked him why, and he said, "Because when you guys are my age, the whole thing is going to fall apart." The statement hung there, suspended in the realm of "maybe we shouldn't go there." Nobody wanted to touch it. After a few moments of heavy silence, my uncle moved on and we were spared. But his statement registered, at least with me. I would have liked to explore what he meant but that was never the nature of our relationship. Whenever we came close to exploring the realm of things better left unsaid, the discussion veered into ambiguous "Teddy Speak" or another funny story.

What? When it all falls apart. I didn't know what he was talking about. How could it all fall apart? The family was everything. It was scary to think it all might end. Unimaginable, really. What Teddy understood better than anyone was how much effort it took to keep it all together, because he had been doing it since 1968 when it all fell on him. If he hadn't stepped up and carried us all on his back for the next thirty-plus years, the family would have disintegrated many years before. The glue that holds a family together is commonality of purpose and shared experience. The glue in our family was also "the legacy." As long as we were serving that, we had commonality of purpose. Not many of us have turned our backs on our legacy and found our own way, myself included. As long as individuals receive personal benefit from their legacy, they will put aside differences to strengthen and promote that legacy.

I REMEMBER when our parents' generation decided to establish the Associate Trustees Committee for the Joseph P. Kennedy Jr. Foundation. The committee was an attempt to pass the baton of social activism to our generation, thus preserving and continuing that part of the legacy. It was their first foray into letting go and sharing power. It was not easy for them. I remember my aunt Eunice coming to me before the first meeting and nervously asking if I was going to lead a revolt and try to move the foundation away from mental retardation to something that had more relevance to me and my generation. I assured her I wasn't, but that tension was always present.

I will share a secret with you: Whenever I meet a new person, I often find a way to let them know sooner rather than later that I am a member of the Kennedy family. I do this because it gives me power and is in fact the most dominant aspect of who I am. In fact, I have gladly subjugated my individual life to the life of being a member of the Kennedy family. Although this book was published because of my family, is about my family, and most likely will be read because of my family, it is also my way of letting go of my family. My declaration of independence—I hope.

I think what my uncle might have been saying that night was that though he never had a choice but to give his life to his family, many of us who followed would not be asked to make that huge a sacrifice and, in fact, would be able to find our own lives, and in doing so, what he had spent his life holding together would cease to exist. Thanks for your sacrifice, Uncle Teddy.

Conclusion

The distinction between past, present and future is only an illusion, however persistent.
—ALBERT EINSTEIN

If I could change anything in my life, being an addict would not be one of them. Whatever wisdom I have gained has come as a result of my struggle with addiction.

SNAPSHOT:

I was invited to Indianapolis to give a talk on substance abuse recovery as the keynote speaker at the annual fund-raising dinner benefiting Fairbanks Hospital. I had been asked because one of the benefactors of Fairbanks was a woman named Susan Simon who was the daughter of Herb Simon, one of the richest men in America and a hearty contributor to the Democrats and my family. I didn't know Susan, but she argued for me to give the keynote because of our families' close relationship.

The day before the dinner I was asked to do some press promoting the dinner. I showed up at the local TV station where I was grilled by a newswoman on what it's like to be an addict. Holy shit. I didn't anticipate this. My history as an addict is no secret, but going public was something different. I got through the interview but was having second thoughts about my decision to put a public face on my recovery.

My next interview was at a radio station overlooking Monument Circle in the center of Indianapolis. This interview was proving less traumatic. I was staring out the giant window overlooking the state Soldiers and Sailors Memorial thinking about a new generation of American kids who were going to get their asses shot at in Iraq and how maybe I should have kept my big fat mouth shut about being a heroin addict, when out of nowhere a man appeared. He was about fifty, African American, and by the looks of him had been living on the streets for some time. He walked up to the window and put a sign on it that read, "Can you help me get sober?" At first I thought it was some kind of miracle. This homeless guy miraculously knew what I was talking about on the radio. That wasn't it. The DJ told me that there were speakers outside broadcasting the show. I motioned to the guy to go over to the doorway, and after the show I went to talk to him with the marketing director from Fairbanks. Let us say the guy's name was Arthur. He had been on the street living in a Dumpster for five years. He had been an alcoholic forever.

> *Arthur:*
> I want to get sober, man.
> *Me:*
> Go to Fairbanks and get some help.
> *Arthur:*
> I've got no insurance.
> *Marketing Director:*
> Take my card and show it to the admitting nurse. They'll
> take you.
> *Arthur:*
> How do I get there?
> *Marketing Director:*
> Take the number 5 bus. It stops across the street.
> *Arthur:*
> I don't have any money.

Me:
Here's five bucks.
Arthur:
Will you be my sponsor?
Me:
We'll talk about that after you get sober.
Arthur:
I don't know, man.

And with that, the marketing director and I got in our car to head to our next appointment. I watched as Arthur shuffled away, clutching the $5 bill I had given him. I was pretty sure he would use it to buy a pint. Later that day I received a phone call from the marketing director.

Marketing Director:
Guess who's here?
Me:
No shit, he actually made it?
Marketing Director:
Yep. Hold on.
Arthur:
Hey, Chris, it's me—Arthur.
Me:
Hi, Arthur. You made it.
Arthur:
Yeah. I wasn't going to come, but I went to the bus stop and
the first bus that came by was going right to Fairbanks
Hospital. I figured it was a sign.
Me:
There are no coincidences, my friend.

Arthur was admitted to Fairbanks Hospital where he got sober. From there he went into sober living, got a job, and began a new life—sober.

I found out later that the radio station where I was being interviewed, where Arthur stumbled upon me, was once owned by the man who provided the initial funding for Fairbanks. There are indeed no coincidences. And whatever doubt I had about revealing my story publicly vanished.

SNAPSHOT:

My mom had been sick for the last three years. In the beginning they told her she would have to bear some terrible things to beat the cancer. She wasn't at all sure she wanted to walk down that road, figuring there was a good chance she might die anyway and she didn't want to give the doctors the satisfaction. My mom never liked doctors very much. There wasn't a whole lot of support for that point of view from those who loved her, so she began the long, difficult battle. After three years of it, pretty much all of her fears had been realized. She was alive, but there was not much of a life left.

I had come to visit her in South Hampton for the weekend with a group of friends. In the previous three years I had not been nearly as patient and unconditional with her as I had seen her be with Aunt Jackie or my grandparents. I have come to understand we don't inherit all of our parent's qualities—good or bad. It was a beautiful September day. The ocean was flat and warm. My mother loved to swim in the ocean almost as much as she liked walking the beach next to it. She could do neither now as she sat in her wheelchair in the great living room surrounded by her beloved paintings and photographs of her family. Frank Sinatra was playing on the stereo, bringing her back to a time of more ease. I came into the living room carrying a stack of folders my sister Sydney had discovered in the basement. I sat down on the sofa and opened the first folder. It was crammed full with the documents and memories of my life. My mom had saved everything. Every scrap of paper that had anything to do with me; letters I had sent her, notes from my teachers, Christmas wish lists, art work, IOUs—my life with my mom was in this file. She had one for each of her children. I don't know why I was surprised.

I heard my whole life that her children were her life but until the moment I opened that folder, I guess I didn't believe it. Now, faced with my mother's meticulous preservation of every shred of evidence I existed—I had to.

I looked at her in her wheelchair. Her eyes were closed and she was in that place where no one could follow. She spent much of her time there and it was rare for me to see her come out.

"I can't believe you saved all of this." I said, without an expectation of a response.

My mom opened her eyes, looked directly at me with a knowing smile, and nodded her head as if to say, "Of course I saved it all, what did you expect I would do?" And with that she closed her eyes and went back to her peace, content in the knowing that I knew what her life had been about.

I returned to the folders and found some notes my mother had made in anticipation of her trip back in 1979 to Mclean Hospital, where she was to endure two days of "family" therapy with me in her courageous attempt to help me get sober. My mom's notes brought me back to the apprehension and tears of those meetings. They also brought me back to the pain. In them, my mom wrote about how much she loved me and how she had done the best she could as a mother in the face of some pretty significant slings and arrows. She thought she had failed me because she wasn't strong enough, there was no man around to pick up the slack, and she was convinced that I was led down the road to ruin by Bobby and David. The truth is, she was plenty strong enough. We all have our own path even if "The Path" we come from is undeniable. I chose mine. I didn't need any guidance from my cousins. Maybe a strong father would have made a difference. Maybe if I had wings I could fly!

THE POINT is I am responsible for my life. I do not regret the past, nor do I wish to shut the door on it. I see today how my experience can benefit others. The lessons of my life thus far have been profound and ordinary. It took a while for me to see them; now that I have, I can move on. Here are some principles I've gotten so far:

I admire my family for all the saving-the-world business, but my experience has shown me that it comes at a cost. And that cost is often borne by those who come after.

The best way to change the world is to change yourself.

If you feel second string it probably means that you have let someone else choose the playing field.

Let go of the myth. It is a lie.

The bliss of those who came before you will never fill you and you will never succeed until you follow your own bliss.

Learn to listen to what is inside you. There is nothing more vital to human existence than honoring one's authentic self.

The worshiping of money, property, and prestige forces a lack of consciousness. If you want to change, you need to put these things aside for a time.

You can't change what you don't acknowledge or what you are not conscious of.

Each of us has our very own good father inside of us. It is a much more powerful father than any representation.

Letting go of being your father's son means you can be whatever you want—even what your father was.

The most important thing I can do as a father is to be honest and not pretend I am something that I'm not.

Learn the difference between what you want and what you need. God is more open to a request than a demand.

Life is gray.

Absolutes are limiting.

Listen to your heart. If you don't, it's never too late to make up for it.

Whatever your true motive is, it will be revealed no matter how cleverly you conceal it.

It is OK to have finite relationships with those whom you are supposed to be in infinite relationships with.

You can make a choice to end a marriage without making somebody wrong.

Kids have their own path and their own God.

I HAVE learned on my journey that we are not necessarily brought to happiness through consumption, power, fame, wealth, and sex. Those who base their lives on these things suffer greatly. My experience has taught me that in understanding the nature of that suffering, the path of emancipation appears, although it is often the road less traveled/trudged. It is not easy to change yourself no matter how much work you do or how aware you become. Inner work is a bitch but it's the only way for someone like me. If there were an easier softer way, I'd have taken it. I tried most of them, and they didn't work.

One of the spiritual traditions I have studied claims that it will take a human being seven lifetimes to become realized and move on. I don't know if this is true, but I am willing to accept that I may have six more trips ahead of me.

I have no regrets for the path I chose. It brought me to the certainty that a life spent in attempting to realize oneself, in service to others, is a life well spent, and to the knowledge that the only infinite high is in one's search for a god of his own understanding. I am more certain of these truths, because of my experience, than I am about anything else except that in the end I really don't know anything.

After a lifetime of trying to be what everyone wanted me to be I have found myself in all that I have come from.

My grandmother Rose wrote in her book, *Times to Remember:* "I hope [my grandchildren and great-grandchildren] will comprehend that the span of any life is short and all the days and hours are precious. I hope they will live life fully while they are alive, in the dimensions of both its duties and its beauties."

When I got sober they promised me a bridge back to life. They didn't lie. I have had *my* life. I have lived it fully *in both its duties and its beauties.*

I want to thank my mom and dad. My mom for teaching me that it is noble to seek to have one's own life and my dad for his class and his heart. I look forward to our next go-round where there may be less pain.

One night after all the pain of my separation had calmed down I was with my kids at my mother's home in South Hampton, New York. My mom bought the house in 1984 and named it Chrisyviro, which is a combination of all her children's names: Christopher, Sydney, Victoria, and Robin. The house is enormous. My mom's intent was to create a place where her children and grandchildren could all be together. This is my family's essence in a nutshell—family. My kids and I were sitting around the living room with all the pictures of family. My mother with her brothers Jack, Bobby, and Teddy. My grandmother Rose with Ronald Reagan. JFK with Khrushchev. My sisters and me with our children. Three generations of my family with each other and on the world stage. My kids and I were playing a game where you pass notepads around with each other's names on them and each person writes down something they would like to know about that person. Matty was eight years old when he grabbed his pen and feverishly wrote on my pad and passed it to me. On it he had written the most important question anybody has ever asked me. "Who the hell are you—Dad?"

It was at that moment that my ambivalence about writing this book vanished, I knew who I was and it was time I told my son. Thanks, Matty!

INDEX

That's right; no index. I purposely have not included one so the members of my family who are in the habit of searching the index and then reading only what is written about them can't.

Everyone is going to have to read the whole book to see what I say about them! I hope it makes you laugh and cry. Finally, let me pass along some wisdom a wise man in L.A. named Milton gave to me. Yes, there are wise men in L.A. He reminds me, whenever I see him, that life is short and that I shouldn't take myself so seriously. His shorthand version for these truths is: LTFU or

Lighten the fuck up!